PRAYER
ASKING AND RECEIVING

PRAYER
ASKING AND RECEIVING

By
John R. Rice
FOUNDER, *The Sword of the Lord*

P. O. BOX 1099, MURFREESBORO, TN 37133

Printed and Bound in the United States of America

CONTENTS

v

when He says "no." (7) Don't be afraid to ask: God will not give bad gifts. (8) Asking for the Holy Spirit.

(1) Sickness is a proper subject of prayer. (2) Prayer for the sick is proper during this age. (3) "The prayer of faith shall save the sick." (4) Is healing in the atonement?

(1) It is not always God's will to heal. (2) But it is usually God's will to heal in answer to prayer. (3) Should Christians use doctors and medicine? (4) Sin hinders healing: should be confessed and forsaken. (5) A personal testimony of healing in answer to prayer.

(1) Christians invited to ask for literally anything they want. (2) It is not wrong to ask it if it is not wrong to want it. (3) Philippians 4:6 says pray about "every thing." (4) Open the door of every closet in your heart to God!

PART THREE: HOW TO PRAY

(1) Jesus in Gethsemane our example. (2) Assurance in prayer. (3) Asking in Jesus' name. (4) Faith comes when praying in the will of God.

(1) The Bible teaches that prayer should be definite, explicit requests. (2) What is wrong with indefinite prayer. (3) How to be definite in prayer.

(1) The great importance of faith. (2) What is faith? (3) How to exercise faith and grow greater faith in God.

All conditions of prayer mentioned in the Bible are simply extra encouragements and opportunities to pray; all fulfilled in asking. (1) God's promises mean exactly what they say. (2) Not extra "conditions," but additional promises. (3) Asking really fulfills all other specific conditions of prayer. (a) Asking in faith. (b) Asking according to His will. (c) Asking in Jesus' name. (d) Where two are agreed in asking. (e) Persistence in prayer. (f) What about hindrances to prayer?

PART FOUR: PERSISTENCE IN PRAYER

(1) Sinners never need to "pray through" to be saved. Trusting Christ gets instant salvation without begging. (2) Bible proof texts that a sinner need never "pray through" to be saved. (3) Bible examples of people saved instantly without "praying through." (4) But Christians ought often to "pray through" with long, continued supplications and waiting on God until God answers their prayers.

(1) What is fasting and prayer? (2) Things we can get by fasting and prayer. (3) Revival brought by prayer and fasting.

PART FIVE: LIMITLESS POSSIBILITIES OF PRAYER

(1) God invites and commands us to ask big things. (2) Bible examples of prayers demanding great things from God. (3) The blessings of big prayers.

(1) The Bible certainly promises miracles in answer to prayer and faith. (2) Christianity, a miracle religion. (3) Miracles of the Bible are given as examples for us.

(1) Some objections answered. (2) Many authenticated miracles in modern times.

PART SIX: SIN AND PRAYER

Daily, regular answers to prayer should be normal for all Christians. (1) Wrong relationships of wives to husbands and of husbands to wives hinder prayer. (2) Prayers blocked by wrongs unrighted, debts unpaid, offended brothers unreconciled. (3) Unforgiveness grieves God and hinders prayers.

(1) Covetousness puts one under a curse, hinders prayer. (2) Self-will, rebellion, disobedience hinder prayer. (3) A disinclination or indifference toward the Bible makes prayer an abomination to God! (4) Any unconfessed, unlamented, unrepented sin grieves God and hinders the prayers of His children. (5) How to get the hindrances removed.

AUTHOR'S PREFACE

Every thoughtful minister must be impressed with the hunger of good Christian people for instruction on prayer. Untaught Christians do not naturally know how to pray though their hearts long after God. John the Baptist taught his disciples to pray; and the twelve came to Jesus saying, "Lord, teach us to pray, as John also taught his disciples." People need to be taught from the Bible to pray as truly as they need to be taught to preach or win souls. And even in their study of the Bible they need help, as the Ethiopian eunuch who was asked by Philip, "Understandest thou what thou readest?" and replied, "How can I, except some man should guide me?"

The great popularity of books on prayer by Andrew Murray, by Bounds, by Dr. R. A. Torrey, by Dr. Blanchard, by Hallesby, by Mrs. Goforth and even by modernists, shows there is a deep hunger in the hearts of the people to learn to pray and to learn to pray aright and get things from God. To meet in some small measure, if I can, this hunger of the people of God and to help men and women and young people really to pray, to ask and receive, is my purpose in writing this book.

Oh, the dearth of real prayer! We have not because we ask not. The churches are powerless, Christians are neither happy nor prosperous in spiritual matters, our loved ones are unsaved, all because we do not effectually, scripturally, get hold of God in prayer. Revival, with the enlargement of God's cause, with the widespread blessing of Christians, with the saving of multitudes of precious souls, surely waits on prayer. When we remedy the prayer life of the people of God, we remedy what is wrong with Christians and churches and open the way for every needed blessing. So I have earnestly set out in this book to teach people to pray according to the Scriptures and to stimulate faith in a God who answers prayer.

Frankly, this book is a book of *Bible teaching* on prayer. It is not a book of philosophy nor reasoning about what is or is not possible or probable about prayer. The book is written on the simple basis that there is a God who has revealed His will in the Bible, an infallible Book. The Bible teaches that God delights to answer prayer. The Bible gives us many great and exceedingly precious promises about what God will do for those who come to Him in prayer, and the Bible clearly gives the conditions for getting things from God. The Saviour said, "Ask, and it shall be given you" (Matt. 7:7), and again, "Ask, and ye shall receive" (John 16:24). So prayer is asking, and an answer to prayer is receiving. In answer to prayer, God miraculously intervenes in human affairs and changes things: changes people, changes weather, changes outward circumstances, changes health, even to the working of physical miracles. So the title of this book is *PRAYER— Asking and Receiving*. To this author prayer is a very simple and blessed matter of going to God daily for what one needs and desires, and getting it, and living in the fullness of joy of answered prayer which Jesus promised in John 16:24: "Hitherto have ye asked nothing in my name: ask, and ye shall receive, that your joy may be full."

This is no untried theory that I bring. Every promise that I write about, I have tried and proved; so I write this book as a matter of personal testimony. I *know* God answers prayer. He has answered mine in thousands of instances. The answers to prayer have been so definite, so clearly out of the realm of probability that an unbiased investigator must be convinced that these answers to prayer were really the supernatural intervention of a loving God who works miracles for His children when they trust Him. Others ought to tell what God has done for them, and so I ought to tell what God has done for me.

To the glory of God let me use the personal pronoun and say I know that the Bible way of prayer actually works. My wife and I prayed two days for a car, and from a totally unexpected source a new sedan was delivered to us the third day. We prayed together over our five-year-old daughter, quarantined with diphtheria, with fever of 105 degrees; and within twelve hours the fever left, and all symptoms of diphtheria disappeared. I was in a prayer meeting in Peacock, Texas, in 1931 when we deliberately asked God for a rain within twenty-four hours. In eighteen hours a flood of rain broke the four months' drought. At Decatur, Texas, some of us prayed for rain when the city lake was about empty. Rain came, filled the lake, and another prayer meeting was called to ask God to stop the rain so special meetings could continue. I saw a woman dying with tuberculosis, sent back from a state sanatorium to die, who had given away her children, instantly healed in answer to prayer, who in a few weeks gained forty pounds and for years has done all of her own housework in fine health. One night I laid out before God the need for $920 for His work. Two days later I received a check for a thousand dollars from a man I had never seen and with whom I had had absolutely no contact. God has given nearly $40,000 for printing bills, multiplied thousands for radio broadcasts, has supported my large family and paid my office workers these years. In hundreds of cases particular needs were met to the penny or the dollar of the amount asked. God has provided all of our needs without any designated salary or agreement with men for sixteen years.

While three of us prayed in Waxahachie, Texas, for a prodigal son in California, he was saved, and two days later his letter came to tell it. We prayed in a Bible conference for an unsaved man, then went to his home and found he had surrendered to Christ twenty minutes before while we were praying. We have felt led to ask God for twenty-five souls in one day, and they came in public profession of faith in Christ. Two of us fasted and prayed for ten souls to be saved in a country church where no one had been saved in two years and when the evangelistic services had proved fruitless; that night twenty-three adults came forward publicly to confess Christ. God has given blessed revivals with a total of perhaps fifteen thousand professions of faith in Christ under this unworthy ministry in answer to prayer. I know the Bible works and that God's promises to answer prayer are true.

As I have preached on prayer up and down the land, most remarkable results have appeared. People have asked and received the salvation of their loved ones; jobs; money for rent, clothes, education. They have received victory over temptations, wisdom from God for their problems.

These chapters were first printed in the weekly evangelistic paper *The Sword of the Lord*. They have led people to pray, and hundreds of letters from readers say that God has seen fit to bless them to many hearts. A woman in Nebraska had been forbidden of the doctors to have a child, threatening almost certain death. She and her husband read some of these articles on prayer, definitely asked of God a baby with perfect protection for the mother. They abandoned the devices used against their conscience, and now a letter tells of a beautiful baby given from God with the mother in perfect health. A minister, after reading one of these chapters on prayer, writes to tell how he had gotten victory over a serious, burdensome problem of five years' standing, praising the Lord because God's way of prayer really works. Others write to tell that the loved ones for whom they prayed are saved, that they got the jobs for which they called on God, that broken health has been restored in answer to prayer. And so, humbly, I dare hope that God will make the book a blessing to thousands as it teaches people to pray according to the Bible, urges them to pray more, and gives remarkable incidents of answered prayer.

Acknowledgments are due the following publishers for permission to quote from their works: The Moody Press, Chicago, for quotations from *Getting Things From God*, by Dr. Charles A. Blanchard, and *Early Recollections of Dwight L. Moody*, by Farwell; Zondervan Publishing House, Grand Rapids, for quotations from *How I Know God Answers Prayer*, by Mrs. Jonathan Goforth, and *Saved or Lost*, by Dr. W. B. Riley; Loizeaux Brothers for quotation from *Praying in the Holy Spirit*, by Dr. H. A. Ironside; Fleming H. Revell Company for quotation from *Divine Healing*, by Dr. R. A. Torrey; to Dr. W. B. Riley for quotation from his book, *Divine Healing*; to Mr. Robert H. Coleman for permission to quote from the song, "Keep On Praying Till You Pray It Through"; to Professor E. T. Tindley for use of verse of his father's song, "Nothing Between"; and to Hope Publishing Company for use of the song, "Have Thine Own Way, Lord." And I owe more than I can express to the work of my own loyal office staff.

The author is conscious of many faults in this book, and covets the reader's charity. In the midst of revival campaigns up and down the land, in the midst of constant duties as editor of *The Sword of the Lord*, I have gone through long, long months of labor. I shall feel wonderfully repaid if wherever people read it, they will really turn to God in believing, persistent, importunate, surrendered, unceasing, expectant prayer.

With a confession of my own weakness, with an earnest exhortation to others that we really come back to the Bible teaching and to Bible examples of prayer, and with a fervent hope that God may use this book to the blessing of thousands, I commit it to God and send it on its way.

As for me, "I love the LORD, because he hath heard my voice and my supplications. Because he hath inclined his ear unto me, therefore will I call upon him as long as I live." Oh, beloved, we have not because we ask not. Ask, and ye shall receive!

JOHN R. RICE

INTRODUCTION

First published in 1942, *Prayer—Asking and Receiving* by Dr. John R. Rice has remained in print without interruption and has become the world's best-seller on prayer (aside from the Bible).

Dr. Rice was one of the mightiest servants of God of the twentieth century. As a pastor he built a strong, fundamental, soul-winning church during the difficult days of the Great Depression. As an evangelist he conducted hundreds of revivals, citywide crusades and conferences on revival and soul winning in which thousands were saved.

As a writer he wrote approximately 200 books and pamphlets which had sold more than 60 million copies at the time of his death.

As an editor he founded the *Sword of the Lord* newspaper and served as its chief for forty-six years. The *Sword* has influenced literally tens of thousands of preachers and Christian workers all over the world.

In the crucibles of his long and distinguished life, Dr. Rice practiced openly and fervently the teachings in this book. He was a man who loved God and was unashamedly given to prayer. He vocally knocked on Heaven's door and was given so much of what he asked for. It's one thing to pray, but it's something else to get answers. Dr. Rice did both consistently.

Prayer—Asking and Receiving is written in warm, simple language, and yet it plows the depths of the Scripture on this great theme.

This collector's edition of this classic volume is not merely an artifact for a dusty shelf: it is a treasury of truth waiting to be explored. It is one of those rare gems which should be read and studied repeatedly.

As you walk your eyes across its pages, it is our hope that you too will grasp the horns of the altar to "ask" of God and "receive" from God through daily, fervent prayer.

—Dr. Shelton L. Smith
President and Editor
Sword of the Lord Publishers

CHAPTER I

A PRAYER-HEARING GOD

"O thou that hearest prayer, unto thee shall all flesh come."—
Ps. 65:2.

"But without faith it is impossible to please him: for he that cometh to God must believe that he is, and that he is a rewarder of them that diligently seek him."—Heb. 11:6.

I. It Is God's Nature to Hear and Answer Prayer

Our God is a God who hears and answers prayer! Prayer-hearing is one of His attributes, a part of His nature. He inspired the psalmist to call Him "thou that hearest prayer" (Ps. 65:2). He selected that title for Himself and delights to be called the God who hears and the God who answers prayer.

God's attributes, His character, are revealed in the titles given Him in the Scripture. An impressive and very helpful book of daily devotions was written by T. C. Horton, *The Wonderful Names of Our Wonderful Lord.* The names and titles and descriptions by which God reveals Himself in the Bible give insight into the character of God. And one of His titles, by His own divine choice, is "thou that hearest prayer"!

God's *mercy* never changes. It is a part of His character, unaffected by changing dispensations. God's *holiness* and His *righteousness* never vary. He is always holy, always righteous. The characteristics and attributes of God are unchanging and everlasting. He says, "I am the LORD, I change not" (Mal. 3:6). "Jesus Christ the same yesterday, and to day, and for ever," says Hebrews 13:8. And even so, God is in all generations, the same God who delights to hear, and does hear, and answer prayer.

"O thou that hearest prayer, unto thee shall all flesh come," said the psalmist. God hears the prayers of all flesh. He just as willingly hears the prayers of a Gentile as of a Jew. God, who is the Creator of all alike, is eager to hear the prayer of every living soul. And He is as willing to hear the prayer of one generation as another. He was delighted with the prayers of Enoch, who walked and talked with Him, and took him on to Heaven bodily, translating him that he should not die. He heard the prayer of Abraham, the "friend of God," and delivered Lot from Sodom and gave Abraham the longed-for child in his old age. Later it was His delight to answer the prayers of Elijah, raising the dead, sending fire from Heaven, giving drouth and then rain, and then taking him to Heaven. He just as readily heard the prayer of Daniel, a captive in far-off Babylon, whose nation was in disgrace, and revealed to him King Nebuchadnezzar's dream, and delivered

Daniel from the lions' den, just as He delivered the other three Hebrew children from the fiery furnace. What did it matter to God whether the prayer was before the Flood or after with Enoch and Abraham? It did not affect the answer to prayer that Elijah was in the land of Canaan and Daniel a captive in Babylon. So in the New Testament, God heard the prayer of the Canaanitish woman and the prayer of the Italian centurion, Cornelius, as readily as He heard the prayer of Peter, the chief apostle. He heard the prayer of the dying thief, or the publican in the temple, or the fallen woman, as readily as the prayer of the upright and godly. If there are ever conditions that hinder prayer, the conditions are on the part of the one who prays and not on God's part. God is the unchanging God who hears prayer, the God who longs to answer prayer, the God who in all generations and with all kinds of people eagerly listens to prayer. It is a part of His nature, as are His mercy, His justice, His righteousness, His omnipotence. "O thou that hearest prayer, unto thee shall all flesh come."

God hears prayer even for the unsaved in many cases. In his helpful little book, *Praying in the Holy Spirit,* Dr. H. A. Ironside says:

"Prayer is almost universal in mankind. 'O thou that hearest prayer, unto thee shall all flesh come.' Unsaved men pray. All nations pray. It is the sense of need, of weakness, that leads men to cry out for help to a Higher Power; and it is wrong to say, as some have said, that the prayers of unconverted people are never heard. The man whom our Lord healed of his blindness said, 'We know that God heareth not sinners.' This is true, in the sense that he meant it. But the cases of Hagar, in the wilderness, the heathen mariners mentioned in Jonah, and other similar instances must not be overlooked. It is wrong and foolish to try to set bounds to the mercy of God. He who hears the prayer of the young ravens when they cry for food, hears the agonized heart-cries of troubled men who are of 'more value than many sparrows' in His eyes. Both Scripture and history testify to prayers answered in wondrous grace, even when those who prayed were ignorant of the One to whom their entreaties were directed."

It is in the very nature of God to answer prayer, even for unworthy creatures.

II. It Is Impossible to Come to God or to Please Him Without Believing That He Is a Prayer-Hearing and a Prayer-Answering God

How jealous God is of His reputation for hearing and answering prayer! In Hebrews 11:6 we are told,

"But without faith it is impossible to please him: for he that cometh to God must believe that he is, and that he is a rewarder of them that diligently seek him."

Here we are told that before anyone can come to God he must believe two things: first, he must believe that there is a God, and second, he must believe that God is a rewarder of them that diligently seek Him, that is, that God hears and answers prayer. No one can come to God, no one can be saved, no one can please God, except he believes God answers prayer!

Here we see what faith is. "Without faith it is impossible to please him." And this faith simply means that one believes that there is a God and believes that He hears and answers prayer. Faith about a particular matter is a confidence that there is a God who will hear prayer about this particular matter. But there is no faith that does not involve a real confidence in the prayer-hearing and prayer-answering nature of God. One cannot know God except as he comes to know this blessed attribute of His: He is a God who hears prayer!

Is it strange that the one attribute of God everyone must acknowledge before coming to Him is the attribute of hearing and answering prayer? When one comes to God, he is not required, necessarily, to think of God as the Creator. He is not required, necessarily, to think of God's attributes and qualities. They are all involved enough in this quality of hearing and answering prayer that when one believes that God "is a rewarder of them that diligently seek him," then he knows enough about God to come to Him and please Him and receive His blessing! In other words, this quality of hearing and answering prayer is the one God most wants to be known. This is the very heart of God's nature. This reveals His power, His wisdom, His grace, His holiness. There is a God, and He answers prayer. That sums up all the creed absolutely necessary to please God and come to Him. All the other things are implied and understood if you know that much about our infinite, blessed, merciful, prayer-hearing and prayer-answering God!

It becomes clear, then, that when we limit God's willingness to answer prayer, we are guilty of a horrible sin of unbelief. Those who lay so much stress on natural law and intimate that God Himself is a servant of nature, limited by rules He Himself has laid down, are guilty of minimizing faith and so are displeasing God and cannot draw as near to Him as they should. To teach, as some do, that in former dispensations God was more ready to answer, more willing to show wonders and signs to His glory in answer to prayer, is striking at the very dignity of God's character, is unbelief in His essential nature as the prayer-hearing God.

Some people believe that God was more willing to send rain or other physical, material, earthly blessings to the Jews in answer to their prayers than He is willing to send the same blessings on Gentile Christians in this age. They speak as if God had limited Himself to earthly blessings to Jews, under the law, and now limits Himself to give only spiritual blessings to Christians under grace. But that would mean that the Jews would have only half a God and we would have the other half of a God! To limit God in His willingness to hear and to answer prayer for those who diligently seek Him is unbelief in the very nature of God Himself! To believe that in apostolic times God was more willing to work miracles than He is today, again limits God. We ought rather to put the limitation on men and frankly confess that we have not because we ask not, that we ask amiss that we might consume it on our lusts (Jas. 4:2,3). We ought frankly to confess that our unbelief makes us unfit to receive the blessings which the apostles and New Testament Christians often received. But we ought never to believe nor intimate that God has changed His plan or His willingness to hear and answer the prayers of those who diligently seek Him, those who trust Him.

There are dispensations in some little arbitrary matters of God's dealings with men. Once there were animal sacrifices, as type and symbol of faith in a coming Saviour. Now "there remaineth no more sacrifice for sins" (Heb. 10:26). Once Jews were forbidden to eat certain kinds of meat as ceremonially unclean to them. Now "every creature of God is good, and nothing to be refused, if it be received with thanksgiving: For it is sanctified by the word of God and prayer" (I Tim. 4:4,5). Once Jewish boys were to be circumcised, but now "neither circumcision availeth any thing, nor uncircumcision" (Gal. 5:6). Once there was a Jewish Sabbath, Saturday, and other ceremonial laws, which Jews were to observe as a shadow of the coming Christ. But Christ has already come, and this handwriting of ordinances has been taken out of the way and nailed to the cross of Christ, so that now no Christian is to be judged concerning "meat, or in drink, or in respect of an holy day, or of the new moon, or of the sabbath days" (Col. 2:16).

I say in small and arbitrary matters, God had dispensations in His dealings with men. The Holy Spirit once was *with* Christians and now dwells *in* Christians (John 14:17). The change came when Jesus was glorified at His resurrection (John 7:37–39; John 20:22). I say there are such dispensational changes, in some matters; but in the great fundamentals that are a part of the very nature of God, there are no dispensations. God Himself cannot change. He never did; He never will.

God always saved people by faith in Christ, no other way, in the Old Testament or in the New (Acts 10:43). God has always been holy, always has been almighty, always has been merciful; and so God has always been the God who hears and answers prayer. This was understood by the psalmist when he cried, under inspiration of the Holy Spirit, "O thou that hearest prayer, unto thee shall all flesh come" (Ps. 65:2). This is why "he that cometh to God must believe that he is, and that he is a rewarder of them that diligently seek him," as stated in Hebrews 11:6. The unchanging, immutable, everlasting God is a God who always has been anxious to hear, and able and willing and mighty to answer, the prayers of those who earnestly seek Him, those who trust Him.

III. Every Attribute of God Is Implied in the Fact That He Hears and Answers Prayer

When one understands that God hears and answers prayer, then he can faintly perceive all the attributes, all the nature of God. All the other qualities or attributes or characteristics of God are implied when we understand that He answers prayer.

First, a prayer-hearing God is a *living* God. He is not an idol of wood or stone or paper. When the priests of Baal on Mount Carmel cried out to their god, "O Baal, hear us," there was none that answered nor that regarded (I Kings 18:26). An idol has eyes, but it sees not. It has ears, but it hears not. It has a mouth, but it speaks not. A God who hears prayer is a living God.

Second, a prayer-hearing and prayer-answering God is an all-knowing God, omniscient. Does God hear the cry of millions of His people in all countries, in all languages, at the same time? Does He even know the hearts of the suppliants? Does He see the faith, does He know the sincerity, or perceive the hypocrisy, in the hearts of those who pray? Then He is a limitless God who knows all things!

Third, if God is able to answer prayer, then He has all power in Heaven and earth. If God answers prayer for rain, He must control the weather. If God answers prayer about crops, He must control the sun, the insects, the moisture, and even the germ of life in the seed itself. Does God answer prayer about health? Then God must have in His hand every corpuscle in the blood, every nerve, every process of metabolism in the human body! Does God answer prayer about revival or about the conversion of a sinner? Then God must have influence on the very souls and consciences and wills of men! If God answered the prayer of Joshua that the sun might stand still in its relation to the earth for about the space of a day (Josh. 10:12,13), then God controls the whole infinite universe. He answers prayer; He has infinite power, limitless power.

Fourth, if God answers prayer and has such infinite wisdom, such almighty power, then He Himself must be the Creator. There could be none other as powerful; there could be none to dispute His right; there could be none other to limit His work or cross His will. Then the God who answers prayer, in the very nature of the case, is the Creator of the heavens and earth.

Fifth, the God who answers prayer, then, is a miracle-working God. To believe that God is a rewarder of them that diligently seek Him, means that one has faith in all that is ever claimed for God. If there is a God who hears and answers prayers, in the sense of the Bible, then of very necessity His work is miraculous, supernatural, not ordinary, but extraordinary; not human, but divine; not limited, but infinite in scope.

"Does God work miracles today?" someone asks. And the answer is, Yes, if He is the God who rewards those that diligently seek Him, if He is still the God who hears and answers prayer, then His ordinary and natural way of working in answering prayer would be by miracles. Every soul saved is a supernatural act, not a natural one. Every time God intervenes and controls nature or changes a plan to make it rain when it otherwise would not have rained, and does it because someone prayed, then that is a miracle. Every time a person gets well in answer to prayer, when otherwise he would not have gotten well, it is a miracle, a divine intervention in natural affairs. As the late Dr. Blanchard, president of Wheaton College, said in one of his books, "If there be a God, He must act like a God." A God works miracles. A God who would cease to work miracles would cease to be a God, in the Bible sense, that is, a personal God who personally hears and answers the prayer of faith.

Sixth, if God answers prayer, then He is a God of infinite love and mercy! God knows none of us deserve to have our prayers answered. We poor sinners deserve only condemnation and forsaking and punishment of death! But God loves sinners. His mercy is boundless. "Where sin abounded, grace did much more abound" (Rom. 5:20). If there is a God who rewards those who diligently seek Him, that is, who hears and answers the cry, the faith, the need of human beings, then God would give His own Son to atone for sin and make it so He could righteously forgive sin and save sinners and keep them out of Hell and make them into His own image and have them forever with Him in Heaven! Ah, when one really believes that God is a prayer-hearing, prayer-answering God, he has the secret to the very heart of God, and he can dimly see and outline all the graces and powers and majesty of the infinite God! A God who hears and answers prayer is a true God. Any God who does not hear and answer prayer has not the power and the grace to create or support the world, or to love and seek and save lost sinners.

With these things in mind we can understand how God longs to be known by the title, "O thou that hearest prayer," and how no one can please Him, no one can come to Him without believing that He is a God who hears and answers the prayer of those who diligently seek Him!

IV. Nature Itself Points to a Benevolent God Who Hears and Answers Prayer

All nature speaks of a benevolent God, a God who made man, who loves him, and who wants to provide all his needs. In fact, the same Psalm 65 which gives God the title, "O thou that hearest prayer," goes straight from the theme of answered prayer to the theme of the bounty of God in nature, and it ends on that theme. Verses 9 to 13 say:

"Thou visitest the earth, and waterest it: thou greatly enrichest it with the river of God, which is full of water: thou preparest them corn, when thou hast so provided for it. Thou waterest the ridges thereof abundantly: thou settlest the furrows thereof: thou makest it soft with showers: thou blessest the springing thereof. Thou crownest the year with thy goodness; and thy paths drop fatness. They drop upon the pastures of the wilderness: and the little hills rejoice on every side. The pastures are clothed with flocks; the valleys also are covered over with corn; they shout for joy, they also sing."

The psalmist speaking by the Holy Spirit seems to say that the God who loves to answer man's prayers has anticipated so many of his needs, has watered the ground that was dry and needed water, has given to the hungry flocks the pasture, and has covered the valleys with corn for man and beast, and these pastures and valleys shout and sing of the benevolent, loving mercy of God! The theme of Psalm 104 is God's care for the cattle of the earth and for mankind through nature:

"He causeth the grass to grow for the cattle, and herb for the service of man: that he may bring forth food out of the earth; and wine that maketh glad the heart of man, and oil to make his face to shine, and bread which strengtheneth man's heart."—Ps. 104:14,15.

"The high hills are a refuge for the wild goats; and the rocks for the conies."—Vs. 18.

"The young lions roar after their prey, and seek their meat from God"!—Vs. 21.

And then of the beasts even of the sea, we are told that

"These wait all upon thee; that thou mayest give them their meat in due season. That thou givest them they gather: thou openest thine hand, they are filled with good."—Vss. 27, 28.

The God that made the animals makes food for them. The God who made the plants causes the rain to fall for them and the sun to shine upon them. The God who made the honeybees made the flowers for them. For every living thing there is a place, a food, a protection, a provision from the hand of an infinite God. And do not these things show that where there is a want, a need, a desire, God wants to fill it? Where there is a hunger, God wants to satisfy it.

This benevolent, loving, all-providing care of man begins as soon as a child is born, yea, long before it. Before the baby is born, God has prepared the mother's breasts, and then a few hours after childbirth, the mother's breasts begin to prepare milk; and the instinctive seeking of the little puckering lips for food is satisfied in the mother's arms and over the mother's heart! And God has provided in nature every kind of food to balance the diet and supply the need of man. Recently scientists were amazed to find there is a thiamine (or a vitamin) to prevent and cure beri-beri, one for scurvy, and one for rickets. God has prepared insulin for the need of the diabetic person. There is no need of the human body but that God has provided for it, and the supply awaits only the finding and applying of mankind!

Does mankind feel the sex instinct surging within him, the need and cry for a mate? So God has given woman to complement man, and marriage as the fulfillment of man's desire and need.

As soon as there begins some shortage of wood on the earth, man discovers that the bowels of the earth are full of coal which God has laid by for man's use! By the time man has invented an internal combustion engine (the ordinary gas or gasoline engine), it is discovered that infinite lakes of petroleum have been stored up for man's need! When man needed iron for tools, he discovered it was already provided and then learned that God had provided alloys to make the hardest steel. And now that man longs for a lighter metal, rust-proof, it is discovered that there are giant stores of bauxite, the ore from which aluminum is made. The earth proves that God loves man, longs to bless him, longs to provide for every need of mankind!

The whole earth shows it was deliberately planned by infinite wisdom, just to fit man's needs. Suppose that the diameter of the earth had been 10,000 miles instead of 8,000 miles. Then the mass would have been almost doubled, and gravity would have been about twice as great. A man who now weighs 170 pounds, of exactly the same size and with the same muscles, would weigh 332 pounds! His muscles would not be strong enough to lift himself; his stomach would not be big enough to hold enough food to provide strength. Life would be intolerable or impossible. Or if the diameter of the earth were only 6,000 miles instead of 8,000, only 2,000 miles less, the gravity would be so much less that air would be much lighter and rarer. Instead of weighing 14.7 pounds to the square inch, the air pressure (and density) would be only 6.2 pounds. But men cannot live without an oxygen tank where the air is less than 7.3 pounds to the square inch. Life would be impossible on this earth if it had not been tailored exactly to fit man's needs. God made it just the right size. Or if three-fourths of the earth's surface were covered by land instead of by water as now, then the earth would be simply a giant desert, with fringes of vegetation around the seas; and the variation of temperatures would be so great it would be impossible for mankind to live! Or if God had made the surrounding atmosphere with another element instead of oxygen, neither animal nor man could breathe. And if the water were not made of oxygen and hydrogen, there would be no living thing in seas and lakes and rivers. Do not these things suggest that God is a God who in His very nature longs to provide what mankind needs?

Nature does not tell of Calvary and redemption, but it does point to an infinitely merciful, benevolent, loving God, whose heart is open to mankind. He who clothes the lilies of the field and notes the fall of the sparrow is the God who hears and answers prayers of those who diligently seek Him and who trust Him. James 1:17 says, "Every good gift and every perfect gift is from above, and cometh down from the Father of lights, with whom is no variableness, neither shadow of turning." God never varies, in any age, nor with any people, from His constant watchfulness to give what men need, what their hearts cry out for, what will make them happy and good. And does not that mean that by very nature God is predisposed to hear the cry of men and is lovingly concerned about whatever want or desire or need is felt by any contrite heart who seeks God's face!

Then if God be a God who hears and answers prayer, let us pray! Prayer, then, becomes the most compelling Christian duty. God never commanded us to sing without ceasing, nor preach without ceasing, nor give without ceasing, nor work without ceasing; but He did command, "Pray without ceasing" (I Thess. 5:17). The apostles after Pentecost demanded the selection of deacons that the apostles might give themselves to prayer and the ministry of the Word (Acts 6:4)—not first the preaching, but first that they should give themselves to prayer!

When Solomon built the temple at Jerusalem and dedicated it to God, God did not say He would be listening for the songs of the antiphonal choirs nor watching for the smoke of the altars where many sacrifices should be offered; but God said, "Now mine eyes shall be open, and mine ears attent unto the prayer that is made in this place" (II Chron. 7:15). Then in Isaiah 56:7 God said, "For mine house shall be called an house of prayer for all people." And Jesus quoted this Scripture as recorded in Matthew and in Mark and in Luke. The temple was primarily a house of prayer for all people. Back of all the preaching, the praying, the prophesying, the singing; back of all religious observances, God intended there should be a living faith in a God who hears and answers prayer, and thus that men should call upon the name of the Lord! There is no pleasing of God without prayer! God is the God who hears prayer. "Without faith it is impossible to please him: for he that cometh to God must believe that he is, AND THAT HE IS A REWARDER OF THEM THAT DILIGENTLY SEEK HIM" (Heb. 11:6).

O Thou God who hearest prayer, put it in our hearts to believe Thee and to pray!

CHAPTER II

WHY PRAY?

I. *Because God insistently commands it in the Bible.*

II. *Because prayer is God's appointed way for Christians to get things.*

III. *Because prayer is God's way for Christians to have fullness of joy.*

IV. *Because prayer is the way out of all trouble, the cure for all worry and anxious care.*

V. *Because answered prayer is the only unanswerable argument against skepticism, unbelief, modernism and infidelity.*

VI. *Because prayer is the only way to have the power of the Holy Spirit for God's work.*

VII. *Because "whosoever shall call upon the name of the Lord shall be saved."*

There are most compelling reasons why everybody ought to pray, why prayer ought to be the most regular and continual thing in our lives. Jesus said that men ought to pray. Here we will give some of the best reasons why people should pray,

I. Because God Insistently Commands It in the Bible

The first good reason for doing anything is that God has commanded it. And God has commanded us to pray. Throughout the Bible are Scriptures with the imperative command to pray.

1. *"And he spake a parable unto them to this end, that men ought always to pray, and not to faint"* (Luke 18:1).

This is a statement, not that some men should pray, but that men, mankind, everywhere and in all times, should pray. It is an impelling duty which Jesus taught.

2. *"Pray without ceasing"* (I Thess. 5:17).

Here is a command without any modification by the context. As long as men in any country, in any language, read the Bible, they will read this plain command to pray without ceasing. Not only ought we to pray; we ought to pray all the time! Prayer should be the continual turning of our hearts to God about everything we need and everything we want until the subconscious mind is continually in touch with God. As a mother in her sleep listens for the cry of her baby, so a Christian's heart can be attuned to God while he is absorbed in daily duties or even when he sleeps!

3. *"Be careful for nothing; but in every thing by prayer and supplication with thanksgiving let your requests be made known unto God"* (Phil. 4:6).

A Christian is to pray literally about everything.

4. *"I exhort therefore, that, first of all, supplications, prayers, intercessions, and giving of thanks, be made for all men"* (I Tim. 2:1).

We are commanded to pray not only at all times, but for all men.

5. *"Praying always with all prayer and supplication in the Spirit, and watching thereunto with all perseverance and supplication for all saints; And for me"* (Eph. 6:18,19).

This passage closes the familiar description of the armor of a Christian, and the final word about how to be strong in the Lord is this command that we are to pray *always* with *all* prayer, with *all* perseverance for *all* the saints. Notice how many *alls* there are. And as the Christians at Ephesus were commanded to pray for Paul, so it is implied that we also should pray for all the ministers particularly, as well as "all saints."

6. *"Watch and pray, that ye enter not into temptation"* (Matt. 26:41).

This command of our Saviour to the apostles is repeated in Mark 14:38; Luke 22:40; and in Luke 22:46. But since we are to "observe all things whatsoever" Jesus commanded the apostles (Matt. 28:20), then we too are to watch and pray lest we enter into temptation.

Besides the above general commands for Christians to pray all the time, for all people and about everything, there are many other commands to pray for specific matters. Many times Paul, in his epistles, by divine inspiration, commanded the readers to pray for him (Col. 4:3; I Thess. 5:25; II Thess. 3:1; Heb. 13:18, as well as Eph. 6:19).

Prayer, then, is a duty expressly commanded for every Christian, all the time, and about everybody and everything. Not to pray is a sin, the sin of disobedience to the plain and often repeated command of God! Lack of prayer is a sin. Doubtless all of our sins and mistakes and failures are prayer sins, prayer mistakes and prayer failures. Samuel said to the people of Israel, "God forbid that I should sin against the LORD in ceasing to pray for you" (I Sam. 12:23). Christians ought to pray because it is so strictly commanded in the Bible.

II. Because Prayer Is God's Appointed
Way for Christians to Get Things

The outside, unbelieving world expects to get things by work or by planning or by scheming or by accident, but God's children are taught that they are to get things by asking and that the reason we do not have is that we do not ask.

James 4:2 says,

"Ye lust, and have not: ye kill, and desire to have, and cannot obtain: ye

fight and war, yet ye have not, because ye ask not."

"Ye have not, because ye ask not"! Fighting, warring, struggling and scheming—these are not God's ways for a Christian to get things. We are to get by asking. And the reason we have not is not "because ye work not," nor is it "because ye plan not." No, it is "because ye ask not." Asking is God's way for a Christian to get things!

You may say that the way for a farmer to grow a crop is to break his ground, sow his seed, plow out the weeds; in other words, that the way to have a crop would be by diligent and intelligent work. But I have seen farmers who worked hard and intelligently, and then there was no rain, and they made no crop! Or storms beat down the wheat before it could be harvested, or boll weevils and pink boll worms ruined the cotton. So human wisdom and human toil cannot be relied upon. No, a Christian is not to depend upon his own toil nor his own planning but to ask of God. To the farmer God's Word says, "Ye have not, because ye ask not." Asking, or in other words, prayer, is God's way for a farmer to succeed.

An unemployed man may think the way to get a job is to make the rounds of all the employment agencies, to take special training for his job, or to get recommendations by men in high places in business. But I have known men to tramp the weary rounds day after day, making applications, only to hear always the same story, "We have all the men we can use," or "too old," or "We only hire men with special training which you do not have," or "We will put you on our waiting list." I say that human efforts to get a job often fail. But, thank God, a Christian has other resources; he can pray and get a job from God! Let us add one explanatory word to the Scripture without changing its meaning at all, and God says, "Ye have not a job because ye ask not for one." Asking is the way to get a job.

In Jackson, Michigan, in 1940 as I preached on prayer, I felt suddenly impressed to speak to a young man on the second seat. Pointing my finger to him publicly, I said, "Have you got a job?" He replied that he did not have.

"If God would give you a job, would you really serve Him with all your heart?" I asked.

He responded, "Yes, I would! And I sure need one."

"Then you go to God tonight and ask Him for a job, and I will pray with you about it," I said. "You say to God, 'Lord, if there is anything in my life that displeases You, if You will show me, I will confess and forsake it. If there is anything wrong with this request for a job, You show me, and I will change my prayer to fit the leading of the Holy Spirit. And if You do not definitely show me what is wrong or lead me to pray otherwise, I am going to expect a job right away in answer to this prayer.'"

The next night he was in the service, and again in the midst of the sermon I felt impressed to speak to him. "Have you got that job yet?" I asked.

"Not yet," he said. But his wife spoke up quickly and said, "You have too; you worked all day today."

"But it is not the job I asked for, and it is not permanent," he replied.

Then I urged him, "Tonight you go to a secret place alone and stay there until God gives you assurance about this matter, and I will pray with you."

The services closed, and I returned to my home in Wheaton. The next week there came a wonderful letter from this young man, telling how he had gotten just the job he had asked for, in the plant and in the department and under the boss which he had specified in his request to God. With overflowing heart he said, "I wish I could tell everybody that the way to get what they need is to ask God for it!"

The Saviour taught us to pray, "Give us this day our daily bread" (Matt. 6:11). The way to get daily bread is to ask God for it.

This does not mean that God wants a Christian to loaf. In fact, the right kind of praying will make a Christian willing to work or to do anything God leads him to do. But it certainly does mean that we should not depend upon our work, but rather, we should depend upon God to give us the results in answer to prayer.

We must remember that God can use means. God can use medicines and doctors to heal the sick. Luke was "the beloved physician" (Col. 4:14). Timothy was commanded to "use a little wine [grape juice] for thy stomach's sake" (I Tim. 5:23). King Hezekiah was healed when Isaiah commanded to place a lump of figs on the boil, which was about to kill him (Isa. 38:21). God can use means, and He may answer our prayers by using human means. He may use an employment agency to give us a job by our diligent application and seeking. He may use our hard work on the farm to make a crop. Certain it is that when God takes charge, He can bring the results out of our poor labors. But remember this, that God does *not always* use human means. Sometimes through ways utterly unexpected and without human instrumentalities, God chooses to work His will in answer to prayer. God can heal the sick without medicine, and sometimes He delights to do it that way in answer to prayer. God can give jobs where you do not have an application in. God can send money that you didn't earn. How well I know, thank God, from blessed experiences that this is true! But the point is that whether God uses well-known means or does it by ways utterly unexpected or even by ways impossible with men, still it is God who gives what we need. And the way for us to get what we need is to ask for it. Praying is God's appointed way for a Christian to have what he needs and what he wants. Every other way may fail. "Ye lust, and have not: ye kill, and desire to have, and cannot obtain: ye fight and war, yet ye have not, because ye ask not."

Suppose there are two men in conversation, one a lost man, the other a saved man, a child of God. The unconverted man says, "These are surely hard times. I can't get a job. I have walked until my feet are sore. I have answered all the advertisements. I just don't get the breaks." And suppose the Christian man answered, "Yes, these surely are hard times. I have walked until my feet are sore too. I have answered all the advertisements in the papers, and yet I can't find a job. You are right. A poor man just doesn't have a chance these days." God forbid! Has the Christian no more resources than a lost man? What good is it to be a Christian if you have no one to answer your prayers, no one to care for your needs, no one to give you what you want! There is no joy, there is no testimony, there is no victory in that kind of Christianity. Thank God, a Christian can confidently pray and say, "My Father, You know I need a job. Everything in the world is in Your hands. So I ask You to give me, Your child, a job so I can have daily bread, so I can care for my family, so I can give to others, and so others may know that God takes care of His children." And for millions God has answered such prayers.

The Christian can sing,

> **My Father is rich in houses and lands,**
> **He holdeth the wealth of the world in His hands!**
> **Of rubies and diamonds, of silver and gold,**
> **His coffers are full—He has riches untold.**

The God who notes the fall of every sparrow, who has clothed the lilies of the field in raiment more gorgeous than Solomon's, who counts all the hairs in the heads of His beloved children for whom Christ died, that heavenly Father has appointed that His children get things by prayer. "Ye have not, because ye ask not."

Praying is God's appointed way for Christians to get things.

III. Because Prayer Is God's Way for Christians to Have Fullness of Joy

Christians ought to be happy. Christians ought to have their wants satisfied. Christians ought not to live defeated, unhappy lives, tormented by needs which cannot be met. So God has appointed that Christians can have fullness of joy all the time by having their prayers answered.

In John 16:24 Jesus said,

"Hitherto have ye asked nothing in my name: ask, and ye shall receive, THAT YOUR JOY MAY BE FULL."

Imagine, if you will, a child whose father loves him so much that he can come day by day and ask his father for anything he needs. If the child in his ignorance asks for something that would cause him trouble and sorrow, the father very carefully explains and teaches the child what would be best, and then teaches him to ask for something far better than that for which he had intended to ask. Thus the child has every desire granted and lives in a blessed state of happiness and joy because his father delights to give him the desires of his heart.

Or imagine a young wife, married to a rich husband who so loves her and delights in her that he gives her everything for which she expresses a desire. Her life is filled with happiness because her husband loves her so much and gives her all the things for which her heart craves.

And that is what God wants to do for His children, only He can do infinitely more. The father cannot change the heart attitude of his child, and so a rich father often finds his son grows indolent and unprincipled, and the father's wealth proves a curse to his son. But God can teach His children and lead them by the Holy Spirit to pray for the things that will bring fullness of joy and no curse. "The blessing of the LORD, it maketh rich, and he addeth no sorrow with it" (Prov. 10:22).

And a young husband has many times spent thousands of dollars trying to make his wife happy; but he could not give health, nor could he give the baby that she desired, nor could he give contentment of mind in the midst of the giddy round of social affairs. So no father and no husband can give fullness of joy. But thank God, that is just exactly what our heavenly Father says He wants to do for us. He wants to give us all we ask, and even help us ask aright. We are to ask and receive so our joy will be full.

Prayer, then, is the secret of constant joy, the secret really of FULL-NESS OF JOY. A rich, full life for a Christian depends on how much and how he prays. If you get on such praying ground that you can get things from God, get all the desires of your heart, get all that you need, then day by day you can live a victorious, happy life. The way to be happy and full of joy is to pray. Prayer is the secret of fullness of joy, and for that reason Christians should pray.

IV. Because Prayer Is the Way out of All Trouble, the Cure for All Worry and Anxious Care

If prayer is the way to get what you want and to be full of joy, as we showed above, then prayer is also the way to get rid of what you do not want and get out of trouble and away from worry and care.

Philippians 4:6,7 says,

"Be careful for nothing; but in every thing by prayer and supplication with thanksgiving let your requests be made known unto God. And the

peace of God, which passeth all understanding, shall keep your hearts and minds through Christ Jesus."

"Be careful for nothing," says the Scripture! Christians should not be full of care or anxious over anything. And the remedy is, "In every thing by prayer and supplication with thanksgiving let your requests be made known unto God." A Christian is to *"pray through" about everything;* thus, day by day he continually has his cares and worries dissolved away, and his heart is left in perfect peace all the time! For God promises to those who bring everything to Him in prayer with supplication and thanksgiving that "the peace of God, which passeth all understanding, shall keep your hearts and minds through Christ Jesus."

Worry is a blighting sin. It is the very opposite of trust. Yet how many Christians are guilty of this sin! They lose their joy, they dwell in uncertainty, their lives are harried by burdens they ought never to carry and by fears they ought never to entertain. And the secret of ending worry and anxious care is to take things to God every day and pray through with prayer and supplication and thanksgiving.

First Peter 5:7 has another way of stating the same command,

"Casting all your care upon him; for he careth for you."

And Psalm 55:22 says,

"Cast thy burden upon the LORD, and he shall sustain thee."

Every Christian ought to be marked by a calm, unworried frame of mind, a deep, settled peace of heart that the worldling can never attain and that the world itself can never give. Here is one of the marks of a really successful, happy Christian, whose cares are all laid on the Lord Jesus. Every Christian ought to be able to boast in the Lord as did David in Psalm 34:6,

"This poor man cried, and the LORD heard him, and saved him out of all his troubles"!

Have you been delivered from all your troubles? Are you continually, day by day being delivered every time you need deliverance from trouble and worry and care? You CAN have this deliverance, this peace, this quietness, this freedom from worry. And the way to have it is to *pray, to pray about everything, to pray through* until you get the peace which God has promised, and then, free of all anxious care, daily end in thanksgiving!

Dr. Walter Lewis Wilson, the beloved physician-preacher, said that years ago he had a motto painted and hung by his desk which said, "Why pray when you can worry?" That expresses the attitude of heart of the average Christian. He worries instead of prays. But prayer is the way to end worries. Prayer is the way to constant peace under any circumstances, anywhere.

Do not misunderstand me. I do not mean that a Christian will never have trouble. But in the trouble he can have the sweetest peace all the time. I do not mean that a Christian will never be sick. But in the sickness he can have the ever-present nearness, consciously, of the Holy Spirit. I do not mean that a Christian will never have any problems. But I mean that he can daily take those problems to God and have them settled, without any fret, without any of the unrest that comes from unbelief. A Christian can take his burdens to the Lord and leave them there day by day and have perfect peace. And the only way he can do this is by prayer, regular prayer with supplication and thanksgiving about every problem.

Are you burdened? Then pray your way out!

> **What a Friend we have in Jesus,**
> **All our sins and griefs to bear!**
> **What a privilege to carry**
> ***Everything* to God in prayer!**
>
> **O what peace we often forfeit,**
> **O what needless pain we bear,**
> **All because we do not carry**
> ***Everything* to God in prayer!**

A Christian can make such a habit of praying about every need, every burden, every fret, every care, every problem until he can obey the command of the Saviour to "take no thought for your life, what ye shall eat, or what ye shall drink; nor yet for your body, what ye shall put on" (Matt. 6:25), and again, "Therefore take no thought, saying, What shall we eat? or, What shall we drink? or, Wherewithal shall we be clothed?" (Matt. 6:31). The heathen people seek after these things, are worried and fretted by these problems, but the Christian has a beloved heavenly Father to whom he can take all his burdens and can seek first the kingdom of God and His righteousness, knowing that all these things shall be added unto him, as promised in Matthew 6:33.

And thus by daily praying through problems as they come, one can learn to "take therefore no thought for the morrow" (Matt. 6:34), but have perfect peace.

Prayer is the way out of trouble, the way to do away with worries and anxious care. Therefore, let us pray!

V. Because Answered Prayer Is the Only Unanswerable Argument Against Skepticism, Unbelief, Modernism and Infidelity

"Without faith it is impossible to please him," says Hebrews 11:6. And what is faith? "For he that cometh to God must believe that he is, and that he is a rewarder of them that diligently seek him." Thus Hebrews 11:6 tells us that no one can come to God unless he believes that God answers prayer.

And what is the answer, then, to infidelity and atheism and modernism? How can we convince those who do not believe in our God? Why, by having our prayers answered, by having such unmistakable answers to prayer as to prove that there is a prayer-answering and prayer-hearing God! The way to answer infidelity is to let God prove Himself by answering prayers.

Argument is sometimes necessary. The Bible proves itself the Word of God. All nature declares there is a God. "The heavens declare the glory of God; and the firmament sheweth his handywork," says Psalm 19:1. There are many, many evidences that there is a God who answers prayer. But the only absolutely unanswerable evidence is answered prayer itself. I can know there is a God who answers prayer if I see the answers to prayer so unmistakably that I cannot doubt.

Thus at Mount Carmel, Elijah gathered the people of Israel together to prove to them that the Lord was the true God and that the idol Baal was no God who could see or hear or help. When the four hundred fifty prophets of Baal cried in vain to their god and he could not answer by fire from Heaven, Elijah built an altar, laid thereon the wood and the bullock, put no fire under, and poured over it twelve barrels of water; and then he prayed that God would send fire from Heaven in the sight of all the people to burn up the sacrifice and prove that He was God. Elijah's prayer was this:

"LORD God of Abraham, Isaac, and of Israel, let it be known this day that thou art God in Israel, and that I am thy servant, and that I have done all these things at thy word. Hear me, O LORD, hear me, that this people may know that thou art the LORD God, and that thou hast turned their heart back again."—I Kings 18:36,37.

Analyze that prayer carefully, and you will see it is a plea that God will prove Himself God by answering prayer. And when the answer should come it would not only prove God is the true God, but it would prove that Elijah was His servant and that Elijah's message was from God.

And so the answer came. "Then the fire of the LORD fell and consumed the burnt-sacrifice, and the wood, and the stones, and the dust, and licked up the water that was in the trench" (I Kings 18:38). And what was the result? What did this answer of prayer do to the infidelity of the people? Verse 39 tells us,

"When all the people saw it, they fell on their faces: and they said, The LORD, he is the God; the LORD, he is the God"!

A visible, definite answer of prayer, in a moment of time, did away with all infidelity of the people, and the whole nation fell on their faces saying, "The LORD, he is the God; the LORD, he is the God"! We ought to pray, then, because God's answer to prayer is proof that can put to rout all the modernism and unbelief.

And until God's people can have definite, remarkable, provable answers to prayer, then we had as well expect that our young people will grow up doubting that there is a miracle-working, prayer-hearing and prayer-answering God. The remedy for unbelief is that God's people will pray and have their prayers answered.

All your argument against modernism, against evolution, against atheism, will fall on deaf ears if along with your argument you cannot give some definite proof in answered prayer. If Christianity is the true religion and if God be a miracle-working, prayer-hearing, prayer-answering God, then the unsaved world has a right to demand that we prove it by having our prayers answered.

How doubts would flee away if we should begin to pray boldly and definitely and expect God to give concrete and specific answers to our prayers day by day!

Notice the power of the argument of Gideon in Judges 6:12,13:

"And the angel of the LORD appeared unto him, and said unto him, The LORD is with thee, thou mighty man of valour. And Gideon said unto him, Oh my Lord, if the LORD be with us, why then is all this befallen us? and where be all his miracles which our fathers told us of, saying, Did not the LORD bring us up from Egypt? but now the LORD hath forsaken us, and delivered us into the hands of the Midianites."

With good reason Gideon answered back to the angel of the Lord and said, "If the LORD be with us, why is all this befallen us? and *where be all his miracles which our fathers told us of*, saying, Did not the LORD bring us up from Egypt?" Gideon felt with reason that if God was with him, he must have the evidence that God would show Himself and prove Himself by answered, definite, concrete manifestations of His power, in answer to prayer. And God did not scorn the plea of Gideon. God did not say, as so many of our beloved but powerless Bible teachers today say, that miracles are all for the past and not for the present. Rather, God was delighted that Gideon demanded evidence of His power. God showed the miracle of fire to consume the offering Gideon brought; He made the fleece first dry and then wet, answering Gideon's prayer. God is perfectly willing to prove that He is the prayer-hearing and the prayer-answering God. And that is the only real remedy for unbelief and atheism.

In Egypt, after God had done for Moses what they could not do with all their enchantment,

"Then the magicians said unto Pharaoh, This is the finger of God."— Exod. 8:19.

A definite answer to prayer convinced these godless, heathen magicians.

God answered Daniel's prayer and revealed to him the dream of

Nebuchadnezzar; then Nebuchadnezzar was convinced and fell on his face, and he said,

"Of a truth it is, that your God is a God of gods, and a Lord of kings, and a revealer of secrets, seeing thou couldest reveal this secret."— Dan. 2:47.

Later God revealed to Daniel the other dream of Nebuchadnezzar (chapter 4), foretelling how the king would live as a beast for seven years. And when the king recovered from his insanity and returned to his throne and glory, the Scriptures indicate that he was truly converted to God (Dan. 4:34–37). Answered prayer is a cure for unbelief.

Acts 13:6 -12 is the story of how Sergius Paulus, a deputy of the island of Cyprus, was wonderfully converted when he saw the answer to Paul's prayer (the prayer is implied but not given), for the blinding of Elymas the sorcerer. Verse 12 says,

"Then the deputy, when he saw what was done, believed, being astonished at the doctrine of the Lord."

We had as well face this question squarely. When the churches of our land again see the startling conversions of drunkards and harlots, with lives transformed, then sinners will come to church and will listen respectfully to the Word of God. And when God's people pray for and get the healing of the sick, get rain when they need it, get jobs, get daily bread, get revivals, all in answer to prayer, then modernism and atheism will lose their hold on the minds of the mass of people in America, and even the unconverted will believe that there is a miracle-working God who answers prayer.

We ought to pray and have our prayers answered as the definite, powerful antidote for unbelief, the only unanswerable argument against atheism and infidelity.

It is not always God's will to heal the sick. It was not always His will to heal the sick in Bible times. But He healed the sick often enough to prove that He was the prayer-hearing God. God did not save every sinner under the ministry of Paul, and He will not save every sinner under the ministry of anybody else. But God was willing to save the most outrageous sinners, and in Bible times He did save them by His wonderful stretched-out hand in such fashion as to convince the gainsayers. And God will do the same today and prove His power the same today if we trust Him.

Even in Bible times, miracles were never a common thing, a plaything of the careless and a reward of the curious. No, no! Miracles in physical matters were always rare and were given only as they could honor the Lord. But God gave faith for them often enough to prove that He is the miracle-working, prayer-hearing and prayer-answering God. And He will do the same today for those who diligently seek Him and give Him a chance to prove Himself.

But this does not apply only to physical miracles. God proves Himself abundantly by saving the souls of those for whom we pray, by giving revivals, by providing for daily needs, by giving peace, by giving wisdom to meet daily problems, by giving fullness of joy and the power of the Holy Spirit. We should pray, then, because answered prayer proves there is a prayer-hearing God. It is the positive antidote for doubts and skepticism, unbelief or even atheism.

VI. Because Prayer Is the Only Way to Have the Power of the Holy Spirit for God's Work

As D. L. Moody well said, it is foolish and wicked to try to do God's work without God's power. But there is no way for Christians to have God's power except by prayer. In Luke 11:13 is this plain promise,

"If ye then, being evil, know how to give good gifts unto your children: how much more shall your heavenly Father give the Holy Spirit to them that ask him?"

Here the Lord is not speaking about the indwelling of the Holy Spirit. The Holy Spirit comes in the human body to dwell at conversion. Ever since Jesus Christ rose from the dead, breathed on the disciples and said, "Receive ye the Holy Ghost" (John 20:22), Christians have the Holy Spirit abiding in them. Every saved person has the Holy Spirit living in his body as a temple (see Rom. 8:9; I Cor. 6:19,20; II Cor. 6:16). But Jesus in Luke 11:13 meant that God will give the Holy Spirit in soul-winning power to those that ask Him. In the same passage He gives a parable of a man who goes to a friend at midnight, saying unto him, "Friend, lend me three loaves; For a friend of mine in his journey is come to me, and I have nothing to set before him." And Jesus said that this man, longing to have bread for a friend, got it only by importunity. And so Jesus teaches us here, a Christian who longs to have the bread of life for an unsaved friend may get it by begging God for it. And then Jesus explains the point of the whole parable by this blessed promise, "How much more shall your heavenly Father give the Holy Spirit to them that ask him?" We may have bread for sinners if we beg God for it, *and in no other way!* "Importunity," Jesus said, was the way a man got bread from a friend for another poor hungry friend (Luke 11:8).

It has always been true that revivals came in answer to prayer. In II Chronicles 7:14 God promised a blessed revival "if my people, which are called by my name, *shall humble themselves, and pray, and seek my face, and turn from their wicked ways."* The Prophet Habakkuk prayed, "O LORD, revive thy work in the midst of the years" (Hab. 3:2). He knew that revivals come in answer to prayer. But what is a revival? Is it not simply that God puts His power upon His ministers and upon His people, and the Holy Spirit of God does His work in blessing the saints and in convicting and saving sinners? So the secret of power on preaching is in prayer. The secret of power on personal soul-winning effort is in prayer. The secret of revival is prayer.

If any Christian longs to have personal, definite enduement of power, the power of the Holy Spirit, then this is the way to have it. Let him seek God's face in prayer with whatever confession and self-judgment and heart-surrender are necessary as he waits on God, until the Spirit of God can fill him and use him.

I want you to notice these Bible instances of where people prayed for the power of the Holy Spirit.

1. Before Pentecost the disciples prayed,

"And when they were come in, they went up into an upper room, where abode both Peter, and James, and John, and Andrew, Philip, and Thomas, Bartholomew, and Matthew, James the son of Alphæus, and Simon Zelotes, and Judas the brother of James. These all CONTINUED WITH ONE ACCORD IN PRAYER AND SUPPLICATION, with the women, and Mary the mother of Jesus, and with his brethren."—Acts 1:13,14.

Following this season of prayer and supplication the Holy Spirit fell on the disciples at Pentecost, and three thousand people were saved and baptized.

2. After Pentecost the disciples needed again to be filled with the Holy Spirit, so they prayed. Acts 4:31 says:

"And when they had prayed, the place was shaken where they were assembled together; AND THEY WERE ALL FILLED WITH THE HOLY GHOST, and they spake the word of God with boldness"!

Please compare Acts 2:4 and Acts 4:31. You will find that these nine words are in both verses exactly alike, "And they were all filled with the Holy Ghost." They prayed before Pentecost, and the power of the Holy Spirit came upon them. They prayed after Pentecost, and the power of the Holy Spirit came upon them. Prayer was necessary after Pentecost the same as before and brought the same results after Pentecost as before.

3. At Samaria Philip preached, and there were many truly converted. But the power of the Holy Spirit for witnessing and soul winning did not come upon the converts until after prayer. Acts 8:14–16 says:

"Now when the apostles which were at Jerusalem heard that Samaria had received the word of God, they sent unto them Peter and John: Who, when they were come down, PRAYED FOR THEM, THAT THEY MIGHT RECEIVE THE HOLY GHOST: (For as yet he was fallen upon none of them: only they were baptized in the name of the Lord Jesus.)"

Be sure to note the distinction the Scripture makes between the Holy Spirit's being *in* a Christian and the Holy Spirit's being *on* a Christian. *In* refers to the indwelling which these disciples already had, as every Christian has had since the day Jesus rose from the dead. *On* means the power of the Holy Spirit's coming upon a Christian for service.

Note that these people received the Holy Spirit, His *power for service, after prayer!*

4. Paul the apostle was filled with the Holy Spirit three days after his conversion, and that in answer to prayer. Acts 9:3–6 tells how Saul was converted on the road to Damascus. He called Jesus "Lord" and said, "What wilt thou have me to do?" But yet Paul went three days without eating or drinking (vs. 9), in constant prayer (vs. 11). What was Paul praying for? The answer is given in Acts 9:17, which says,

"And Ananias went his way, and entered into the house; and putting his hands on him said, Brother Saul, the Lord, even Jesus, that appeared unto thee in the way as thou camest, hath sent me, that thou mightest receive thy sight, AND BE FILLED WITH THE HOLY GHOST."

Paul was filled with the Holy Ghost *after three days of fasting and prayer.* Then he "straightway" began his preaching ministry in the power of the Holy Spirit.

5. Paul and Barnabas were especially filled with the Holy Spirit for their missionary journey in answer to prayer. In Acts 13:1–4 we have the story of a group who met in fasting and prayer until the Holy Spirit said, "Separate me Barnabas and Saul for the work whereunto I have called them." Then we are told, *"AND WHEN THEY HAD FASTED AND PRAYED, and laid their hands on them, they sent them away. So they, BEING SENT FORTH BY THE HOLY GHOST, departed unto Seleucia; and from hence they sailed to Cyprus."* And no wonder there were many marvels of souls saved by the working of the Holy Spirit through these people who had been filled with the Holy Spirit after fasting and prayer and waiting on God.

The way for a Christian to have the power of God for His service is to pray.

6. It was Paul's constant prayer for other Christians that they should be filled with the Holy Spirit. In Ephesians 1:15–19 Paul mentions his prayer for the Ephesian saints, that God

"May give unto you the spirit of wisdom and revelation in the knowledge of him...And what is the exceeding greatness of his power."

That is a prayer that they might be filled with the Spirit and have His power. Again in Ephesians 3:14–19 the same object of prayer is mentioned.

"For this cause I bow my knees unto the Father of our Lord Jesus Christ...he would grant you...to be strengthened with might by his

Spirit...that ye might be filled with all the fulness of God."

Paul was praying for these Christians to be filled with the Holy Spirit. His power comes in answer to prayer.

Prayer, unceasing supplication to God, was the secret of the power that came at Pentecost and resulted in the saving of so many souls. Prayer, heart-broken, sin-confessing, penitent prayer, was the secret of power every time the saints of God had seasons of revivals and every time individuals were filled with the Spirit of God for His blessed service. We ought to pray, then, because prayer is God's appointed way for us to have the power of the Holy Spirit to do His work.

VII. Because "Whosoever Shall Call Upon the Name of the Lord Shall Be Saved"

In Romans 10:13 we are told that "whosoever shall call upon the name of the Lord shall be saved." A lost sinner, then, may pray to God for salvation. So, in Luke 18, we see the poor publican beating upon his breast and crying out, "God be merciful to me a sinner," and see him going down to his house justified, saved that very day. Thus we read the sweet story of the dying thief who turned to Jesus, on the cross beside him, and said, "Lord, remember me when thou comest into thy kingdom." And we hear the sweet promise of the Saviour beside him, "To day shalt thou be with me in paradise" (Luke 23:39–43). So lost sinners have a right to pray, and everyone who genuinely calls on the Lord for salvation will be saved.

Of course, it is made clear in the Bible many, many times that heart-faith is the deciding factor in salvation. "Believe on the Lord Jesus Christ, and thou shalt be saved," said Paul and Silas to the Philippian jailer (Acts 16:31). Jesus said to Nicodemus, "Whosoever believeth in him [God's only begotten Son] should not perish, but have everlasting life." Again Jesus said, "Verily, verily, I say unto you, He that believeth on me hath everlasting life" (John 6:47). One who puts his trust in Christ is saved, instantly, has everlasting life. So it is clear that no one has to go through a formal prayer in order to be saved. There need not be words aloud; there need not be any of what people generally call prayer. Faith is a turning in the heart to depend on Christ. And God hears the faintest cry of the heart without a whisper of breath, without a moving of the lips.

But often the trembling steps of faith are taken with more ease when one prays, consciously putting into words his cry for mercy, his dependence. How many sinners have been able to trust the Lord with more assurance when they put into words the plea of the publican's prayer, "God be merciful to me a sinner." So, dear friend, if you who read this are unsaved, feel perfectly free to call on God for mercy and forgiveness, and be assured that God will hear, that He does hear, that He has heard already, when you call on Him for forgiveness and salvation. Anyone who has faith enough to ask God sincerely for mercy and forgiveness has faith enough to be sure God has heard him, for Jesus said, "Him that cometh to me I will in no wise cast out" (John 6:37). And any sinner may claim the sweet promise that "whosoever shall call upon the name of the Lord shall be saved."

And now in conclusion, let us remember these seven reasons why we ought to pray: 1. It is commanded plainly of God that Christians ought to pray always about everything and about everybody, with all prayer and supplication. 2. Prayer is God's appointed way for Christians to get things. 3. Prayer is the way for Christians to have fullness of joy. 4. Prayer is God's cure for worry, the way out of trouble and anxious care. 5. Answered prayer is God's way of stopping the mouths of unbelievers, God's unanswerable argument against infidelity. 6. Prayer is the way to have the power of the Holy Spirit for God's blessed work. 7. "Whosoever shall call upon the name of the Lord shall be saved." Therefore, beloved brethren, let us pray! Oh, how many and how weighty are the reasons that Christians should pray!

CHAPTER III

PRAYER IS ASKING

"Ask, and it shall be given you."—Matt. 7:7.

"For every one that asketh receiveth."—Matt. 7:8.

"Ask, and ye shall receive."—John 16:24.

"Ye have not, because ye ask not."—Jas. 4:2.

"How much more shall your Father which is in heaven give good things to them that ask him?"—Matt. 7:11.

"And all things, whatsoever ye shall ask in prayer, believing, ye shall receive."—Matt. 21:22.

"How much more shall your heavenly Father give the Holy Spirit to them that ask him?"—Luke 11:13.

"If ye shall ask any thing in my name, I will do it."—John 14:14.

Although surrounded much of the time by a wife, six daughters and a number of secretaries, I am continually astonished at the ways of women. When I was first married, my wife and a young lady friend insisted on going "window-shopping." Since I was broke, I felt a great deal of unease about the proposal, until I learned that they did not plan to buy anything: they were merely going to "shop." And gradually I learned that a woman can shop half of a day without really expecting to bring anything home!

And so it is that people often "pray." They "pray" and "pray" but do not get anything; indeed, they do not *expect* to get anything. That is not the reason they "pray." But though they call it praying, really it is not real prayer if it does not come with a definite petition, asking something from God.

My wife and daughters do not see how I get any fun out of buying shoes. I walk into a certain chain shoe store and order a certain conservative-style, low-quarter shoe in black calf, size ten, like others I have worn before, and pay $3.60, have my old shoes wrapped up, and walk out. The whole transaction takes about ten minutes. I go after shoes of a certain kind and get them and go home. I do not "shop," in the woman's understanding of the term. Rather, I buy. And that is what prayer is. Prayer is asking something definitely from God.

Notice again the Scriptures at the head of this chapter. Matthew 7:7, 8 says:

"Ask, and it shall be given you; seek, and ye shall find; knock, and it shall be opened unto you: For every one that asketh receiveth; and he that seeketh findeth; and to him that knocketh it shall be opened."

Prayer, then, is asking. Or in other words, it is seeking and knocking. One who prays is expecting to receive. One who knocks is expecting something opened. One who seeks is expecting to find something. That is what the Bible says prayer is, really: asking, seeking, knocking. Real prayer is *asking for something.*

In James 4:2,3 the Scripture says:

"Ye lust, and have not: ye kill, and desire to have, and cannot obtain: ye fight and war, yet ye have not, because ye ask not. Ye ask, and receive not, because ye ask amiss, that ye may consume it upon your lusts."

Christians have not because they *ask* not, and they have not because they ask amiss. That Scripture says that it is not fighting or warring or desiring or worrying, but it is asking that gets things from God. PRAYING IS ASKING.

There are two principal words in the Greek New Testament translated *ask.* One is the word *eperotao*, which means *to ask, to inquire*, as asking questions. But the word used about prayer is *aiteo*, which means *to ask, to crave, to desire, to call for*, always meaning *asking for* something. I have just counted about thirty times that this word is used about prayer in the New Testament. And it is properly translated *ask.*

Modernists do not believe that prayer really changes things. So the modernist does not accept the plain Bible teaching that prayer is asking and the answer is receiving, that prayer is seeking and the answer is finding, that prayer is knocking and the answer is that God opens the door—the Bible doctrine that God is primarily "thou that hearest prayer" (Ps. 65:2), that He is "a rewarder of them that diligently seek him" (Heb. 11:6). And since they do not believe the Bible doctrine that prayer is asking and that God really answers, that prayer really changes things, modernists and unbelievers teach that prayer is largely a meditation and communion. At most the modernist believes only that prayer can do some good inside us, that it is a spiritual enjoyment. And so modernists discourage concrete requests and call such prayer selfish.

Dr. Harry Emerson Fosdick, noted modernist, in his book *The Meaning of Prayer* says,

"There are some who still think of prayer in terms of childish supplications to a divine Santa Claus" (page 22). And again he says, "Many foolish prayers are offered by the well-meaning but unintelligent with the excuse that they are childlike in their simple trust....To pray to God as though He were Santa Claus is childish." "Childishness in prayer is chiefly evidenced in an overweening desire to beg *things* from God" (page 23). Then this unbeliever, who denies that Jesus was the virgin-born One, paying for our sins, denies the veracity of the Bible, prates about prayer as 'friendship with

God.' To the modernist prayer is nice but does not get things from God. Prayer does not change things.

And many Bible believers fall into this snare, this doctrine that prayer is merely spiritual fellowship, that we do not really get things from God but that after we pray we feel stronger to get them for ourselves or are perhaps resigned to do without them! How far is this from the Bible teaching on prayer!

I once visited a home in Chicago where for purposes of exercise they had an "electric horse." As a horseman of long experience in my youth, I was asked to ride the electric horse. I got on, pressed the button, and presto, galloped and galloped, arms flapping, coattail waving! The action was a fine imitation of the gallop of a horse. But it was only an imitation after all, for I pressed the button, the galloping stopped, and I got off exactly where I got on! I had not been anywhere at all! And that is exactly like the prayer of a modernist, purely for exercise and not to get things from a prayer-hearing, prayer-answering God!

Prayer is not meditation, not adoration, not even communion in the ordinary sense. Prayer is *asking God for something*.

I. Prayer Is Not Praise, Adoration, Meditation, Humiliation nor Confession, but Asking

Again let me press upon your heart and mind that prayer is asking, and not anything else.

Prayer is not praise, though praise is blessed. "Whoso offereth praise glorifieth me," says the Lord (Ps. 50:23). "Let every thing that hath breath praise the LORD," says Psalm 150:6. David said, "Bless the LORD, O my soul: and all that is within me, bless his holy name" (Ps. 103:1). Praise is blessed. It is the duty of every grateful heart. But we must remember that praise is not prayer and prayer is not praise. Prayer is asking.

Prayer is not adoration. Adoration is good. We ought to adore Him whom the angels adore. But adoration is not prayer, and prayer is not adoration. Prayer is always *asking*. It is not anything else but asking.

Prayer is not meditation. It is proper to meditate day and night in the Word of God (Ps. 1:2). Quiet devotion and meditating upon the Word of God and upon the Lord's blessings are fine. Every Christian ought to take such times for meditation. But remember that that is not prayer. The Bible never calls it prayer, and we sin against God and misuse the Scriptures and pervert the truth, when we call such things prayer. Prayer is not meditation. Prayer is asking.

Humiliation is not prayer, though it is certainly proper for Christians to humble themselves before God. James 4:10 says, "Humble yourselves in the sight of the Lord, and he shall lift you up." And we are told that "he that humbleth himself shall be exalted" (Luke 18:14). But humiliation is not prayer. The Bible expressly separates them. Second Chronicles 7:14 says, "If my people, which are called by my name, shall humble themselves, and pray." So humiliation is one thing, and prayer is another thing. Humiliation is preparation for prayer, perhaps, and humiliation is always proper in a Christian. But humility and humiliation are not prayer. Prayer is asking.

Even confession is not strictly prayer. It is proper for Christians to confess their sins, and the Bible many times commands it; but confession is one thing, and prayer is another. In Daniel 9:4, Daniel tells us, "And I prayed unto the LORD my God, and made my confession, and said." Daniel both prayed and made confession. If you will read through that long passage which tells us of Daniel's prayer and confession together, you will find that much of it is confession but that after confession came the brokenhearted requests of Daniel 9:16–19 that God would turn His anger and fury away from Jerusalem and forgive the sins of His people and restore the nation and the holy city, Jerusalem, and the temple. Confession is proper, but confession, strictly speaking, is not prayer. Prayer is ASKING. And asking is prayer, and nothing else is really prayer.

In Philippians 4:6 the Lord says, "Be careful for nothing; but in every thing by prayer and supplication with thanksgiving let your requests be made known unto God." Note that prayer is one thing and that thanksgiving is a separate thing. With this as a key thought, go through the Scripture, and you will find that often the Scripture speaks of prayer and supplication, prayer and confession, prayer and thanksgiving. Thus, the heart of prayer is to ask something from God. Everything else is an incidental which is not essentially a part of prayer. Asking is prayer, and prayer is asking.

So when God invites us to pray He invites us to ask things of Him.

II. Bible Prayers Were Asking

Consider the Lord's Prayer, the model prayer, which Jesus gave us in Matthew 6:9–13. The Saviour commanded us: "After this manner therefore pray ye: Our Father which art in heaven." And then follows a series of requests as follows:

1. "Hallowed be thy name": that is, may I and others speak reverently of Thee and not take Thy name in vain. It is a request.

2. "Thy kingdom come. Thy will be done in earth, as it is in heaven." This is a prayer for the second coming, a request that Jesus may come quickly, and that He soon will reign on the earth and put down all of His enemies. It is the prayer that John the beloved prayed by divine inspiration in Revelation 22:20: "Even so, come, Lord Jesus."

3. "Give us this day our daily bread."

4. "And forgive us our debts, as we forgive our debtors."

5. "And lead us not into temptation."

6. "But deliver us from evil."

And then follows a very simple argument as to why our heavenly Father can give us these things and should do it: "For thine is the kingdom, and the power, and the glory, for ever. Amen."

The Lord's Prayer is petition, all the way. We are plainly commanded to pray like this daily. When the Bible speaks of prayer, it always means asking.

Throughout the Gospels Jesus gave examples of prayer. He said prayer is like a man knocking at a door and saying, "Friend, lend me three loaves." It is like a widow before a judge, saying, "Avenge me of mine adversary." It is like a son asking bread or a fish or an egg of a father. According to Jesus, prayer is a very simple business; and anybody who can ask for things can pray.

The actual cases of prayer mentioned in the New Testament are likewise very simple examples of this. The people who prayed in the New Testament really asked for what they wanted, and got things.

The publican in the temple prayed, "God be merciful to me a sinner," and he went down to his house already saved, forgiven (Luke 18:14)!

Peter, about to sink in the waters of Galilee, cried out, "Lord, save me" (Matt. 14:30).

Blind Bartimaeus by the roadside cried out, "Jesus, thou son of David, have mercy on me" (Mark 10:47). And then more definitely still he prayed, "Lord, that I might receive my sight" (Mark 10:51). And he did receive his sight.

The thief on the cross prayed for salvation, saying, "Lord, remember me" (Luke 23:42), and the Lord saved him that day and took him to Paradise.

The Syrophenician or Canaanitish woman prayed, "Have mercy on me, O Lord, thou son of David; my daughter is grievously vexed with a devil" (Matt. 15:22), and again, "Lord, help me" (Matt. 15:25). And she kept praying and asking it until she got what she asked; that is, until her daughter was healed.

In fact, the only "prayer" I recall mentioned in the New Testament that is held up to scorn is the prayer of the Pharisee in Luke, chapter 18. He "prayed" in public long and loud, but he did not ask for a thing! That is the kind of a prayer that God hates!

We are so weak and sinful, and God is so strong and mighty and gracious, that the only possible relationship that would be righteous and proper between us and God is that we should be asking and He should be giving. When man becomes occupied with how much he could do for God, it is blasphemy and unbelief. But when poor, self-confessed sinners begin to call on God for what He so graciously and lovingly offers, then that is proper and legitimate prayer.

Do you really ask God for things when you pretend to pray?

Too many people only "window-shop" when they "pray." They do not go after anything, and they do not bring anything home.

Prayer is not a lovely sedan for a sight-seeing trip around the city. Prayer is a truck that goes straight to the warehouse, backs up, loads, and comes home with the goods. Too many people rattle their trucks all over town and never back up to the warehouse! They do not go after something when they pray. They do not ask, and therefore they do not receive. Much of our so-called praying is not asking, and so it is not really praying.

III. Hypocrisy in So-called Praying That Does Not Ask for Something

In churches all over the land pastors are accustomed Sunday morning to going through the rigmarole of "the morning prayer." But usually it is not prayer at all: it is a well-planned, pious speech or sermonette. It includes praise, adoration, thanksgiving and theology. It is addressed more to the people than to God in most cases, I fear. Its aim, I suppose, is to create a reverent atmosphere, to comfort the people and edify them. But the aim of the so-called "morning prayer" is very rarely really to get things from God! It does not ask, and it does not receive. It is not real prayer.

Dear pastor, test your public prayer by this measurement: Was it answered? Did it expect an answer or require one? Most preachers believe that God answers prayer, I hope, and yet I never heard a pastor say, "I've just had a glorious and definite answer to my 'morning prayer' of last Sunday." No, no, the average Sunday "morning prayer" was not intended to be answered. It was not asking anything. Really, it was not prayer. It was a professional part of a formal service.

Sometimes in the address there are some elements of real prayer, and this is not meant to be a wholesale criticism of my dear brethren in the ministry. But how sad God must be over our perversion of the doctrine of prayer and because of our failure to ask anything of God.

In revival services it is my joy to have many ministers of the Gospel attend. They are the best men in the world, and I want their love and sympathy and help and prayers more than I want the love and sympathy and help and prayers of any other group in the world.

But as a result of long and sad experience, I have grown accustomed to leading the prayer myself when we come to a serious crisis in a revival service and there is desperate need for God to work.

How many, many times when we have come to the close of an earnest revival sermon, and when sinners have held their hands asking that Christians pray for them that they may surrender to Christ and trust Him for salvation, I have asked some minister to lead in prayer and had not a prayer, but a sermon or an exhortation. I have asked Dr. Blank to lead us in prayer that these earnest and convicted sinners may this moment trust Christ and be saved. Instead, he has addressed God and then talked around the world, thanking God for Jesus Christ, thanking God for the Gospel and the Bible, thanking God for our free country, thanking God for the sermon and for Christian fellowship, and then has come to the close of his so-called prayer, without ever once earnestly begging God to save these sinners who sit in the congregation before him and who are already convicted and wanting to be saved! I am not exaggerating when I say that again and again I have had this heartbreaking thing happen.

People ordinarily, at least in their public "prayers," do very little praying. They sometimes praise God and sometimes exhort the people and sometimes, perhaps, simply go through a form of beautiful and eloquent words without any special heart-feeling or crying out to God for anything definite. I say that that is generally true.

I say this is pretty generally true about *public* prayer. Of course, I cannot say about *private* prayer except about my own. Too often I find that in my own secret prayers I have a tendency to be indefinite and to follow a form and to say the words which are customary, instead of really beseeching God for definite things. I think that probably in private prayer people are not so tempted to make a showing before men, and probably secret prayers tend to be more sincere.

I am not saying that exhortation to the people is wrong. I think it is often blessedly used of God. I am not saying that public praise is wrong. I know that public praise is many times commanded and certainly ought to be used to glorify God. But these things *ought not to take the place of prayer.* And they *ought not to be called prayer.* Prayer is asking. If it is not asking, it is not prayer in the Bible sense.

Oh, beloved reader, I beg you in Jesus' name that when you come to pray, you ask things of God! Bring your wants and wishes before God and make definite requests and expect definite blessings! God is rich with blessings that He longs to give, and He but waits for us to ask, that He may give.

When my oldest daughter was three years old, she taught me a shocking lesson. In our prayer at the table I found that she waited until I drew near the end of my prayer, and then she began to say, "Amen!" "Amen!"

"Amen!" It seemed strange. I was puzzled. How did she know when I was drawing near the end of my prayer?

And upon careful examination I found I was saying approximately the same thing in every prayer. I could start my prayer and let it go like a phonograph record, and my mind could wander here or there while my lips went through the pious phrases and the platitudes that long before had meant something but now had become a commonplace form with no heart-cry to God. And my three-year-old baby girl, who was hungry and glad when the prayer was through, could anticipate the close of the prayer. She knew just what came next because I had said the same thing so many times!

My spiritual face was certainly red! I found with shame that I had drifted into a kind of formalism in my thanks at the table. I was a Pharisee, a hyp-ocrite. Of course, I was a very well-meaning hypocrite, as all Pharisees are, but nevertheless there was a fundamental insincerity in following a certain form and using pious terms which had more or less lost their meaning. Shame, shame on us that when we pretend to pray we usually do not really ask anything from God!

This means, of course, that much that we call prayer is not prayer at all. And all over the world our foolish pretense of praying, when we do not ask anything and do not get anything, has encouraged unbelief, has cast doubt upon God and the Bible, and millions do not know that there is a God who is ready and willing to answer prayer marvelously. Millions do not really believe that prayer changes things. To millions, prayer is no more than a quiet meditation, which may do subjective good to the one who prays, like good exercise, a form of self-discipline, but which does not, they think, receive any objective results from God.

Prayer is asking. The Lord Jesus said that "every one that asketh receiveth." James said by divine inspiration, "Ye have not, because ye ask not."

Under any other definition of prayer, there might be some place for form and ceremony, but not since prayer is asking. Since prayer is really asking something from God, then it must come from the heart.

No wonder that in Isaiah 44:3 the Lord says, "I will pour water upon him that is thirsty." Real asking comes from a thirst of the heart.

Mark 11:24 says, "What things soever ye desire, when ye pray, believe that ye receive them, and ye shall have them."

Heart's desire is back of honest prayer. It is all right to pray aloud. It is all right to pray in a whisper. But since prayer really comes from the desire of the heart, it may overleap the incidental matters of words and sentences. The heart-cry may be manifested in tears or in groans or in quiet, expectant faith. But real prayer, prayer that *asks* something from God, must come from the heart. Oh, what an abomination is this fake kind of "praying" that is not the honest petition of the heart.

Long ago my father was a country preacher. Once when he held services in a certain church, a dear brother prayed long and eloquently. He said, "Lord, come down and meet with us today in this church house. Lord, come right down through the roof right now; I'll pay for the shingles!" Either that was a very figurative way of expressing what his heart desired, or it was not prayer at all.

Too much of our praying is like the incantation of a witchdoctor or the rites of some modern cult; that is, they may have rhythm or eloquence or beauty and aesthetic form, but they are not genuine prayers when they do not ask for things. The modern tendency to have pipe organ music during prayer is because we are not really praying at all. We say we seek reverence, but actually we are seeking some form of aesthetic beauty, some appeal to the senses.

When a lady orders groceries, she does not quote poetry.

When the dispatcher gives orders to a trainman, they are not written on engraved stationery. He does not use classic illustrations or ponderous words.

When a beggar asks for a dime for a cup of coffee and a "hot dog," he does not talk about the glowing sunset.

Brother, come to God, asking for what you want, and go home with it! Let us really learn to pray by asking things from God.

CHAPTER IV

THE ANSWER TO PRAYER IS RECEIVING

"And whatsoever we ask, we receive of him."—I John 3:22.

"...if his son ask bread, will he give him a stone? Or if he ask a fish, will he give him a serpent?"—Matt. 7:9,10.

In the preceding chapter I showed that *prayer is asking.* Prayer is not adoration; it is not meditation; it is not even praise and thanksgiving. Prayer is not just spiritual exercise. No, prayer is asking. There ought to be adoration and meditation and thanksgiving, to be sure, but these are not prayer; prayer is asking. So we are told, "Ye have not, because ye ask not" (Jas. 4:2). We are promised, "Ask, and it shall be given you; seek, and ye shall find; knock, and it shall be opened unto you" (Matt. 7:7). Many, many Scriptures show that prayer, in the Bible sense, is asking God definitely for something.

Now there is another side to that truth. If prayer is asking, then the answer to prayer must be receiving. It is the will of our loving heavenly Father that we should be able to come to Him day by day, ask what we want, and receive it.

Preachers have a way, when faith grows dim and weak, of making alibis for the fruitlessness of their prayers. For example, preachers sometimes say, "God answers prayer three ways. He may say, 'Yes,' or He may say, 'No,' or He may say, 'Wait awhile.' "

Of course that statement is intended to mean that a Christian ought to be content for the will of God to be done and to be satisfied with anything God gives. But actually, it teaches exactly the opposite of what the Bible teaches about prayer. It makes us think of prayer as a mystical, indefinite matter, by which one may get what he wants, or may not, as if there were no way to know what is the will of God. It leaves the impression that there is not much use of praying, because God will do what pleases Him anyway without any meddling of ours, so why should we pray? And anything that makes prayer indefinite and makes the answer seem uncertain is contrary to the plain teaching of the Word of God.

Sensible people would not be content with any such slipshod and indefinite arrangement about asking and receiving in any other realm of life. Suppose I should drive into a filling station to buy gasoline and say, "I want ten gallons of gas, please. And check the oil." I expect the affirmative answer—that is, I expect to get just what I ask for. How surprised I would be if the attendant should say, "No, I am sorry, but I don't think you need any gas," and would refuse to fill my empty tank; or if he should say, as some preachers say God does, "Wait awhile. When you have waited there until I think you deserve it, I'll get you some gas." Or I should be even more surprised if, instead of gasoline, the attendant should fill up my tank with soapsuds or alcohol or mud! This "yes" or "no" or "wait awhile" would not seem sensible, I say, to people in any other matters of asking and receiving; and yet they speak in that foolish way about prayer!

Suppose that a young man has learned to love devotedly a certain young woman and has cause to believe that she loves him. Suppose he then asks her to marry him, but she refuses. Would the young man then go along happily saying that he had received his request, that his request was answered? No, and neither should a Christian be content until he can be in such close touch with God that he can get exactly what he asks for and rejoice in a "yes" from God in answer to his prayers.

I. The Scriptures Teach That an Answer to Prayer Is Getting What You Asked For

Our modern way of thinking so indefinitely of prayer and expecting nothing when we talk to God, was not the way of Bible Christians. And the Bible promises clearly teach us to expect God to give us just what we ask for when we pray aright. According to the Bible, a genuine answer to prayer is simply getting what you ask for. See how clear this is in the Scriptures.

For example, Jesus said,

"Ask, and it shall be given you; seek, and ye shall find; knock, and it shall be opened unto you: For every one that asketh receiveth; and he that seeketh findeth; and to him that knocketh it shall be opened."

Now, in this Scripture if *asking* is prayer, then *receiving* is the answer to prayer.

In these words of Jesus, if *seeking* is prayer, then *finding* is the answer to prayer.

If *knocking* is prayer, then *having the door opened* to us is God's answer to prayer. There is not a hint here that a Christian should expect God to say, "No," or "Wait awhile."

Again in John 16:24 Jesus said, *"Ask, and ye shall receive."*

Here if *asking* is prayer, then *receiving* is the answer to prayer.

In James 4:2 we are told that *"ye have not, because ye ask not."*

If *asking* here is prayer, then God's Word says that *having* is the answer to prayer.

Dr. Charles A. Blanchard in his book, *Getting Things From God,* has helped me greatly on this matter. Dr. Blanchard, in his chapter on "What Is an Answer to Prayer?" says:

"I have repeatedly heard beloved brethren say that when God declined to do the things which His children desired, the answer was as real as when He granted the things which they desired. The statement is sometimes made in this manner: 'God says sometimes "yes" and sometimes "no." "No" is as really an answer as "yes," so that prayer is always answered.' It has ever seemed to me a cruel trifling with the souls of men to teach in this way. Of course, I do not mean to charge those who thus speak, with intentional cruelty or trifling. Nevertheless, that which they do seems to me a heartbreaking piece of work."

Then Dr. Blanchard gives the example of a mother who prays for the life of her child, but not praying acceptably to God, and the child dies; the example of a businessman in difficulty who prays, but not according to God's will, and becomes a bankrupt, his business in ruin; and the example of a man who is tempted who prays for help but does not pray aright and so falls into shame, with his family broken up, the church embarrassed, and the neighborhood demoralized. To all these, Dr. Blanchard says, some good ministers answer, "Oh no, God has not refused your prayer. He has not failed to answer your prayer. He has just said 'no.'" And Dr. Blanchard says,

"I do not believe that this teaching is true, and I am sure it would not be a comfort to a mother whose heart lay cold and heavy under the shadow of the little grave.

"...I do not believe this teaching to be true, and I do not believe it to be a comfort or help to anybody. I think it would tend to make infidels rather than Christians."

Then Dr. Blanchard says:

"An answer to prayer is a granting of the thing which a child asks of his heavenly Father, according to the directions which his Father has clearly set down. If a saint prays for healing for himself or his child or his friend, and God answers his prayer, the sick person will be recovered. If a saint prays in scriptural fashion for relief from financial difficulties, he will be relieved. If he prays in scriptural fashion for victory over the powers of evil, he will obtain victory. An answer to prayer is a granting of the thing desired. Saying 'no' to a request is not an answer to prayer in any real, substantial meaning of the expression. When God answers prayer He says 'yes.'"

And again Dr. Blanchard says:

"Let me once more record my conviction that answered prayer is prayer which accomplishes the results desired. To say that the answer may be 'yes' or 'no' and that the latter is as really an answer as the former, seems to me trifling with the sore hearts and the great needs of man."

As Dr. Blanchard so well teaches, if the proper answer of prayer is a "yes" answer, and if a Christian who prays in a normal and scriptural manner should receive that for which he prays, then when a Christian does not get what he prays for, the Christian should begin a thorough investigation. He knows that God is not wrong. He should set out to discover by the Word of God and by the leading of the Holy Spirit why his prayer has not been accepted and answered. And this makes prayer a simple and understandable business, and the way to full and blessed answers to prayer will soon be open to honest, surrendered, Bible-believing hearts.

II. How to Pray in the Will of God for a "Yes" Answer

All of us know that the average Christian does not usually get exactly what he asks for from God. On the contrary, the average Christian expects nothing of the kind. His prayers are indefinite: they do not pointedly and plainly ask for concrete, definite answers. Ordinary prayers are not really meant to be answered. The ordinary "prayer" is not *asking*, and it does not expect an answer of *having*.

Doubtless this is the reason that so many Christians condition nearly every request with the words, "if it be Thy will." We ask God to send a revival "if it be Thy will." We ask God to save sinners for whom Christ died and over whom He yearns with inexpressible longing, "if it be Thy will"! We ask God for the things He has *promised* to give, the things which He *longs* to give, the things for which He has entreated us to ask; and then we ask and put a question mark by it—God forgive us! We put an *if* in our prayers about whether God is willing to save souls or give revivals or keep His word! But that *if* is not a sign of submission to the will of God—it is a sign of our unbelief. It is a sign of our stumbling about in the dark in our prayers, with no assurance that God will hear us and give us the things for which we ask.

Suppose that in the pulpit your pastor should put an *if* about the virgin birth of Christ, as you put an *if* about His keeping His promises—would you like that? Suppose there is a doubt, an *if*, an uncertainty, an ambiguity about every doctrine a preacher preaches, with no certainty, no ring of victory, nothing you can absolutely depend upon, in the way the Word of God is proclaimed and taught—would you like that? Well, do you think God would like that? No more does He like us to come with such unbelief, such stumbling, doubting, uncertainty to ask for the things which He has promised and which He wants to give. No, God wants us to find out how to pray according to His will for things which can honor His great name, and then He wants us to expect definite and exact answers to those prayers. If we ask for bread, He wants us to expect bread, and not a stone. If we ask for fish, He wants us to expect fish, and not a snake. If we ask for an egg, He wants us to expect an egg, and not a scorpion. He wants praying to be on the basis of asking and receiving as simple as that of a child and his own father.

And for that kind of praying, there are certain important requirements. Before we can pray in the will of God with the certainty of getting what we ask for, certain important conditions must be met, which I will name:

1. First of all, there must be a full surrender to the will of God. There can be no happy, successful prayer life for a rebellious child of God. Psalm 37:4 says,

"Delight thyself also in the LORD; *and he shall give thee the desires of thine heart."*

Remember that when Jesus taught us to pray, He said the very first requests we are to make are these, "Hallowed be thy name....Thy will be done in earth." God is our Father, and children should be subject to their father. We are not our own. We are bought and paid for, redeemed with the awful price of Calvary. There can be no victory in prayer except as the heart humbly bows and says, "My Father, show me how to pray in Thy will. I want to ask what will please Thee. I want to have what You want me to have." Every Christian who wants to be able to pray for certain definite things and get exactly what he prays for, day after day, should first pray, like the disciples of old, "Lord, teach us to pray" (Luke 11:1). God delights to answer the prayer of a surrendered heart, wholly surrendered to His will.

In James 4:2 is the remarkable and blessed promise, "Ye have not, because ye ask not." God has so many wonderful things that He longs to give us, and He only waits for our asking. And yet the next verse tells us that "ye ask, and receive not, because ye ask amiss, that ye may consume it upon your lusts." Wicked hearts that seek to have success in prayer without first getting on the praying ground of a surrendered heart, are doomed to disappointment. No doubt here is a great secret of our lack of faith and lack of enthusiasm and lack of success in prayer: we ask amiss that we may consume things on our own lusts.

Sometimes a wife wants her husband saved, and she prays for him; yet her motives may be all wrong. It may be that the wife thinks, *If my husband were saved, it would be so much easier on me. He would take me to church. He would be kinder in the home.* So she prays for the thing that God really wants to do, longs to do; but God cannot righteously answer her prayers. God needs to make the wife's heart right before He can save her husband. So many Christians hinder the answers to their own prayers, prayers that God would delight to answer, if it could be done to His glory, without His encouraging sin. Oh, how important it is that the heart should surrender to the Lord Jesus!

We need to pray with the words of the sweet hymn by George C. Stebbins:

Have Thine own way, Lord!
  Have Thine own way!
Thou art the Potter;
  I am the clay.
Mould me and make me
  After Thy will,
While I am waiting,
  Yielded and still.

Have Thine own way, Lord!
  Have Thine own way!
Search me and try me,
  Master today!
Whiter than snow, Lord,
  Wash me just now,
As in Thy presence
  Humbly I bow.

Have Thine own way, Lord!
  Have Thine own way!
Hold o'er my being
  Absolute sway!
Fill with Thy Spirit
  Till all shall see
Christ only, always,
  Living in me!

Dear Christian, if you really are tuned in to Heaven by a heart submitted wholly to the will of God, then you are ready to learn how to pray so you can ask God for exactly what you want and get it.

2. Next, we must have a heart-understanding of God's Word, so we may know the will of God. How can we ask with any assurance that God will be pleased to give us what we ask, unless we know something of His will? For this reason Jesus said:

"If ye abide in me, and my words abide in you, ye shall ask what ye will, and it shall be done unto you."—John 15:7.

Here, asking just what we want and getting it is said to depend upon our abiding in Christ and His Word abiding in us. We cannot know the will of God without familiarity with the Word. In Psalm 1:1–3 and in Joshua 1:7–9 the prosperity of a Christian in everything is conditioned upon his meditating day and night in the Word of God and walking therein. It is not enough just to read the Word of God. It should abide in us. We should love it, should meditate in it, should absorb it until it colors all our lives and thoughts. Then when we come to ask something from God and can say honestly, "My dear heavenly Father, I have found in Your Word that You want me to have thus and so and that it would honor Thy name. You have said for me to ask for it, so I claim Thy promise and believe Thy Word and take what Thou hast promised me"—we can certainly expect the answer and get exactly what we prayed for.

For example, notice the sweet promise of I John 1:9 that "if we confess our sins, he is faithful and just to forgive us our sins, and to cleanse us from all unrighteousness." Knowing that verse, any Christian in the world can get instant forgiveness for any sin he is willing to confess with his whole heart; and he can get cleansing too. He has the Word of God for it! It would be a sin for a Christian to doubt that God is ready instantly to forgive and cleanse any Christian who honestly confesses that sin. Or take the implied promise in the Lord's Prayer when the Saviour taught us to pray, "Give us this day our daily bread." Any Christian familiar with the Word of God can pray for daily bread and get it, knowing already it is God's will. It would be a mistake to pray, "if it be Thy will," about a thing which God has already clearly told us is His will.

On the other hand, if a Christian be thoroughly endued with the Word of the Lord, he could not honestly ask for the great wealth of the world, to the ignoring of spiritual values. If he knew and loved and believed the words of the Saviour in Matthew 6:33, "But seek ye first the kingdom of God, and his righteousness; and all these things shall be added unto you"; he would certainly know that spiritual blessings are far more important than great wealth, that to seek first the kingdom of God would bring the greatest happiness, the greatest peace and the greatest prosperity. He would know that one who really seeks first the kingdom of God will have food to eat and garments to wear, beside the peace of God which passeth understanding.

I am saying that one cannot pray in the will of God without knowing the Word of God. The Bible is the revelation of the heart of God. It is the revelation of all that is good and right and true and pure. When you understand from the heart the teachings of God's Word and when you meditate therein day and night, then you can pray knowing that what you ask for is in the will of God and that it will both please and honor Him to hear and answer your prayer and give you what you ask for. And prayer that is not based on the Bible is likely not to be pleasing to God. And groups of Christians who put great emphasis on prayer and little emphasis on the Word, are usually fanatical extremists, who may enjoy emotional ecstacy but who do not always pray in the will of God and do not get, many times, the things for which they ask.

3. Next, to pray in the will of God one needs the leadership of the Holy Spirit. Without the Holy Spirit's guidance, our poor carnal minds would get only the bare letter of the Bible and not understand the will of God; for

spiritual things are spiritually discerned. And there are a thousand details on which we need to know the mind of God, about which the bare letter of the Word of God does not give information: What shall be the theme of my next sermon? To which sinner should I speak first about his soul? How shall I approach him? Should I ask God for a new car or do with the old one for awhile? Does God want my children to take music or not? Shall I send this money to foreign missions or give it to the local church? What part of the Scripture shall I read in my devotions today? Does God want me to take this business venture? Thus, there are a thousand questions about which one needs the personal and detailed guidance of the Holy Spirit of God, or we cannot certainly pray in the will of God and be assured that we have a right to expect exactly what we ask.

But, bless God, every Christian can have the Holy Spirit to help him pray.

"Likewise the Spirit also helpeth our infirmities: for we know not what we should pray for as we ought: but the Spirit itself maketh intercession for us with groanings which cannot be uttered. And he that searcheth the hearts knoweth what is the mind of the Spirit, because he maketh intercession for the saints according to the will of God."—Rom. 8:26,27.

No, we do not know what to pray for as we ought, but our infirmity in this matter is helped by the Holy Spirit. He makes intercession for us with groanings that cannot be uttered. And then our prayer, led and dictated by the Holy Spirit, reaches the heart of God; and we get what we ask because the Holy Spirit "maketh intercession for the saints *according to the will of God.*" The Holy Spirit can pray always "according to the will of God." So any prayer that is inspired and guided and aided by the Holy Spirit can be assured of an answer. When one prays according to the will of God, then that prayer will be answered. Someone has well said that any prayer that begins in Heaven will certainly not be rejected there.

The Holy Spirit is called "the Comforter" by our Saviour (John 14:16,26; John 15:26; John 16:7). This "Comforter" is a translation of the Greek word *parakletos*, meaning "one called alongside." So the blessed Holy Spirit is alongside of every Christian. Better yet, the Saviour said in John 14:17, "Ye know him; for he dwelleth with you, and shall be in you." The Holy Spirit dwelled *with* the apostles before the resurrection. But the Saviour promised that after He would be glorified, the Holy Spirit would be *within us.* So when Jesus rose from the dead, He breathed on the disciples and said, "Receive ye the Holy Ghost" (John 20:22). Now from that time, every saved person has the Holy Spirit abiding in his body. Romans 8:9 says, "But ye are not in the flesh, but in the Spirit, if so be that the Spirit of God dwell in you. Now if any man have not the Spirit of Christ, he is none of his." The Spirit of God dwells in us who are saved; and if anybody does not have this Spirit of Christ, this Holy Spirit, dwelling in him, he is not saved. First Corinthians 6:19,20 says, "What? know ye not that your body is the temple of the Holy Ghost which is in you, which ye have of God, and ye are not your own? For ye are bought with a price: therefore glorify God in your body, and in your spirit, which are God's." The body of every Christian is the temple of the Holy Spirit of God who dwells within. And, oh, how eager this blessed Holy Spirit is to comfort us and to guide us into all truth and teach us.

In fact, this Holy Spirit of God is also "the Spirit of Christ," as Romans 8:9 says. Jesus promised the heartsick disciples on the night before the crucifixion, "I will not leave you comfortless: I will come to you" (John 14:18). And He explained that He would come in the Person of the Holy Spirit of God. And John 14:26 says, "But the Comforter, which is the Holy Ghost, whom the Father will send IN MY NAME, he shall teach you all things, and bring all things to your remembrance, whatsoever I have said unto you."

So the blessed Holy Spirit makes known to us the will of Christ and calls to our remembrance what He has said in His Word and teaches us all things we need to know, as we submit ourselves to Him and with fervent hearts meditate on God's Word. So Christians, then, have a blessed and sure way of knowing the will of God. If they pray according to the plain promises of the Word and if they are led and helped by the Holy Spirit, then their prayers will be pleasing to God. God can put in the hearts of Christians what He wants them to pray for, what will honor His name, what will prosper His cause, what will be for the happiness and good of His children. And when we pray thus according to the will of God, we can get exactly what we pray for.

And since the Holy Spirit is Christ's own personal representative, His Spirit, His Comforter, then one who is led by the Holy Spirit can honestly pray in Jesus' name.

Every prayer that is honestly presented in Jesus' name will be answered. That is the express statement of John 14:13,14. Let us read it again: "And whatsoever ye shall ask in my name, that will I do, that the Father may be glorified in the Son. If ye shall ask ANY THING in my name, I will do it." There it is as plain as day. Anything under Heaven, asked in Jesus' name, will be given.

But how often we lie to God about this matter! People have fallen into the custom of saying at the close of their prayers, "This we ask in Jesus' name. Amen." But are we always asking in Jesus' name? Do we really mean, "Father, in Thy Word I have found what You have promised, and the Holy Spirit has made clear this petition is exactly what Jesus wants. Here He puts His endorsement on the prayer, and I know You will give it because

Jesus wants it"? Is that really always true about the prayers where we add the formality, "in Jesus' name"? I believe it is not. I know it is not, because many such prayers do not get the answer they seek; and that proves they are not really given in Jesus' name.

With the above things in mind, it seems to me that there are clearly these elements in getting ready to pray: First, we should surrender our own will and decide we will be willing to have God's own will, whatever it is, wherever it leads, and whatever it costs. Second, we should eagerly seek in the Bible to find what is the will of God on the subject and to pray according to the expressed will of God written down in His Word. And third, we should earnestly submit ourselves to the Holy Spirit for guidance and seek to have clear leading from God as to what we should pray for, and how. And if the Holy Spirit of God gives a divine expectancy, a conquering faith, then we may be sure God will answer the prayer. And no matter how I feel, if I have surrendered my own will and am earnestly trying to find just what God wants me to pray for, and if I pray according to the written Word of God and pray as the Holy Spirit leads out and as He prays with me and helps me in prayer, then I can be bold in my praying! I can claim and have the best God has for me!

I suggest that you go over your prayer list. Criticize and weigh carefully every item. Are you asking this for a personal, selfish reason? Is it according to the written Word of God? And does the Holy Spirit specially lead you out in prayer for this? If you have given up your own will and if it stands the test of the last two points, then you may with holy boldness storm the gates of Heaven to get the answer to your prayer, and say like Jacob, "I will not let thee go, except thou bless me" (Gen. 32:26).

Now, beloved Christian, will you put this teaching in practice? Will you begin to pray definitely, asking God for concrete things? And will you seek to pray in the will of God and then expect day by day, regularly, complete answers to prayer, receiving from God exactly what you ask Him for?

Remember that prayer is ASKING.

Remember that an answer to prayer is HAVING.

Therefore, "ask, and ye shall receive, that your joy may be full" (John 16:24).

"Ye have not, because ye ask not" (Jas. 4:2).

"Ask, and it shall be given you; seek, and ye shall find; knock, and it shall be opened unto you: For every one that asketh receiveth; and he that seeketh findeth; and to him that knocketh it shall be opened" (Matt. 7:7,8).

If you do not get just what you pray for, then you should set out today to find what is wrong with your prayers. Do not claim to have the answer until you get what you pray for. Either change your prayers so that God can righteously answer them, or correct any fault and sin that grieves the Spirit and hinders your prayers. Then if nothing is found that hinders the affirmative answer you seek, and if you are assured after prayerful study of the Word of God and opening your heart to the quiet voice of God's ungrieved Holy Spirit, that your prayer is according to the will of God, then you should wait before God insistently, with supplication and importunity, insisting on receiving the thing you have asked for!

Prayer is asking, and the answer to prayer is receiving.

Prayer is seeking, and an answer to prayer is finding.

Prayer is knocking, and an answer to prayer is having God open the door to you.

Prayer is asking, and the answer to prayer is having!

O Christians, I beg you, enter into your privileges, and get the things you want and need and ask for from God!

CHAPTER V

PRAYING FOR DAILY BREAD

I. How God Gives Food, Clothes, Money, Jobs, Cars, Other Material Blessings in Answer to Prayer

When Jesus taught His disciples the model prayer, He said,

"When ye pray, say, Our Father, which art in heaven. . . . Give us day by day our daily bread."—Luke 11:2,3.

Jesus plainly commands us Christians to pray for our daily bread. And of course He meant not only bread, but all our necessary food, and other material necessities.

In Matthew 6:9–13, Matthew gives the Lord's Prayer, or the model prayer, and the request is, "Give us this day our daily bread." Then following that in the same chapter the Saviour commanded us not to lay up for ourselves treasures on earth, and said, "Take no thought for your life, what ye shall eat, or what ye shall drink; nor yet for your body, what ye shall put on" (Matt. 6:25), and then reminded us that our heavenly Father feeds the fowls of the air and clothes the lilies of the field.

So there can be no doubt that the Saviour intended us to pray for bread and clothes and all the material blessings. All of our physical needs are matters to be taken up with our heavenly Father in trusting prayer. And when the Lord Jesus commanded us to pray for daily bread, He implied forcibly that the heavenly Father will surely grant this request. How bold we ought to be when we come to our own heavenly Father and ask Him for bread for today!

How many wonderful miracles God has worked, recorded throughout the Bible, simply to give people necessary food!

God gave the children of Israel manna from Heaven full forty years, six miracles a week, year in and year out, that the people simply might be fed (Exod. 16:35)! And God was so anxious for people to remember His willingness to give daily bread that He had the children of Israel to put a pot of the manna away to keep in the holy of holies through the centuries to remind them of God's willing and loving providence (Exod. 16:32–34). But the Lord cared as much for their clothes as for their food, and He saw that their garments waxed not old and that their shoes did not wear out for the forty years (Deut. 29:5)! And He gave the quail when they were hungry for meat (Exod. 16:13; Num. 11:31). He gave them water out of a rock when they were thirsty (Num. 20:11). He made the bitter water of Marah sweet (Exod. 15:25).

Food, drink, clothes—these are matters to be taken up freely between a child and his father, between a Christian and his heavenly Father!

God clave a hollow place in the jawbone of an ass with which Samson had killed a thousand Philistines, and there came out water that he might drink so he would not perish (Judg. 15:15–19).

God fed Elijah with ravens (I Kings 17:3–6). Twice a day Elijah had bread and meat brought from ravens, and drank of the brook. Then God sent him to the home of a widow in Zarephath, and the handful of meal in a barrel and the bit of oil in a cruse neither wasted nor failed, but God miraculously multiplied them to feed His prophet and the widow and her son (I Kings 17:9–16). God is definitely interested in the comfort and welfare of His people. God even sent an angel to bake a cake of bread for the discouraged Elijah and to refresh him with water (I Kings 19:5–7).

It is remarkable how many miracles of the Saviour were done to provide somebody with physical necessities. The first miracle the Saviour did was to turn water into wine in Cana of Galilee (John 2:1–10). When Jesus planned to call Simon Peter and James and John to follow Him and be His disciples, He said to Simon, "Launch out into the deep, and let down your nets for a draught," and the nets "inclosed a great multitude of fishes: and their net brake" (Luke 5:4–8). How impressive that this was a miracle of food! Then the Saviour later fed five thousand people with five little barley loaves and two small fishes. And again He fed four thousand people on another occasion. These are miracles of food. Then when Jesus had risen from the dead He went to Galilee, where the disciples had fished all night, catching nothing; and again He filled their nets, this time with 153 great fishes (John 21:11).

Meantime He Himself had built a fire of coals and cooked their breakfast by the lakeside (John 21:5–12). The Lord Jesus was interested in food, and how glad He was to supply it for hungry people!

And Paul rejoiced because the saints at Philippi had sent him food and other good things by the hand of Epaphroditus; and he wrote to say, "I am full, having received of Epaphroditus the things which were sent from you, an odour of a sweet smell, a sacrifice acceptable, wellpleasing to God. But my God shall supply all your need according to his riches in glory by Christ Jesus" (Phil. 4:18,19). Paul took this food as being sent from God and promised that these beloved saints who cared for God's apostle should likewise have all their needs provided.

How often I have met the sin of unbelief as regards God's willingness to give physical blessings! Frequently people tell me, "Earthly blessings were for the Jews, but God gives to Christians heavenly blessings." I do not know who invented that wicked alibi of unbelief; I have known many good men to quote it. But it is certainly not true. God is as willing to give daily bread to Christians in the New Testament as in the Old Testament. His plan has never changed. In James 1:17 we are told, "Every good gift and every perfect gift is from above, and cometh down from the Father of lights, with whom is no variableness, neither shadow of turning." On this matter of supplying Christians' needs, God never varies: there is never a shadow of turning away from His goodness in providential care for His own!

I know that God gives great spiritual blessings in answer to prayer, but I am equally sure that He longs to give us our daily bread and raiment and to supply all our physical, material needs.

Every Christian should read the life story of George Müller, the man who built orphan houses at Ashley Downs in Bristol, England. There he housed over two thousand orphans; and the money for every building, the money for every meal, the supplies for all the workers came in answer to prayer without ever taking a public collection and without ever appealing to any man for money. Hundreds of missionaries were supported, many thousands of copies of the Scriptures were circulated, millions of tracts were printed and given out, schools for poor children were established and maintained; and in George Müller's lifetime over seven million dollars in money came in simply in answer to prayer, without ever asking a soul for a penny! (See *George Müller of Bristol*, by A. T. Pierson, published by Revell.)

George Müller abundantly proved that God answers prayer about food and clothes and the ordinary necessities of life.

Let no one think that to pray for material things marks one as less spiritually minded. No, the opposite is true. One who gets his prayers answered about daily bread will be more likely to pray for the salvation of sinners and more likely to get what he prays for!

Repeatedly in the Bible we are encouraged to pray for material things because God gave His Son to die for us. In Romans 8:32 we are encouraged with these blessed words, "He that spared not his own Son, but delivered him up for us all, how shall he not with him also freely give us all things?" If God loved us enough to let Jesus die for us, He loves us enough to answer our prayers and give us all things needed, even material things.

II. A Personal Testimony to Answered Prayer in Material Things

This is not theory with me. I feel impelled to give my personal testimony and say that I *know* God answers prayer about material things: about food, about clothes, about money, about jobs, about automobiles. I can say like David, "This poor man cried, and the LORD heard him" (Ps. 34:6). I can say with him, "The young lions do lack, and suffer hunger: but they that seek the LORD shall not want any good thing" (Ps. 34:10). In literally hundreds of detailed cases God has supplied our needs in answer to prayer. I think it will glorify the Lord and encourage the saints for me to tell briefly some of the things that God has done for me in answering prayer about material things.

In January 1916, I was twenty years old, living on a stock farm near Dundee, a little cow town in west Texas. God stirred my soul with a desire for an education, yet I knew of no way to get money to go to school. My father did not have it. I had about $9.35 besides my horse and saddle. I had tried to borrow money at the bank, had tried two well-to-do friends, had tried to sell my horse. But it was a time of financial stringency everywhere, and I could not borrow the money and could not sell my horse. I remember that on the thirteenth day of January, as a cold mist was falling, I went out by the woodpile, through the pea-patch, crawled through the fence, and walked over the hill to a place of prayer I had. It was in the brakes in a bare ravine under a chaparral bush. There I went down on my face and prayed. I told God that I would do anything He wanted me to do: I would preach the Gospel, or I would be a gospel singer or do anything else that He should clearly lead me to do. I told Him I would give carefully a tenth of my income besides freewill offerings through the years. Then I told Him that since this burden was on my heart, it must be from Him and I must ask Him to give me the means to go through college. I promised Him I would go and I would look to Him to open the way before me.

I had been reading the little book *How to Pray* by Dr. R. A. Torrey (one of the very best; every Christian ought to read it). I packed my little trunk which Mother left when she died and told my father I would send him word when to ship it to me. Then I saddled my horse and rode away through the rain toward Decatur, Texas, to Decatur Baptist College.

On the way I talked to the Lord and told Him I would try every way to borrow money on my horse or to sell the horse for the money for the first tuition. I rode twenty-five miles and the next day walked into the Power State Bank at Archer City, Texas. Speaking to the cashier I said, "Mr. Power, I would like to borrow some money on my horse. I am going to college." He did not even look at the horse but reached for a bank note and said, "Mr. Rice, how much money do you want?"

That stumped me! I hadn't ever gotten that close to getting the money before! But I said, "Well, I would need to get $60 for the first payment on tuition."

"How long do you want it?" he asked, waiting to fill in the due date.

"I could pay it back in six months, I think, when I am back home in the harvest," I said. So he made out the note for $60, payable in six months, and I signed it.

A man standing at the window spoke up and said, "Mr. Powers, you told me you couldn't let anybody have money for longer than three months in these hard times we are having!"

"But this young man is a friend of mine and did me a special favor once," the cashier said. The favor was that I had once taken ten minutes to show him what I had learned from a book about grafting high-grade peach branches onto old trees for his orchard!

I rode on to Decatur College. God gave a job when the president told me at first that there was no job to be had. Soon I was milking cows and waiting on tables to pay my board. But another payment would be due on tuition soon, and I took it earnestly to God in prayer. Soon the president, Dr. J. L. Ward, who was a great blessing to me and wonderfully kind, called me to his office and said, "John, can you teach a class in arithmetic for some backward boys who are not ready for the junior college course in algebra and geometry?" I assured him that I could, and soon I was making enough money to pay my tuition.

But I had few clothes. They were worn thin, and in my room late at night I patched my worn trousers. They became so thin and their strength so uncertain that I got to the point of carrying my cap behind me when I walked, to hide the patches!

One night I said to my roommate, Riley Whatley, "Riley, I am going to have to leave school if I don't get some clothes. I have gone as far as I can with patching these trousers." Riley suggested that we pray, and there together in our room we bowed in prayer; and God gave sweet assurance. That was Friday night. On Sunday afternoon there came a long-distance call from my uncle in Gainesville, Texas, a generous and godly man who is now in Heaven. He said, "John, how much money do you need for some clothes?"

"How did you know I needed any money for clothes?" I asked.

"Well, I think a boy would always need clothes when he is in school," my uncle said. And after a little further talk he said for me to be looking out for a check. I had told him $15 would buy the suit I needed, but the check was for $20; and I bought a blue serge suit, a cap, and shoes with that $20! Later I paid back every dollar of it, bless God; but my heart is blessed every time I remember how God answered prayer again and again and again!

I went on through junior college and then through university and two years in the seminary with eight months out for time in the army, and yet I did not lose a day out of school for lack of money. I had a Backer who supplied my needs. God answered my prayers!

And God has not changed since that time. He still answers prayer for all kinds of material needs: for jobs, for food, for clothes. In January 1941, I told in a radio broadcast from Grand Island, Nebraska, the story above of how God answered my prayers and helped me through school. An unhappy lad in Kansas State College had tuned in and heard the story. He was heart-sick because of all the wickedness on the campus and the atheism and delib-erate godlessness in the classrooms. He had long been praying that God would send him the means to go to Wheaton College, but he had no money. When he heard how God had answered my prayers, his heart thrilled, and he said, "God can take care of me too, and I am going to Wheaton College!" When his roommate came in, he was packing his clothes and told how, though he had no money, he believed God would help him get to Wheaton, Illinois, and that He would furnish the means for his tuition and board in that great Christian school. He hitchhiked to Wheaton College. Within two hours after he arrived in town he had a job to pay his expenses and a place to work for his board. Later he told me the story and now works part-time in my office, paying his own way through school.

In the summer on his father's farm in Kansas he prayed that God would open some way for him to make enough money to come back to school. He felt impressed to buy a secondhand threshing machine. When it wouldn't work he stopped and prayed, and God showed him what was wrong. Soon he had paid for the machine four times over, threshing grain for neighbors, and had enough money for his next year's tuition in college.

In 1926 I resigned as pastor of the First Baptist Church, Shamrock, Texas, to enter full-time evangelistic work. I felt impressed to have a spe-cial time of dedication to God, and I entered into a covenant with Him like this: "Lord, I'll look after Your work, and You look after me and my fam-ily." I gave up $10,000 life insurance. My wife and I agreed that we would trust in the Lord and not in men. I decided not to have again a regular salary and never to set any kind of price on my services for God either as pastor or evangelist. These fifteen years since, God has cared for me and my fam-ily. I have six children, but God has cared for the eight of us in the family without any lack. Workers in my office, looking to me alone for support, have numbered six much of the time, besides other part-time workers.

In the last ten years God has given me in answer to prayer about $36,000 for printing gospel literature. Printing bills often run as high as $1,000 a month. I have had daily radio services totalling several years' time, spend-ing thousands of dollars; and yet God has given it, every penny. Praise His name! And all these things and many more God has given in answer to prayer.

For example, for six months in 1931–32 I had a daily radio broadcast on WBAP at Fort Worth. The broadcast fee alone was $25 a day. Two secre-taries were needed to keep up with the work, besides the expenses of my family and thousands of pieces of literature given away. Day by day we went to God in prayer, and God sent the money. I had no church to help on the expenses. I did not take public collections for the broadcast. And on the radio by agreement with the station I was never to make any special appeal for funds. I could only say, "This broadcast is maintained by the freewill offerings of God's people." Yet every week there was money in hand to pay the broadcast fee, to pay the workers, and for the necessities of life. And the way it came was by daily, believing prayer.

One day, as was our custom, Mrs. Rice, one of the secretaries and I agreed to pray for $30 to come that day. We expressly named $30 in our prayer and agreed in asking God for it. The morning mail came about nine o'clock and contained among many letters offerings totalling $13.50 for the radio broadcast. The noon mail came with letters asking Bible questions, telling of blessings received through the broadcast, but with no money. The afternoon mail came about three o'clock with other letters but with no money. I had someway expected, though we had not specified, that the $30 would come in the mail that day. Most of the money for our needs came by mail, nearly all of it.

However, I went into a study and began to dictate a Bible lesson. Later a secretary came to the door and said, "Brother Rice, Mrs. W_____ wants to see you." I invited her to bring the lady in, and she came to thank me for the blessings received from the radio broadcast.

As she talked a bit about the blessings she had received through my Bible teaching, she opened her purse and handed me a one-dollar bill. She said, "I will never forget how my heart was thrilled the first time I ever heard you at an Epworth League meeting explaining the Scriptures. And now to think of the joy I have in hearing you on the radio every day!" Tears came in her eyes, and she said to me, "Give me that dollar back!" And she handed me a five-dollar bill instead.

"My neighbor, a Catholic woman, has been listening to you," she said. "She had seemed so hard to reach and so far off from God, but now I am beginning to believe that she may get saved. It is wonderful what the broadcast is doing for people who hear." Then suddenly she said, "Here, give me the five-dollar bill, and I will give you ten instead!" So she gave me a ten-dollar bill instead of the five and continued speaking about the blessings they had received. As she told how her husband had been blessed by the broadcast, she said, "I believe Frank would want me to give you everything I have in my purse except just carfare to get home!" With tears in her eyes and with trembling lips she handed me back the five dollars and the one dollar, and then in her coin purse she found coins totalling fifty cents and handed them to me.

With happy steps she left the office and went away, and I turned again to the Bible study lesson I was dictating to a stenographer. But in the back of my mind things began to add up—$13.50 plus $10 plus $5 plus $1 plus 50¢—exactly $30! My heart ran over with joy. Thirty dollars that day was better than fifty dollars, because it was exactly what we asked for!

Solemnly, earnestly, in the fear of God I say unto you that again and again, many, many times, God has that definitely and that specifically answered my prayers for material matters and even for money. I KNOW that God answers prayer. He has answered *my* prayers.

With less than $10 in cash, in July 1932 I went to Dallas, feeling definitely impressed of God to begin an open-air revival campaign and to organize a new church in Dallas of which I should be the pastor. Not a dollar had been promised by any friend for this purpose. Very few people in Dallas knew me. We had no seats, no money for electric lights, for advertising, for radio time; no money for living expenses. I found a vacant lot which God seemed to tell us to use, and I paid five dollars for the first week's rent. I had announced on the radio that on a certain day I would meet on that lot any who might want to come to help build benches. That morning enough money came to buy a load of lumber, the seats were built, and the work began. Time would fail for me to tell of how the work grew, how the great brick tabernacle, 90 by 146 feet, was built, with all of it paid for in cash, how the congregation of the new church grew to 1,400 members and more, and how thousands of souls professed faith in Christ in seven and a half years. But God gave all the material things in the heart of the Depression, in answer to prayer.

I prayed for a car and got one in three days from totally unexpected sources. I prayed earnestly in a time of distress, and God gave in two days' time a check for $1,000 from a man I had never seen, who had never seen me; and between us there had never been a word by mail.

And through these fifteen years since I determined to trust wholly in the Lord, there has been an unending stream of wonderful answers to prayer about material things. This week, for example, we needed $500 for a printing bill. I had been reading the life of C. T. Studd and, before knowing that this amount would be needed, had decided to set apart anything I might have in the bank and apply it on printing bills. Other money was at hand for *The Sword of the Lord* and through the sale of gospel literature, but there was not quite enough. And, behold, here came a letter with a check for $25 from a church in Mississippi. After prayer they had felt impressed that they should have given me more for a revival three years ago. But God's timing is perfect. (Later: today, Saturday, we sent the last of the $500. Praise God!) Solemnly I tell you that the definite provision of God for our needs is a regular and unfailing thing, and that literally thousands of prayers for particular, definite material needs have been answered.

Let us believe, then, that all the promises about answers to prayer apply to matters like daily bread, jobs, and money for clothes or for the coal bill.

"What things soever ye desire when ye pray, believe that ye receive them, and ye shall have them" (Mark 11:24). This means dollars and cents!

"If ye shall ask **ANY THING** in my name, I will do it" (John 14:14). This means anything in the world that you need and want when you pray!

Oh, may God teach us to pray from our hearts, in sincere faith, the prayer He taught us to pray, "Give us this day our daily bread."

CHAPTER VI

ASKING BREAD FOR SINNERS

Or, How to Get Soul-Winning Power

(An Exposition of Luke 11:1–13)

I. "Lord, Teach Us to Pray"

The disciples often heard Jesus pray. Luke 9:18 says, "And it came to pass, as he was alone praying, his disciples were with him." So in Luke 11:1 we find that the disciples quietly waited while Jesus poured out His heart in prayer:

"And it came to pass, that, as he was praying in a certain place, when he ceased, one of his disciples said unto him, Lord, teach us to pray, as John also taught his disciples."

There was nothing formal nor ordinary in the prayer of Jesus. To hear Jesus pray would carry one, surely, into the very holy of holies! Can you imagine the groanings, the tears, the happy, childlike faith, the urgency with which Jesus prayed? How the disciples marveled and grew hungry-hearted as they heard Jesus pray!

I do not know other things that were in the prayer Jesus prayed, but I know one note that could not be lacking. He was come to seek and to save that which was lost. It was to this end that He was born. His compassion for sinners, His burning zeal to save them, the love and grace which carried Him to the cross were surely manifested in His prayer that day while the disciples quietly waited. And when Jesus closed His prayer and looked up, one of the disciples, moved so deeply by hearing Jesus pray, said to Him, "Lord, teach us to pray, as John also taught his disciples."

John the Baptist had taught his disciples to pray. What a lesson is that for preachers! We should teach people to pray. Christians do not automatically become great men and women of prayer just as soon as they are born again. Prayer is an art that requires teaching. Every pastor and teacher should set himself to training people in Christlike prayer. So this disciple asked Jesus, "Lord, teach us to pray." Christians should study how to pray. They should ask God to teach them to pray. They should train themselves in Christlike prayer.

The entire passage of Scripture in Luke 11:2–13 was given by Jesus in response to this earnest request that He teach His disciples to pray. Let us study these verses carefully. Let us learn to pray as John taught his disciples to pray and as Jesus taught His disciples to pray. We should learn to pray in the spirit with which they prayed. We should pray for the same kind of things for which they asked. And we should pray with assurance and according to the will of God. We should get our prayers answered as they did.

Suppose we approach this Scripture reverently, then, with a heart fully committed to learn from this Scripture lesson just how to pray as Jesus taught His disciples.

The first thing, then, is to come with the same hungry heart the disciples had and pray the same prayer. I suggest that every reader stop just now and search his heart a moment. Then, can you pray the prayer of this hungry-hearted disciple? If you can, then bow your heart before God and earnestly, sincerely pray this prayer:

"Lord, teach me to pray."

Let us look to Christ to teach us through this Scripture. And as the Holy Spirit interprets it to our hearts, may we be taught to pray so that we may pray as Jesus did and as He taught His disciples to pray, even as John taught his disciples also to pray.

II. Grade School Praying: "The Lord's Prayer"

Jesus then gave His disciples the model prayer, which multitudes simply call "the Lord's Prayer." Do not quibble about the name. The Lord Jesus gave it as a model for prayer. Let us learn to pray as Jesus here taught His disciples to pray:

"And he said unto them, When ye pray, say, Our Father which art in heaven, Hallowed be thy name. Thy kingdom come. Thy will be done, as in heaven, so in earth. Give us day by day our daily bread. And forgive us our sins; for we also forgive every one that is indebted to us. And lead us not into temptation; but deliver us from evil."—Luke 11:2–4.

This prayer is simple and universal in its usefulness. Every Christian, from the most ignorant child to the most profound scholar, can approach God, saying, *"Our Father which art in heaven."* And everyone should approach reverently, *"Hallowed be thy name."* And all of us alike ought to pray for the Lord's return and His kingdom on the earth. How many, many times the saints of God have uttered these words, *"Thy kingdom come. Thy will be done in earth, as it is in heaven,"* without realizing that thus we are to pray regularly for the return of Christ. That is the blessed hope of the Christian (Titus 2:13). And John said, "Even so, come, Lord Jesus" (Rev. 22:20).

Note that this prayer is for common, everyday needs, universal needs of the people of God. *"Give us day by day our daily bread."* We have a right to pray for our daily needs. Food, clothes, shelter, a job, physical necessities—all these are included in God's will for a Christian. Christians do not always get what they *want*, but Christians *ought* to get all they *need*. I believe that just as confidently as a child comes to its mother or father for food, so any Christian ought to come to God for daily needs, physical, material needs. God is the Maker of this world, and "every good gift and every perfect gift is from above, and cometh down from the Father of lights" (Jas. 1:17). The God who fed Elijah with ravens, and made the meal and the oil last all along for the widow and her sons and the prophet of God (I Kings 17:2–16), and the hand that fed five thousand people with five loaves and two fishes, can still feed the saints of God and supply their needs. God is our Father. All the heavens and the earth are His, and He will as gladly clothe His children as He does the lilies of the field. He will as gladly feed His beloved as He does the fowls of the air. It is well to note that this prayer should be a model for prayers every day. We need not use these exact words, but we ought at least to pray in the spirit of this prayer every day. We are encouraged to pray today for today's bread. Tomorrow we need to pray again for tomorrow's bread.

"And forgive us our sins." Every Christian needs to pray that prayer every day. We are saved, and yet we are saved sinners. Every day, according to the teaching of our Saviour, we should come to God and get all the hindrances removed. By confessing our sins, we are cleansed and forgiven them, as is faithfully promised in I John 1:9. And when we come to God for daily cleansing and forgiveness, let us remember to forgive others.

I know that when one turns to Christ for salvation and depends upon Him in simple faith, he gets all of his sins forgiven: sins of the past, of the present, and of the future. All these sins, every one, have been laid upon Jesus Christ, who has paid for them. The one who trusts in Christ has everlasting life and never will come into condemnation but is passed from death unto life (John 5:24). But there is a secondary sense in which Christians need forgiveness every day. After I am already a child of God, my sins grieve God and must be dealt with. My sins cannot send me to Hell, but they can break God's heart, can hinder our fellowship, can grieve the Holy Spirit, can ruin my testimony and my happiness. Daily every Christian needs his sins cleansed and forgiven. And one sure token of a genuine and sincere repentance for sin is our willingness and gladness to forgive all those who sin against us. And this Scripture agrees with the beatitude, "Blessed are the merciful: for they shall obtain mercy" (Matt. 5:7). Be sure that you learn this secret of daily, conquering prayer. Forgive and be forgiven every day.

"And lead us not into temptation; but deliver us from evil." Every Christian needs daily leading. We should daily beg for divine guidance to keep us out of temptation. David rejoiced in the Twenty-third Psalm: "He leadeth me in the paths of righteousness for his name's sake." And we must daily ask God to keep us from the hands of the evil one. Prayer is a mighty

weapon against temptation. Daily let us call on God for bread, for forgiveness, for guidance, for protection from sin and the temptations of Satan.

This is the common school of prayer, the elementary grade of Christ's school in prayer. Every Christian should learn to pray in the spirit of our Lord's model prayer.

We must note, however, that all of the petitions included in the Lord's Prayer are personal and for self. Every Christian is invited to ask for bread for himself, forgiveness for himself, guidance for himself and deliverance for himself. Every Christian should learn these elementary kindergarten steps in prayer. But let us remember that these are, after all, simply the first steps in prayer. God has far greater teaching on prayer that He wants to give us.

III. Bread for Others—Christ's College Course in Prayer

It is important to note that after the Lord's Prayer, quoted above, from the mouth of the Saviour, there is no "amen." The lesson in prayer is not over. The simple elementals of prayer have been taught, and now the Lord Jesus goes on further into the marvelous realm of intercessory prayer, prayers for others. Here He teaches the disciples to enter into His own brokenhearted burden and pleading for the salvation of sinners. In Luke 11:5–8, Jesus continues the lesson on prayer, as follows:

"And he said unto them, Which of you shall have a friend, and shall go unto him at midnight, and say unto him, Friend, lend me three loaves; For a friend of mine in his journey is come to me, and I have nothing to set before him? And he from within shall answer and say, Trouble me not: the door is now shut, and my children are with me in bed; I cannot rise and give thee. I say unto you, Though he will not rise and give him, because he is his friend, yet because of his importunity he will rise and give him as many as he needeth."

Blessed is the man who has a friend. But here we see illustrated the man who has two. There is the Friend nearby who has plenty of bread, and there is the other friend, who, in his journey, has come to him and is hungry. Every Christian has these two friends. One Friend is God, who has plenty of bread for sinners. The other friend is the sinner himself. Every Christian in the world stands between God and the lost world. We are the channel that God has chosen to carry bread to sinners. Jesus said to His disciples concerning the five thousand who waited, hungry—yea, famishing and weak— "Give ye them to eat" (Matt. 14:16). When Christ furnished the bread, the disciples carried it to the waiting thousands who had not bread. And so here the disciples are taught to pray as the man who so desperately needs bread for one friend and so goes to another friend and pleads until he gets all he needs.

Some Christians make the mistake of never separating from unsaved sinners. They are not a peculiar people. They are like Lot down in Sodom, who called the men of Sodom "brethren" and lost his testimony so that "he seemed as one that mocked unto his sons in law" (Gen. 19:14). We should not be conformed to this world. It is true that we are in the world and we must have contact with sinners, but we should not live as they do. Saved people must be different if lost people are to come to us for the bread of life.

But other Christians go to the opposite extreme. They feel that this world is not their home, that they here have no continuing city; therefore, they make much of their heavenly friends who have plenty of bread, but they never carry any to the other friends who have none. Some Christians try so hard to be sanctified and separated that they do not love sinners, they do not win souls. You can be sure that Jesus was holy and sinless and otherworldly. No one ever could accuse Him of compromising with sin, and yet the Pharisees were astonished at His love for sinners. "And the Pharisees and scribes murmured, saying, This man receiveth sinners, and eateth with them" (Luke 15:2). It is remarkable how Jesus loved sinners, ate with sinners, preached to sinners, forgave sinners.

Here, then, God has left Christians as the link between two worlds, the link between God and man. I know that Christ is the one mediator between God and man, the one atonement for sin; but in some sense Christians enter into the mediatorial work of Christ. In some sense we are to be intercessors like Christ. Paul said he was one who "fill[s] up that which is behind of the afflictions of Christ in my flesh for his body's sake, which is the church" (Col. 1:24). I wonder if you, dear reader, have been in kindergarten so long, as regarding Christ's teaching on prayer, that you have never learned to pray for others, have never entered into the burden and soul-agony of Christ for sinners, have never sought and found the bread of life for sinners and carried it to them with power and blessing.

Here Christ offers to teach the disciples to pray like Moses. He came down from Mount Sinai to find his beloved Israel dancing naked about the golden calf, and saying, "These be thy gods, O Israel, which have brought thee up out of the land of Egypt" (Exod. 32:8). Moses took radical steps to destroy the idol and convict the people of their sins and stop the plague. Then he went with a broken heart back up to the mountain to pray. God threatened to destroy the nation and to make of Moses and his descendants a great nation. But Moses said, "Oh, this people have sinned a great sin, and have made them gods of gold. Yet now, if thou wilt forgive their sin—; and if not, blot me, I pray thee, out of thy book which thou hast written" (Exod. 32:31,32). Moses' compassionate, intercessory prayer prevailed with God, and He did not destroy the nation, though they had sinned so grievously. That is not the simple and elementary praying taught in the Lord's Prayer.

That is not kindergarten praying, but the praying of a master. This is Christ's college course in prayer.

Here Christ would teach us to pray as Esther prayed for her nation of Jews to be saved from the hands of wicked Haman who had plotted to destroy them all.

Here God would teach us to pray as Daniel prayed in the ninth chapter of his prophecy—"By prayer and supplications, with fasting, and sackcloth, and ashes," interceding for the whole nation of Israel; or again when he ate no pleasant bread, either flesh or wine, nor did he anoint himself with oil, till three whole weeks were fulfilled (Dan. 10:3).

Christ here would have us enter into the travail of soul which Paul the apostle had so that he could write even under infallible, divine inspiration, "I say the truth in Christ, I lie not, my conscience also bearing me witness in the Holy Ghost, that I have great heaviness and continual sorrow in my heart. For I could wish that myself were accursed from Christ for my brethren, my kinsmen according to the flesh" (Rom. 9:1–3). Most of us pray for ourselves. We could not say like Paul in Romans 10:1, "Brethren, my heart's desire and prayer to God for Israel is, that they might be saved."

Here Christ would teach us to enter into His experience in the Garden of Gethsemane, yea, into the very agony of the cross itself. Christ died to save sinners. For this purpose He left Heaven and came to earth, and was despised and abused and betrayed and deserted and spit upon and scourged and mocked and stripped and nailed to the cross and slain. Christ paid the price to get the bread of life to sinners. He Himself is that Bread. None of us can ever take His place. None of us can atone for man's sin. Christ, in the Garden of Gethsemane, "went a little further" than anyone else, and of course He is God's only Saviour, the only mediator between God and man (I Tim. 2:5). But still it is true that He has granted that Christians who will, may learn to enter into the intercessory work of Christ, to bear His burdens, suffer His travail, and so carry the bread of life from God to the sinner. That is the meaning of this parable when Jesus taught His disciples to pray, not only the little prayer for daily needs but the great prayer of intercession for others. Christ wants us to learn the prayer of travail for souls, the prayer of intercession for others, the prayer that will give us bread for sinners.

IV. Confession Before Importunity

We started out by asking Jesus to teach us to pray. Then we must pray the kind of prayer that He puts in our mouths. We often pray the words of the Lord's Prayer, or the model prayer, but why not take it to heart to pray also this other model prayer given us in Luke 11:5,6: "Friend, lend me three loaves; For a friend of mine in his journey is come to me, and I have nothing to set before him"? This is a prayer asking for bread, but it is much more—it is a prayer of humble confession. How Christians do need to pray this prayer:

"A friend of mine in his journey is come to me, and I have nothing to set before him."

Every Christian who reads this is the best Christian somebody knows. Many a wife writes to me and says, "Brother Rice, pray for my husband," or, "Please go to see my husband and try to win him to Christ." But again and again such dear women urge, "Do not let him know that I sent you." Wives say to me, "You know how it is, Brother Rice. Husbands won't listen to their own wives." Or mothers or fathers say, "Brother Rice, pray for my boy. I hope God will send somebody to win him. You know, boys and girls don't pay much attention to mothers and fathers. An outsider can do more with them." But that is an alibi that will not stand up. It is really not true. If a mother is what she ought to be, she can have more influence over her own boy than anyone else in the world. If a Christian wife is out-and-out for God and filled with the Holy Spirit, she can win her husband more quickly than anyone else can.

Here is the teaching. Jesus teaches us that we must admit our responsibility. We must frankly confess to God that there are certain ones God has sent our way, "friends" to whom we owe the bread of life. One of you who reads this is a wife, and God gave you a husband. He is dearer to you than life itself, dearer than any other earthly friend could be. God sent him your way. God depends upon you to give him the bread of life. If you do not do your part, if you have not the power to win him, then surely his case may be well-nigh hopeless.

I know wives who have lived with husbands for thirty years and never won them to Christ. I know brothers who have grown up with brothers; they have worked together and played together. Oftentimes they have been nearly inseparable, and yet the Christian brother has not been able to win his unsaved brother to Christ. I know fathers into whose hands and homes and hearts God has put little children. They love Daddy, follow after Daddy, imitate him, almost worship him. And yet I have seen such children grow up around their father, and he never once had the bread of life for them.

I tell you, we cannot escape the responsibility of blood relationship and the responsibility of intimate friendship and association. If there is someone who is near and dear to you and is unsaved, then God expects you to take to him the bread of life. Even the rich man in Hell acknowledged his obligation to his five unsaved brothers (Luke 16:27,30). He knew that, following his example, they too would go to Hell unless they were warned, and he pled that one should be sent even from Heaven to warn his five brothers that they should repent lest they come to that place of torment where he was already! You cannot escape your responsibility, I say, to the friend or wife or husband or son or daughter or mother or neighbor that God has sent your way.

Multitudes of you who read this long to win souls, but never do. You pray for souls to be saved, and sometimes timidly you invite them to church or tell them that you pray for them. And yet you do not get them saved. Why? Why? WHY?

This simple prayer that Jesus teaches His disciples to pray gives us the answer. You dear Christians simply do not have what it takes. You do not have upon you the power of the Holy Ghost. You do not have the holy boldness, the deep concern, the travail of soul, the burning words, it may be, or the tears, or the example that God will use to win that soul to Himself! You, if you are honest, must pray this prayer of confession, "A friend of mine in his journey is come to me, AND I HAVE NOTHING TO SET BEFORE HIM"! You do not have the bread of life to set before sinners. You do not have what it takes. God meant for you to have, you could have had, you may yet have, the bread of life for sinners.

Let me suggest, then, Reader, that you drop very quietly before God and bow your head. Pray this simple prayer of confession. Mean it from your very soul. Acknowledge in these words your failure, your barrenness, your shallowness as a Christian, your lack of fruit-bearing. Pray it now in your heart. Perhaps it will help you if you bow your head and close your eyes and earnestly and contritely, with a confession of your failure, pray these words: "O God, a friend of mine (husband or brother or neighbor or son or daughter or sweetheart) has come to me, and I have nothing to set before him. I ought to be able to win him to Christ, but I haven't done it."

Alibis and excuses here will do no good. If you are to learn to pray as Jesus is trying to teach you in these verses, then you will pray the prayer that is directed.

Here is the shameful reason for the fruitlessness of Christians all over the land. Here is why preachers have no souls saved, why churches have no revivals, why Sunday school teachers do not win their pupils, why fathers and mothers and wives do not win their loved ones to Christ. The simple fact is that God sent loved ones our way that we ought to win and that we could win if we had the bread of life, the power of the Holy Ghost upon us. We do not have what it takes to win souls. God has certainly bread for sinners. His dear, compassionate, bleeding heart has prepared a way for all mankind, and His seeking Spirit will never be satisfied until His house is filled and the wedding table is furnished with guests. God has bread for sinners, but that bread must be carried by Christians. There is bread for you to carry to your loved one. I beseech you today, go and beg for it, plead for it, with confession, with tears, with travail of soul, until God answers from Heaven and gives you power that you need, the wisdom and leadership and the message that you need to win souls. There is a Friend who has bread, plenty of it, for every sinner. There is someone whom God has brought to your door, to your life, who needs the bread. God means for you to get the bread which He has in abundance to give to the poor sinner who has none. Confess today your lack, your fruitlessness. Make your confession, admit your sin, and then stay and get the bread!

This is a sad prayer, isn't it? "I have nothing to set before him." It is like the disciples who frankly shrank from the task of feeding the five thousand, and said, "There is a lad here, which hath five barley loaves, and two small fishes: but what are they among so many?" (John 6:9). And they said that even if there were two hundred pennyworth of bread, it would not be enough for so great a multitude. And yet Jesus said to them, "Give ye them to eat."

Do you remember when Jesus came down from the Mount of Transfiguration and found the disciples who did not go surrounded by a multitude? A father with his poor, demon-possessed son came to Jesus. He had brought his son to the disciples to cast out the devil, and they could not cast him out! And since the disciples could not cast out devils, the father doubted whether Jesus could. But Jesus did. Then the disciples came to Jesus and said, "Why could not we cast him out?" They saw they had failed. They confessed their need. All over the land Christians and preachers ought to be confessing that friends in their journey have come to us and we have nothing to set before them. God has bread for all the sinners, but we have not been able to carry it to them.

V. Importunity, or "Praying Through," for Bread for Sinners

Read again the Scripture with which we began, Luke 11:5–8:

"And he said unto them, Which of you shall have a friend, and shall go unto him at midnight, and say unto him, Friend, lend me three loaves; For a friend of mine in his journey is come to me, and I have nothing to set before him? And he from within shall answer and say, Trouble me not: the door is now shut, and my children are with me in bed; I cannot rise and give thee. I say unto you, Though he will not rise and give him, because he is his friend, yet because of his importunity he will rise and give him as many as he needeth."

In the parable which Jesus gave us in Luke 11:5–8, teaching us to pray, the man came to his friend at midnight to beg of him, "Friend, lend me three loaves." It was at midnight; that would seem to indicate unusual urgency. Blessed is the Christian who is willing to break up the ordinary routine of his life for prayer and soul winning. I dare say that God never specially blesses with an outpouring of the Holy Spirit in soul-winning power upon a Christian who is not willing to take extraordinary measures to receive it.

I say the friend came at midnight and pounded upon the door and woke up his neighbor, saying, "Friend, lend me three loaves." And so many of you came to God too. You have prayed that God would save your husband, or you prayed that God would save your son or your neighbor. You prayed that God would make you a soul winner. Surely, you thought, that kind of prayer is according to the will of God. And yet, if you tell the truth, many of you who read this will have to admit that God did not answer it. You asked for power, but you did not receive it. You asked that God would help you to win some loved one that He had put in your home or that He had caused to cross your path, and yet God did not give you that bread for sinners. Isn't that true?

Here Christ is teaching us to pray. He teaches us to come to the Father as to one who has plenty of bread, and ask Him for bread for sinners. Well, since He teaches us to pray such a prayer, does He teach us to expect an answer? Does everyone who asks for the bread for sinners get it?

Let's read again what the Lord Jesus said about this kind of praying for soul-winning power, praying for bread to give to sinners:

"And he from within shall answer and say, Trouble me not: the door is now shut, and my children are with me in bed; I cannot rise and give thee."

Thus, the Christian who asked for bread to give to sinners is taught by the Saviour to expect rebuff, to expect no favorable answer at first. How strange this seems to us! Surely it seems that God would gladly give soul-winning power to everyone that asks it, bread for sinners to everyone who wishes to carry the bread. And yet, according to this parable, the bread is not forthcoming. The man within simply answers, 'No, my children are with me in bed, and I cannot rise and give thee.' Isn't it strange for God to say, 'Trouble Me not; don't bother Me. I don't have any time nor disposition now to give you bread for sinners'? And yet that is what the Scripture seems to teach! What can Jesus mean by these words?

I think I can help you to see it by this illustration. The little child longs to be able to use the axe with which his father cuts down big trees and splits the stove wood, and yet the father carefully keeps the keen-edged instrument from the child when he asks for it. Or will the mother immediately turn over an expensive sewing machine to the little girl the first time she wants to use it to sew? Or what foolish parent would turn an expensive, high-powered automobile over to the little fellow the first time he wants to drive it? And so, I tell you, it is foolish to expect the infinite God to place the dynamite of Heaven in the hands of a careless Christian who does not know the travail of soul that Christ had and has not entered into the burden for sinners and the sense of shame over sin. How can God give to the light-hearted Christian who casually asks to be filled with the Holy Spirit, asks to be made a great soul winner—how can God, I say, give him the power to defeat Satan, to transform lives, yea, put in his hands all the infinite power that raised Jesus Christ from the dead?

"I say unto you, Though he will not rise and give him, because he is his friend, yet because of his importunity he will rise and give him as many as he needeth."—Luke 11:8.

Underline the most important word in verse 8, quoted above. What is it? You are right, it is *importunity*. God does not give soul-winning power to people simply because they are friends of Christ. You say you are saved and that gives you the right to come and say, "Our Father, who art in Heaven," and to ask for daily bread and forgiveness of sins and guidance and deliverance from the evil one. But here in this lesson on intercessory prayer, Jesus tells us that the friend will not rise and give to his neighbor the bread that he needs because he is his friend. Friendship is not enough in that case. But "because of his importunity," his pleading, his insistence, his begging, "he will rise and give him as many as he needeth."

Certainly God means for us to get this lesson: there are some blessings that a Christian will never have without pleading, importunate waiting on God! Those who want soul-winning power, want to be able to carry the bread of life to sinners, must learn the secret of *"praying through"!*

I believe that in asking many things it is wrong not to expect the blessing at once. For instance, I know that God is ready to save instantly any sinner who will call upon Him for mercy and trust Him for salvation. I believe that a sinner can trust Christ immediately and be saved. I do not believe there needs to be any long period of waiting or mourning or seeking God when a sinner is willing to trust in Jesus Christ. For that reason I do not usually use what is generally called a "mourner's bench." I like for sinners to come with deep earnestness, and I believe it profitable to have a place to teach them the Word of God, and I think it well even to have sinners to pray and ask God for forgiveness. But I do not want to leave the impression that God is hardhearted or that He is indifferent about saving a soul or must be begged into it. That is not true. God is able and willing to save instantly everyone that comes to Him for salvation.

I think that many ordinary affairs ought to be easily settled between the Christian and God. I believe that a Christian ought not to need to pray long for daily bread, I mean bread for today and asked for in the will of Christ and in simple faith. I believe that it does not take a Christian long to get his sins forgiven when he is willing to forgive others and confess his own sins honestly. Surely one does not need a long period of waiting before God is willing to forgive His own penitent child and to cleanse him from unrighteousness. I say, some things a Christian can get from God the moment he is willing to come God's way with all of his heart and trust Christ for it.

But here Jesus plainly teaches that importunity is God's way of getting soul-winning power.

Before Pentecost a hundred twenty gathered in an upper room. "These all continued with one accord in prayer and supplication, with the women, and Mary the mother of Jesus, and with his brethren" (Acts 1:14). There was intercession, there was begging, supplication, waiting, before the power of the Holy Ghost came upon them at Pentecost.

When Paul was saved on the road to Damascus, then he was three days and three nights without food (Acts 9:9). And the angel of God brought the word to Ananias: "Behold, he prayeth" (vs. 11). For three days and nights after his conversion Paul fasted and prayed. What for? Evidently for bread to give to sinners, for the soul-winning power of the Holy Spirit. For when Ananias came to him he said, "Brother Saul, the Lord, even Jesus, that appeared unto thee in the way as thou camest, hath sent me, that thou mightest receive thy sight, and be filled with the Holy Ghost" (Acts 9:17). Paul got salvation for himself instantly when he surrendered to Christ. He got power to witness to others and get others saved only after heartbreaking periods of fasting and prayer. Again the one word, *importunity*, spelled the way to have bread for others.

D. L. Moody prayed, he tells us, for two long years, beseeching God to pour upon him the power of the Holy Spirit. Ever since two godly women had called his attention to his need for the power of the Holy Ghost upon his ministry, he had earnestly sought this blessing. It did not come until one day as he walked down Wall Street in New York City after long, long waiting on God.

In the case of Cornelius (Acts 10), as in the case of Charles G. Finney, the time of waiting and pleading came before salvation.

There are too many problems to explain here, but certain it is that in this college course on prayer, this lesson in advanced praying, intercessory praying, unselfish praying, Jesus means to teach us that *importunity* is the way to power. God does not give the power of the Holy Spirit simply because we are friends of God, but because we wait before Him until we are fitted to receive His blessing. How foolish we should be to expect the marvelous power of the Spirit of God to be given us freely, without any confession of sin, without any weighing of motives, without any pleading with tears, and without any transformation of life as we wait before God.

Certainly many Christians do not carry bread to sinners because they are not willing to wait and knock at the door and rattle the doorknob persistently and incessantly until the Friend within will arise and give them as many loaves as they need because of their importunity. Oh, may God teach us to pray, teach us to pray importunate prayers that will not be denied, that we may have bread for sinners!

VI. God Does Not Always Mean "No" When He Says "No"

Here is encouragement, then, for every child of God who has longed to win souls but never has. God has sent someone your way for you to win to Christ. A friend in his journey has come to you, and you have had nothing to set before him, and when you asked God, He seemed to say "no." He seemed to disregard your prayer. You never received the power you requested, and you never bore fruit as you longed to do. But you can! God did not mean "no" when He said "no." He simply meant for you to keep on asking and praying and for you to refuse to be denied. How eagerly God waits for His people to pray. Importunate praying, insistent praying can change even the plan of God. How gladly He will give bread to those who wait before Him with importunity just as the man pictured in the passage rose and gave his neighbor as many loaves as he needed, not because he was his friend, but because of his importunity.

In Matthew 15:21–28 we have a blessed example of the fact that God does not always mean "no" when He seems to say "no." A Canaanitish woman came to Jesus crying, "Have mercy on me, O Lord, thou son of David; my daughter is grievously vexed with a devil." But Jesus "answered her not a word." Finally Jesus "answered and said, I am not sent but unto the lost sheep of the house of Israel." Was she discouraged? Did she quit praying? No.

"Then came she and worshipped him, saying, Lord, help me."

Again Jesus discouraged her, saying, "It is not meet to take the children's bread, and cast it to dogs."

But see the faith in this woman's heart as she said, "Truth, Lord: yet the dogs eat of the crumbs which fall from their masters' table." If she was a dog, then she insisted she was Jesus' dog.

How Jesus exulted! He said, "O woman, great is thy faith: be it unto thee even as thou wilt."

And she went home and found her daughter well from that very hour!

Preachers have a way of sometimes getting the letter and not the spirit, so I doubt not that the disciples hung about greatly bored because it seemed that Jesus had insulted the woman to send her away deliberately. If they believed simply the outward indication of His language, they had a right to think that Jesus cared nothing for Gentiles, that to Him they were only dogs, and that He would do nothing at all for this heathen woman who cried after Him. But the woman did not listen to the letter of the words of Jesus. If He seemed not to care, her faith cried out that she knew He did care, He did love her, He did love her daughter! If He seemed to send her away, yet she believed that He came to save, and to save Gentiles as well as Jews. By faith she trusted in the goodness of His heart and was not discouraged by His words. I tell you that the Lord Jesus does not always mean "no" when He seems to say "no"! And when you asked for power, asked for bread for sinners, God did not mean you could not have it when the answer was delayed. He did not mean that there was not bread enough and to spare for all; He simply meant that He wanted you to wait and mean business for God. He wanted you to "pray through." As certain as the Bible is true, there is power for those who seek it with all their hearts. Oh, Lord Jesus, teach us to pray, to pray the importunate prayer so that we may have bread for sinners, as many loaves as we need.

Notice carefully Luke 11, verses 9 and 10:

"And I say unto you, Ask, and it shall be given you; seek, and ye shall find; knock, and it shall be opened unto you. For every one that asketh receiveth; and he that seeketh findeth; and to him that knocketh it shall be opened."

I think it would be more accurate if we should translate these verses, "I say unto you, Keep on asking, and it shall be given to you; keep on knocking, and it shall be opened unto you. For every one that keeps on asking receiveth; and to him that keeps on knocking, it shall be opened."

The form of the language in the Greek involves a continued asking and seeking and knocking. Blessed assurance God gives here that everyone who really keeps on asking receives, and everyone who really keeps on seeking finds, and everyone who keeps on knocking at the door of God for bread for sinners will have the door opened and bread given—yea, as many loaves as he needs for the sinner God sends to him!

VII. Don't Be Afraid to Ask: God Will Not Give Bad Gifts

It is a sad thing that fanatics have taken all the blessing out of many Scriptures for Christians. Some people have so grievously erred in regard to the power of the Holy Spirit that many, many Christians fear to ask for His presence and power. Many earnest preachers and teachers fear to speak upon certain passages of the Scripture lest they be misunderstood and lest they should be accused of teaching fanaticism, a jabber in unknown tongues, a false claim of sinless perfection, etc. But Christ knew the doubts that would arise in people's hearts when He gave this lesson on prayer, and He answered those doubts.

Dear friend, you need not fear to ask for bread for sinners. Christ will not give you an evil spirit nor an unholy jabber nor a false testimony. Christ will not turn you over to folly. You may ask, unafraid, knowing that when you ask for bread you will get bread and not a stone, or you will get fish and not a serpent, and you will get an egg and not a scorpion. Hear again these tender assurances of the Saviour:

"If a son shall ask bread of any of you that is a father, will he give him a stone? or if he ask a fish, will he for a fish give him a serpent? Or if he shall ask an egg, will he offer him a scorpion? If ye then, being evil, know how to give good gifts unto your children: how much more shall your heavenly Father give the Holy Spirit to them that ask him?"—Luke 11:11–13.

You love your child. If he asks for bread you would not give him a stone. And all the more if he, with a compassionate heart, asked bread for another that you loved dearly and wanted to see fed, you would not give him a stone. You, weak and ignorant and sinful as you are, would not betray the confidence of your child. You would not give a poisonous snake instead of fish, nor a scorpion or stinging lizard to the little fellow who confidently pled for an egg. So then Jesus reminds us, "If ye then, being evil, know how to give good gifts unto your children: how much more shall your heavenly Father give the Holy Spirit to them that ask him?"

We may feel perfectly safe to wait on God. Do not be discouraged. Do not listen to the taunts of those who say it is unnecessary, but ask and receive the power of the Holy Spirit.

VIII. Asking for the Holy Spirit

Strangely, Jesus did not put in exact words until the very close of this lesson on advanced praying, that He was teaching the disciples to *pray for the Holy Spirit!*

How many, many preachers and teachers hate the idea of praying for the Holy Spirit. They are willing to pray for revivals, pray for the conviction of sinners, pray for power on their preaching, pray for divine wisdom in their messages, and yet they fear to pray for the Holy Spirit Himself, who really brings revivals, who convicts sinners and converts them, who gives wisdom and power and leadership to the man of God! When we pray for bread for sinners, we really mean that we need the power and wisdom of the Holy Spirit of God to come upon us and enable us to do what otherwise we could not do. We want the Holy Spirit of God to make us fruitful soul winners.

The Scofield Reference Bible is the best reference Bible in the world, I believe, but in the footnotes on this Scripture, the editors make a bad mistake. Dr. Scofield says:

"To go back to the promise of Luke 11:13 is to forget Pentecost, and to ignore the truth that now every believer has the indwelling Spirit."

To be sure every believer now has the indwelling Spirit, but Jesus is not here teaching the disciples to pray for the indwelling of the Holy Spirit. Rather, He is teaching them to pray for the soul-winning power of the Spirit. Surely neither Dr. Scofield nor any informed man would say that every Christian has the soul-winning power of the Spirit. And that is what Jesus here urges us to pray for. We are to pray with holy begging, with urgent pleading, that the Holy Spirit of God will help us to carry the bread of life to sinners. There can be no other meaning to the teaching of Jesus here. The disciples were never taught to pray for the indwelling of the Holy Spirit, and if they had prayed for His indwelling, their prayer would NOT have been answered. For Jesus had plainly stated in John 7:37–39 that the Holy Ghost would not be given in the sense of making His headquarters in the Christian's body until Christ should be glorified, that is, raised from the dead. Any praying for the indwelling of the Holy Spirit could never be answered before Jesus rose from the dead and breathed on His disciples and said, "Receive ye the Holy Ghost" (John 20:22). And after that time it would not do any good to pray for the indwelling of the Holy Spirit, for every saved soul has the Holy Spirit dwelling within him. No, Jesus meant that Christians should pray for the Holy Spirit to anoint us or fill us or empower us to make us soul winners; that the Holy Spirit of God would enable us to carry the bread of life to sinners. And that is the only way soul winners are made. Do not let anybody steal this precious verse, Luke 11:13, away from you. God still gives the Holy Spirit in soul-winning power to those who ask Him importunately and will not take "no" for an answer.

Those who think this part of the Bible is out-of-date should remember that the book of Luke was not written until long after Pentecost. Why should the Holy Spirit ever have inspired it, and why should God have written down this sweet promise that men who ask for the Holy Spirit could have Him to make them soul winners, if the promise were already out-of-date before it was written down? Beware lest Satan steal away the riches of the Bible from you by having men tell you that part of the Bible is out-of-date and was not meant for you. God is still eager to have bread taken to sinners. Friends in their journey through life come to you, and you have nothing to set before them. But God has bread enough for all, and He will give it if you knock at His door with importunity.

There is a way to power, to fruit-bearing. You too may enter with Moses and Paul into the travail of soul that Christ had for sinners. You too may enter into the miracle-working power of the Holy Spirit in saving sinners. But it is not a light and frivolous matter. It is not gained by flippant or half-hearted praying.

Some ministers have a way of saying to people who seek for the power of the Holy Spirit that they should simply go home and believe that they have the power, that already they have the Holy Spirit and they have all they need. Well, suppose that the neighbor at midnight would say to the man who was outside pounding upon his door, "Go on home and believe that you have bread for your friend that has none, and it will be all right." Well, that is not what the friend who had the bread said to his neighbor. And if the neighbor had acted on such advice, he would have gone home without the bread, however hard he tried to believe it was in his hands. The power of the Holy Spirit is real and definite, and we may know whether or not the breath of God is on us to win sinners. We may know whether or not we have bread for sinners. And we may have the bread if we mean business, but I want you to know there is a price to pay. You may have the bread if you are willing to knock at the door and wait before God until He gives you as many loaves as you need. And while you pray and wait, God will search out your heart, will show what displeases Him, will bring you to confession and forsaking of sin, will help you count the heavy cost. Whatever needs fixing, God can fix, in your life and heart as you wait and plead for bread for sinners—that is, for the power of the Holy Spirit to win sinners.

CHAPTER VII

PRAYING FOR HEALING

"Is any among you afflicted? let him pray. Is any merry? let him sing psalms. Is any sick among you? let him call for the elders of the church; and let them pray over him, anointing him with oil in the name of the Lord: And the prayer of faith shall save the sick, and the Lord shall raise him up; and if he have committed sins, they shall be forgiven him. Confess your faults one to another, and pray one for another, that ye may be healed. The effectual fervent prayer of a righteous man availeth much."—Jas. 5:13–16.

How many times our Saviour, in His brief earthly ministry, heard the cry of the sick for healing! And how willingly the Saviour answered their prayers and healed the sick.

The leper said, "Lord, if thou wilt, thou canst make me clean" (Matt. 8:2).

The centurion at Capernaum said, "Lord, my servant lieth at home sick of the palsy, grievously tormented" (Matt. 8:6).

A certain ruler worshipped Jesus, saying, "My daughter is even now dead: but come and lay thy hand upon her, and she shall live" (Matt. 9:18).

A woman diseased with an issue of blood twelve years came behind Jesus, touched the hem of His garment, and yet there was a prayer in her timid heart (Matt. 9:20).

Two blind men followed Jesus, crying and saying, "Thou son of David, have mercy on us" (Matt. 9:27).

The Syrophenician woman, "a woman of Canaan," cried to Jesus saying, "Have mercy on me, O Lord, thou son of David; my daughter is grievously vexed with a devil" (Matt. 15:22).

When Jesus came down from the Mount of Transfiguration, there came a certain man, kneeling down to Him and saying, "Lord, have mercy on my son: for he is lunatick, and sore vexed: for ofttimes he falleth into the fire, and oft into the water. And I brought him to thy disciples, and they could not cure him" (Matt. 17:15,16).

As Jesus departed from Jericho once, two blind men sitting by the wayside heard that Jesus passed by and cried out, saying, "Have mercy on us, O Lord, thou son of David" (Matt. 20:30). All these and many other cases recorded in the Gospels were prayers for healing; and Jesus answered these, every one! On a number of occasions, multitudes brought their sick people to Jesus for Him to heal. If the personal ministry of Jesus shows anything about His tender heart, then He loves to heal the sick, He is glad to hear prayers for healing.

I. Sickness Is a Proper Subject of Prayer

In James 5:13 we are given the plain instruction,

"Is any among you afflicted? let him pray."

Afflicted could be translated *suffering.* So people are to pray for themselves when they suffer. And then verse 14 continues,

"Is any sick among you? let him call for the elders of the church; and let them pray over him...And the prayer of faith shall save the sick, and the Lord shall raise him up."

Clearly, sickness should be an occasion for prayer. We are commanded to pray when we suffer ourselves, and the elders of the church are to be called officially too to pray for the sick. Then in James 5:16 we are told,

"Confess your faults one to another, and pray one for another, that ye may be healed."

Though the sick may pray for themselves, it is proper also for the elders of the church to pray, and individual Christians are to confess their sins one to the other and to pray one for the other, in order that they may be healed.

If there were no particular and specific command, like this, to pray for healing of the sick, yet many other passages of Scripture authorize us to pray for anything we want or need. For instance, in Mark 11:24 Jesus said, "What things soever ye desire, when ye pray, believe that ye receive them, and ye shall have them." That *"what things soever"* would certainly include the healing of our sick bodies. And again in John 14:14 Jesus promised, "If ye shall ask any thing in my name, I will do it." Those words *"any thing"* certainly would cover healing of the body. And Philippians 4:6 commands us: "...in every thing by prayer...let your requests be made known unto God." If there were not a single specific promise in the Bible which mentioned healing of the sick in answer to prayer, yet any believing Christian would have a right to call on his heavenly Father for healing in the light of these general promises clearly meant to cover every need of a Christian.

Besides, sickness is evidently the attack of Satan. Job's sickness was brought on by the direct attack of Satan (Job 2:4–7). Jesus healed one woman, whom, He said, "Satan hath bound, lo, these eighteen years" (Luke 13:16). And then of Paul's thorn in the flesh, we are told it was a "messenger of Satan" (II Cor. 12:7). Sickness and disease come from Satan. God permits them as He permits sin and permits certain results of sin. And often God overrules sickness to His own glory. But generally, it is proper to say that sickness is from Satan.

And thus, may not God's own children call on their heavenly Father to help them in the attack of Satan on their bodies? Surely the very nature of sickness means that we ought to pray about it and have a perfect right to pray about the healing of our bodies.

And even better is the sweet thought that God is our heavenly Father. He has an infinite compassion for us. As Jesus Himself went about doing good and was moved with compassion by the sickness and the sorrows of the people, so He has compassion upon us now, and our dear heavenly Father has loving compassion upon His children. "Like as a father pitieth his children, so the LORD pitieth them that fear him" (Ps. 103:13). If there were not a line in the Bible upon which to base our hope except this—that God is our heavenly Father and we are His dear children, redeemed at infinite cost— then surely that alone would give us a right to look up in His face and tell Him of our woes and ask Him for help in our sufferings and sicknesses. Jesus said, "If ye then, being evil, know how to give good gifts unto your children, how much more shall your Father which is in heaven give good things to them that ask him?" (Matt. 7:11). The relief from pain, the healing of disease, the strength for our daily tasks—surely in many, many cases, at least, these are good things for which we have a right to ask our heavenly Father. A father's love and compassion is enough to guarantee that He is concerned about our sickness. Sickness is a proper subject for prayer.

Christians ought to pray alone when they are sick. Or Christians ought to call for their pastors or for church officials to pray. It is perfectly legitimate to have prayer in public services, just so it is sincere prayer, God-honoring prayer, and not a racket and not connected with false doctrine. And Christians ought to pray privately one for another, confessing their faults one to another. Sickness is a proper subject for prayer.

Years ago I was troubled with tonsillitis. Every winter I had a wretched time with sore throat and fever. One can feel so much like dying with tonsillitis, and not be very sick! The family doctor insisted that I should have my tonsils removed, and at last, reluctantly, I consented. A certain day was set for the operation. That morning in my devotional reading I read II Chronicles 16. How startled I was to read in verses 12 and 13, "And Asa in the thirty and ninth year of his reign was diseased in his feet, until his disease was exceeding great: yet in his disease he sought not to the LORD, but to the physicians. And Asa slept with his fathers, and died in the one and fortieth year of his reign." I was not ready to 'sleep with my fathers,' so decided I should seek God first, before the physicians.

Immediately I told my wife that I had sinned in settling any matter about my health without a season of prayer. I postponed the tonsillectomy; I went to the Lord in earnest prayer for my throat. Soon thereafter I had occasion to talk to a doctor who was an earnest Christian. He said to me that if I would take his counsel, I would never need to have my tonsils removed. He gave me a diet list; I left off fried foods, fats and sweets and began to use more fruit juices and eat more green vegetables, and I have never had tonsillitis from that day to this!

How often we commit the sin of Asa who "in his disease...sought not to the LORD, but to the physicians." That does not mean that Asa sinned in having physicians. It means that he sinned in not looking *first* to the Lord, and in that he was trusting men instead of God. The Bible never indicates that it is wrong, under certain circumstances, to use doctors and medicine. But always, we may be sure, it grieves God when His children think first about human help and human remedies. The very first thing anybody ought to do about sickness is to *pray!*

In Dallas, Texas, once in a church prayer meeting, we had many testimonies of remarkable answers to prayer for healing of the body. Some had been healed after spending hundreds of dollars on hospital bills and doctor bills and after long weeks of suffering. Some had been healed who had been given up by good doctors to die. The testimonies were blessed. At the close of the testimony meeting a dear old Christian lady rose and said, "Brother Rice, if the time ever comes when I am sick and the doctors can't help me and when medicine doesn't do any good, I'm going to call on you and this church to pray for me!" How like the rest of us that is—we call on God when other things have failed. How glad He would be if we called on Him first; and then, as He directed, we could use medicine and doctors as He led, and give God the glory when He healed. Or if He gave faith for healing without doctors and medicine, we could take the blessing He gave and thank Him for it. Christians ought to look first to God in every trouble and in every need. And so when Christians are sick they should pray, and others should pray for them.

No doubt there are many, many Christians who are sick who ought to be well, and would be, if they came in Jesus' name to God in prayer according to the scriptural plan. It is not *always* God's will to heal the sick, we know; but *usually* it is His blessed will, and certainly always we should pray. In those cases where it is not God's will to heal the sick, He will make His will known to humble and surrendered hearts. Meantime, whenever we are sick, let us pray.

II. Prayer for the Sick Is Proper During This Age

Dr. H. A. Ironside says (*Our Hope* magazine, August 1942), "No instructed Christian can help acknowledging the power of the Lord to heal the body as well as to save the soul. He who credits the miracles of the New Testament, as every sincere Christian must, necessarily recognizes the healing power of God....God can heal. God has healed. God does heal. He heals in answer to prayer. He heals where there is no prayer at all by the recuperative power of nature. He heals, as in Hezekiah's case, by the use of means.

He has often healed in answer to the prayer of the individual who was sick, or of others who prayed for him. There are too many reputable testimonies at the present time to such healings to question them for a moment."

Some pestiferous, ultrasmart Bible teachers go about chopping up the Bible, making new dispensations at will, and dividing them up between Israel and the church! They sometimes say, "Physical blessings were for Israel, and spiritual blessings are for the church," although the Bible never says anything of the kind. Some notes in the Scofield Reference Bible lean too much toward this ultradispensational teaching. Dr. R. A. Torrey, in his book *Divine Healing* says:

"It is said by some that the Epistle of James was written to Jewish believers, and therefore it does not apply to Gentile believers. But God in His Word very definitely tells us that what applies to Jewish *believers* applies to Gentile believers, that *'in Christ Jesus'* 'there is neither Jew nor Greek' (Gal. 3:28).[1] This splitting up of the New Testament and giving one part to Gentile Christians and another part to Jewish Christians, has absolutely no warrant in the Word of God, in fact is against its plain teaching. There are some who would take away from us Gentiles pretty much all of the New Testament except the latter Epistles of Paul, but they are riding a hobby for which there is no warrant whatever in the Bible itself. They are not *'rightly dividing the word,'* they are *mutilating* the Word, and stealing from the greater part of God's children what really belongs to them."

These ultradispensationalists say that the book of James was primarily to Jewish believers and not to Gentile Christians. Even the Scofield Reference Bible has a subhead before Hebrews, James, I and II Peter and Jude, calling them "The Jewish-Christian Epistles," as if they were essentially different from the rest of the New Testament. But this is not true. It is true that James addressed his epistle "to the twelve tribes which are scattered abroad." But that was when the only Christians there were, were Jewish Christians. James was probably the first epistle written in the New Testament, and was written to all those who were Christians. But it is also true that the book of Galatians was addressed "unto the churches of Galatia," and that Romans was addressed "to all that be at Rome." And no one doubts that they are messages for us, the spiritual successors of the Christians in that day.

But fortunately we do not have to guess as to whom the Holy Spirit meant to address in these writings. Notice in James 5:14 that it is *elders* who are to be called to pray, not a *rabbi; elders of the church,* and not *rulers of the synagogue.* This is a message to Christians in churches, and not to Jews in synagogues. And notice particularly in James 5:3, "Ye have heaped treasure together for the last days." James, chapter 5, is fitting for the last

1. The Scripture text employed by Dr. Torrey has been changed by the editor to the KJV.

days. And verse 7 says, "Be patient therefore, brethren, unto the coming of the Lord." This epistle of James, and the last chapter particularly, is fitted for the days just preceding the Lord's return. Again in verse 8, we are told, "Be ye also patient; stablish your hearts: for the coming of the Lord draweth nigh." And again, verse 9 in this same fifth chapter of James says, "Behold, the judge standeth before the door." So in this chapter, at least four times (that is, in verses 3, 7, 8 and 9) the last days and the second coming of Christ are mentioned. It could not be clearer than it is that the Lord meant these blessed commands and promises about praying for the healing of the sick, to be claimed in these last days when the coming of the Lord draws nigh and when the Judge stands at the door. Do not let anyone take away from you the book of James—it belongs to Christians of this age.

III. "The Prayer of Faith Shall Save the Sick"

Let us make sure that we understand God's condition of healing. He says,

"The prayer of faith shall save the sick."

Dr. R. A. Torrey in his book *Divine Healing* calls attention to the fact that it is not attending three days in a certain kind of public service, nor saying over and over to one's self a certain formula; but it is the prayer of faith that saves the sick. Dr. Torrey's words: "Not *intense carnal excitement* [that] temporarily *galvanize*[s] him into brief activities, from which there is an appalling reaction, often leaving the poor victim of the religious charlatan worse than ever, and not infrequently sending him to the insane asylum or the cemetery."

For instance, the oil does not heal. The oil mentioned here was not medicine. Dr. W. B. Riley says, "The 'oil' here is the symbol of the Holy Ghost, and is applied as such. It is hardly medicinal, for if God is any sort of a physician, He is not a quack who would prescribe oil for all diseases." In Bible times kings, high priests and prophets were anointed with oil, setting them apart, or sanctifying them, to a special work for God. Leviticus 8:10–12 shows that the Tabernacle, the altar, and the vessels and the laver and its base were all anointed, "to sanctify them," and that Aaron was anointed "to sanctify him." Any man who is to serve God acceptably must serve in the power and anointing of the Holy Spirit, and the oil is a symbol of this Holy Spirit. And every saved person has the Holy Spirit abiding in his body. And every Christian, if he wants healing, should recognize the fact that the Holy Spirit has a right to take charge and use this body, as one dedicated wholly to God. To anoint one with oil for healing would simply mean that the one anointed is dedicated to God and that we trust the Holy Spirit of God to heal the body, if it be God's will. Dr. Torrey says, "The Holy Spirit is the One who does the healing, if it really is *Divine* healing. In

Romans 8:11 we read, 'But if the Spirit of him that raised up Jesus from the dead dwell in you, he that raised up Christ from the dead *shall also quicken your mortal bodies by his Spirit* that dwelleth in you.'[1] Now that refers, as the text itself and the context (vss. 20–23) clearly prove, to the future resurrection of our body by the Holy Spirit, and not to our present healing, but, nevertheless, *it shows the quickening, i. e., life-giving, power of the Holy Spirit in our physical bodies."*

Now this passage in James says in verse 13, "Is any among you afflicted? let him pray." There is prayer for the sick without anointing with oil. And again in verse 16, "Confess your faults one to another, and pray one for another, that ye may be healed." There is mutual prayer of Christians for one another, without anointing of oil; yet it is prayer for healing. But verses 14 and 15 suggest, "Is any sick among you? let him call for the elders of the church; and let them pray over him, anointing him with oil in the name of the Lord: And the prayer of faith shall save the sick, and the Lord shall raise him up." The anointing with oil is proper, under some circumstances; but it is not the oil that heals, and the oil is not essential. It is the prayer of faith that saves.

The twelve disciples sometimes anointed the sick with oil. In Mark 6:13 we are told, "And they cast out many devils, and anointed with oil many that were sick, and healed them." However, in many, many other cases of healing in the New Testament, there is no mention of anointing with oil.

Anointing with oil is sometimes a help to our faith. It reminds us that the Spirit of God dwells in the body of the sick Christian. Thus, by doing just what the Scripture suggests by anointing the sick with oil, we are encouraged to expect His blessing; and we make it more real to ourselves that God has invited us to pray for the healing of the sick. But whether we use oil or do not, it is the prayer of faith that saves the sick. In the Bible there is no mention of anybody's anointing with oil, except elders of the churches. But any Christian has a right to pray for his own healing or for the healing of a friend or loved one.

Modern evangelists who have so-called "divine healing services" and say that it is always God's will to heal the sick, often lay the blame for their failures on those who come to be healed. A poor sick person comes to be prayed for, the evangelist announces that it is God's will to heal this person and to restore him to perfect health, always, and then when the disappointed sick person is not healed, the evangelist disclaims all responsibility and says that the sick person simply did not have faith in God or that some other sin was in the way. But note here that it is the faith of those who do the praying that settles the matter! "Is any sick among you? let him call for the elders of the church; and let them pray over him, anointing him with oil in

1. The Scripture text employed by Dr. Torrey has been changed by the editor to the KJV.

the name of the Lord: And the prayer of faith shall save the sick, and the Lord shall raise him up." If the professional divine healers, who go about teaching that it is God's will to heal every sick Christian, are right, then these divine healers must be great rascals, for they do not pray the prayer of faith in such a multitude of cases, and the sick person is not healed. And in every case they are to blame, if it is really true that it is God's will to heal every sick person. No, it is not always God's will to heal the sick; but when the elders are called on to pray, then it is *their* faith that will guarantee the healing of the sick.

Of course, individual Christians may pray for themselves, and it may be that both the sick person and his friends alike join in prayer and join in faith.

Now faith is a gift of God. Romans 12:6 says, "Having then gifts differing according to the grace that is given to us, whether prophecy, let us prophesy according to the proportion of faith." And I Corinthians 12:8, 9 says, "For to one is given by the Spirit the word of wisdom; to another the word of knowledge by the same Spirit; To another faith by the same Spirit." The Holy Spirit gives faith. When God's Word has a plain promise to us, it would be sin not to believe the promise and risk God. For example, every lost person can instantly trust Christ and be saved. But about an individual problem, not covered by a great and general promise in the Bible, we must depend upon the Holy Spirit to show us the will of God. If God's Holy Spirit gives us faith for healing, then our prayer for healing will be answered. But if it is not God's will to heal, and if God's Holy Spirit does not give us any assurance that it is the will of God, then all of our willpower will not create faith. Where God gives the faith, God does the healing. Where God is not pleased to heal in a particular case, He will not give faith for healing.

Faith is not an emotion, but it is simply a resting upon the revealed will of God, whether that will of God is revealed in His Word or by revelation of the Spirit. Sometimes people say they have faith when they are depending upon the word of the preacher. Sometimes people say they have faith when, like Christian Scientists or like mind healers, they have said over and over to themselves that they are well or that they are getting better every day, etc., until they almost make themselves believe it. But mental suggestion, hypnotism, psychology are entirely different from faith in God. When we know that we are asking according to the will of God as revealed in His Word, and the Holy Spirit makes us sure that it is His will to do the thing we ask, then we have God-given faith. And in such cases we can claim the answer and expect it. "The prayer of faith shall save the sick, and the Lord shall raise him up."

IV. Is Healing in the Atonement?

There has been much loose talk over the question of whether or not Christ purchased redemption and healing for our bodies in His death on the cross. And I am sorry to say that much of this loose talk has been done by otherwise sound Christian men who were irritated with the Pentecostalists and others who claim that healing is in the atonement and that therefore every Christian ought at once to claim perfect healing on the basis of the atonement just as he takes salvation by faith at once.

In Matthew 8:16,17 is a clear Scripture on this question. It says:

"When the even was come, they brought unto him many that were possessed with devils: and he cast out the spirits with his word, and healed all that were sick: That it might be fulfilled which was spoken by Esaias the prophet, saying, Himself took our infirmities, and bare our sicknesses."

You would do well to read those two verses again carefully. The reference is to Isaiah 53:4, "Surely he hath borne our griefs, and carried our sorrows." It is remarkable that the New Testament translation, as given by the Holy Spirit, is even more emphatic than the Old Testament promise, that Christ carried our infirmities and our sicknesses. The Greek word for *sicknesses* in Matthew 8:17 could be translated *diseases*. And we remember that Isaiah 53:5 says, "And with his stripes we are healed."

It is foolish to fight the plain teaching of these verses. Jesus Himself took our infirmities and bare our diseases. Dr. R. A. Torrey spoke of the saying that "physical healing is in the atonement" in his book *Divine Healing*; and then Dr. Torrey said, "I think that that is a fair inference from these verses when looked at in this context." And as the beloved S. D. Gordon, author of the "Quiet Talks" series of books, said, surely every good thing we have comes, not as a result of our own merits, but as a result of the merits of Jesus Christ, and is paid for on the cross. If a Christian comes to pray for healing and prays in Jesus' name, he is praying properly. Surely it is not too much to say that every good thing God ever gives us was purchased by Jesus Christ.

But Dr. Torrey hastened, as I do, to call attention to the fact that we do not now receive all that is purchased for us. It is wonderful to be saved, to have our sins forgiven; but every Christian ought to know that that is only a part of his inheritance—there is more coming later! At the second coming of Christ, at the resurrection of the Christian dead, when our bodies are changed like unto Christ's glorious body, then we will inherit all that was bought for us on Calvary, but not before. Then we will have perfect health, perfect bodies, with all the mark and stain of sin gone, but not before. Then Christians will not wear glasses nor walk with canes nor have false teeth nor be bald-headed nor have dandruff nor halitosis nor athlete's foot! These things are bought for us on Calvary and are to be delivered when our salvation is complete. But no one will have perfect and permanent healing of all disease till then.

I think we may safely say that all the people who ever were healed, were only partly healed, except Enoch and Elijah who were translated and given glorified bodies at once. Jesus raised Lazarus from the dead, but Lazarus died again. The "perfect soundness" of the poor lame man healed at the gate of the temple, mentioned in Acts 3:16, was only a *relative* soundness. By human standards he was perfectly well, but by the standards of the angels who know no sickness nor disease, who never are tired or weak or sick and who never die, his body was still imperfect and subject to the weight and wages of sin. People who think they are perfectly well have yet the decay and weakening going on in their bodies that will lead them to death, sooner or later, unless the Saviour comes speedily. There is a susceptibility to disease, a tendency toward death in every living human being. So in some sense, healing, in this present age, is always relative. No one living has perfect health as the angels have, as Adam had in the Garden of Eden before he ever sinned. And that perfect health will be ours only when Jesus comes and changes our vile bodies to be like unto His glorious body.

That is a plain statement of the Scriptures. Romans 8:18–23 says:

"For I reckon that the sufferings of this present time are not worthy to be compared with the glory which shall be revealed in us. For the earnest expectation of the creature waiteth for the manifestation of the sons of God. For the creature was made subject to vanity, not willingly, but by reason of him who hath subjected the same in hope. Because the creature itself also shall be delivered from the bondage of corruption into the glorious liberty of the children of God. For we know that the whole creation groaneth and travaileth in pain together until now. And not only they, but ourselves also, which have the firstfruits of the Spirit, even we ourselves groan within ourselves, waiting for the adoption, to wit, the redemption of our body."

Here we learn that our salvation is largely in the future. We already have everlasting life, and the Holy Spirit has been given to us. He, the Holy Spirit, is "the firstfruits" of salvation; but we are still waiting "for the adoption, to wit, the redemption of our body." The redemption or salvation of the body was purchased on Calvary. Christ did really bear our infirmities and our sicknesses there. In that sense, perfect healing is in the atonement, but it is a part of the same salvation which we get when we trust in Christ. It is not a separate matter. When one trusts in Christ for salvation then he is forgiven and saved, without any further struggle or seeking or agonizing. That is, he has the Holy Spirit come in to regenerate him and make him a child of God, and the same Holy Spirit abides in his body as the firstfruits of salvation. And the completion of his salvation will come in due time when

Jesus comes and when the resurrection of the Christian dead takes place and the bodies of living saints are changed, in a moment, in the twinkling of an eye. Then we will have "the adoption, to wit, the redemption of our body."

Freedom from all sin was purchased for us at Calvary too. Absolute sinless perfection is in the atonement. But none of us have yet attained it. "If we say that we have no sin, we deceive ourselves, and the truth is not in us" (I John 1:8). But when Jesus comes, the sin question will be settled once for all. *Now* we have *forgiveness of* sins. *Then* we will have *complete erad-ication* of sin. We have the firstfruits of salvation, but when Jesus comes, we get the completed salvation. So now we live in hope for that which we have not yet attained, the Scripture says, and we groan within ourselves, "waiting for the adoption, to wit, the redemption of our body."

Then it is true that bodily healing is in the atonement, in the same sense that our resurrected bodies are provided for in the atonement. Christ Himself rose from the dead, and all of us who are His will likewise be raised from the dead by the same Spirit. And then, in our resurrected bodies, we will have received the adoption and redemption that are pro-vided on Calvary. And then we will be done with all sin and will be perfect like Christ.

CHAPTER VIII

PRAYING FOR HEALING, Continued

I. It Is Not Always God's Will to Heal

Yes, healing is in the atonement, in that sense, but it is never taught in the Bible that God intended Christians always to claim and have perfect health and perfect healing during this life.

Many Bible cases make that clear.

Dr. R. A. Torrey, in his little book *Divine Healing,* calls attention to the following instances in the Bible where people who were in the will of God were sick: (1) In II Kings 13:14 we read: "Elisha was fallen sick of the sickness whereof he died." And when you read the story you will see that Elisha was not out of communion with God, but rather was in most intimate fellowship with God and that on his dying bed he made remarkable prophecies as the mouthpiece of God, even while he was "sick of the sickness whereof he died."

(2) In II Timothy 4:20 Paul says, "Trophimus have I left at Miletum sick." Here the godly Paul himself did not get Trophimus healed, and we have no indication that either Paul or Trophimus was to blame.

(3) In Philippians 2:27 we read that Epaphroditus "was sick nigh unto death." And verse 30 in the same chapter tells us that it was because of his earnest love for Christ and devotion to His work that he "came nigh unto death." Epaphroditus wore himself out, nearly killed himself, in serving Christ. So sin was not to blame for his sickness, and there is not a hint of that here.

Besides the above, there is the classic example of Paul the apostle, who had a thorn in the flesh, and after he had thrice sought the Lord, still it was not removed (II Cor. 12:1–10). God did not remove Paul's thorn in the flesh, despite Paul's earnest and repeated prayers. Rather, He plainly revealed to Paul that that temptation, that "messenger of Satan" sent to buffet Paul, would be used of God to keep Paul humble and broken and dependent upon God. "My strength is made perfect in weakness," the Lord said to Paul. And noble Paul set a proper example to us all, when, instead of mourning and being downcast, immediately changed his prayer to fit with the revealed will of God, and said, "Most gladly therefore will I rather glory in my infirmities, that the power of Christ may rest upon me." Paul saw that sometimes sickness is better than health, and that the best Christian is sometimes permitted to suffer in order that God can bestow His power upon him.

Certainly it is not always God's will to heal. When God promised that "all things work together for good to them that love God" (Rom. 8:28),

He included sickness in His "all things."

How much blessedness has come because of the sufferings of Christians! Stephen was martyred. If his bones could honor the Lord in being broken, could not ours, sometimes? If Timothy's weak stomach was not healed but needed careful moderation and use of fruit juice, why may not Christians today sometimes have weak stomachs to the glory of God? If Job suffered, if Paul suffered, if Timothy had often infirmities, if Trophimus and Epaphroditus could be sick to the glory of God, then sometimes that may be true of you too. It was for the glory of God that Lazarus was sick and died (John 11:4). Then it was to God's glory that he should be raised from the dead. But it was not to the glory of God for Lazarus to stay well, so again he died, as does everybody else, no matter how good he may be.

Read the story of David Brainerd, the man of prayer, and see how earnest his prayer life, how strong his faith, how marvelous the answers God gave to his prayers; and then explain how he died of tuberculosis before he was thirty, perfectly content to go, assured that it was God's perfect will for him, the best promotion he could have! Sickness, like all the other things that follow a sinful race, can be used of God for His glory and for our preparation for His service and for Heaven.

My mother died when about twenty-eight years old; on her deathbed she made us promise to meet her in Heaven, had us sing "How Firm a Foundation, Ye Saints of the Lord," and looking up, declared that she saw Jesus and her baby. And so, literally filled with the Spirit and rejoicing, she went home to Heaven. Was her sickness God's will? I, who have missed her so much for forty years, feel certain that it was.

And every divine healer who teaches that it is God's will that every Christian should have perfect health, sooner or later finds that sickness comes upon him, and sometimes with it the breakdown of all his faith, and even insanity. And the sickness eventually results in death, even for the most spiritually minded, the best Christians, those who claim sinless perfection and those who claim perfect health from God alike. "It is appointed unto man once to die," says the Scripture (Heb. 9:27); and death proves that no man has yet lived (save Enoch and Elijah, who never died) who has attained either perfect health or perfect righteousness this side of the grave.

So, although Christ "Himself took our infirmities, and bare our sicknesses," as we are plainly told in Matthew 8:17, and though Christ's death on the cross did surely guarantee for all who are born again by faith that one day our bodies will have perfect redemption as well as our natures, we do not yet possess all that is bought for us. Healing of the body may not be instantly claimed in every case, as forgiveness of sins may be instantly received always by penitent faith. Perfect healing, along with the resurrection of our glorified bodies, is in the atonement made by Christ, we are taught by Romans 8:18–23. But that "adoption, to wit, the redemption of our body," certainly is not wholly ours until Jesus comes.

II. But It Is Usually God's Will to Heal in Answer to Prayer

One who comes to pray for healing, either for himself or for another, must come saying, "Nevertheless, not as I will, but as thou wilt" (Matt. 26:39). Before any of us can demand of God or claim healing, we must, with surrendered hearts, be ready to have sickness continue or death come, if that be God's will. But thank God, it is usually God's will to heal the sick. We know that a large percentage of sick people would get well without a physician, without medicine. God put healing forces in nature, and the body itself tends to combat disease. That surely shows that usually health is God's plan and that disease is usually of Satan. We know that God's great compassion and love toward His dear children is greater than that of an earthly father. He never wants us to suffer except when it is for our own good and thus for His own glory. He who "spared not his own Son, but delivered him up for us all, how shall he not with him also freely give us all things?" (Rom. 8:32)—that is, all things truly good and for our happiness and welfare. Unless He sees that the sickness Satan has brought may be turned to our best interest, better than health for the time, then we may be sure He is eager to heal our sickness.

Often, about health as about everything else a Christian needs, it is true that "ye have not, because ye ask not."

Yes, thank God, it is usually God's will to heal His own, so He invites us to pray. "Is any...afflicted? let him pray." And we are to call the elders of the church to pray also, as God leads. And individuals are to "confess your faults [sins] one to another, and pray one for another, that ye may be healed" (Jas. 5:13,14,16). Not every sinner we pray for is saved, not every sick person we pray for gets well; but nevertheless, prayer gets many lost sinners saved, and no doubt many a sick person is healed in answer to prayer, who would otherwise die or remain an invalid. So the first duty about sickness is to pray about it.

In my own experience, I have sometimes felt clearly, after I prayed about the sick, that God had some good reason for keeping them sick, and I could not have faith for their healing. In a few cases I felt that sin was in the way, and God would not heal because His blessing was prevented by sin. God must not appear to endorse sin or ignore it. Sometimes I have felt that the Christian would not wait on God in faith but preferred to trust doctors and human help; sometimes there was known sin in the life, worldliness, covetousness, unforgiveness or some filthy habit. *But in the great majority of cases where Christians seemed honestly to forsake sin and wait*

on God to find His will about sickness, He has healed the sick! Healing is
the normal and to-be-expected thing for a Christian in the will of God.

I think sometimes a Christian should be hungry for Christ's sake and
sometimes be out in winter's cold without a bed or without sufficient
clothes for Christ's sake. We should be willing to suffer for Him, and Paul
and many other of the best Christians have suffered these things. *But usu-*
ally that is not God's will. Ordinarily, Christians should pray for and get
daily bread and sufficient clothing. And so, I believe, ordinarily Christians
can go to God in sickness and be healed. So Christians should learn to go
earnestly and confidently to God in prayer every time they are sick, and ask
for healing. If the Holy Spirit plainly reveals that it is not God's will to heal,
then we, like Paul, should gladly accept the will of God, knowing it is better than anything else we can ask. Remember, prayer is not *telling* God; it
is *asking* God. But unless God does reveal that He has other plans, after we
earnestly seek to know His will and to make it ours, then we have a right to
wait confidently on God for healing.

I think I ought to say that in literally hundreds of cases I have had my
prayers for the sick answered, some slowly, some suddenly, some at once,
and others only after long waiting on God. So I believe it is usually God's
will to heal His children when they are sick, provided they confess and forsake their sins and seek His face with a surrendered heart, asking for healing.

III. Should Christians Use Doctors and Medicine?

Some traveling evangelists who draw big crowds by their healing meetings claim that it is a sin to go to a doctor, or at least that for a Christian it
shows lack of faith in God. But that teaching is not found in the Bible; it is
inconsistent with common sense and with God's way of doing His work in
other realms.

There are a number of Scriptures which show there is no sin in consult-
ing physicians, if it be done in faith, depending on God to use the doctor;
and no sin to take medicine if it be in faith, depending on God to bless and
use the medicine which He Himself has supplied in nature for mankind.

A typical case of healing in answer to prayer in the Bible, where God
used means in the cure, is that of King Hezekiah. Isaiah 38:1–5 says:

"In those days was Hezekiah sick unto death. And Isaiah the prophet, the
son of Amoz, came unto him, and said unto him, Thus saith the LORD, Set
thine house in order: for thou shalt die, and not live. Then Hezekiah turned
his face toward the wall, and prayed unto the LORD, And said, Remember
now, O LORD, I beseech thee, how I have walked before thee in truth and
with a perfect heart, and have done that which is good in thy sight. And
Hezekiah wept sore. Then came the word of the LORD to Isaiah, saying, Go,

and say to Hezekiah, Thus saith the LORD, the God of David thy father, I have heard thy prayer, I have seen thy tears: behold, I will add unto thy days fifteen years."

What a wonderful case of answer to a prayer for healing! And did Hezekiah instantly get out of bed, call all the doctors imposters, and vow he would never take another dose of medicine? He did not! The way he got well is told in the same chapter, Isaiah 38:21, which says, "For Isaiah had said, Let them take a lump of figs, and lay it for a plaister upon the boil, and he shall recover." From the similar account in II Kings 20:8 we learn that by the third day King Hezekiah was well enough to go to the house of the Lord. It was not instant healing, it was not without means, but it was divine healing, I think even miraculous healing, healing in answer to prayer.

In I Timothy 5:23 the Holy Spirit had Paul tell Timothy, "Drink no longer water, but use a little wine for thy stomach's sake and thine often infirmities." I have no doubt the wine prescribed here was simply the "new wine" of Bible language, that is, grape juice. But it was to be used, certainly, as a medicine. And if the juice of grapes may be pressed out and used for medicine, why may not the juice be pressed out of figs to make "syrup of figs"? And why may not the oil be pressed out of castor beans and used for medicine (castor oil), and why may not other things which God has provided in nature be used, prayerfully and gratefully, for the human body's health, when they are specifically fitted for the use?

Dr. Frost, of the China Inland Mission, in his book, *Miraculous Healing*, calls attention to the foolish inconsistency of those who would eat figs and thank God for their naturally healthful laxative effect but who would, if the juice were pressed out and put in a bottle, feel that it would be a sin to take it for the same result!

Jesus used spittle mixed with clay to heal a blind man. Why, I do not know, except to show that He could use means and that His healings need not necessarily be instantaneous. But Jesus used a fish, a hook and Peter, to get money for taxes (Matt. 17:27). He had the ten lepers go show themselves to the priest, and in the act of going they were healed (Luke 17:14). He used five loaves and two small fishes to feed the five thousand people, though He could as easily have done it without them. He used the disciples to carry the food. He used baskets for picking up the fragments. When He made His triumphal entry into Jerusalem, He rode a donkey when He could have flown. Why should not God use means, when He chooses, to answer prayer for healing of the sick?

God can save a sinner without the use of any human aid, but certainly He does not usually do so. If God can use a man with his consecrated wisdom and love and skill in winning a soul, why should He not use a doctor, a pharmacist or a nurse with his consecrated skill in healing the sick?

Luke is called "the beloved physician" (Col. 4:14), and the Bible never condemns the prayerful use of doctors and medicines. But men should not trust doctors instead of God.

Sometimes I have felt clearly led to pray and trust God for healing, without doctors and without medicine, and He has answered graciously and wonderfully. I have known a number cases in which doctors failed and God seemed to be glorified in doing His wonderful work without them. One such case was called to mind yesterday as I read what I had written for *The Sword of the Lord* dated April 19, 1935. It blessed my heart so, I reproduce it here.

"GOD HEALS SICK IN ANSWER TO PRAYER

"Brother J. A. Middleton Is Wonderfully Healed

"Near the first of March, Brother J. A. Middleton, an earnest Christian man and treasurer of the Fundamentalist Baptist Tabernacle in Dallas, was taken seriously and dangerously ill. He was unable to work and was confined to his bed with such agonizing pain that the doctors felt compelled to give him unusually large opiates. Much of the time he was delirious, and for long periods he had no recollection of what transpired about him. The pain was so bad that doctors said that something must be done at once. After all medicines had failed he was taken to St. Paul Hospital in Dallas. His physician frankly said, 'I do not know what is the trouble.' Four other good doctors were called in. Their answer was the same. They did not know where the seat of the trouble was that was causing such violent illness and pain, but all agreed that something must be done at once. They decided that the tonsils should be removed. If that did not settle the difficulty, the optic nerve must be clipped. If that did not stop the pain, they would do something else.

"The tonsils were removed. Still the illness was not cured. Recovering from the tonsil operation, Brother Middleton was brought home, yet taking regular injections in the arm, still under the care of the physician.

"On Sunday night, March 24th, I was called to Brother Middleton's home to pray for him. He was in such pain that he buried his face in the pillow and rolled from side to side, trying to keep control of himself. I had been praying for him for weeks, while I was in the Oklahoma City revival and after I returned. Many members of the church had been praying. But now the doctors had failed, five of them, the best they had known to consult. Brother Middleton had spent two weeks in the hospital.

"Anointing With Oil, Following the Bible Command

"It seemed time to get the matter settled with God. So there in Brother Middleton's home we agreed that we could do exactly what the Bible said, 'pray over him, anointing him with oil in the name of the Lord,' according to James 5:14. Mrs. Middleton, Mrs. Rice and I got down on our knees and confessed our sins to each other and to God. We wanted to fulfill every detail of what God commanded. Remember that James 5:14–16 says:

" 'Is any sick among you? let him call for the elders of the church; and let them pray over him, anointing him with oil in the name of the Lord: And the prayer of faith shall save the sick, and the Lord shall raise him up; and if he have committed sins, they shall be forgiven him. Confess your faults one to another, and pray one for another, that ye may be healed. The effectual fervent prayer of a righteous man availeth much.'

"After confessing our sins and quoting God's promise, I put my hands upon Brother Middleton's head and prayed that if it would please and honor Him, He would heal Brother Middleton either without any known medicine, without doctors, or with doctors and medicines, just as He chose, but so that everybody would know that God did it, not the doctors. Then Mrs. Middleton prayed, then Mrs. Rice, then Brother Middleton. We promised God that if He would heal we would give Him the glory and that we would tell about the anointing with oil as well as the prayer of faith which actually gets the healing. While we were on our knees, God gave us some faith that He had heard our prayers.

"Mrs. Middleton, after our prayers, said, 'I don't want Mr. Middleton to go back to the doctor tomorrow. If he is willing, we will just trust the Lord and Him alone.' Brother Middleton answered, 'That is just what we will do.' After a time of quiet conversation, Mrs. Rice and I went to our home late that Sunday night.

"God Heals

"Before we left that night Brother Middleton's pain was a great deal lighter. By the next morning he was better. The next day he did not go back to the doctor. Wednesday came, and again he did not keep his appointment with the doctor. The doctor phoned to know why, urging him to come back the next Saturday. Saturday Brother Middleton went to see the doctor but refused to have an injection in his arm and had the doctor to dismiss his case, so he would be free to go back to work. Brother Middleton had lost twenty-five pounds, but he rapidly regained his strength. The following Friday he went back to work, and today (Friday, April 12th) he has worked one week. After losing exactly thirty days' work, after a $115 doctor bill, after a $150 hospital and nurse's bill, after losing his tonsils and after almost unbearable pain, God healed Brother Middleton in answer to prayer and following the anointing with oil. I say, praise the Lord for answered prayer and for proof that God is just the same and that the Bible is still up-to-date! We promised God to give our testimony, and we are doing it here and now that everybody may be encouraged to call on God in time of sickness or any other time of need. Besides that, I want people to be encouraged to take the Bible literally and follow it literally.

"King Asa 'Sought Not to the LORD, but to the Physicians'

"Gathered around that bed of pain Sunday night, March 24th, we read II Chronicles 16:12, 13, which says:

"'And Asa in the thirty and ninth year of his reign was diseased in his feet, until his disease was exceeding great: yet in his disease he sought not to the LORD, but to the physicians. And Asa slept with his fathers, and died in the one and fortieth year of his reign.'

"We had prayed but depended on the doctors. We decided not to be like Asa but to depend on the Lord. So we followed the explicit Bible command and prayed for Brother Middleton, anointing him with oil in the name of the Lord."

In the above case God plainly showed that He could heal without doctors, and in that case we all felt that He chose to do it. But in the case of my tonsillitis, it was a Christian doctor to whom I was directed, after prayer, who after examination prescribed a diet and, temporarily, certain medicine which led to a permanent cure, so that the operation I had long dreaded was wholly unnecessary. What God wants, I am sure, is for Christians to pray and follow His clear leading; then trust in Him to heal, using human means, and to bless our best wisdom; or if He so leads, trust Him to heal without medicine and doctors. In any case, whether with medicine or without, it is God who does the healing. He should have the glory; our trust should be in Him, not in men.

Elijah was well fed when God miraculously sent food by ravens and he drank at the brook Cherith. But the food, brought by unusual miraculous means, and the water from the brook, a most ordinary, unmiraculous source, were both from God. It would be stubborn willfulness for a Christian to say he would never trust God to heal without medicine. But it would be just as stubborn and just as unreasonable for a Christian to say he would never take medicine. When Christians pray, they are not *telling* God; they are *asking* Him. Every prayer, to please God, must be offered with a surrendered heart, willing for God to answer in His own way, for His own glory.

IV. Sin Hinders Healing: Should Be Confessed and Forsaken

When there was no sin, there was no sickness. All disease and suffering came to mankind as the fruit of sin. People suffer, sometimes, when it is not their own sin that causes the suffering. Job is a classic example. People suffer also for Christ's sake, sometimes. But if there had been no sin, there had been no suffering; and often, at least, suffering can be traced directly to the sins of the one who suffers. So one who asks God for healing should carefully consider whether there are sins between him and God. Sin must be considered in the healing question. James 5:15 says,

"And the prayer of faith shall save the sick, and the Lord shall raise him up; and if he have committed sins, they shall be forgiven him."

It is thus inferred that sin may have caused the sickness. And the next verse, James 5:16, says,

"Confess your faults one to another, and pray one for another, that ye may be healed."

The word *faults* here could be translated *sins*. So those who pray for healing should confess their sins. Certainly they should confess their sins to God, but here we are told to confess our sins to one another when we pray one for another, that we may be healed.

God does send sickness because of sin, as is shown throughout the Bible. Miriam (Num. 12:10), Uzziah (II Chron. 26:19), and Gehazi (II Kings 5:27) were all struck with leprosy because of their sins. King Jeroboam had his hand withered because he attempted to seize the prophet of God (I Kings 13:4). In the New Testament, King Herod was smitten of God, and worms ate him because he took honor as a god (Acts 12:23). Ananias and Sapphira were struck dead at Peter's words (Acts 5:5–10).

Elymas the sorcerer was made blind for his sin in resisting the Gospel before the deputy, when Paul preached (Acts 13:11).

When Jesus healed the impotent man at the pool of Bethesda, He told him, "Behold, thou art made whole: sin no more, lest a worse thing come upon thee" (John 5:14). When He healed the palsied man, borne of four and let down through the roof, He said, first, "Son, thy sins be forgiven thee." Then later, He said, "But that ye may know that the Son of man hath power on earth to forgive sins, (he saith to the sick of the palsy,) I say unto thee, Arise, and take up thy bed, and go thy way into thine house" (Mark 2:5,10,11). And then the man was healed at once. But his sins were first forgiven. That should teach us that forgiveness is far more important than healing of the body. But surely it also shows that often sins need to be forgiven before God can honorably heal the body.

We are told that in Corinth many Christians ate the Lord's Supper unworthily. They had divisions, some came drunk to the Lord's table, and some were guilty of even grosser sins. For this reason there was sickness among them, and some Christians died prematurely because of their sins. The Holy Spirit had Paul write them,

"For this cause many are weak and sickly among you, and many sleep. For if we would judge ourselves, we should not be judged. But when we are judged, we are chastened of the Lord, that we should not be condemned with the world."—I Cor. 11:30–32.

So sickness, for a child of God, is often the chastening of the Lord. Every Christian who is sick or weakly, therefore, should judge himself, carefully confessing every known sin and forsaking his own way in any matter that may be contrary to God's way.

Mrs. Jonathan Goforth, famous missionary to China, tells in her book, *How I Know God Answers Prayer*, of remarkable answers to prayer, among them the wonderful healing of a Chinese woman's little daughter with an enlarged spleen. But she also tells how at about the same time her own little girl was sick of the same disease, and despite all her prayers the child died. She said she could not explain the failure to get the answer to her prayer except that at that time she held a grudge against a fellow missionary, and she indicates that that sin may have withheld the answer her heart craved.

Dr. Charles A. Blanchard, in the splendid book on prayer *Getting Things from God*, tells of a sickness of his wife that continued despite many prayers. Finally it was decided to have an operation as a last resort. Then Dr. Blanchard was reminded of a certain coldness or neglect in his own heart which the Holy Spirit showed him was a sin. Earnestly he confessed his fault to God, and at once there came a change for the better, and his wife was soon well, without an operation.

Beloved Christian, if you want God to heal your body, first earnestly search whether there be sin in your life, unconfessed and unlamented and unforsaken. "Confess your faults one to another, and pray one for another, that ye may be healed."

V. A Personal Testimony of Healing in Answer to Prayer

Jesus said, "Ye shall be witnesses unto me" (Acts 1:8). There is a place for expounding the Word of God, but there is also a place for personal testimony. In Dr. A. J. Gordon's great book, *The Ministry of Healing*, are given many, many authenticated cases of marvelous answers to prayer for healing of the sick. Dr. John Roach Straton, late pastor of the Calvary Baptist Church, New York City, gives some heartening and stirring examples of healing in answer to prayer, true stories, including his own, in his book of sermons, *Divine Healing in Scripture and Life*. Some of the most remarkable, miraculous healings are related by Dr. R. A. Torrey in his little book *Divine Healing*. Other marvelous healings are related in books and *China's Millions*, published by the China Inland Mission. Even though we cannot agree with all the doctrinal teachings of men like Dr. Straton and Dr. A. B. Simpson and with some evangelists now living who make much of public healing services, yet those familiar with them who love God and believe in answered prayer will rejoice at their personal testimony of how God healed them in answer to prayer. Not all professed healings really happened. The facts have been greatly exaggerated about many cases, and there have been many hurtful things about the modern movement which has big public healing services. Ofttimes it has seemed a racket to make money and exalt man, and has left many Christians in despair, since they have been taught that it is their own fault they are not healed. Yet despite the failures of men, both in doctrine and life, there are many well-known and blessed cases of healings, even miraculous healings, in answer to prayer, and in them every child of God can rejoice and can take courage. The evidence is overwhelming that many have been miraculously healed. God is the same. Jesus Christ is the same. The testimony of millions is that God has, in loving compassion, answered their prayers for the healing of the sick.

So I can say, I too have seen the answer to my prayers for the healing of the sick. It is both a duty and a joy to tell it.

When I was a boy of about fourteen, my father was seriously sick. We lived in Dundee, a little cow town in west Texas. Long strain had so seriously affected my father's health that a specialist in Fort Worth had told him he must be away from business and go to the mountains for months or he would die. When he went on with his work, the inevitable breakdown came, and he hung between life and death. The family physician called in the other local doctor; finally both said the case was without hope. One night they announced to my stepmother that my father would not live till morning; that there was no hope. I knew little about the Bible, although I had been saved. But I knew that God answered prayer. I think I may never have read James 5:12–16. Certainly I had never heard a sermon nor read an article about divine healing. Yet my father was a devout, believing Christian, and I knew that he had often told of remarkable answers to prayer. As instinctively as a child asks his father or mother for food, I felt I must pray. I went out to the barn, and as I passed the buggy shed I heard a voice; I listened and heard my sister, two years older than I, weeping and begging God to spare our father. I went on to the barn, kneeled down in a horse stall and prayed. I came back into the house, and in the "front room" I heard someone praying; it was my stepmother. I went to bed and to sleep with a calm assurance that the doctors were mistaken and that my father would live.

The next morning my father opened his eyes and looked around him strangely. He had for days, as I recall, been either half conscious or delirious. Now he sat up in bed and said, "Where are my pants?"

My stepmother, half laughing, half crying, said, "What do you want with your pants? You are sick; you must stay in bed."

"I am going to town," he said. "I am all right." And he would not be denied. He got up, dressed, and went to town, while my stepmother frantically called the doctors. After he returned to the house, the doctors saw him and marveled, said it was simply unreasonable, and went away dumbfounded!

Later my father went again to the specialist in Fort Worth, told him about the whole case. "Who was your doctor?" said the specialist. "Why, a country doctor, Dr. Robinson," my father answered. The specialist then said my father was the luckiest man alive to have happened on such a physician, that not one doctor in a thousand could have done what that country doctor did; that if he ever had similiar trouble he must go to that doctor, wherever he might be! But I know it was not that country doctor, but the Great Physician Himself, who healed my father in answer to prayer.

It now seems to me most remarkable; then it seemed to me the most natural thing in the world that God should answer such prayers. In those days, with the people I knew, evolution was a joke, a man who doubted the Bible was a fool, God was real. I do not remember that I told anybody about our prayers; I think God let me hear my sister's and stepmother's prayers because He planned for me to tell it. How warm it makes my heart now to remember it! My father lived nearly twenty years longer to the glory of God.

In 1927 I had a daily broadcast on radio KFQB, Fort Worth. I began to preach on prayer, partly because it came naturally in a series of messages on the Gospel of Luke; partly, I think, because I had gotten such a blessing from the little Moody Colportage book *How to Pray* by Dr. R. A. Torrey. A woman in Oklahoma wrote me that her married daughter had been bitten by a spider and was desperately sick. Her life was despaired of. She had heard my radio messages and felt led to ask me to pray for her daughter. I did pray. In a few days, two or three, I think, a letter came saying that the afternoon I prayed the sick woman suddenly felt well, got out of bed, and took up her housework. The decayed flesh had dropped out, from the poison, leaving a hole; but now, at once it began to heal. My heart was greatly blessed by this incident and several others where God gave me faith to ask for sick people to be healed and then wonderfully answered prayer.

After that my own older daughter, then five years old, had a sore throat. We carefully attended her at home, but when after a few days her throat seemed worse and fever ran to 105, we took her to our family doctor. He examined her throat, checked her temperature and pulse, and gravely shook his head. "John," he said, "I am afraid it is diphtheria. Wait here till I see." He took a culture from her throat, smeared it on a glass slide, sent it to the laboratory in the same building. Soon the report came back that diphtheria germs were clearly present. It was an advanced case. The doctor gave the little girl diphtheria antitoxin and had our home reported to the health department and quarantined.

When we returned home and put the child to bed, I said to my wife: "I have been praying for other people and telling them that God answers prayer, and now I am going to pray for my own. I want to kneel by this bed and stay here until I have assurance from God that Grace will get well and that He has taken complete charge of the case." She said she would do the same. We knelt in prayer, reminding God of how we had given the child to Him when she was born, reminding Him of His promises, and telling Him that if He would heal her we would praise Him, would give Him, instead of the doctor, the glory, and would earnestly try to raise the child for Him. Soon I felt assured that God had heard and the answer was ours. My wife felt the same, so we rose from our knees, after thanking Him.

That afternoon the fever went down; that night or the next day it was gone entirely. Grace wanted to get up, but we would not let her. Then she asked to play with her dolls in bed, and they were given her. Now and then she would ask me, "Daddy, am I still sick?" I would have to say that I did not know—that I knew she would soon be well and everything was all right, but I felt she should stay in bed till a doctor or nurse examined her. We sent for the health nurse to examine her to see whether we should be kept under quarantine. The nurse came, was puzzled, said the child seemed perfectly normal, but since it was a proven case of diphtheria, we should keep her in bed and the house would be under quarantine until the doctor examined her. The doctor came in a day or so, said the danger was passed, the child seemed perfectly well. He had the quarantine lifted. I know that God healed my child in answer to our prayers. God may have used the doctor and medicine—I think He did—but it is certain that He could do it either with or without the doctor. I have never felt it dishonored God to use any means we could use in faith, if the dependence were on God. But God did the healing.

In 1931 I was in a tabernacle revival campaign in north Fort Worth, Texas. One night a young woman asked me to pray for an unsaved young woman friend who was near death in St. Joseph's Hospital. She had quarrelled with her husband that day and had taken four bichloride of mercury tablets in a glass of water, and now was expected to die. It had happened that day; she had been rushed to the hospital. We prayed that night; the next morning I was in that Catholic hospital to see her. (In Catholic hospitals it is often much easier than it is in other hospitals to deal with the sick concerning their need for Christ.) First I showed her that she needed a Saviour and told her I would be willing to pray for her body if first she would trust Christ as her own Saviour. Soon she claimed Him, though desperately sick. Then I read to her God's Word about praying for the sick. When she confessed her sin and promised to do right about her home if God would heal her, we prayed, and I left. Outside the room I asked the nurse about her chances, and she said the doctor said there was no chance at all. I reminded her that God could do more than men dreamed, and she replied. "But you do not understand; even if the poison did not kill her, the lining of the stomach is destroyed, and she could never digest food; she cannot get well."

I went away remembering the red rash over the sick woman's face, her heavy breathing, her humble turning to God; and I continued to pray. The next morning I saw her again, and the nurse said the doctors had decided there was one chance in a thousand. Loved ones had come from Oklahoma to see her before she died. The next time I called, the doctors thought there might be one chance in ten. A day or two later they said there was an even chance that she would live. I went out of town for revival services and when I returned, found that she was well, had gone home with her father and mother who had come to see her die! I understand that her home was reestablished happily. God does answer prayer!

Again about 1931 in Fort Worth, Texas, a Mrs. Kelly called me by telephone, asked me if I would go to see a woman, Mrs. Jewel Duncan, and pray for her, anointing her with oil in the name of the Lord. I have her signed statement somewhere. I said that if it were the woman's own request and if she were a Christian, I would. I was reluctant about it because I knew the fanaticism that sometimes accompanies praying for the sick. I do not recall that I had ever anointed anyone with oil before, but there it was in the Bible, and I could not explain it away as many do in unbelief. So I agreed.

When I arrived at the home, a sign on the door said, "Do not knock." The nurse was gone, so I stepped inside. In the bedroom lay Mrs. Duncan. I already knew that she was dying with tuberculosis. She had spent two years in the state sanatorium for T.B. patients, and then was sent home to die. Already arrangements had been made to give away the two little boys. Humanly speaking, there was no hope. She had resisted until the last the idea of having a preacher pray for her, because she said that was not the way Baptists believed. But the fact that I was a Baptist preacher and that doctors gave no hope at all led her earnestly to seek the Lord and ask for me, whom she had heard, I think, on the radio, to come to her home to pray for her.

She could barely whisper. I talked quietly about God's power, His willingness to answer prayer whenever it would honor His name, His blessed promises. Then I asked her several questions: 1. Did she know she was saved? 2. Was she willing to confess to God any sins He would bring to mind? 3. If God would heal her, would she give her life to Him in consecration and tell openly what He had done in healing her? To all these she answered in the affirmative. By this time the nurse had come in, and she got for me a bottle of olive oil. I put oil upon the sick woman's forehead in the name of the Lord, reminded her that it represented the Holy Spirit who lived in her body and who must heal her if she were to be healed. Then I quietly prayed, sitting by the bed. I felt peace in my heart and went away.

I was called out of town for two revival campaigns. A few months later I spoke in Fort Worth, and after the service among those who came to greet me was Mrs. Kelly. She brought forward a fine-looking woman and said,

"You know this lady, don't you?" I did not and said so. Then Mrs. Kelly told me it was Mrs. Duncan, for whom I had prayed about six months before. She was the picture of health. She told me she had felt immediately strengthened after I prayed for her, anointing her with oil in the name of the Lord. Within two weeks after that she was up and going about. Now she had been doing all her own housework, her children had been brought back home, she never had another indication of the tuberculosis which after a fight of years' duration had brought her to the door of death. She wept for joy as she told me how strong and well she was. Four years later I preached in Commerce, Texas; this woman was in the audience and came weeping as soon as I entered the building, to tell me God had wonderfully kept her well. Later she wrote me a lovely letter of testimony, which I still have. God simply kept His word that "the prayer of faith shall save the sick, and the Lord shall raise him up."

I do not feel that there was any merit in what I did, except that it was simple obedience, and I believe that thousands of others can have as remarkable answers to prayer as that if they only obey God's simple command and pray for the sick, believing the Bible and giving God a chance. And ministers and elders of churches should be willing to anoint the sick with oil, when it is requested in the Bible manner and when they can do it in the name of the Lord. Surprising and blessed results follow God's way, many times.

CHAPTER IX

PRAY FOR ANYTHING AND
EVERYTHING YOU WANT

"What things soever ye desire, when ye pray."—Mark 11:24.

"Ye shall ask what ye will, and it shall be done unto you."—John 15:7.

"He shall give thee the desires of thine heart."—Ps. 37:4.

"If ye shall ask any thing...I will do it."—John 14:14.

"In every thing by prayer...let your requests be made known unto God."—Phil. 4:6.

One afternoon in the midst of a revival campaign, I spoke at Sherman, Texas, under the shade of the trees on the courthouse lawn. I suppose seventy-five or a hundred people had gathered that weekday afternoon to hear the message on prayer. My text was, "Ask, and it shall be given you; seek, and ye shall find; knock, and it shall be opened unto you: For every one that asketh receiveth; and he that seeketh findeth; and to him that knocketh it shall be opened," found in Matthew 7:7,8. After I had earnestly tried to show that God is eager to give in answer to our prayers and stressed the plain words of our Saviour that "every one that asketh receiveth," a Baptist deacon rose in the audience and said, "Brother Rice, I believe in prayer; and I know God answers prayer, but I do not believe God wants us to pray about literally everything. Why, you talk as if you could even pray and get a- a- [he was searching for a preposterous thing], as if you could even get a *barrel of pickles!*"

The people laughed, but I told him plainly, "Yes, anybody who needs a barrel of pickles should pray for them, and I thank God that God has given me things a whole lot greater and seemingly more unlikely than a barrel of pickles."

What shall we ask for when we pray? That is answered many times in the Bible. We are to ask for everything we want! Anything that you have a right to want, you have a right to ask for. Every Christian should take every desire to God in prayer. It is a sin to want anything that you cannot honestly pray for, and you should ask God to remove the desire, if it is wrong. And if the desire itself is not wrong, then you ought to ask God to fulfill it!

Elsewhere we will discuss the conditions to be met when we pray, but we are inquiring now, "What shall I ask for when I pray?" And the Lord answers back in His Word many times that we are to ask for whatsoever we desire. We are to let our requests in everything be made known to God. We are to carry everything to God in prayer.

It is strange and sad how stilted and artificial has become the modern conception of prayer. Many people think that one cannot pray acceptably without many "Thou's" and "Thee's," without a certain formal theological discussion at the beginning of the prayer, thanking God for Christ, and at the end of the prayer, adding the stereotyped formula, "This we ask in Jesus' name."

And as people have set and limited opinions about the proper *manner* of prayer, so they have most limited views of the proper subjects for prayer. Some teach that Jews in the Old Testament properly asked for earthly blessings, but that Christians in the New Testament can properly ask only for spiritual blessings! Some think it is wrong to ask for rain, for jobs, for money or for particular, definite daily bread, despite the Saviour's model prayer.

Likewise, other people think that on very great matters it is proper to pray, but on small matters it would not be right to take God's time nor ask His help.

But Christians need to break away from these traditional limitations on prayer and learn from the Bible that a Christian has a right to pray about anything and everything.

I. Christians Invited to Ask for Literally Anything They Want

In the Scriptures quoted at the beginning of this chapter, I have, for the moment, deliberately omitted the conditions God has placed upon Christians' asking for anything they want.

Jesus surely meant to invite us to ask for anything we want when He said in Mark 11:23,24,

"For verily I say unto you, That whosoever shall say unto this mountain, Be thou removed, and be thou cast into the sea; and shall not doubt in his heart, but shall believe that those things which he saith shall come to pass; he shall have whatsoever he saith. Therefore I say unto you, WHAT THINGS SOEVER YE DESIRE, when ye pray, believe that ye receive them, and ye shall have them."

He asked us to pray for "what things soever ye desire." Anything in the world you want, even to the casting of a mountain into the sea, is included in the boundaries of legitimate, normal prayer for a Christian! The condition of faith is given, to be sure. We are not here discussing the condition but calling your attention to the wonderful, unlimited invitation to pray for the things your heart desires, whatever they may be.

In John 15:7 the same thing is taught. Jesus said,

"If ye abide in me, and my words abide in you, ye shall ASK WHAT YE WILL, and it shall be done unto you."

Here "what ye will" is the proper subject for prayer. Anything in the world your heart wants, you should pray for.

And is that not the meaning too of Psalm 37:4? There we are told, *"Delight thyself also in the LORD; and he shall give thee THE DESIRES OF THINE HEART."*

A Christian's prayer should coincide with the desire of his heart. Whatever his heart desires, that a Christian should ask for.

Literally, "any thing" may be requested by one of God's children in prayer, according to the sweet invitation of the Saviour Himself. In John 14:13,14 Jesus said,

"And WHATSOEVER ye shall ask in my name, that will I do, that the Father may be glorified in the Son. If ye shall ASK ANY THING in my name, I will do it."

"Whatsoever" means anything in the world. And then Jesus, knowing the unbelief of our hearts, simply said, "If ye shall ask any thing in my name, I will do it." Christians ought to ask for anything, literally anything, they want from God!

II. It Is Not Wrong to Ask It If It Is Not Wrong to Want It

Every Christian ought to get his heart's desires and his prayers in accord. Anything you have a right to want, you have a right to pray for. If you do not have a right to pray for it, then it is wrong to want it. About any particular matter, the Christian ought to ask for what he wants or quit wanting it.

Just imagine that the Lord Jesus should knock at the door of your home and say, "I have come to supply your needs, to supply every legitimate want, to make you fully happy. Take Me into your home and tell Me every lack, every need, every desire." If there were things in the home that were disgraceful: vile music, licentious literature, worldly habits that defile the Christian's body, bad companions—no doubt you would be ashamed and would start housecleaning. If you were conscious of the Saviour's literal presence, no doubt it would make a difference in what you wanted. But also, thank God, you would feel more free to ask Him for what you needed in the home. Since He came to your home for that very purpose, you might say, "Lord Jesus, You see there is not enough food in the home to satisfy the hunger of the children. You have it all, dear Jesus; give us the food we need." You might say, "Dear Lord, You see the good wife is so frail and does not have the strength she so badly needs to care for the home and teach the children and to prepare their food. Lord, give her more strength." Or you might say, "Dear Lord, we do not love each other as we ought here; we are quarrelsome and critical. We do not mean to be. We are so sorry. Won't You please help us to be patient and loving as Christians ought." I say, if Jesus really came to live in your home or to visit it just to satisfy your heart's desires and to tell you He was eager to give you what you wanted, I think you would surely make your requests known and tell Him *anything* you needed or wanted. Well, that is exactly what He says for you to do. If you want it, pray for it! If it is not right to pray for it, then it is not right to want it. In that case you should pray about it and ask God to fix your "wanter" so you could want things according to His will, want things that a Christian would have a right to want and have a right to pray for. It is shameful and wicked to set our hearts on anything that we cannot honestly talk to God about. But anything we have a right to want, anything we have a right to work for, anything we have a right to try to buy or plan about, that we have a right to pray for too! Ask for anything you want!

III. Philippians 4:6 Says Pray About "Every Thing"

Really your heavenly Father wants to be taken into all the secrets and longings and desires of your heart. He wants no desire hidden from Him, but every desire turned into a prayer. In Philippians 4:6,7 the Lord says to us,

"Be careful for nothing; but in every thing by prayer and supplication with thanksgiving let your requests be made known unto God. And the peace of God, which passeth all understanding, shall keep your hearts and minds through Christ Jesus."

"In *every thing*...let your requests be made known unto God."

Here is the cure for worry. Anxious care; fretting; the lined, harassed faces and the troubled hearts that come from frustrated desires and troubled uncertainty about the future, can all be done away with if you will come to God and ask Him frankly and boldly for everything you want and stay there until He answers!

Worry is a horrible sin. Worry is the opposite of faith and trust. John Wesley said, "I would no more fret than to curse and swear." And God's cure for worry is to pray about *everything*.

I remember a dear Christian woman, devout and very useful, who came to me in Wheaton, Illinois, after hearing me preach on prayer, and said, "And to think that all these years I have put up with that faded, worn old rug in my living room! I've been burdened about it, I have been ashamed of it, I have planned and planned, but I was never able to buy another. I felt that it was all right to pray about lost souls but that it would be wrong to ask God for a rug. Thank God, I have found that He is willing to answer prayer about little things and He wants us to talk to Him about everything. I'm going home right now and ask God to give me a new rug!"

What a Friend we have in Jesus,
All our sins and griefs to bear!

What a privilege to carry
***Everything* to God in prayer!**

O what peace we often forfeit,
O what needless pain we bear,
All because we do not carry
***Everything* to God in prayer!**

IV. Open the Door of Every Closet in Your Heart to God!

Mother is at home, but oh, how she longs to hear from the daughter who is in the city. She wants to know about every new dress, every new friend, every night's entertainment, every raise in wages. Mother wants to hear every secret, wants to see every snapshot, delights in every confidence. And so it is with Father too, though he may not say so much about it. It is one of the saddest things in the world when parents feel their children slipping away from them. When children no longer take parents into their confidence, the parents grieve.

And so it is with God about His own children. How dear we are to Him! I have never understood why. I think when I get to Heaven I will ask God to tell me why He wanted us, why He sought us, why He could not do without us! I have wondered why God wanted to come in the Garden of Eden and walk with Adam, even when he was perfect and sinless. And much more I have wondered why God runs after us poor, fallen creatures. But He does! And He wants us to take everything in the world to Him, share every burden with Him, every joy, tell Him every heart-cry, express to Him every longing!

And since I learned this blessed secret, it has done wonders for my own inner life. I have found that I ought, and that I may, freely take every desire of my heart to God. He wants me to pray about literally everything. And that means that I open every closet door. He knows it anyway, so why should I try to hide it? And if God loves me more than a father loves his child, why should I not tell Him about anything I want, anything I need? And even if I have a want, a desire that is not according to His will, should I not tell Him about it? Should I not ask Him to reconcile my desires with His will? I have resolved before God that I will never want things that I cannot talk to God about. And when I take the things to Him, He cures the desires that are evil by helping me to confess them, and He also gives me a blessed confidence that I have a right to ask my heavenly Father for anything in the world that I want.

O Christian, do not shut God out of a single corner of your heart! Tell Him everything! Ask Him for literally everything your heart desires! The presumption is that God wants you to have everything you want. Unless it would do you harm or dishonor Him, He would certainly want you to have your heart's desire. So pray for everything you want, meet God's conditions and get it. Or if you take a matter to God and He shows you He does not want to give it to you, then ask Him to take that hurtful desire, of which He does not approve, out of your heart. Ask Him for anything you want, or stop wanting it!

CHAPTER X

PRAYING IN THE WILL OF GOD

"Nevertheless not as I will, but as thou wilt."—Matt. 26:39.

"O my Father, if this cup may not pass away from me, except I drink it, thy will be done."—Matt. 26:42.

"And this is the confidence that we have in him, that, if we ask any thing according to his will, he heareth us: And if we know that he hear us, whatsoever we ask, we know that we have the petitions that we desired of him."—I John 5:14,15.

"And whatsoever ye shall ask in my name, that will I do, that the Father may be glorified in the Son. If ye shall ask any thing in my name, I will do it."—John 14:13,14.

Successful prayer is for those who love the Lord and are surrendered to His will. An unsaved man may pray, like the publican in the temple who prayed, "God be merciful to me a sinner," or like the dying thief who prayed, "Lord, remember me." And those men were heard and saved, as millions of other sinners like them have been heard and saved when they prayed. Sinners may pray and should pray; but if they expect to be heard, they must be willing to surrender to the will of God, willing to love and serve Him. It is true, God's mercy is so great that He sometimes answers the vilest sinners, but throughout the Bible it is made clear God delights to answer prayer, but that He cannot do it regularly for those who hate Him, those who do not want His will.

So, if you want your prayers answered, seek to pray *in the will of God*, not contrary to His will. Seek to pray for things that can please Him, honor Him, and not for the things that grieve Him or hinder His blessed business or encourage sin.

God loves you, loves you so much that His love could only be measured by the gift of His own dear Son, the awful price of Calvary. He is so anxious for your happiness and welfare that if you find the prayer He would have you pray, the one He is most willing to answer, it will include a larger number of the best things, the happiest things, than any prayer you could even think of without His help. "He that spared not his own Son, but delivered him up for us all, how shall he not with him also freely give us all things?" (Rom. 8:32). To pray in the will of God does not mean asking less, but more. And praying for just what God wants you to have will result in far more happiness than if you could have everything you wished with some of it outside the will of God. In this matter, loving surrender is not only right; it is wise. What God wants to give you is just exactly what you would want if you knew enough to want it, if you knew as God does, just how happy it would make you and how long the blessing of it would last. Thus, knowingly to pray contrary to the will of God is folly, and for God to answer such prayers would wrong you as much as it would wrong Himself.

The Lord Jesus in His earthly ministry and life could say truly, "I knew that thou hearest me always" (John 11:42). The Father heard and answered every prayer that Jesus ever prayed, except, I think, the prayer on the cross, when He did not pray in His own right but prayed as a lost sinner would have prayed, when He was in the place of dying, condemned sinners, an alien from God. Then Jesus prayed not "My Father," but, "My God, my God," and God forsook Him, as He was in the place of all the sinners in the world, that He might receive us, clothed in Christ's righteousness, and in His stead. So Psalm 22:2 says of Jesus on the cross, "O my God, I cry in the daytime, but thou hearest not." But with that exception, God heard and answered every prayer that Jesus ever prayed. Always, except then, Jesus came as one perfectly in the will of the Father and was never denied. Would you like always to be heard when you pray? Would you like to be able to get things from God as easily as His own Son, the dear Lord Jesus, got whatever He prayed for? Then "let this mind be in you, which was also in Christ Jesus."

I. Jesus in Gethsemane Our Example

This most striking example of the Saviour's surrender to the will of the Father is when He was bowed down in the Garden of Gethsemane under the weight of the sins of the world, when His soul was "exceeding sorrowful, even unto death," He said (Matt. 26:38), and when "his sweat was as it were great drops of blood falling down to the ground" (Luke 22:44). There Jesus prayed, saying,

"O my Father, if it be possible, let this cup pass from me: nevertheless, not as I will, but as thou wilt."—Matt. 26:39.

Then again He prayed, saying,

"O my Father, if this cup may not pass away from me, except I drink it, thy will done."—Matt. 26:42.

Then a third time, we are told, He prayed, "saying the same words." Facing the most awful suffering, Jesus, without hesitation, said to His Father and our Father, "Not as I will, but as thou wilt."

But this scriptural incident has been greatly misunderstood, I am convinced. Many have taught that here the Lord Jesus was begging the Father that He might not have to go to the cross and only reluctantly submitted to the thing He did not want to do and tried to avoid. Some commentators have supposed that Jesus thought there might be some other way to save sinners besides the cross. But all this seems foolish in the light of other Scriptures. First, Hebrews 5:7 refers to these very prayers, tells us what Jesus prayed for, and that the prayer was answered. "Who in the days of his flesh, when he had offered up prayers and supplications with strong crying and tears unto him that was able to save him from death, and was heard in that he feared." So in the garden, Jesus prayed to be saved from death that night when He was near death, and He was heard and saved from death. Satan would have forced the bitter cup to His lips that night, killing Him so that the Scriptures would not be fulfilled, so Christ should not die on the Passover Day, so He should not hang on a tree, so He should not die between two thieves, so He should not die "according to the scriptures" (I Cor. 15:3,4). If Satan had succeeded, God's will would have been thwarted, the Scripture would not have been fulfilled, and the death of Christ would not have saved anybody. But Christ prayed, in effect, 'Father, You know I am willing to die. I came into the world to die and have never shrunk from it. I would even be willing to die tonight, though I know You would have to raise Me up to die again tomorrow in the appointed way, at the appointed place, on the foretold date. I ask You to defeat Satan; let this cup pass from Me tonight. My blood is breaking from My veins; I am sorrowful even unto death; I will die here if You do not help. So if it be possible, let this cup pass from Me tonight. But You know I seek not My own will. Not as I will, but as Thou wilt.' And Jesus "prayed through" and was heard, and the cup did pass from Him till the morrow, and the Father who was able to save Him from death did save Him. Christ's prayer was answered. Let no one think that Christ was simply resigned to the cross. Rather, He hastened toward it! He said, "I have a baptism to be baptized with; and how am I straitened till it be accomplished!" (Luke 12:50). He also said, "Therefore doth my Father love me, because I lay down my life, that I might take it again. No man taketh it from me, but I lay it down of myself. I have power to lay it down, and I have power to take it again. This commandment have I received of my Father" (John 10:17,18). Long before Jesus came to this world and every day of His life here, He was perfectly surrendered to go to the cross.

What I am saying is that Jesus did not fearfully, reluctantly resign Himself to the will of the Father, asking one thing but consenting to another. No, JESUS PRAYED IN THE WILL OF GOD, NOT AGAINST IT, and got what He prayed for. And the example He gave is not that we are to ask for our own way, being willing to give it up. Rather, it is that we may know God's will and ask for that all along, as Jesus did.

No doubt we will not always know as perfectly as Jesus knew the will of God. Perhaps it was largely for our example that He prayed so repeatedly, "Thy will be done," and, "Not as I will, but as thou wilt," since the incident is clearly recorded by Matthew, Mark and Luke, as if the Holy

Spirit wished to emphasize it. Every Christian should have this explicit understanding with God about every prayer, "Not as I will, but as Thou wilt." Oh, may we learn to pray with hearts surrendered to the will of God!

II. Assurance in Prayer

When we know we pray in the will of God, how confident we may be of getting our prayers answered! In I John 5:14, 15 is this sweet assurance:

"And this is the confidence that we have in him, that, if we ask any thing according to his will, he heareth us: And if we know that he hear us, whatsoever we ask, we know that we have the petitions that we desired of him."

How sweet to pray, knowing that God gladly listens, since we are asking things according to His will. And thus praying, often we can literally *know* without any doubt that we are to receive the things we have requested.

That is one reason for taking delight in the Lord, in His Word, His work, His will, His sweet presence through the Holy Spirit's conscious communion. For Psalm 37:4 says,

"Delight thyself also in the LORD; and he shall give thee the desires of thine heart."

That is another way of saying that the way to have your prayers answered is so to delight in God's will and be so surrendered to His loving plan that you and the Lord will see eye to eye, and He can afford to risk you with anything your heart desires! That is praying in the will of God!

Jesus meant the same thing, I think, when He said in John 15:7,

"If ye abide in me, and my words abide in you, ye shall ask what ye will, and it shall be done unto you."

Abiding in Christ must mean at one with Him, agreed with Him, surrendered to His will, trusting joyfully in Him. But to love and trust Christ is not enough if you would have your prayers answered. If you do not know His will, what would please Him, then no matter how you love Him, how surrendered to His will you might be, you could not expect Him always to answer your prayers. So the condition is added, 'and if my words abide in you.' You need to know the Bible, *from the heart*, so that Christ's words really live in you; and then, abiding in Him, you can ask anything you want and get it. So a loving heart-reception of the Word of God is a part of praying in the will of God. We know the will of God largely through the Bible.

How strange it is that some people learn only the letter of the Bible and never get the Spirit's message. Several years ago a good man sold Bibles in a revival campaign I conducted. He had read the Bible through each year for twenty-two years, he told me, and at that time was reading the New Testament through each month. I feel sure he was a sincere, good man. Yet he told me he had not yet decided about whether a saved person already possessed everlasting life so that he could never be lost. And when we spoke of the second coming of Christ, he was not sure whether he was a premillennialist; and he thought perhaps one must be baptized to be saved. He had read the Bible many, many times but got only the letter. So the Scripture never indicates that *reading* the Bible is enough for a Christian. If you would know the will of God so you can pray in His will, with confidence in getting an answer, you must have the Word abiding *in your heart.*

So Psalm 1:2,3 says about the blessed man,

"But his delight is in the law of the LORD; *and in his law doth he meditate day and night. And he shall be like a tree planted by the rivers of water, that bringeth forth his fruit in his season; his leaf also shall not wither; and whatsoever he doeth shall prosper."*

And is not that as blessed a promise as a Christian could ask? It is really a prayer promise; it is almost the same as saying that one who meditates day and night in the Bible will have everything he asks for; that God will prosper everything he does, give him everything he wants. That could only be because he so earnestly seeks, with the heart, to know the will of God that all his prayers are according to God's will and God can safely trust him with anything he wants!

III. Asking in Jesus' Name

Many times we are taught to pray in Jesus' name. John 14:13,14 says:

"And whatsoever ye shall ask in my name, that will I do, that the Father may be glorified in the Son. If ye shall ask any thing in my name, I will do it."

Anything you ask in His name, God will give it you! Then why do we not get everything we ask? For do we not nearly always close our prayers with the words, "we ask in Jesus' name. Amen"?

And John 16:24 invites us to ask in Jesus' dear name.

"Hitherto have ye asked nothing in my name: ask, and ye shall receive, that your joy may be full."

So the way to get our prayer answered, so our joy may be full, is to ask in Jesus' name.

But here, I am convinced, many of us are forgers, putting Christ's name to a prayer where He would not sign it, using His name trying to secure things He would not endorse! The Bible does not promise to answer any prayer that *we say* is in His name, but rather any prayer that is really asked for His sake, because that is what He wants and what He would ask for. "In Jesus' name" is not to be used simply as a magical formula. In fact, I do not think it was specially intended as words to be said in a prayer. That phrase is not in the model prayer given by our Lord, nor was it used in any prayer recorded of New Testament Christians.

We say "in Jesus' name" as a commonplace phrase, a part of formal ritual, in prayers that get no answer; and that proves they were not really asked for Jesus' sake, not really asked just to please Him. But Bible Christians prayed in the will of God, often, without mentioning the fact that it was in Jesus' name they asked it. This condition of successful prayer is not a matter of words but of heart. No one can pray in Jesus' name without knowing what the Lord Jesus wants and without wanting just what He wants in that particular matter. Really, to pray in Jesus' name simply means to pray in the will of God.

IV. Faith Comes When Praying in the Will of God

Believing, having faith about the answer, is many times stressed in the Bible as a certain way to secure the answer to our prayers. Mark 9:23; Mark 11:22–24; and Matthew 21:22, with other precious promises, show that all things are possible to him that believeth, that whatever you desire, you may have if you believe and do not doubt. Elsewhere we shall try to show how to have faith in God and how to grow stronger in faith, but here I call attention to the fact that faith is a gift of God (I Cor. 12:9). And no one can have faith in God for things not in God's will. Faith really is a divinely given confidence that the thing asked is pleasing to God and that He will therefore give it. When we pray in the will of God, with a heart fully surrendered to His way, eager to do and have done His will, and when we know by the sweet leading of the Holy Spirit and by the Word of God what is His will in the matter of the prayer, the faith grows in the heart and confidently claims the blessing which it knows it will please God to grant. So faith is only possible when praying in the will of God, but it is easy to have faith that God will do the thing we ask when we know it is in the sweet will of God.

O Christian, submit your will to God's will! Turn away from any rebellion, any willful wanting of your own way, that displeases God. God wants you to have your heart's desires, wants you to be happy, prosperous and successful. He wants you to be filled with the Spirit, to have soul-winning power and all the blessings that are bought for the Christian. But God cannot do much for you except as you humble your heart and surrender to God's will, wherever it shall lead you. Even if you do not know at once the will of God, surrender in advance and promise God, "I'll go where You want me to go! I'll do what You want me to do! I'll be what You want me to be!"

In this book I have told as a humble, personal testimony of many times that God has answered my prayers. I believe there is a great need for personal testimony by those who know by many actual experiences that God is wonderfully ready and willing to answer prayer. However, when I tell of marvelous answers to my prayers, I find that sometimes people bring me their burdens thinking that I can get an answer for them when they could not get an answer for themselves, as if God were more willing to hear me pray than to hear them. Always that grieves me.

The plain truth is that any Christian has as much right to pray as any other Christian. And ofttimes the very reason why you cannot get your prayers answered is the same reason that someone else could not get a prayer answered for the same thing. If you are not praying in the will of God, then it would be foolish for me to urge God to do that which was not according to His will. Or if there is a hindrance in your life, then that hindrance would still block the answer to your prayers, doubtless, even if many other devout Christians should join in prayer for the thing you want for yourself. So what you need to do is to make sure that your heart is surrendered to the will of God, that you find His will the best you know from His Word and by the leading of the Spirit, and pray in the will of God. God is as willing to hear your prayer as the prayer of anybody else in the world, if you can come acceptably, praying in His will.

CHAPTER XI

DEFINITE PRAYING

"What things soever ye desire, when ye pray."—Mark 11:24.
"Give us this day...."—Matt. 6:11.
"Friend, lend me three loaves."—Luke 11:5.

I was only a young Christian, about eighteen, in the cattle country of west Texas, when a dear country preacher R. H. Gibson took me with him to a rural community for revival services at the Black Flat schoolhouse. The first Monday morning, after one day's services, he and I went out early to pray. He read some verses of Scripture from his little Testament and then said, "Can we agree on something definite to ask God to give us in the service tonight?" We talked it over prayerfully and finally agreed that it seemed that God was laying it on our hearts to pray for five souls to be saved that night. And so we prayed, he first and then I, asking God to give us five souls in the evening service. That night five souls were saved and came out publicly, openly, for Christ so definitely that no one doubted their salvation.

The next morning we rejoiced together in our place of quiet prayer out among the rocks and waited on the Lord to see if He would lead us again to know just how many we should ask. After a quiet time of discussion we each felt led to ask for three souls to be saved that night. We prayed, each of us, for three souls. That night three people were happily converted and came out in open profession of faith in Christ. Later we named particular people in our prayers and felt clearly led to ask for their conversions in the services that evening. The evening we prayed for Bill Palm to be saved he trusted Christ as his Saviour. (Later he was my roommate in college.)

In those few days it dawned upon me that God wanted Christians to pray for *definite objects*, to be explicit in their requests.

In any matter of daily living, we make our requests definite. We never go into a restaurant and say, "Bring me some food." No, we carefully select from the menu just what we want and think we can pay for. Perhaps we say, "I want the small steak, cooked medium; some French fried potatoes and spinach. I want black tea, hot, with cream; and orange Jello dessert." When you go to buy a meal, you are definite.

No woman ever goes into a grocery store and says, "Please give me a basket of groceries." Rather, she selects a certain brand of whole wheat bread, perhaps; selects the best-looking head of lettuce, three grapefruit, and asks at the meat counter for two pounds of her favorite bacon. We are very definite in making our requests known about other matters. Then why do we not pray definitely also?

No man whose house is on fire calls the fire department and says, "It may be my house is on fire. I saw some smoke coming out the roof a bit ago, but I have not investigated. Could you come out someday, if it pleases you, and put it out?" No, no! And yet many a Christian will pray about an unsaved loved one who is lost and may die any moment and go into eternal torment, and will say, "Lord, if it be Thy will, someday before it is too late, save my brother."

The modern idea and the modern practice about prayer are so indefinite that they are silly and wicked. Prayer is very definitely asking God for something. It ought to be as specific as a sick man's calling a doctor, as a housewife's giving an order to the groceryman, as an unemployed man's asking for a job, as a child's asking for an ice cream cone.

I. The Bible Teaches That Prayer Should Be Definite, Explicit Requests

The model prayer the Saviour taught us all to pray is certainly explicit. A Christian is taught to pray about his food:

"Give us this day...."

In other words, God wants the Christian, instead of praying in lump sums and indefinite terms, to ask for exactly what he wants that day. This means that the Christian who is in the will of God should be expected often to have his prayers answered *the same day he prays!* Happy is the Christian who can confidently ask his heavenly Father, "Give me my food this very day."

The disciples heard Jesus praying and said, "Lord, teach us to pray, as John also taught his disciples" (Luke 11:1). So Jesus taught them to pray by the example of a man who goes to his friend at midnight and says,

"Friend, lend me three loaves."

Not just, "Lend me some bread," nor, "Have you got anything to eat in the house?" but rather, exactly and definitely, "Lend me three loaves" (Luke 11:5). What a thrilling example of definite praying Jesus gave us!

But this idea is inherent in all the promises throughout the Bible about prayer. For example, in Mark 11:24 Jesus said,

"What things soever ye desire, when ye pray, believe that ye receive them, and ye shall have them."

There are many marvelous truths in this promise, but note that Jesus certainly meant that a Christian ought to have certain definite desires in his mind when he prays and then ought to be able to trust God and get exactly those things from God which he requests. Prayer, in the Bible sense, is getting down to brass tacks and asking God for exactly what you want. Prayer is not only asking, but it is *asking something*. It is hardly prayer if it is not definite.

How many times the great men of God in the Bible knew exactly what they wanted and insisted upon it and got it!

I am reminded of Gideon, who prayed thus,

"If thou wilt save Israel by mine hand, as thou hast said, Behold, I will put a fleece of wool in the floor; and if the dew be on the fleece only, and it be dry upon all the earth beside, then shall I know that thou wilt save Israel by mine hand, as thou hast said."—Judg. 6:36,37.

The next morning Gideon got up, and sure enough, the fleece was so full of water that he "wringed the dew out of the fleece, a bowl of water"!

That was a very definite prayer with a definite answer. But Gideon was encouraged to change his specifications and prayed again,

"Let me prove, I pray thee, but this once with the fleece; let it now be dry only upon the fleece, and upon all the ground let there be dew."— Judg. 6:39.

And sure enough, the next morning it was dry upon the fleece; and there was dew on all the ground! Gideon knew exactly what he wanted as an evidence from God, and God seemed delighted to give it!

How refreshing is the beautiful story told in Genesis, chapter 24, of the old servant of Abraham who was sent back to the land of Ur to get a bride for Isaac. Verses 12 to 14 give us his prayer as follows:

"And he said, O LORD God of my master Abraham, I pray thee, send me good speed this day, and shew kindness unto my master Abraham. Behold, I stand here by the well of water; and the daughters of the men of the city come out to draw water: And let it come to pass, that the damsel to whom I shall say, Let down thy pitcher, I pray thee, that I may drink; and she shall say, Drink, and I will give thy camels drink also: let the same be she that thou hast appointed for thy servant Isaac; and thereby shall I know that thou hast showed kindness unto my master."

Isn't that a definite prayer? He asked that God would send to him the very girl He wanted to be a bride for Isaac. He even gives the very sentence she is to say: "Drink, and I will give thy camels drink also." And while he was yet speaking, we are told, Rebekah came out, gave him water, and offered to water all his camels; and succeeding events proved she was God's answer to his prayer and to Abraham's prayer. And if men and women should pray as definitely about mates today, in the same spirit, no doubt God would direct them just as clearly to happy marriage, under His clear guiding.

How definite was the request of Moses when he asked that the ground open and swallow Korah, Dathan and Abiram and their families (Num.16). And so Elijah prayed for drought and got drought, prayed for rain and got rain, prayed for fire from Heaven and got fire from Heaven! And when

Joshua asked for the sun to stand still, he told the sun exactly where to stop in the heaven and then turned and ordered the moon, giving explicit directions where it should stay in its relation to the earth.

"And he said in the sight of Israel, Sun, stand thou still upon Gibeon; and thou, moon, in the valley of Ajalon."—Josh. 10:12.

How blessedly definite were the prayers of the Bible characters who got things from God!

In fact, the definiteness of some of these men of God, in their requests, became so bold as to seem to us almost arrogant. They seemed to command God, and God even seemed to delight to obey! They knew exactly what they wanted; they asked it, gave specific instructions about it, almost demanded it, and got it! Peter seemed just to take it for granted that anything he said about Ananias and Sapphira, God would do; and at his word they were stricken dead (Acts 5:1–10)! And Peter seemed to feel a perfect *carte blanche*, as if he had a signed blank check from God so that he could simply announce to Æneas, who had kept to his bed eight years, sick of the palsy, "Æneas, Jesus Christ maketh thee whole: arise, and make thy bed." "And he arose immediately," the Scripture tells us (Acts 9:34)!

And Paul the apostle could say with a loud voice to the impotent man, "Stand upright on thy feet"! And the man leaped and walked (Acts 14:10)! Or he could say to Elymas the sorcerer, "Thou shalt be blind, not seeing the sun for a season" (Acts 13:11); "and immediately there fell on him a mist and a darkness," we are told. The Bible is full of examples of men who knew exactly what they wanted and seemed to be in such agreement with God that they demanded and got exactly what they had in mind, to the last detail! *That is definite praying!*

Elijah went around for years with the key of Heaven in his pocket! God had given him such assurance that he could announce to the king, "As the LORD God of Israel liveth, before whom I stand, there shall not be dew nor rain these years, but according to my word" (I Kings 17:1).

This knowing exactly what you want and asking it, demanding it, expecting it, and knowing that it is in the perfect will of God to give it, seems to be God's will for Christians; for Isaiah 45:11 says:

"Thus saith the LORD, the Holy One of Israel, and his Maker, Ask me of things to come concerning my sons, and concerning the work of my hands command ye me."

Blessed is the Christian who is so in the will of God, who so knows the mind of God, who has such definite desires that concerning the work of God he can command God and have exactly what he asks!

II. What Is Wrong With Indefinite Prayer

A little consideration will show that indefinite prayer not only fails to get things from God, but it shows a sinful state of heart that must grieve God greatly.

First, indefinite prayer is often a mere formality and is insincere. Many people pray day after day for things that they do not really desire. But Mark 11:24 stipulates "what things soever ye desire, when ye pray." How could God answer prayers that do not represent a sincere desire?

Some people pray to be heard of men. Think how many of our public prayers are indefinite, not asking anything of God and not getting anything! For example, the secretary of a preacher in an Illinois city not long ago told how the minister who employed her had already written out his public prayers for the next four months! So in not one of those prayers would the preacher be praying, "Heavenly Father, save my next-door neighbor who is here today." In not one of those prayers would the pastor be praying, "Lord, heal Mrs. Smith, who was taken to the hospital this morning with acute appendicitis." In none of those prayers would the pastor be praying, "Lord, help us to give five hundred dollars today to send this missionary to China." No, such written prayers are likely to be mere formalities. We may say such prayers to please others. Or we may say them out of sense of duty, feeling that there is some merit in praying, whether we ask for anything or get anything or not. Or we may pray such prayers simply as a matter of habit. Many Christians say the same words, day after day.

And this is the danger of a "prayer list." The other day a woman said to me, "Haven't you been to our church before? Then you are on my prayer list, and I pray for you every day." But I had *not* been to the church before; she was not familiar with the names on her prayer list and would run through them by rote. I have found it wise, when people ask me to pray for them, to stop just then and pray, if it is a matter that I can conscientiously take to God and make a request of Him. But I never promise to pray every day for anybody. I sometimes say, "If God lays it on my heart and brings you to mind, I will pray about it." The prayer that is not sincere, the mere formal saying of prayers, surely is an abomination to God. And indefinite prayer is often just that, an insincere formality.

Spurgeon, writing on I Samuel 1:10–13—"She [Hannah]...prayed unto the LORD, and wept sore....she spake in her heart"—said:

"For real business at the mercy seat give me a homemade prayer, a prayer that comes out of the depths of my heart, not because I invented it, but because God the Holy Ghost put it there and gave it such a living force that I could not help letting it out.

"Though such words are broken and your sentences disconnected, if your desires are earnest, if they are like coals of juniper, burning with a vehement flame, God will not mind how they find expression. If you have not words, perhaps you will pray better without them than with them. There are prayers that break the backs of words; they are too heavy for any human language to carry."

Indefinite prayer usually reveals that there is no burden, no urgency in the heart. Very cheerfully, a woman said to me some time ago, "Well, I have been praying for my husband twenty-three years, and he is not saved yet; but I am asking God to save him before he dies." Her lightness of heart alarmed me, and I felt led to say to her, "If you do not come to mean business and get to praying in earnest, your husband is likely to go to Hell!" If it is sin for a lost man to go on in sin without concern, expecting to be saved sometime before he dies, then would it not be a sin for his wife to be content for him to go on in his sin and be saved just sometime before he dies?

At Paris, Texas, a Christian woman told me about her fine, sixteen-year-old son who was unsaved. "But I am sure he will be saved some of these days," she said. When I urged her to bring him to the revival services and make sure he was saved, she said she was not worried; he was such a good boy, and she knew that she could win him some of these days. But a few nights afterward as the sixteen-year-old boy rode home on his bicycle late one night, he was bitten by a black widow spider. A number had recently died from the bite of this poisonous kind of spider. She called the doctor at once; and as soon as the boy was cared for, she called me, at 11:00 at night, and told me weeping, "I'll never sleep until I know he's saved. I have just waked up to see that he might die and go to Hell any moment!" I rushed across town in a car. With his distressed mother standing by his bedside pleading with him, the boy quickly was convicted of his sins and was soon led to trust Christ as Saviour.

I say that where there is no definiteness in prayer, it is because there is no urgency, no real burden, no heart desire. So when we pray, God wants our fallow ground broken up (Jer. 4:3; Hos. 10:12). How appropriate to our prayer life is that warning, "Woe to them that are at ease in Zion" (Amos 6:1), and again, "As soon as Zion travailed, she brought forth her children" (Isa. 66:8). Indefinite prayer is prayer with no burden.

When a neighbor says, "Come over to see me sometime," I may answer, "Yes, I will, and you come to see me sometime too." But in fact both of us are only being polite. "Sometime" never comes. Recently a good man said to me, "Please don't make any other plans for Sunday, as we want you to have dinner at our house. We have a nice young chicken; and my wife will plan things so she need not stay away from church, so please come!" And I knew they wanted me, since plans were so definite, and I did go; and how sweet was the fellowship!

But one of the worst things wrong with indefinite praying is that it proves we have not found out the will of God, so we do not know exactly what we should pray for. When we pray about a sinner's being saved and say, "If it be Thy will," we are simply confessing that we have no will about the matter; and it may be we are confessing that we are not even familiar with the Scriptures and do not know the tender heart of God and His concern over every poor lost soul. Of course we dare not pray very definitely and dogmatically, demanding that such things happen on a certain day or in a certain way, unless we have a clear leading that this is the will of God. How wicked it would be, how presumptuous to pray in such detail without having any idea as to whether or not it would please God and fit in with His plans and glorify His name!

Of course we ourselves would not know, with our carnal minds, but "likewise the Spirit also helpeth our infirmities: for we know not what we should pray for as we ought: but the Spirit itself maketh intercession for us with groanings which cannot be uttered. And he that searcheth the hearts *knoweth what is the mind of the Spirit, because he maketh intercession for the saints according to the will of God"* (Rom. 8:26,27). This indicates that formal, indefinite, general praying is the result of not being led of the Holy Spirit. We do not know the mind of God. We have no assurance that we are in His will. Very likely we have grieved the Holy Spirit by our sins, or we have quenched Him by ignoring His plan.

Nothing is clearer in the Bible than that men of God who got wonderful answers to prayer were led by the Spirit of God. They were definite in their praying because they knew what to pray for. They knew what they wanted, and they knew that God was willing to give these definite things.

Oh, my beloved readers, indefinite prayer must often prove our insincerity, our formality. It proves that there is no burden, no real heart-desire, in our prayers. It proves that we have not found the will of God, have not made ourselves familiar with His plans by the Word of God and by the Holy Spirit's leading.

III. How to Be Definite in Prayer

If you want to become definite, businesslike, efficient in prayer, God will help you. I suggest the following steps:

1. Set out to weed out any objects of prayer about which you are not definite. If you have a long list of things for which you pray in a halfhearted way, without any real conviction, and about which you cannot ask God for some definite answer, with boldness, then confess to God that your praying is halfhearted and formal and to some degree insincere. Quit praying for things to be heard of men or because you think it is your duty in a general sense or that people expect you to pray for these things. Set out to pray for

things about which you have a genuine desire and about which you ought to expect some definite answer.

2. Next, set out to search the Scriptures and find in them the will of God. If you are praying for somebody to be saved, then prayerfully, earnestly search the Scriptures to find out the will of God and how He feels toward the salvation of sinners. Meditate, for instance, on Luke, chapter 15, the parables of the lost sheep, the lost coin, and the lost Prodigal Son, and come to see the passion of Christ for sinners. If your heart really becomes affected with the concern Christ has for sinners, then you can pray more definitely for their conversion.

At Kingman, Kansas, I spoke one afternoon in a Bible conference for more than an hour on prayer and urged people to be definite, to mean business when they prayed. I showed by many Scriptures why we may be bold in praying for the conversion of sinners. When the service was over, a nurse came to me, a young woman who had been a Christian about a year. With her face shining with a light from Heaven, she said, "So that is the way to pray, is it?"

I answered, "Yes, that is the way to pray!"

"Well, then, tonight I am going to have my two brothers saved!" she said. "I have been praying for them now for a year, but I have been praying, 'Lord, save my brothers before it is too late.' Now I am going home and ask God to save them tonight!" And off she marched home.

I was troubled. I thought, *Is she risking my word, or is she really trusting God?* But she went home and spent the time in prayer and that night had sweet assurance in her heart that God was going to save her twin brothers.

That night an uncle came in fourteen miles and was wonderfully converted. Then the nurse's mother, seeing her own brother wonderfully saved, came to the front weeping and confessed she had been a backslider, she had not been concerned about her own children as she ought to be. Then I saw coming down out of the balcony two fine young men, seventeen years old, twins. The pastor was with them, and they came openly to claim Christ. It may be that God had to get the uncle to wake up the mother and that He needed to arouse the mother before He could reach the boys; but God did not deny the earnest, fervent prayer, the definite request, of that young nurse who asked God to save her brothers that very night, depending on the Word of God and its clear promises.

I say that a study of the Word of God will help us to be definite in our prayers. As we meditate on God's Word we will see how much He longs to give us and how freely He has offered to answer our prayers. We can find what things are in His will and so be more bold in praying for definite objects, at definite times.

3. Next, it often takes some waiting on God before one is able to have in mind clearly what he ought to pray for. Let the Holy Spirit talk to you. Ask God to show you the things that are wrong in your life, to help you to judge and turn away from any sin that grieves God. Then ask the Holy Spirit to lead you clearly into desiring the things that are right, and let Him lead you in praying. Anytime you can pray a prayer that you know is put in your heart by the Holy Spirit, then you can be bold in demanding an answer, and you will know you are asking according to the will of God and that you will receive your request. Definite praying does not mean that you try to make God come to your viewpoint. Rather, it means finding just what the Lord wants to give you, what He wants you to ask for, and then praying the prayer that the Holy Spirit lays on your heart.

In 1931 I went for a series of revival services with the First Baptist Church of Peacock, a little town in west Texas. That midwest Texas town was in the clutches of a terrible drought. It had not rained for months. Crops were utterly ruined. Even normally it was too dry to raise corn, but in that particular year even drought-resistant crops, as milo maize and cane, were blighted, and their tops were all sere, brown and dead. Water holes were dried up. The pastures were in some places almost as barren as a floor. Frequently as one drove down the lane, he would smell dead cattle, starved to death. Some farms were deserted, and people had traveled far to get work and earn a little income to live on.

As we went into the revival services, my heart got more and more burdened about the barren country. I felt that God wanted to show His power. So I promised God that just as soon as the Christian people began to be aroused and concerned over their sins and over their lost loved ones, I would call a meeting of confession and prayer, begging God to send a rain, as well as a revival.

God's Holy Spirit took hold of the people; and they began to have broken hearts, to seek God and to want souls saved. I took courage and called a meeting for prayer, telling the people I felt definitely led to pray for a rain. I felt that the Holy Spirit had put the matter in my heart. Many agreed to pray with me. We publicly asked God to send a great rain and to send it within twenty-four hours. I announced to the public that we would expect a rain in twenty-four hours and that if it came after that time it would not be the one we were asking for and that we would not count our prayers answered. There was no evidence of any kind in the heavens that we should expect a rain. The next day the sun beat down pitilessly on the barren land. At the morning service at 11:00 o'clock that weekday, we again prayed for rain and begged God to send it by the night service so that all could know that God answered definite prayers. I announced that if the rain did not come within twenty-four hours, it would not be an answer to our prayers.

God put it in my heart to pray that definite prayer, and I felt that He would hear it. After noon my wife set about to wash some clothes and sent our little girl Grace, then five years old, to borrow a tub of a neighbor woman who had offered it. It was about two o'clock. Suddenly black clouds began to roll up swiftly from the southeast. In a few minutes there came a mighty wind. Mrs. Rice had to rescue the little girl and catch the washtub, rolling across the prairie! The tabernacle where we had been meeting was blown off the blocks that supported it. Downtown in the stores the scoffers and the wicked had been saying, "Praying for rain may be all right in east Texas, but it won't work in west Texas. That fool young preacher will see; there will not be a rain by tonight." Suddenly the plate glass windows of a store were blown in, and then there came a flood of rain. The scoffers were scattered. Then there was a great downpour over the town and for about five miles in each direction. What a rain it was!

We had services that night in the Methodist church. People came, filled the seats, sat in the windows, all the building would hold. But they did not come in their cars; the roads were deep in mud; and they came in farm wagons and buggies and on horseback and wading with rubber boots. God sent the rain. And we had a right to be definite and bold about it because the Holy Spirit had put it in our hearts.

Wait on God. Submit to the Holy Spirit. He knows how to pray according to the will of God, so let Him lead your praying.

4. Another way to be definite is to go on record. I often feel a need when I pray to take pencil and paper and write out certain definite requests and number them 1, 2, 3, etc. Often I make confessions of sin the same way. As honestly and fairly as I can, I wait before God until He lays on my heart things that grieve Him, certain matters in which I have failed or sinned; and then I write them out plainly on a piece of paper. I keep that before me for a few days until I feel I have gotten the victory and God knows and I know that I have honestly judged those sins and tried to put them away and have confessed them to God. (But you may be sure I do not leave that list of confessed sins around where anybody else can see it!)

And so I often write down definite requests. For example, in a little prayer notebook I occasionally jot down on the left-hand page a prayer request and the date and the names of any who agree with me in that earnest request. On the right-hand page I leave a blank space for the day when the prayer is answered. And there I mark down the answer and the date, and I praise the Lord.

On December 11, 1937, I wrote down the following: "For new book on soul winning to be printed by Moody Colportage. Claimed by John R. Rice, Fairy Shappard, Eula Lee, Viola Walden, Lola Mae Bradshaw." (The four young women were working in my office.) Three years later, on August 29,

1941, my little book *The Soul-Winner's Fire* was printed as one of the Bible Institute Colportage series. I know it helped me to be definite to write down that request, and it helped me to believe God. Now the record of definite answer fills my heart with joy and increases my faith.

Often you will start out to pray for things and soon find that it is not the will of God. If the Holy Spirit does not help you pray, then consider. Perhaps you are not praying according to God's will. So change your prayer as the Spirit leads. Do not keep an old prayer list and try to follow it when you have no sense that God is pleased with the prayers.

Ofttimes, it is well to put your request in words to other people. Perhaps two of you can agree as touching a certain matter. If possible, agree on exact dates, or numbers, or amounts. For example, a few weeks ago I was in revival services at the Berean Baptist Church, Grand Rapids. As the pastor and I prayed before the service Sunday morning I felt impressed to ask God for twenty-five souls to come out publicly to claim Christ that day, and I prayed for that number definitely. At the morning service I think there were only two. In the afternoon service I told how God had answered many of my prayers, and there were one or two others who claimed the Saviour. When the pastor and I met together before the evening service, I reminded him of my prayer and felt ashamed that all the wonderful answers to prayer I had mentioned had been given years before. So definitely and earnestly I reminded God that I had been telling how He answered prayer and now I wanted Him to answer a definite prayer that day—to see that, in that evening service, we got the rest of the twenty-five souls we had asked for.

The Lord wonderfully blessed in the service that night. A seventy-four-year-old man who had come in twenty miles was saved. Many others were saved, coming with tears. A mother who had been a backslider thirty-five years, she said, came back to Christ; and with her was her adult daughter who came to accept the Saviour for the first time. When the service was over, the pastor showed me the names of twenty-five people who had come out during the day, openly claiming Christ as Saviour or as backsliders who came again to take up their cross and live for God. He remembered two others who had been saved whose names he did not have, but he had the names of twenty-five! I know it helped me when I told the pastor that I expected twenty-five to answer the invitation that day. You can be definite, *when the Holy Spirit lays it on your heart*, by setting goals or agreeing with others.

Elsewhere I have told about a recent campaign for trial subscriptions to *The Sword of the Lord*. We asked God for 5,000 trial subscriptions. We posted that number on the office wall, and every day in the office prayer meeting at ten o'clock the workers prayed for 5,000 trial subscriptions in that brief campaign. I announced in *The Sword of the Lord* that we hoped for that number. We set a definite time for the campaign to close. My secretary felt led to give trial subscriptions to thirty friends. When what we thought was the final mail came, we found her thirty made exactly 5,000 trial subscriptions! But one of the workers thought she had helped God too much, and they prayed again. The next day mail from stragglers came in, to make 5,030 subscriptions, that is, exactly 5,000 without the thirty subscriptions she had given! Not one less and not one more than exactly the 5,000 we had agreed upon openly and had prayed for definitely!

Later other subscriptions came in, but it seemed that God was patiently showing us, just as He showed Gideon, that it was His delight to answer definite prayer. For Gideon He first made the fleece wet and all about it dry. And then when Gideon prayed again, He made the fleece dry and all about it wet. And for us God gave exactly 5,000 subscriptions including the secretary's special gift of thirty. Then when that was questioned, God made it exactly 5,000 without the thirty specials. And then later, when every doubt was settled and all of us knew that God had exactly and definitely answered prayer to the letter, He sent other subscriptions, as if to say He had more yet if we would but ask!

Beloved readers, let us be definite in our praying and give God a chance to show His mighty power and willingness to answer. Ask God definite things; expect definite answers.

CHAPTER XII

"HAVE FAITH IN GOD"

"Have faith in God."—Mark 11:22.

"Without faith it is impossible to please him."—Heb. 11:6.

"Whatsoever is not of faith is sin."—Rom. 14:23.

"If ye have faith as a grain of mustard seed, ye shall say unto this mountain, Remove hence to yonder place; and it shall remove; and nothing shall be impossible unto you."—Matt. 17:20.

In this chapter I want to lay on your heart the enormous importance of faith. You will see that faith is the very first requirement for coming to God, and no one can please God without it; that we are commanded to have faith in God, that unbelief is therefore a wicked sin, rebuked by the Saviour, which all should confess and forsake with penitent hearts; and that everything God has is promised in answer to the prayer of faith. Then second, we will see what faith is and what it is not. And third, we will show how everyone who will may grow an abounding, masterful, conquering faith.

I. The Great Importance of Faith

1. *You cannot please God without faith!* Hebrews 11:6 says,

"But without faith it is impossible to please him: for he that cometh to God must believe that he is, and that he is a rewarder of them that diligently seek him."

You cannot come to God unless you believe that there is a God and unless you believe He really hears prayer. And the Scripture plainly says, "Without faith it is impossible to please him."

Faith, then, is the very first requirement for anyone who would do anything pleasing to God. Without faith you cannot be saved. Without faith you cannot pray acceptably. Without faith you cannot live victoriously. Without faith you cannot be pleasing to God in any wise. Faith is the first requirement for pleasing God.

2. *Faith is plainly commanded as a duty.* Jesus, on a morning walk to Jerusalem from the little town of Bethany where He had spent the night, cursed the fig tree, and it withered away. They returned in the night, and the next morning the disciples saw the fig tree withered away and were astonished. Jesus turned to them and commanded them,

"Have faith in God"!

And then He told them that even mountains could be removed and cast into the sea by faith, that they could have what things soever they desired if they believed. "Have faith in God" is a plain command. Christians are commanded to have faith, and can have faith.

Jesus said to Thomas,

"Reach hither thy finger, and behold my hands; and reach hither thy hand, and thrust it into my side: and be not faithless, but believing."— John 20:27.

Oh, to every Christian the Lord Jesus cries out, 'Investigate for yourself the proof of God's promises. Give God a chance to prove Himself. Be not faithless but believing.'

3. *Unbelief is a sin.* Many people believe that faith is more or less an accident and that one cannot be blamed if he does not have faith in God. Quite generally it is supposed that some people have great faith because God picked them out to give them great faith, that others do not have much faith but cannot help themselves. However, on the contrary, the Bible plainly teaches that unbelief is a sin since every Christian can and should have faith for all that God offers.

The wickedness of unbelief is clearly implied in the Scriptures. If "without faith it is impossible to please God," then unbelief, of course, is displeasing to God and is sin. If Jesus commanded, "Have faith in God," then one who does not have faith in God is disobedient and rebellious. All the Scriptures on the question imply that a Christian can have faith in God whenever he needs faith and that not to do so is a sin.

There are many direct Scriptures which teach the moral guilt of unbelief. In the case of a Christ-rejecting sinner, Jesus said to some,

"Ye will not come to me, that ye might have life."—John 5:40.

It is clear that unbelief is a wicked decision of the will. People who are lost do not trust Christ because they do not want to. Jesus, in John 3:19–21, said:

"And this is the condemnation, that light is come into the world, and men loved darkness rather than light, because their deeds were evil. For every one that doeth evil hateth the light, neither cometh to the light, lest his deeds should be reproved. But he that doeth truth cometh to the light, that his deeds may be made manifest, that they are wrought in God."

Unbelief in Christ as one's own personal Saviour involves a moral guilt, involves a moral choosing of sin and rejection of Christ and righteousness.

And Hebrews 3:12 warns Jews plainly that they should beware *"lest there be in any of you an evil heart of unbelief, in departing from the living God."*

Unbelief is the sin of a wicked heart, departing from God intentionally, turning away from light.

John 12:37–40 explains that despite the miracles of Christ, many Jews would not believe on Him, and tells us why. Quoting Isaiah, the Gospel tells us that God had blinded their eyes and hardened their hearts, lest they should see and understand and be converted. Because of long, deliberate rejection of the light, God hardens the hearts of people so they cannot believe. Unbelief, then, grows out of other sins.

Likewise II Thessalonians 2:9–12 tells us of the man of sin who will come with lying wonders to deceive certain people, "because they received not the love of the truth, that they might be saved. And for this cause God shall send them strong delusion, that they should believe a lie: That they all might be damned who believed not the truth, but had pleasure in unrighteousness." Thus, it is certainly clear that God becomes grieved by men's preference for sin and their pleasure in unrighteousness and so sends strong delusions on Christ-rejecting sinners who continue in sin until finally they cannot believe. Lack of faith is a sin which proceeds from a deliberately wicked heart that chooses sin and refuses to seek the light and test God's promises and goodness.

And for Christians too the Scriptures say that unbelief is a sin. Romans 14:23 plainly says,

"For whatsoever is not of faith is sin."

Any element of a Christian's life that does not involve a constant dependence upon God, a belief in His Word and His promises, a reliance on His faithfulness, is wicked.

Hebrews 12:1 commands Christians to "lay aside every weight, and the sin which doth so easily beset us." What is that besetting sin? It is the sin of unbelief! Throughout the preceding chapter God has held up for our admonition and example the heroes of the Faith. We are commanded to be like them and to lay aside the besetting sin, that which is ever ready to trip us, our unbelief. Unbelief is sin.

Jesus often rebuked unbelief in His disciples. In Mark 4:40 He said to them, "How is it that ye have no faith?" Again in Luke 8:25 He said unto them, "Where is your faith?" In Mark 16:14 we are told that Jesus "upbraided them with their unbelief and hardness of heart." There is a plaintive sadness in the words of Jesus in Luke 18:8, "Nevertheless when the Son of man cometh, shall he find faith on the earth?"

Since unbelief is such a wicked sin, how earnestly we should seek to uncover every tendency to it, to confess it penitently. And how eagerly we should seek to please God by exercising faith.

4. *Faith can get anything in the universe, with nothing impossible.* How marvelous is faith! Jesus says in Matthew 17:20, "If ye have faith as a grain of mustard seed, ye shall say unto this mountain, Remove hence to yonder

place; and it shall remove; and nothing shall be impossible unto you."
Literally, "nothing shall be impossible unto you." And again Jesus said in
Mark 9:23, "If thou canst believe, all things are possible to him that
believeth." And then in Mark 11:24 He said, "What things soever ye desire,
when ye pray, believe that ye receive them, and ye shall have them." We are
plainly and unconditionally promised that "the prayer of faith shall save the
sick, and the Lord shall raise him up" (Jas. 5:15). So it is clear that if you
will believe God, you can have anything you ask. With faith, nothing in
earth or Heaven is impossible, and nothing unattainable.

Of course, this means that one must have faith about each particular
thing to get it. Faith about salvation will not get a job. Faith about a job will
not get healing for the body. Faith about one prayer will not get another one
answered. One must be so in harmony with God that one can base each of
his requests on a blessed promise or on the known will of God to get each
prayer answered.

Naturally, faith is not a device by which any poor wicked man can have
his own will, irrespective of God's will. Nothing about prayer is ever
intended for that or ever attains to that. Faith is a grace, or a gift, by which,
in a particular matter, one can ask for things in the will of God and having
a divinely based confidence, he may receive whatever he asks.

It is of surpassing importance, then, for every Christian to learn what
faith is, to learn how to have faith and how to suppress and forsake his
unbelief for a whole life of victorious faith.

II. What Is Faith?

1. *A Bible definition.* A Bible definition of *faith* is given in Hebrews
11:1:

*"Now faith is the substance of things hoped for, the evidence of things
not seen."*

Substance could be translated *assurance,* and *evidence* could be translated *conviction.* Faith, then, is a certain conviction, an assurance, an evidence that we will get the thing we hope for and ask for. By faith one sees
the thing that is invisible. By faith one holds what is intangible. One who
has faith has the substance of the thing hoped for and has the evidence of
that which is not yet seen by human eye. Oh, the blessed confidence and
assurance of faith!

The faith mentioned in the Bible is nearly always faith in God. But the
above definition is a general definition. In the case of sickness, one may
have confidence and assurance based upon a good doctor. That is faith, but
it is not necessarily faith in God. A depositor may have confidence and
assurance that his money will be perfectly safe in the bank. That is faith, but

it is faith in the bank and not necessarily faith in God. A child has sweet confidence that food will be forthcoming when he is hungry, that a home will be maintained, that his needs will be supplied. That is faith, but it is faith in his parents and not necessarily faith in God.

2. *It is important to see that not every confidence, not every assurance, is faith in God.*

A woman wrote me in greatest disappointment. She had asked God for a baby girl and felt that she had perfect faith that God would send a girl, but instead He gave her a baby boy. We know that God had not promised her the baby girl. He had not promised it by the Bible, and He had not promised it by His Holy Spirit in her heart, or He would have given it, for God always keeps His promises. There was nothing in the nature of God that made it wrong for Him to send a baby boy. Hence, we know that woman's confidence was not real faith in God. She may have had confidence in *her prayers.* Possibly she had prayed and prayed until she felt, *Well, surely now that I have begged God so much, He will have to send me a girl. I am going to believe it and expect it.* She may have analyzed circumstances and decided that since a girl would be so much better (she thought) for her and for her husband, who also wanted a baby girl, and for the little boys, who wanted a sister, therefore God, knowing how necessary it was, would give a baby girl. But in that case God knew better what she needed than she did, and her decision was not based on the leading of the Holy Spirit nor on the Bible but on her own understanding of circumstances. So she got a baby boy instead of a baby girl. I have no doubt in the long run she will find that God's way was the best for everybody concerned. And surely, if she draws nearer the Lord, she will see how foolish it was to grieve over the good gift that God gave. The confidence she had was not faith in God.

People may have assurance that they are saved when they are not. Their assurance may be on false grounds. One believes he is saved because he has been confirmed. Another says that he pays his honest debts, that he does none of his neighbors harm, that he provides for his own family, that he is as good as church members, and therefore he believes that he deserves salvation. I say, such people may have an assurance, but it is a false assurance. It is not based upon God's promise. God has not promised to save those who are confirmed. God has not promised to save those who live good lives, who pay their debts and are good to their families or who join churches or who try to practice the Golden Rule. So if people have faith in their own self-righteousness, or have faith in the words of false teachers, or have faith in the church or its ordinances to save them, then their faith is misplaced. It is not faith in God and is not saving faith. You see, then, that not every assurance in the heart is real faith in God.

What we call faith may sometimes be a self-deception. A Christian

Scientist practitioner may teach a sick man to say over and over, "There is no such thing as evil. Sickness is only an error of mortal mind. I am well, completely well. I have no pain." And the Christian Scientist may induce a state of mind whereby he thinks he is not sick, he ignores the pain and the evidence of his senses and actually thinks he is well. And if his disease is one in which the mental attitude may be decisive, perhaps he will get well. A large percentage of our suffering is really mental. Worrying and fretting are great enemies of our health. A confident, happy mind has much to do with recovery from sickness in some cases. But if his sickness is not mental and cannot be affected by the attitude of mind, then the Christian Scientist may die, as Christian Scientists do, as everybody else does. He has assurance, an assurance based on self-deception. It is not faith in God. In such a case, if God does not through other agents and means see fit to heal him, He would not heal the man because of that self-induced confidence. The Christian Scientist may have assurance, but it is not based upon any promise of God, and God is under no obligation to give what is expected.

I do not say that Christian Scientists never really pray to God nor that they never get their prayers answered. Doubtless they sometimes do, despite their false doctrines. But I say their normal teaching that there is no sin, no sickness, that sin is only an error of mortal mind, is not faith in God. It is a self-induced attitude of assurance and confidence which is not based upon God's Word nor upon His faithfulness, and is not faith in God. Instead of *faith* healing, Christian Science healing, Unity healing, etc., should be called *mental* healing. There is such a thing as mental healing, but let us not confuse it with the matter of faith in God.

3. *It is only as we come to know the will of God, through the Bible and the Holy Spirit, that we can have faith in particular matters.*

As an example, in the matter of salvation we have the full assurance of repeated statements in the Bible that God is willing to save every sinner that comes to Him, depending on Christ. "Him that cometh to me I will in no wise cast out" (John 6:37). That is so clearly taught in the Bible that every time a lost sinner depends on Christ for salvation he may know he is instantly saved, then and there. I know that my sins are forgiven. I have full assurance that I am God's child, that He will take me safe to Heaven, that I already have everlasting life. "He that believeth on the Son hath everlasting life" (John 3:36). That assurance is so strong it has become practically a certainty. That assurance is based on the infallible Word of God which I have proven true over and over again. God never turns down nor dishonors such faith. Since God says He loves sinners, since Jesus says He died for sins, since God says He is willing to accept the price Jesus has paid for our sins and that all who will come to Him through Christ will be received and not one cast out, it is easy to have faith in God for salvation. No sinner ever

really wanted to come but could come. The only way people can have difficulty getting saved is when they want to be saved some other way or when
they do not know what God has so plainly promised. Saving faith, then, is
simply a confidence that God will do what He plainly said He would do. So
faith in that case is based upon the Word of God.

After one has trusted Christ for salvation, believing God's Word, he
receives an added assurance of salvation as he comes out to confess Christ
openly and sets out to live the Christian life. Then he has the sweet witness
of the Spirit that he has been born again. The Holy Spirit puts in his heart
the cry of a child for his father, "Abba, Father," and he does not have the
spirit of bondage to fear. Now this added assurance that He is God's child
is based on the testimony of the Holy Spirit in his heart that he has been
received of God. So in some sense, then, faith is the assurance that what the
Holy Spirit says in the heart is true.

Faith is based on the Word of God. It may also be based upon any direct
revelation of the Holy Spirit. The Holy Spirit wrote the Bible. The Holy
Spirit may also give particular and definite promises in the heart of a Spirit-
led person. But still, the faith in each such case is based upon what God has
promised. God will do what He says He will. When I believe that, risk that,
that is faith in God.

Some people have an idea that faith in God is simply an independent
method by which one can get whatever he wants, irrespective of the will of
God in the case. But faith is not a way of getting things God does not want
us to have. Rather, faith is a way of getting things God does want us to have
and has planned for us. We never get most of the great things God has for
us and would delight to give us. But faith will open the doors to the bounties and riches of Heaven and give joys and blessings and powers and victories and abundance which are in the will of God for us. There is no such
thing as having faith in God, outside the known will of God.

Not long ago I received a letter saying to me, "Brother Rice, will you
please pray the prayer of faith with me about this," and the writer mentioned an object of prayer which I had no evidence in the world it was God's
will to give. It may have been; it may not have been God's will. I did not
know how it would particularly honor the Lord. There was no Scripture that
applied in the case, as far as I knew in my ignorance of the details, and I did
not know how truly the person who made the request would honor God if
He granted it. And the Holy Spirit did not reveal to me that it was clearly
the will of God. Therefore, of course, I could not "pray the prayer of faith"
in the matter, as the writer so naively requested.

Anytime you can find a clear promise in God's Word that He will do
such and such a thing and believe it and risk it and depend upon it, then you
have trusted God, and your faith will be rewarded with the thing desired.

Or anytime you have a clear revelation by the Holy Spirit that your prayer request is in the will of God, will honor Him and that He will do it, then that is faith in God and will be rewarded. But such leadings must be in accord with the Word of God. We must "try the spirits whether they are of God" (I John 4:1).

If you ever hear people say that they have trusted God or that they had faith about a matter and still did not get it, you may assure them that they did not really have faith in God. Faith is *always* rewarded, without any exception in the world. God is trustworthy. He keeps His promises. He does what He says He will do. He always does what He has given anyone assurance He will do. Faith is the assurance that God will do a thing because He has promised to do it.

Some ultradispensationalists say that the great promises of answers to the prayer of faith, promises to remove mountains, to work miracles, promises like Mark 11:24, Matthew 17:20 and Mark 9:23, are not for this age. They say that no matter what faith people have, still God will not do such things now. But they are utterly, wickedly mistaken. Real faith is from God. Whatever God says, He will do. God never gives faith unless He will answer it. And faith, true faith in God, is always based on what God has agreed to do and what He says He will do. It is an assurance based on either the Word of God or what we know to be the character and nature of God, as revealed by His Holy Spirit. Faith always presupposes a promise and that God will keep His word. God is under obligation *always* to answer the prayer of faith because such real faith in God is always based on an obligation that God has assumed, a promise which He has given. In any dispensation, anywhere, if God gives a definite assurance that He will do a thing, He will do it, to any limit; and absolutely nothing is impossible to the one who is given definite faith about a particular matter. Faith is really depending on God's faithfulness to do what He agrees to do.

4. *Faith may be based on the known mercy of God without a definite promise.* Faith may be based on a plain word of God in the Bible. Faith may be based upon a clear and tested impression given by the Holy Spirit that God wants us to do a certain thing and that He will lead us and bless us. And so faith may be based upon what we know of the nature of God. Knowing God's holiness, we know He will not sin. We know how merciful He is; and if there are no elements in a situation that demand judgment, the very nature of God may demand mercy. In such a case, knowing what God is like, we may know what He wants to do and will do in certain circumstances. God will always do right, will always act in accordance with His own righteous and merciful nature. Of course we must learn what God is like and what He will do from a heart-knowledge of the Word of God and the blessed teaching of the Holy Spirit. Men do not by wisdom find God. So this faith, based

on the general assurance that God's nature obligates Him to act in a certain way and to answer certain prayers, must still grow out of the Bible and be wrought in us by the Holy Spirit.

An example of this kind of faith is that of the Syrophenician woman who came to Jesus to beg for the healing of her daughter who was grievously vexed with a devil, as recorded in Matthew 15:22–28. When He said, "I am not sent but unto the lost sheep of the house of Israel," and again when He said, "It is not meet to take the children's bread, and cast it to dogs," still she did not believe His pretended indifference. He pretended that He came only to heal and save Jews and no one else. He meant, I think, to try her faith and teach His narrow-minded disciples a needed lesson. He pretended that He, like other Jews, thought of Gentiles as only dogs, not fit to call on God. But God's Holy Spirit had already revealed to her that Christ was really merciful and loving, that He came to seek and to save all who were sinners. So she would not believe He was as indifferent as He appeared to be. And to Christ's own delight she insisted that if she were a dog, she was His own dog and had a right to the crumbs from the table. He said to her with joy, "O woman, great is thy faith: be it unto thee even as thou wilt." Her daughter was healed that very hour. She had faith in what she knew Jesus was. She knew He was merciful, though He did not outwardly appear to be so. She knew He was sent to save Gentiles the same as Jews, though He did not immediately answer her prayer. That was genuine faith, faith in what she knew Christ to be, faith in Him as He was revealed in her heart by the Holy Spirit, instead of what He pretended to be to test her faith and evidently as a lesson to the disciples. *Christ was obligated to be merciful!* Christ could not be indifferent, could not be a respecter of persons, could not hate Samaritans as other Jews did. Since Christ was God, the God of all flesh, the Saviour of the world, she knew He was as willing to hear her as to hear anybody else. Her confidence, her assurance, her faith were based in the Christ she knew. Whether she had seen Him work miracles before or whether she had seen the compassion in His face as He healed others or whether she was an utter stranger and the blessed Holy Spirit had simply and directly revealed it in her heart, we do not know. But she trusted Him to do what He, from His loving mercy, was constrained to do. Her faith was based on an intimate understanding of the real will of Christ and the real character of Christ. Oh, that we might know Him better so that we might always pray according to His will and believe how compassionate, how tender, how willing to bless us is He!

III. How to Exercise Faith and Grow Greater Faith in God

Can *anybody* have faith in God; I mean faith enough to live victoriously, get prayers answered regularly, faith enough to please God? Most certainly anyone can! And can anyone grow a really great faith, like the heroes of the Bible and like other men for whom God has done marvels? I believe they can. George Müller, the man of faith and prayer, founder of the orphanage at Bristol, England, who got seven million dollars by prayer, says, "Some say, 'Oh, I shall never have the gift of faith Mr. Müller has got.' This is a mistake—it is the greatest error—there is not a particle of truth in it. My faith is the same kind of faith that all of God's children have had. It is the same kind that Simon Peter had, and all Christians may obtain like faith. My faith is their faith, though there may be more of it because my faith has been a little more developed by exercise than theirs; but their faith is precisely the faith I exercise, only, with regard to degree, mine may be more strongly exercised."

About His best spiritual gift, is God partial? Is not salvation free to all on exactly the same basis? And does not the Bible say that "God is no respecter of persons"? We remember that at Pentecost, "they were ALL filled with the Holy Ghost" (Acts 2:4). And again, when they prayed "they were ALL filled with the Holy Ghost" (Acts 4:31). And I Corinthians 12:7 tells us plainly that "the manifestation of the Spirit is given to EVERY MAN to profit withal." These things would lead us to believe that great faith, triumphant, happy, victorious faith, is possible for every Christian.

Otherwise, God would be a party to the sin of unbelief, which is unthinkable. But not to have faith in what God has promised is a sin. Not to believe God will do what He said is to make God a liar. And in Hebrews 12:1 we are plainly commanded to "lay aside every weight, and THE SIN which doth so easily beset us." That besetting sin is unbelief, and we are commanded to lay it aside. Therefore, every one of us may lay it aside; every one of us can have a victorious, triumphant faith in God.

Surely, then, every Christian should set out to develop and grow and act on confident faith in God in every detail of life. Let us study together here some ways to have faith:

1. *Learn the Word of God.* We are plainly told that "faith cometh by hearing, and hearing by the word of God" (Rom. 10:17). Originally the Word of God was principally gotten by hearing instead of reading. There were few copies of the Word of God, all copied by hand. Most people could not read. Most people then got the Word of God secondhand. So faith came by hearing—that is, hearing the Word of God. But the essential point is that faith principally comes by familiarity and heart-understanding of the Word of God. If you want to have faith in God, you must know His Word.

That is true, first of all, because faith is based upon God's promises. If God said He would do a thing, He will. If God made a proposition, He will stick to it when it is accepted. God's guarantees are always fulfilled. But you will not know what God has promised unless you learn His Word. So one who wants to please God with a faith that gets prayer answered and gets for him all that God wishes to give him should set out to find the blessed promises of God. Search for them through your Bible, read them with delight, mark them for quick reference, memorize them so that the blessed assurance of them may sink into your soul. Learn God's promises if you would come to depend upon Him.

Then you should take these promises to heart. Take them as personal to yourself. Search out the Scriptures; meditate over them lovingly; pray for the Holy Spirit to help you understand them that you may get exactly what is the sense of God's promises and how they are to apply to you. Only as you get the exact meaning of God's promise can you know what He has obligated Himself to do and what you can count on His doing. This comes through an understanding of the Word of God. The Holy Spirit builds faith in the heart by the means of God's Word, particularly His blessed promises.

Modernism, then, cuts the taproot of faith. It teaches people that the Bible is not reliable, that it is not really the Word of God, that the promises cannot be relied upon. The acceptance of the Bible as what it claims to be, the very Word of God, infallibly correct, to be absolutely trusted, is necessary to faith. You would not be willing to receive a check that you knew was forged. You could have no faith in it. Unless you believe the Bible really is God's Word and that the promises are His and that He is really obligated to make them good, you will never risk them, depend upon them, and act on them in faith.

The ultradispensationalist, like the modernist, does great harm to faith. Those who chop up the Bible, saying most of it is for the Jews, part was for a transitional period, and only a few of the epistles are really written for Christians today, mutilate the Bible and thereby mutilate the basis of faith. God's promises are *yea* and *amen*, but they do no good to one who does not believe them and apply them to himself.

So believe the Bible, and then count it as the very Word of God, to be believed in childlike sincerity. Then set out to find exactly what are God's promises for you. As you learn God's promises in their proper settings and become familiar with the things God has obligated Himself to do for those in your circumstances, then you can grow more and more to depend on God's Word. Faith comes thus by the Word of God as you learn His promises.

In the second place, our faith comes through the Word of God as we become familiar with God's nature. When I read the story of how Jesus saved the dying thief and said, "To day shalt thou be with me in paradise," I do not read therein any express promise to me, but I become familiar with the tender compassion of Jesus. I learn how He loves sinners, how quick He is to forgive! And I naturally think in my heart, *If Jesus loves that poor sinner, He loves me too. And if He saved that poor sinner immediately after a*

*simple prayer of faith, "Lord, remember me," then He would save me the
same way.* As I read how Jesus stilled the waves of the sea, I learn to know
of His power. As I read how He fed the five thousand with the five barley
loaves and two small fishes of a little boy, I come to have more confidence
that Jesus cares about hunger of the body and that He can do, oh, so much
with so little! As I read the Bible I find that Jesus cleansed the lepers, healed
the sick, opened the eyes of the blind, forgave the fallen woman and the publican alike. And so, in the Bible, I have become familiar with the tender heart
of God, His mighty power, His approachability, His eagerness to bless.

That is a reason for reading all the Bible. A Christian should read it again
and again. The historical part, rightly interpreted, along with the devotional
Psalms; the crisp, businesslike Proverbs; the Gospels; the Epistles; the
Prophets, all reveal the nature of God as the One who answers prayer. As
you see what God has done for others, you see what you have a right to
expect Him to do for you.

In John 15:7 we are told, "If ye abide in me, and my words abide in you,
ye shall ask what ye will, and it shall be done unto you." That blessed
promise evidently means that if we abide in Christ and so surrender our
will to His—and particularly as His Word, the Scriptures, abides in us, and
as we become familiar with His promises and His nature—we can ask for
anything we want and get it. Faith comes by hearing, and hearing by the
Word of God. No one who does not make much of the Word of God can
ever have faith.

That is the reason, no doubt, that Proverbs 28:9 says, "He that turneth
away his ear from hearing the law, even his prayer shall be abomination."
There is no such thing as right praying, prayer that really gets things from
God, the prayer of faith, except as it fits in with the spirit of God's Word.
To become familiar with the Bible, with a heart-familiarity, is to become
familiar with God: who He is, how He acts, and what He has promised to
do. Let no Christian ever believe he will grow strong in faith except as he
grows strong in a love for and in enjoyment of and in a heart-surrender to
the teachings of the Bible.

2. *Surrender fully to the leading of the Holy Spirit and to the will of God.*
The will of God is found in the Bible and in the leading of the Holy Spirit
of God to a surrendered Christian heart. And let no one think he can be great
in prayer or great in faith except as he abides in Christ with a surrendered
heart to the will of God. Prayer is not a way of taking from God things He
does not want you to have. Rather, prayer is intended to find what is God's
sweet will and then to ask for and receive all that God has for us. And what
God has for us is so much richer and better and happier than what we can
desire in our own will that there is no comparison. Praying in the will of
God means bigger prayers, not smaller ones, and bigger answers, not

smaller answers. Praying in God's will means not so much giving up as getting. Let there be no mistake: real faith is exercised only in the will of God. God never gives faith for things contrary to His will.

Nothing is as fatal to confidence about prayer as known sin in the heart. First John 3:20–22 says:

"For if our heart condemn us, God is greater than our heart, and knoweth all things. Beloved, if our heart condemn us not, then have we confidence toward God. And whatsoever we ask, we receive of him, because we keep his commandments, and do those things that are pleasing in his sight."

If your heart condemns you that you are not in God's will, that you do not keep His commandments, that you do not ask for things according to His will, then of course your heart will condemn you when you come to pray, and you will have no confidence, no faith to receive your request from the Lord.

So each Christian, in growing faith, should make sure that he is fully surrendered to the will of God. And the will of God is found in the Bible and in the leading of the Holy Spirit.

That means that we need the Holy Spirit of God rightly to interpret God's Word. The Bible is "the sword of the Spirit." So the Spirit can interpret and use His own writing, the Word, better than anyone else. Self-willed, haughty people sometimes get the letter of the Word without the Spirit, but to know the mind of God we need to wait humbly on God's Spirit.

And there are no real understanding of the Bible and no real approach to the holy of holies of God's gracious fellowship without a heart-surrender to God's will. No one can know the Bible intelligently who does not let the Bible apply to his own heart. One who reads the Bible with childlike surrender and honest acceptance will find that the Scripture points out his sins, rebukes his unbelief, and presses on him faults to be corrected, duties to be done. The Bible is not only for the head; it is for the heart and the will. So to get the real impact of the Scripture, we must surrender our lives to the blessed leading of the Spirit of God.

I have often felt that it is folly and sin to pray to be filled with the Holy Spirit except as we plan to go about the holy business of winning souls as God has commanded us. So if you want the Word of God to be used to grow faith in your heart, you must surrender to God's will and let yourself be made over. It is not enough that "my words abide in you" as Jesus requires in John 15:7. But even before that, He requires that "ye abide in me." When the heart rests in Jesus and the will is centered in His will and we humbly await His pleasure and make Him Lord, then we can approach the second condition of John 15:7, and His words can really abide in us, and we can ask what we will. So faith grows out of our knowledge of the Word, but even more it grows out of our full surrender to the Word of God, as interpreted to us by the blessed, sweet Holy Spirit.

3. *Act on the faith you have.* Every child of God already has faith in God. You meet the requirement of Hebrews 11:6, at least in part. You do believe that there is a God and that He is a rewarder of them that diligently seek Him. You feel that your faith is weak. You often wonder how you can have more faith. Well, one way to grow a great, robust faith is to act on God's promises. Put God to the test. He will prove Himself, and you will have a stronger assurance than ever before that you can rely on God's faithfulness.

To doubting Thomas, Jesus said, "Reach hither thy finger, and behold my hands; and reach hither thy hand, and thrust it into my side: and be not faithless, but believing" (John 20:27). So doubting Thomas did put his finger in the nail-prints and put his hand in Jesus' side and then fell in adoration and in strong faith before Jesus, saying, "My Lord and my God." To the other disciples Jesus made a similar proposition: "Handle me and see; for a spirit hath not flesh and bones, as ye see me have" (Luke 24:39). Never think it is wrong to give God a chance to prove Himself.

In Malachi 3:10 the Lord said, "Bring ye all the tithes into the storehouse, that there may be meat in mine house, and prove me now herewith, saith the LORD of hosts, if I will not open you the windows of heaven, and pour you out a blessing, that there shall not be room enough to receive it." "Prove me now," says the Lord. God is perfectly willing for you to try Him out.

Suppose you try Him, then, on the tithing business. Should Christians tithe, or is that simply an ordinance for Jews in the Old Testament? And does it really pay to tithe, when people are very poor and do not have money for even the necessities of life? The quickest way to settle that is not by argument. Give God a chance, and He will prove it!

I remember that day when on a farm in west Texas I went out by the woodpile, through the pea-patch, crawled through the strands of a barbed wire fence and down in the brakes and knelt under a chaparral bush and committed certain things to God. I told Him I would tithe. I promised that if He wanted me to preach I would preach, if He wanted me to sing I would sing. I told Him that I was going to college and would risk Him for my needs.

How could I ever forget that holy hour! For God went with me as I saddled my sorrel horse and rode off to college with about $9.35 in my pocket. I worked my way through junior college and university. I played football, I was active in college debating, I was president of a literary society and of the University Christian Association, I took voice lessons, and yet I did enough outside work to pay my expenses. How I earned a scholarship and how there was always a job awaiting me I could never explain except that I had a covenant with God, and I put Him to a test. And since then, I have had such a boldness on this matter that I have no trouble about daily provision.

Why do you not set out by God's grace to put Him to the test first on the money question, trusting Him fully in material matters? Start out today to give God the tithe and then freewill offerings beside. Tell Him that all of it is His and that by His help you will risk Him—that He may have it all or any part He chooses. And you will find that God proves Himself in daily supply. "Seek ye first the kingdom of God, and his righteousness; and all these things shall be added unto you" (Matt. 6:33). That is a good place to start trying God out and growing your faith by using it.

You can win souls. God's Word is clear, in Psalm 126:6, that if you really go, weeping, bearing precious seed, you shall doubtless come back rejoicing with sheaves. And Jesus in the Great Commission plainly promised that if we go to win souls and baptize them and teach them to go, "Lo, I am with you alway." Why do you not, in your timidity, your conscious ignorance, your faltering, even your unbelief, just set out to see if God's Word can be trusted on that point? Go earnestly, with real labor, really searching out lost people. Go with a broken heart of concern and holy compassion wrought in you by the Spirit of God. Go with the Word of God which is the precious seed. And as certain as God's Word is true, you will come back with some sheaves and with rejoicing. You will not win everybody you speak to, just as no fisherman gets a fish for every bait and just as no farmer gets a stalk of corn for every seed, but you will get some fruit if you go God's way. Why do you not try it and see? And when you have tried it once, you will know then that the Word of God is true, you will know it in a way you never knew it before. A *teacher* may become a modernist, but a real *evangelist* cannot become a modernist. For God's Word proves itself when you try it out.

Why do you not, in the first time of trial and testing, resolve simply to act as if there were a good God who would be exactly what He promised and would care for His own? You may have doubts about it; I think the Hebrew children, brought before Nebuchadnezzar for refusing to bow before the great image in the plain of Dura, did not know that God was going to save them out of the fiery furnace. They *thought* so, they *hoped* so, but very possibly they trembled. And they said, "If it be so, our God whom we serve is able to deliver us from the burning fiery furnace, and he will deliver us out of thine hand, O king. But if not, be it known unto thee, O king, that we will not serve thy gods, nor worship the golden image which thou hast set up" (Dan. 3:17,18). They believed God would deliver them, but they were resolved to try it anyway. Even if they should die in that furnace, they would do what they knew God wanted them to do and leave the results with God.

And when the One who was "like the Son of God" came and walked with them in the fiery furnace; when their garments did not even receive the smell of fire but only their bonds were burned off and they were free men; when they came forth to face the astonished and converted King Nebuchadnezzar and his princes, those Hebrew young men had a greater faith in God!

Oh, how my heart rejoices when I look back through some testing times in my own life when I resolved I would give God a chance. A committee of good men, strict denominationalists, waited on me, demanding that I cease my contention about modernism and evolution as taught in certain denominational schools; and they threatened I should be blacklisted by the denomination, that I would never be invited to revivals, that my family would suffer want and that my ministry would wane. When the opposite proved true, as I put God to the test and depended on Him, what a great victory I had!

Again, a wicked man from personal spite slandered me and had a pastor and church cancel a proposed revival campaign. Without money for a return trip, I drove 1,800 miles for the revival campaign anyway. That church, when it saw the evidence, reconsidered; and the revival effort grew into a big united campaign with eight or nine churches in an auditorium seating 2,200 people, which continued for six weeks with hundreds of souls saved and the whole city shaken and blessed! How my heart has leaped for joy upon every remembrance of that testing!

Debts once pressed me sore, accumulated on my weekly evangelistic paper, *The Sword of the Lord*, and in printing tracts. It was a labor of love, and the burden had seemed to get too heavy for me. Satan tempted me through a good church and preacher. If I would remain over an extra Sunday in a certain campaign, a good offering was promised. But I did what I knew I ought to do and went home with the $25 offering they gave me for ten days, and the next day came a check for $1,000 to pay those haunting, crushing debts. Never since that time have I been so burdened or tried about printing gospel literature, and now more money is spent on printing each month than I then spent in a year. My faith grew because it was tested and I found God keeps His promises.

GOD IS TRUSTWORTHY! GOD WILL DO WHAT HE PROMISES! And anybody in the world can know that if he will only give God a chance to prove it. Take God at His Word, risk Him, depend upon Him, and your faith will grow by leaps and bounds!

Did you know that faith is not primarily feeling? No, primarily, faith is acting. Read again that great hero chapter, Hebrews 11, and you will find that every one of these "by faith" *did something!*

"By faith Abel offered...."

"By faith Enoch was translated."

"By faith Noah...prepared an ark."

"By faith Abraham...went out."

"By faith he sojourned."

"By faith Abraham, when he was tried, offered up Isaac."

"By faith Isaac blessed Jacob and Esau concerning things to come."

"By faith Jacob, when he was dying, blessed both the sons of Joseph."

"By faith [of the parents] Moses...was hid three months of his parents."

Go on through the chapter, and you will see that by faith people did things. Abraham accounted that God was able to raise up Isaac, so he offered him. God met Abraham, and it was not as hard to trust Him anymore.

Why do you not, then, act on God's promises? Try God out. Put yourself in the place where if God's Word is true you will be blessed and if God's Word is not true you may be ruined. And when God works out His plan and does what He promised to do, your faith will have greatly grown. The life that is lived on the daily basis of "I will do what God tells me to do, and I will risk Him to take care of the results," is sure to be a life of daily expanding faith, as God makes His faithfulness known.

I told you about the time when I knelt under a chaparral bush as a lad before I rode off to college. Years later, in 1926, I gave up a happy pastorate, with a regular salary and a nicely furnished parsonage. The church had doubled its membership; we had built a nice new building; we had had hundreds saved. People wanted me to stay, but I felt God calling me to go out into the white harvest field of evangelism. I made a solemn covenant with God. I said, "Lord, You look after my business, and I will look after Yours. I will give up all regular salary and not look to man but will look to You. I will give up my $10,000 government insurance. I promise You not to fret about daily bread. I believe You will supply all my needs, and I here and now lay myself on the altar to go anywhere You say, to do what You tell me, and to risk You to care for me and my family."

Praise His name, God has kept His part of that bargain. He has kept my growing family and supplied all our needs. He has provided about $35,000 for printing gospel literature. He has provided many thousands of dollars for radio bills, and day by day, sometimes meal by meal, God has provided our needs bountifully, and we have lived a life of resting in God's faithfulness. I know a lot more about God than I did when I entered into that covenant. My faith is much stronger. Your faith too will grow, if you really take God up on His proposition, if you try Him on His promises and promise to prove His faithfulness!

4. *Faith comes by asking for it.* If you want more faith, then ask God for it. Several Scriptures make it clear that we have a right to pray for faith and

that God gives faith in answer to sincere prayer.

Romans 12:3 warns us not to think of ourselves more highly than we ought to think, "but to think soberly, according as God hath dealt to every man the measure of faith." Faith, then, is a gift of God.

In I Corinthians 12:9 we are told that faith is given by the same Holy Spirit who gives wisdom and knowledge and the gifts of healing and miracles, of prophecy and other such gifts. Faith is a gift of God. Then we have the same right to pray for that as we have to pray for knowledge and wisdom and for other good things. It is in the same passage mentioned as a manifestation of the Spirit. And I Corinthians, chapter 12, closes with the exhortation, "But covet earnestly the best gifts." Christians ought to want and ought to ask God for faith.

Jesus said, "If ye then, being evil, know how to give good gifts unto your children, how much more shall your Father which is in heaven give good things to them that ask him?" (Matt. 7:11). Jesus invites us to ask the Father for all good things. Faith is a good thing and is certainly within the province of prayer.

The disciples, in daily contrast to the victorious life of Jesus, felt their utter lack of faith, so they came to Jesus prayerfully and said, "Increase our faith" (Luke 17:5). They prayed for faith. And we may be sure that they got it. It may not have come all of a sudden, without any intermediate experiences. It is likely, rather, that in answer to the prayer, Christ made their hearts sensitive to His words and helped them through their listening to His word and by seeing His marvelous answers to prayer and by proving Christ and the heavenly Father many times; that through these things their faith grew and grew, until they could heal the sick, cast out devils, face mobs and imprisonment and death all with a smile. And Peter even raised the dead, by faith. Christ did answer their prayer and increased their faith.

A father brought his poor devil-possessed boy to the disciples while Jesus was on the Mount of Transfiguration, and they could not heal him. Almost in despair the father brought the boy to Jesus and said, "If thou canst do any thing, have compassion on us, and help us." Jesus replied, "If thou canst believe, all things are possible to him that believeth." And then the father, so conscious of his unbelief, cried out with tears and said, "Lord, I believe; help thou mine unbelief" (Mark 9:22–24). The father had a little faith, and he prayed for more faith. And Jesus did help his unbelief. Jesus wonderfully healed the afflicted son, and that day the father went home, I am sure, with abounding, triumphant faith in a Saviour who worked miracles in answer to prayer. He had seen the miracle. The evidence of the marvel walked down the road beside him on the way home!

And so we ought to pray, "Lord, I believe; help thou mine unbelief"!

In conclusion, I hope you are not complacent, not content with your unbelief. I hope there is a hunger of heart to know God better and to see Him work wonders in your life. Well, the first thing to do is to confess the sin of unbelief. Without faith you cannot please God. Not to have it is failure and rebellion. Unbelief is a wicked sin. Faith can get anything in the universe with nothing impossible. Admit to God how far short you have fallen of asking for or expecting the things you would have a right to pray for. Uncover the barrenness of your life, the coldness of your heart, the powerlessness of your testimony before God! If you are a pastor, why not count out before God the pitifully small results of your ministry? If you are an evangelist, why not compare yourself with Finney and Moody and Torrey and Chapman and Sunday and with Bible preachers, and admit to God that unbelief is the cause of the fruitlessness? Unbelief has lost the power of God. Oh, may God help my own heart to take this lesson in penitence and confession today on account of my unbelief, my littleness of faith!

CHAPTER XIII

JUST PRAY

All Conditions of Prayer Mentioned in the Bible Are Simply
Extra Encouragements and Opportunities to Pray;
All Fulfilled in Asking

Do you want something from God? Then just pray! Prayer gets things from God, and the one great condition of getting things is asking for them.

Some Scriptures give special promises for those who ask *in faith*. Others mention that we can get anything we want if we ask anything *according to His will*. Again we are told that whatsoever we shall ask *in Christ's name* we can have. Then *if two are agreed* they can have what they ask for. *Persistence in prayer* is encouraged too; and those who cry day and night to God will be heard speedily. But all these are *enlargements* of promise, and not *limitations*. These are *promises*, not strictures. All these are to make prayer easier, and not to make it harder. All these promises are simply elaborations of the general promises that we can get things just by praying, simply by asking.

I. God's Promises Mean Exactly What They Say

Let us go back again to Matthew 7:7,8, where Jesus said, "Ask, and it shall be given you; seek, and ye shall find; knock, and it shall be opened unto you: For every one that asketh receiveth; and he that seeketh findeth; and to him that knocketh it shall be opened." Now, the dear Lord Jesus was always honest and always exactly accurate. He means here just exactly what He said. If you ask, you shall receive. If you seek, you shall find. If you knock, it shall be opened unto you. And the only possible limitation to that promise, since it means exactly what it says, is in the amount of asking. Literally I understand the Greek to mean "be asking," or "keep on asking, and it shall be given unto you," and "keep on seeking," and "keep on knocking." Evidently what Jesus meant for us to do was to take this promise at literal face value. If there were not another verse in the Bible, this one is all true. All that it implies is true. It is not right to try to find one verse in the Bible to hamstring another, to take away its meaning. All the verses in the Bible are meant to fit exactly. Every other verse in the Bible rightly interpreted would mean the same as this means: that those who ask receive from God; and that if you want things from God you are just to pray, simply to ask for them!

The same thing is the implication of James 4:2: "Ye have not, because ye ask not." It is not right to read into this verse what it does not say. It is not right to search through the Bible and try to find other Scriptures that will limit this verse and make it mean less than it says. Hundreds of times I have read Matthew 7:7, 8 and James 4:2 to congregations and have asked them if they believed it, that everyone who asked received, and that just by asking we could get things from God. In every single case that I ever gave people a chance to reply, some said, "Yes, that is true if we ask according to God's will," or, "If you do not ask amiss," or, "If you ask in faith." And many times when I pressed the matter, some have frankly said, "No, I do not believe it." Now that is practical infidelity. Any verse of the Bible may be believed. Any one is so perfectly stated that it means exactly what it says. And certainly these two passages expressly say that by asking (perhaps continual asking, if necessary) one can get things from God without limiting this promise by other conditions.

How well the Scripture says that unbelief is our besetting sin (Heb. 12:1). We preachers and Bible teachers have grown into the habit of searching through the Bible trying to find other Scriptures to modify the great promises. Some do that way about salvation. They say glibly that they believe in salvation by faith in Christ. But they add that you also have to be baptized, have to keep all the commandments, have to be faithful till death, even though you are saved by faith in the blood. But if it is of works, it is not of grace. If baptism is essential to salvation, then salvation is not wholly by the blood and is not received simply by faith. Thus do men wickedly search through the Bible to make it contradict itself and use one verse of Scripture to tear down another. It is true that the Bible has many simple and varying statements about the plan of salvation. In John 1:12 it is receiving Christ. In John 6:37 it is *coming* to Christ. In Matthew 10:32 and in Romans 10:9, 10 it is *confessing* Christ. In John 3:16 and many other passages the plan of salvation is stated as *believing* in Christ. But the context in every case shows that all these are simply different ways of making it plain that anybody in the world who comes trustingly to Christ will immediately be received, forgiven and saved. These different promises do not give different ways of salvation. They do not even give different steps in the same way to salvation. Salvation is not obtained by long, detailed processes and meeting difficult requirements. Salvation is one simple step to Christ. And if some poor sinner does not understand one way of explaining it, then God gives another explanation to enlighten his poor, darkened mind. But any sinner can safely depend upon any single promise in the Word that offers salvation. When he honestly receives Christ or honestly comes to Christ or sincerely confesses Christ or when he repents or when he trusts, it is all the same thing: God receives him with open arms and for Christ's sake forgives his sins. The extra promises are to make it easier to be saved and not to make it harder.

II. Not Extra "Conditions," but Additional Promises

And so on the matter of prayer, God has given many, many promises so that by many terms He may make it clear how eager and willing He is to answer our prayers. Some preachers in teaching about prayer search through the Bible for every "condition" they can find. Then they proceed something like this: "Now, God is a hardhearted God. He really does not want to answer your prayers, and He will not answer them unless you meet every single requirement. Now here I have found barriers on the road to God. If you get your prayers answered you must climb over every single barrier mentioned in these conditions." Bible teachers sometimes leave the impression that one must unlock a half dozen or more gates before he can get a single prayer answered, and if one has every key but one, he cannot get anything from God. But this is shameful and wicked. The so-called "conditions" are really *promises*, and any Christian who meets a single one of God's promises can get everything that promise of God has offered.

I think this illustration will help you to understand how eager God is to hear our prayers and how He has provided many, many various promises, trying to encourage us to pray. A visitor at a farmhouse, it is said, saw one large hole and three smaller holes at the bottom of an outside door. So he curiously asked the farmer what the holes were for.

"They are for the cat and the kittens," replied the farmer.

"But," said the visitor, "why wouldn't one large hole do? Why can't the kittens go through the same hole as the mother cat?"

"No, that wouldn't do," said the farmer. "When I say, 'Scat,' I mean scat, and every kitten needs his own hole!"

And so every Christian needs his own promise. The blessed promise of God in one verse is just what one Christian needs to stir his faith. But the same promise arouses no spark of hope and faith in the breast of another. So God gives the other Christian another promise.

During one season of prolonged prayer for a definite object, I memorized and delighted in and said over and over in the night John 14:13, 14 and was assured that since I was asking it in Jesus' name my prayer would be granted. At another time I could not seem to get victory alone, and so I found the full assurance I needed when I got a friend to claim with me the promise in Matthew 18:19, "If two of you shall agree on earth as touching any thing that they shall ask, it shall be done for them of my Father which is in heaven." And then there was a long period of time when I delighted daily in that wonderful passage in Mark 11:22–24 that if one would believe he could have whatsoever he said. No one promise can properly reveal the infinite, loving care of our heavenly Father and His willingness to hear His children! It takes all the promises in the Bible, taken at face value, to make us realize how eager God is to hear us pray, and how willingly He will give us what we desire! The truth is that asking, just praying, is the way to get things from God. All these extra promises are intended to encourage us to ask.

III. Asking Really Fulfills All Other Specific Conditions of Prayer

If you study prayerfully all these specific "conditions of prayer," you will find that asking really fulfills them all; that they are not barriers between a Christian and God but rather open doors so the Christian can come through any one of them or all of them. So anxious is God for us to approach Him in prayer and ask for all we need!

1. *Asking in Faith*

Faith is more often mentioned as a condition of prayer than anything else. Remember these marvelous promises of Jesus.

"According to your faith be it unto you."—Matt. 9:29.

"Verily I say unto you, If ye have faith as a grain of mustard seed, ye shall say unto this mountain, Remove hence to yonder place; and it shall remove; and nothing shall be impossible unto you."—Matt. 17:20.

"And all things, whatsoever ye shall ask in prayer, believing, ye shall receive."—Matt. 21:22.

"If thou canst believe, all things are possible to him that believeth."—Mark 9:23.

See also Mark 11:22–24; Matthew 21:21; Luke 17:6. Every Christian should dwell on these promises and as far as he is able, should claim them. Nothing can be clearer than that faith can get all that God has to give.

But it is well to remember that faith is a relative matter. Suppose that on the left-hand side of a piece of paper you write "utter unbelief." Then at the far right-hand side of the paper write "absolute certainty." Now draw a line from one to the other between those two, and any point on that line will be faith. People speak of "perfect faith," but really there is no perfect faith. As soon as you reach certainty, it is knowledge and not faith. Faith is made up of two parts: belief and unbelief. One may have both at the same time. Remember the father who came to Jesus and said, "Lord, I believe; help thou mine unbelief" (Mark 9:24). And that father, who had some unbelief and some belief, got his prayer answered and his boy healed! When you take all the unbelief out of faith, then it is certainty or knowledge, and not faith at all. For example, when we get to Heaven in glorified bodies and are already entered into the eternal blessings there, we will not have faith about salvation. It will be knowledge. I have faith in a check, until I cash it. Then after that I do not have faith in the check. I already have the cash money, and faith has become a certainty. Before the check is cashed I *believe* that the man who signed it has the money in the bank. But after the check has been cashed, then I *know* that he had the money in the bank.

As a few of us students talked together about the things of God when we were in seminary, a student minister said, "If you have any doubt in your heart when you pray, you had just as well quit praying. God will never answer a prayer when there is any doubt in your heart." That grieved me and greatly troubled me then, for I could hardly say of my faith, even when strongest, that I had no doubt. But I soon learned that the young man was mistaken, very greatly mistaken; for God answers our prayers not in relation to our doubts, but in relation to our believing. One can have doubts and faith at the same time. And Jesus said that if one had faith as big as a mustard seed he could move mountains. The father who said with tears, "Lord, I believe; help thou mine unbelief," had doubts, but he had belief too. And he had faith enough to have his boy healed.

A most comforting example from the Bible is that in the twelfth chapter of Acts. There we find a group of earnest Christians spending the night in prayer at the home of Mary, the mother of Mark. They are spending the entire night in prayer; for Peter, the chief apostle, is in prison and is to be slain tomorrow. Wicked Herod has already killed James, the brother of John, and now to please the wicked Jews he is willing to kill Peter. Oh, how fervently these dear Christians prayed!

I can imagine their prayers were something like this: "Oh, Lord, we can't spare Peter! He's the chiefest of the apostles, the boldest preacher of all. Stephen has been stoned; James has been killed with the sword. Oh, Lord, deliver Peter. This night, Lord, bring him out of that jail and deliver him!" Yet their hearts were very heavy in the midst of their prayers, for it seemed impossible for Peter to get out of jail. Sixteen soldiers were on constant guard over this one man within the locked jail. Peter was even sleeping between two soldiers and was bound with two chains. But God heard their prayers.

He sent His angel who woke up Peter, broke off the chains, opened the doors, and brought Peter out into the city. Peter then bethought himself of dear Sister Mary's home and came to report his wonderful deliverance. He knocked at the front gate again and again. The elder Christians were too busy praying to go see who it was. So they sent a little girl named Rhoda. When she heard Peter's voice and knew who it was, she forgot to unlock the gate and ran gladly to tell the praying group, "Peter is here! It is Peter himself knocking at the gate! Peter is out of jail!" They stopped praying long enough to say, "Thou art mad." They thought she was crazy when she announced that their prayers were answered! When she insisted that it was surely Peter, they said, "It is his angel." They thought Peter had already been killed and his spirit was at the door! But Peter kept on knocking, knocking at the front gate; and when finally they let him in, "they were astonished," says the Scripture.

I have laughed again and again at this incident. All night long they had been praying for Peter to get out of jail, and then they did not believe it. But they had faith enough to pray, and that is not all; *they had faith enough to get the answer!* They had many doubts. Who can blame them? But they also had a brokenhearted, pleading, clinging faith that would not let God go until the answer came.

I say that faith can get anything that God has. But if you have faith even too little to measure, even less than a grain of mustard seed that it takes to move mountains, then keep on praying.

The truth is that asking fulfills the requirement of faith, at least in part. For everyone who really prays has some faith, or he would not pray. That is made clear in Romans 10:13, 14 which says,

"For whosoever shall call upon the name of the Lord shall be saved. How then shall they call on him in whom they have not believed? and how shall they believe in him of whom they have not heard? and how shall they hear without a preacher?"

"Whosoever shall call upon the name of the Lord shall be saved." But the Bible has elsewhere many times said that those who *believe* on the Lord Jesus Christ shall be saved. Does *calling* here fulfill the requirement of *believing*? Yes, for the next verse says, "How then shall they call on him in whom they have not believed?" No one calls on God unless he believes there is a God. No one asks anything of God unless he believes that there is a God who answers prayer. No one asks anything of this God who answers prayer unless he has some reasons to hope that even his own prayer will be answered. Calling is believing.

Then how wonderfully clear it is that all who really earnestly and sincerely ask, have some faith in their hearts, or they would not ask. And we have a right, then, to take at face value the words of Jesus, "Ask, and it shall be given you; seek, and ye shall find; knock, and it shall be opened unto you: For every one that asketh receiveth; and he that seeketh findeth; and to him that knocketh it shall be opened." And again we have a right to believe that "ye have not, because ye ask not." It is well to grow in faith. If God gives you, out of His great mercy, a large, vigorous faith, then use it and be glad. But let us remember that asking too is proof of faith. If you want anything from God, JUST PRAY! For asking fulfills all God's requirements.

And suppose a Christian's faith is weak; where can he grow better than on his knees and waiting before God in asking? The place to grow faith is the place of prayer. If you ask in weak faith and begin to get some prayers answered, then your faith will grow. As you prove God, you will grow more and more to see His willingness to answer prayer, what things hinder prayer, and will feel greater freedom to call on God.

So those who pray already have some faith. And those who continue to pray will grow in faith. Simply asking, earnestly and with a surrendered heart, meets all God's requirements about prayer, including the requirement of faith.

2. *Asking According to His Will*

This is another requirement or "condition" for answered prayer. First John 5:14,15 says,

"And this is the confidence that we have in him, that, if we ask any thing according to his will, he heareth us: And if we know that he hear us, whatsoever we ask, we know that we have the petitions that we desired of him."

That is a wonderful promise. But, mark you, God is talking here about *knowing*, and not about believing. Any Christian who knows that he is asking just what God wants to do and asking according to His will about it, knows that God hears him and that he already has the petition he desired of God. And if you reach, in some particular, this wonderful condition of absolutely knowing that you are asking according to God's will, both as to the what and the how of your prayer, that is a wonderful confidence. Take care that you are not discouraged if you do not have such absolute confidence, for this Scripture does not say that those who do *not* know that they are asking in accordance with God's perfect will will *not* receive anything of God. Asking according to His will is the perfection of asking. It is true that if we ask something clearly contrary to the will of God, we should not expect to receive it. But if we ask something clearly in the will of God, we should expect to receive it. And if we ask earnestly for that which we have no reason to believe is against God's will, we should expect to receive our request. God gives us all He can give and still do right.

We are human; we are weak; we are imperfect in knowledge. We do not even perfectly understand the Bible. We are only imperfectly submissive to the leading of the Holy Spirit. So often we do not perfectly know the will of God. Can we, then, never get our prayers answered in such cases? Oh yes, we may! My children do not always know they will get what they ask from me. But they have sincere hope, a belief that they will get many things, without absolute knowledge of it. And so they come and ask, and for their asking they are rewarded.

God really has many reasons which we do not perfectly understand for wanting us to have what our hearts desire and what we crave. Often the thing we dimly hope for and ask for with fear and trembling is the very delight of God's heart to give! We must never measure God's willingness to give by our imperfect understanding of His willingness. He is "able to do exceeding abundantly above all that we ask or think." Both God's ability and His willingness to answer prayer are greater than our ability to ask.

Children, in their asking of parents, go more by their wants and seeming needs than by a perfect understanding of the resources and plans of their parents. And so we frail children of God have a right to come in our ignorance, in our poverty, in our littleness and unworthiness to ask of God all we want and all we need. We have been taken into God's own family. We are the dear children of His heart. God has bought us to Himself at such infinite price in the death of His Son that it is shameful and wicked to think He would be reluctant in His giving or unwilling to answer prayers. So when there is no known reason why our request would be against the will of God, we should in most cases presume that it is in His will. If after honest searching of our motives and an honest examination of the Word of God and a quiet listening to the voice of the Holy Spirit to find what kind of things please God and will be according to His dear will—after that, if we have no rebuke from God or no leading that the thing we desire is against His will, we have a right to come boldly with our requests. For when a born-again child of God comes to his own loving heavenly Father, crying out for his heart's desire, then the presumption is in favor of his getting what he desires.

We know that anybody in the world may freely come to God for salvation. We are already plainly told that it is God's will to save all that come to Him through faith in Jesus Christ. But Romans 8:32 tells us, "He that spared not his own Son, but delivered him up for us all, how shall he not with him also freely give us all things?" Anyone who has been to Calvary for salvation is earnestly urged, then, to be perfectly free to come back for everything else that is needed.

I am saying that our relationship as the born-again children of our dear heavenly Father means that already God has a predisposition to answer our prayers and that unless it is wrong or hurtful, then it is likely according to His will.

So the Scripture, I John 5:14,15, is precious, but it is not meant to be a limitation on our prayer. If you perfectly know the will of God, then ask with all the more boldness. If you do not perfectly know the will of God, then you know that He loves you, that He has given His Son for you, and with Him is just as willing freely to give us all things.

And let us remember this: the way to find the will of God is to pray. While we wait before God, asking, He will help us to modify our prayers if they are not according to His will. His blessed Spirit, who is a prayer-helper to every surrendered Christian, will show us the things that are according to the will of God.

"Likewise the Spirit also helpeth our infirmities: for we know not what we should pray for as we ought: but the Spirit itself maketh intercession for us with groanings which cannot be uttered."—Rom. 8:26.

And this blessed Holy Spirit "maketh intercession for the saints according to the will of God," says Romans 8:27. It is *while we pray* that we best learn what is the will of God. Praying is the way to get our prayers corrected so they can be heard, so they will please God. Then if you want anything from God, JUST PRAY! Simply asking, if it be sincere, honest asking, will lead to asking in the will of God and to meeting all the conditions for answered prayer.

3. *Asking in Jesus' Name*

John 14:13, 14 says,

"And whatsoever ye shall ask in my name, that will I do, that the Father may be glorified in the Son. If ye shall ask any thing in my name, I will do it."

And John 16:24 says,

"Hitherto have ye asked nothing in my name: ask, and ye shall receive, that your joy may be full."

Of course these Scriptures do not mean that we are simply to add onto our prayer the label, "We ask in Jesus' name." It is nowhere said that we are to put such a phrase in our prayers. Saying it does not make it so. Bible Christians often told other people they did things in the name of the Lord, but I do not recall a single Bible prayer in which people told God they were asking in the name of the Lord. God would know without our saying. But to ask in Jesus' name simply means that we know it would please and honor the Lord Jesus and we are making the request for His sake. And the instruction is for us and not for God. We need to check ourselves to see that we ask things for Jesus' sake. We do not need to tell God that it is for Jesus' sake. He knows.

Now here is a blessed promise. Anything we ask because Jesus wants it, we have a right to expect. God will surely give it. This is the same as asking according to His will mentioned above. John 15:7, "If ye abide in me, and my words abide in you, ye shall ask what ye will, and it shall be done unto you," means the same thing. If we are in conscious full surrender to the will of God, and if we have His words abiding in us so well that we know the perfect will of God, then manifestly it will be easy to get the things we want. We will ask things that Jesus wants and get them.

But do you think that no Christian ought ever to pray for his own local and particular needs because he himself is God's child and has a claim on his heavenly Father? Do you think that my four-year-old baby girl, when she is hungry, would need to come to me and put up an argument like this: "Daddy, you will get more honor among men if you don't let me starve. You will probably preach better. You will have more friends. So, Daddy, for your own sake, won't you give me a glass of milk?" Do you think all of that is necessary when my baby is hungry? No, no! She is my own baby. I love her. The very fact that she is hungry and needy puts an obligation on me. I want her to love me, to wish to please me. I want her to be interested in all my work, my happiness, my welfare. But when all that is taken for granted, my own daughter still has a perfect right to come to her daddy to ask for what she wants.

I say it is well for us to ask in Jesus' name when the matters are those which primarily concern His kingdom. And in some sense, of course, every matter concerning our own welfare touches in some point the honor that is due the name of Jesus.

But if we are frank and honest, we will see that when we ask for help in winning a soul, and when we ask for food when we are hungry, we are praying in two different realms. Certainly, when I am asking for the salvation of a soul, I know the Lord Jesus is more concerned than I am, and of course I ought to be far more concerned that Jesus be honored in the matter than that some personal wish of mine should be fulfilled. I should ask for the salvation of that soul in Jesus' name primarily, though my own heart needs the comfort and encouragement of seeing a soul saved. And perhaps it may be my own blood brother, and the earthly ties are strong, and my heart cries out in love for my brother, longing to see him have the happiness and peace and security which I have; yet in that matter, Christ's will ought to be first in my mind.

However, when I pray for daily bread, there is a slightly different emphasis. In the model prayer we are simply taught to pray, "Our Father which art in heaven....Give us this day our daily bread." Asking in Jesus' name is proper and is certain to get results when we can do it. But every born-again child of God has a shortcut when it comes to asking for daily provision and needs. He too is God's child. If God wants to please His Son, Jesus, then God also wants to please all His other children. This is not blasphemy. Many, many times in the Bible we are taught that we stand before the Father much like Jesus Christ does. We are heirs of God and joint heirs with Christ. Christ is our elder Brother. "As he is, so are we in this world" (I John 4:17). Asking in Jesus' name is always proper. And if we can do it honestly, there is the certainty of answer. But if you do not know that you can meet that condition, you still have the open door that every child has with his loving father.

These various promises are not a series of barricades, all of which we must climb over to get anything from God. No, rather, they are different avenues of approach. If you cannot come through one, then God makes another for you. And if you do not know that you can ask in the name of Jesus, yet you have a right to come and say, "My Father." Do you think a hungry baby has to argue with its mother long and profoundly to get food? No, but rather she knows the hunger-cry and is eager to hold the little one to her breast. The mother has as much need to give as the child has to receive. And so God has as much predisposition to answer our prayers as we have to call upon Him.

I think if you study prayerfully and reverently, you will understand what I mean when I say that it is best, of course, to come in Jesus' name, but that even in our own names, as the born-again children of God, we have precious rights and inheritances, we make bold claims since we are already accepted in the Beloved. It is not that we deserve anything, but God loves and gives to us according to our needs and not according to our deserts; according to His mercy and grace and not according to our worthiness. It is well to ask in Jesus' name. But simply asking gets things from God too. The very fact that we can say, "Our Father," involves Jesus' name, for it is through Jesus Christ that we were born into the family of the Father and have a right to ask of Him what we need.

4. *Where Two Are Agreed in Asking*

it shall be done for them. Matthew 18:19 says,

"Again I say unto you, That if two of you shall agree on earth as touching any thing that they shall ask, it shall be done for them of my Father which is in heaven."

But again let us see that this is not an extra condition of prayer which all must meet. Rather, it is simply an extra encouragement to pray, an extra promise. When two people can agree, not simply to ask a thing, but when they are agreed as touching the thing they shall ask, the Scripture says that they shall receive. That simply means that with two people each would be encouraged to believe because the other believed. It means that with two people carefully listening to the Holy Spirit's instructions, they would feel surer of His leading when He helped them to pray for certain things. If one person understands the Scripture to promise a certain thing and if the second person comes to exactly the same opinion and says, "Yes, I too believe that God's Word authorizes us to make this request, to pray this prayer," then naturally they can be more bold in prayer. Two people might each check the other to see that the prayer is not selfish. We are even commanded, "Confess your faults one to another, and pray one for another, that ye may be healed." So when hearts are knit together and guided by the Word and by the Holy Spirit, they can receive from God the things they are perfectly agreed upon in their prayer.

But it is still true that if one trusts the Lord, he may move mountains if there is not another person in the world to agree with him in prayer. If one meets God's promises, those promises are plain and sure. If one is led by the Spirit of God, he may be just as sure that he prays in the will of God as if there were a thousand praying. We do not need a group of prominent citizens to bring political influence upon God when we pray! We do not need the "pull" of somebody else, seemingly more favored of God than we are, when we come to pray. "God is no respecter of persons." The weakest of His children stands before Him, in some measure, in all the beauty and worth of Jesus Christ who has taken his place. So if you can get someone else perfectly agreed with you on the petition, to help you ask God for it, you may do so with assurance. But be sure that God does not require this before you can get your prayers answered. This is not a condition but simply an extra opportunity for prayer.

Do you remember that the greatest answers to prayer in the Bible followed the petition of only one person? Moses alone prayed before God until He agreed to spare rebellious Israel, and God repented when He had planned to blot them out of His book (Exod. 32:9–14). At the faith and command of Joshua alone, the sun stood still in the heavens for about the space of a full day (Josh. 10:13). King Hezekiah alone prayed, even against the discouragement of the Prophet Isaiah and the revelation from God that he was to die. God heard him and added fifteen years to his life (Isa. 38:5)! Elijah alone in Israel prayed, and it rained not for three years and six months. Again he prayed and it rained. Again he alone prayed, and the fire came down from Heaven to burn up the sacrifice and turn the hearts of all Israel back to God! Peter put everybody else out of the room and kneeled down by the body of Dorcas and prayed, and she was raised from the dead (Acts 9:40). And again and again in history, one person has prayed, and God has done marvels. If others agree with you in prayer, that is blessed. If they do not, still all the resources of Heaven are at your command if you simply pray. Just ask God, and in this sincere, earnest asking, all God's conditions are met.

5. Persistence in Prayer

Persistence in prayer has the promise of an answer. Now the parable of the unjust judge and of the widow who troubled the ungodly judge so that finally he gave her her petition, as he said, "lest by her continual coming, she weary me"; then promised,

"And shall not God avenge his own elect, which cry day and night unto him, though he bear long with them? I tell you that he will avenge them speedily."

Persistence in prayer has the promise of an answer. How many precious promises are given to those who wait upon the Lord. They shall not be ashamed, they shall inherit the earth, they shall renew their strength, and the Lord is good to them. And waiting certainly means persistence in prayer. And all the instances in the Bible where people fasted and prayed are implied promises that if we continue steadfastly in prayer, we too shall see the blessing.

But is not persistence simply asking? Is it not simply praying and keeping on praying? There is no time limit on prayer. Sometimes the heart-cry in the fraction of a second is heard and answered. Sometimes people have waited on God for years before they got the desire of their hearts. But these cases all alike are covered by the blessed promise, "Ask, and it shall be given you; seek, and ye shall find; knock, and it shall be opened unto you: For every one that asketh receiveth; and he that seeketh findeth; and to him that knocketh it shall be opened" (Matt. 7:7,8). In fact, the very tense used here implies that one who persistently asks and persistently seeks and persistently knocks, receives and finds and has God's door opened to him.

So I say that asking covers all the conditions, all the requirements to get things from God.

Yes, to teach that we ought to be persistent in prayer is to teach the truth; but that is not all the truth. The full truth includes the fact that many, many times God hears those who pray about a matter only once and then drop it. The truth includes the fact that people oftentimes ask of God and in despair they give up and faint, but a merciful and kindly God who loves His own frail and weak children, does not forget as easily as we do; and He often gives the answer that was desired and longed for, even when the one who prayed has ceased to expect it! How often I have prayed for something, and then because of lack of faith or because I was overwhelmed it seemed with other duties or interests, I have dropped the prayer; then later the answer has come, and I have hardly remembered at first that I had asked for the thing I was so glad to get! Oh, God does not answer us according to our merits but according to His grace! God is more faithful to answer than we are to ask. "For he knoweth our frame; he remembereth that we are dust." He knows the desire of our heart, the earnest need, even though we do not have faith to expect it or strength to continue praying. Persistence in prayer is fine. Oh, that we were more steadfast in daily taking to God all of our needs and claiming all of His bounties! Persistence is a part and parcel of asking. But even weak asking often gets great blessings from God. And when the Saviour gave us a wonderful promise about the answer that comes to persistent praying, He was not putting that as a limitation on prayer nor as the absolute minimum requirement. No, no. In that the Saviour was only making a broader promise for those who seemed not to have much faith or for those who could not, they felt, ask wholly in Jesus' name or who could not meet some other precious promise. This is simply another open door to God for those who feel they cannot enter in as well by some other promise.

So if you want things from God, just pray; simply ask God! Earnest asking meets all God's requirements.

6. *What About Hindrances to Prayer?*

Can just simply praying get hindrances out of the way so God will hear our prayers? Yes, undoubtedly! Honest, earnest asking will lead to the cure of everything that is wrong with our prayers. We are told that wrong relationship between husband and wife hinders prayer (I Pet. 3:1–7). Being unreconciled to our brother hinders prayer (Matt. 5:23, 24); so does unforgiveness (Matt. 6:12,15; Mark 11:25,26; Matt. 18:21–35). Any loved sin, unrepented, unlamented, unforsaken, turns away God's face and hinders our prayers (Isa. 59:1,2; Ps. 66:18; I Pet. 3:12). And James 4:3 says, "Ye ask, and receive not, because ye ask amiss, that ye may consume it upon your lusts." So it is quite clear that sometimes evil motives and covered sin make it so God cannot answer our prayers. In such cases what shall we do?

The answer again, first of all, is simply to pray! For there is something in praying that tends constantly to correct all the hindrances to prayer. Anyone who consciously, earnestly seeks God has already turned in his heart toward the way out of his troubles. And if he will follow it honestly and earnestly, he will be led out into the clear light of sweet fellowship with God and unhindered prayer!

This is made quite clear by the teaching of our Saviour in Matthew 5:23,24, where He says, "If thou bring thy gift to the altar, and there rememberest that thy brother hath ought against thee; Leave there thy gift before the altar, and go thy way; first be reconciled to thy brother, and then come and offer thy gift." Did you notice the significant statement, "and *there* rememberest that thy brother hath ought against thee"? Where is it that your sins are brought to mind? Where is it that God will remind you of the hindrances to your prayers? It is in the very place of prayer itself! If you want God to show you what is wrong, then try to pray. At the very place where you come to talk to God, to make your gift to God, to ask God's blessing, there God is most likely to reveal the things that grieve Him.

Nowhere in the world is the conscience so alive as in the place of prayer! How many, many times I have found it true, that I did not know anything was wrong between me and God, I did not know He was grieved with me, until I began to pray; and there the blessed Spirit of God began to point out the things that were wrong. Many others can live with their consciences all right, except when they try to pray!

One dear woman told me, "Every time I've tried to pray for fourteen years, God has seemed to say to me, 'What about that $800?'" She was left a widow and wickedly burned down her little home and collected $800 insurance. Often she did not remember it, but every time she tried to pray, God brought that sin to remembrance! So if you really want to know what is wrong between you and God, just draw near to Him and begin to pour out your heart. Ask Him for anything you want or need. Be honest with God, and He will be honest with you. If there are things grieving His Spirit, if there are things that block His blessing, do you not think He will tell you so?

And where else would be a better place to have things made right than in the secret closet of prayer? Do you think you would be as apt to have your evil lusts fixed while at the theater? Do you think your covetousness would be as likely to be cured in the business house? Do you believe your intemperate eating will be most likely cured at the table with many delicacies spread out temptingly before you? Do you think your hot anger will be best overcome as you go to contend with your brother? No, no! The place to remedy whatever is wrong with your prayer life is at the place of prayer. Go wait before God. Open your heart honestly to the searchlight of the Holy Spirit. God's finger will surely press upon the sore spot, if you are honest and really want to please Him, if you are really trying to find His will and get His blessing.

Sometimes a hasty prayer does not seem to bring results. One may go on through the little forms of thanksgiving at the table and of public formal prayer, but give any Christian a half-night alone with God or a day of fasting and prayer, and as sure as his heart wants things made right, all the things that grieve God will be brought to light. The Spirit will help the honest Christian to judge them, to confess them and forsake them.

Oh, it is wonderful how prayer—I mean honest, surrendered, loving, persistent prayer—can remove every hindrance between man and God and cure all the ills of our poor, frail Christian lives. Enough prayer, just so it be honest and sincere prayer to God, really seeking God, can cure all hindrances and meet all God's requirements for getting His blessing! You may need to leave the place of prayer, "leave there thy gift before the altar," to be reconciled to a brother before you finish the prayer. Or you may, like Zacchaeus sliding down the tree into the presence of Jesus, make solemn vows to restore fourfold all you have gotten by false accusation and to give half you get to the poor. But nevertheless, the place to settle that is in the presence of Christ, and nowhere else! So if you want anything from God, JUST PRAY!

I would not wait until I got everything fixed. I would not wait until I grew in faith. I would not wait until I had the victory. I would come just as I was, today, and pray. Keep on praying and waiting on God until God fixes all that is wrong, until God gives you the faith you need, until God modifies your prayer or increases it to fit His plan. What you really need to do is simply to pray and honestly seek God. Asking, continually asking, meets God's requirements and completes all the conditions that are necessary to have answers to our prayers.

CHAPTER XIV

"PRAYING THROUGH"

I. No Lost Sinner Need Ever to "Pray Through" to Be Saved.
Trust in Christ Brings Instant Salvation

II. Christians, However, Should "Pray Through"
About Many Things

The Preacher, wise King Solomon at Jerusalem, wrote in Ecclesiastes 3:1,2: "To every thing there is a season, and a time to every purpose under the heaven: A time to be born, and a time to die; a time to plant, and a time to pluck up that which is planted."

And that saying is true. A thing which is proper at one time may not be proper at another time.

When we speak of "praying through," different people according to their background and experience think of two entirely different things. One group of people think of a sinner mourning and begging God for salvation until after long hours of prayer, perhaps, he "gets through to God," as people say. Other people, when we speak of "praying through," think of one who is already a Christian taking his burdens to God and waiting on God until he gets the answer to his prayers. The term "praying through" means entirely different things to different people. We will discuss both meanings here in the light of the Word of God.

I. Sinners Never Need to "Pray Through" to Be Saved. Trusting Christ Gets Instant Salvation Without Begging

The "praying through" doctrine is certainly out of place when applied to the plan of salvation. Some people teach that a sinner, in order to be saved, needs to wait on God and pray and weep and mourn. The theory is that if one prays long enough and earnestly enough, God will finally hear his prayer and save him. Such people use the phrase "getting through to God." They tell how sinners "weep their way through" or how they "pray through" and finally gain the victory and God saves them. And Christian workers who think in such terms urge sinners to keep on praying until they get saved. And if one makes a bright profession, then they say that he "came through gloriously."

Such good people often have what they call a mourner's bench or an altar where sinners are asked to kneel and pray. I remember in my boyhood hearing a good Baptist preacher say, "I guarantee that if you will come to the mourner's bench three nights in succession, you will be saved." No such guarantee is found, of course, in the Bible. I can guarantee something far better than that: if you will trust Jesus Christ the tenth part of a second, committing yourself to Him, He will save you. In fact, the tenth part of a second is too slow for the way God really saves a sinner who trusts Him.

This idea of sinners' "praying through" for salvation is utterly foreign to the Bible. It is unscriptural and hurtful and wrong. I do not mind having sinners put in words their acceptance of Christ as Saviour. I do not mind if a sinner wants to pray and say the words of the publican in the temple, "God be merciful to me a sinner." Perhaps putting the matter in words may sometimes help to make it definite in his mind. But it is certainly foolish and unscriptural to think that any wording of prayer is essential to salvation. It is certainly foolish and unscriptural to believe that any process involving any set length of time is necessary for a sinner to be saved.

I believe that everywhere the invitation that we ought to give to sinners is that they should trust Christ with their whole heart, turning from sin honestly, and then claim Christ openly as Saviour. And we ought to make it clear, as the Bible does from one end to the other, that the very instant a sinner will turn from his rebellion and trust in Christ, then he is saved already and has everlasting life. I think that inquiry rooms are sometimes useful. It is good for a Christian worker to take the Bible and after a sinner trusts Christ to show him the sweet assurances of God's Word that he is already saved, when he has trusted Christ. Certainly it is wise to use the Word of God with unconverted sinners and show them that if they will penitently and honestly trust Christ, He will instantly save them. But the whole idea of mourning in order to be saved, of long seeking after God before He will hear and forgive, is utterly unscriptural. It dishonors God. It beclouds the plan of salvation. It exalts man and man's feelings and man's experience and man's profession, instead of exalting God's marvelous grace to save any sinner instantly on the first turning of childlike faith.

I find often that if churches have an altar where lost sinners are expected to kneel to plead and mourn for salvation, it is unwise to use it. It is best that everyone may understand that salvation is not gotten by knee-action nor public mourning nor by a process of saying certain words or working up certain feelings.

Man, carnal man, has an insatiable desire to be saved by his own works or his own feelings or emotions or experiences, instead of by simple faith. The idea of God's unmerited grace is alien and foreign and distasteful to the carnal mind. Most of the world wants to be saved by its good works. And if good Christians are forced by the Bible to abandon the idea of salvation by works, then they like to substitute salvation by feeling, by earnestness, by certain experiences and emotions. There is no special way a person has to feel in order to be saved. There is no special experience one has to go through, emotionally, in order to be saved. One who believes in Christ, in the sense of committal, dependence, trust, is already born again. Thus, there are people saved who do not remember any emotional crisis and cannot prove by their experience emotionally that they are saved. People often say, "I know I am saved because I was there when it happened." That sounds good, but that is not *the Bible way* to tell that you are saved. I was there when it happened when I was born the first time too, but I do not remember anything about it. I would not know the day I was born, nor who was my father, nor who was my mother, nor who was the doctor, nor how much I weighed, from the simple fact that I was there when it happened. No, the truth of the matter is that I took my mother's word for it. She cherished the day carefully, and she it was who taught me to call her "Mama" and to call my daddy "Papa" and to remember December 11th as my birthday. So I take my first birth and the details about it on the authority of one who knows. And that is the only sure way to know about the second birth too. God's Word tells me that if I trusted Him, I am saved, forgiven. And that is the sure evidence.

To be sure, I later found that there were certain physical similarities and mental and spiritual similarities between my mother and my father, and me. I have evidence within me that I am their child. And so a Christian may have evidence in his own heart that there has been a change, that he is born again. But he must not depend upon his own observation nor opinions in such matters. Let him have the twofold witness, first from the Word of God that when he trusts Christ he is saved; and second, of this Holy Spirit within him that tells him his sin is forgiven; and then he may know he is saved.

Because one had a crisis of great emotion does not prove that he is saved. Because one has a great period of depression and sense of failure and condemnation does not prove that he is lost. The unconverted may have a time of emotional crisis and ecstasy without being saved. You may be sure these people who believe in "praying through to God" for salvation do not believe that they are saved because they pray, until they reach a certain climax of emotion, a certain feeling. But the Bible knows nothing about being saved by feeling. It teaches being saved by faith. And one who trusts God can take His simple word for it that Jesus died for him and loves him and is willing to change his heart at once.

Along with the doctrine of "praying through" for salvation, it would naturally follow that if you know you are saved by *getting* the feeling, then you will believe you are lost when you *lose* the feeling. Most of the people who insist on a time of mourning and pleading and begging God in order for a sinner to get saved, believe that the sinner when he loses his good feeling has lost his salvation. Since they depend somewhat on man's faithfulness in prayer in *getting* saved, it comes natural for them to depend on man's faithfulness in life to *keep* saved.

Such a doctrine dishonors God. It would show man the active one in his salvation and God finally persuaded to cooperate with man. It pictures a God who is hardhearted and indifferent but who can be finally won over by a sinner's pleading. How wicked and unjust that is! What a slander on a God who gave His only Son to die for sinners! How evilly that misjudges the God who sends His Holy Spirit seeking after sinners continually and woos them with every mercy and with the witness of everyone He can get to carry His message! The truth is that no sinner ever sought God but that God had been seeking him long before. No sinner ever became willing to be saved but that God was willing all the time, even while the sinner was yet a rebel. If God has already provided for the salvation of every sinner who will trust Christ, and if He has freely offered salvation and promised it instantly to those who trust Christ, then a sinner can be instantly saved; and there is never any reason for a sinner to delay salvation a moment.

In fact, persistent praying and mourning and pleading on the part of a sinner is sometimes outright sin. It is a human substitution for the one thing God commanded him to do. God commands that the sinner repent. And that means, not a long period of penance as Roman Catholics translate the word in their Bible, but rather an instant turning of the heart from sin to trust Christ. God commands that every sinner everywhere look to Jesus and be saved. And if you spend your time in pleading instead of accepting freely what God has already offered, you not only disobey God, but you make Him out a liar as if He were unwilling to give what He has plainly promised. The only way a lost sinner can obey the Lord in this matter is to trust Christ instantly and depend on Him for salvation, believing that He does, yea, has already done, what He promised to do, as soon as the sinner trusts in Him.

In Dallas, Texas, in an open-air revival one night a number of people came to trust Christ as Saviour. They came to the front to take my hand, after a clear Bible message and after the invitation had made it insistently plain that they were simply to turn their hearts from sin and trust in Christ for salvation and a new heart and everlasting life. Those who came forward were dealt with by me personally. In a few words I probed into their hearts the best I could to see that they came admitting they were wicked sinners and needed forgiveness and if they now at once, wholeheartedly, were putting their trust in Christ. They were a happy bench-full of people when we had the benediction. Then a woman came forward and said to me:

"Brother Rice, don't you think we had better get these people on their knees?"

"Well, praying is always all right," I said, "but what for?"

"To get them to 'pray through,'" she answered.

"But Christ has already 'PAID through,'" I said, "and so a sinner never has to *'pray through.'"*

Christ has done so much for man's salvation, that now man does not have to do anything—neither working, nor keeping commandments, nor weeping, nor praying, nor mourning—but simply to accept what Christ has done for him. The instant there is a living faith in the heart, surrendering to and trusting Jesus, the sinner is saved.

II. Bible Proof Texts That a Sinner Need Never "Pray Through" to Be Saved

There are two kinds of proof in the Bible that a sinner never needs to "pray through" in order to be saved.

First, there are the plain precepts, showing the plan of salvation. Again the Scriptures make it clear that instant salvation is available to those who believe. Consider the following:

"But as many as received him, to them gave he power to become the sons of God, even to them that believe on his name."—John 1:12.

"For God so loved the world, that he gave his only begotten Son, that whosoever believeth in him should not perish, but have everlasting life."—John 3:16.

"He that believeth on him is not condemned: but he that believeth not is condemned already, because he hath not believed in the name of the only begotten Son of God."—John 3:18.

"He that believeth on the Son hath everlasting life: and he that believeth not the Son shall not see life; but the wrath of God abideth on him."—John 3:36.

"Verily, verily, I say unto you, He that heareth my word, and believeth on him that sent me, hath everlasting life, and shall not come into condemnation; but is passed from death unto life."—John 5:24.

"And this is the will of him that sent me, that every one which seeth the Son, and believeth on him, may have everlasting life: and I will raise him up at the last day."—John 6:40.

"Verily, verily, I say unto you, He that believeth on me hath everlasting life."—John 6:47.

"To him give all the prophets witness, that through his name whosoever believeth in him shall receive remission of sins."—Acts 10:43.

"And by him all that believe are justified from all things, from which ye could not be justified by the law of Moses."—Acts 13:39.

"Believe on the Lord Jesus Christ, and thou shalt be saved, and thy house."—Acts 16:31.

No honest reader of the above verses can say that they involve a "praying-through" process in order to be saved. No, they teach instant faith in Christ. The instant one trusts in Christ, he already has everlasting life.

So many other Scriptures which deal with the plan of salvation make it clear that it is instantaneous.

For instance, John 6:37 says,

"Him that cometh to me I will in no wise cast out."

That coming is by faith, of course, a believing act of the heart. It is another way of saying the same thing. But it does not say, "Him that cometh and keeps on coming and keeps on coming unto Me I will in no wise cast out." No, no! There is no time element in that coming. The instant a sinner in his heart comes to God, he has salvation.

Just so in John 1:12 quoted above, "As many as received him" were saved. And the receiving is simply to say "yes" to Jesus and let Him come into the heart. It could not possibly require any prolonged process. When the door is unlocked, the Saviour comes in. When the heart says "yes," the Saviour does what He has longed to do and has been begging to be allowed to do.

In Romans 10:13 we are told:

"For whosoever shall call upon the name of the Lord shall be saved."

But to call, in the sense of that verse, simply means to call once, and it does not mean a prolonged begging and pleading. Nothing like that is taught either in that verse or any other verse in the Bible. The soul that asks Jesus for mercy gets it. The very asking is simple evidence of the faith in the heart, willingness to receive what God has long been offering the sinner. It is not that any certain outward calling is necessary to salvation, for it is not. Rather, one who calls on the Lord simply shows by that and proves that he has trusted. In the following verse, Romans 10:14, the Scripture explains:

"How then shall they call on him in whom they have not believed?"

One who calls on Christ has already trusted Him, and the calling is simply the evidence and proof of the faith that instantly saves. The one who calls has already trusted.

Again, a similar thought is involved in the words of Jesus in Matthew 10:32:

"Whosoever therefore shall confess me before men, him will I confess also before my Father which is in heaven."

One who claims Christ is saved. Certainly it does not take long to own or claim Christ. Again, it is not the confession that saves. Joseph of

Arimathaea was a disciple of Christ and was saved, though he was a secret disciple and had never openly confessed Christ. Confession does not save. Rather, it is the proof that one has trusted Christ in the heart. As little time as it takes a poor sinner to claim Christ as Saviour, in less time than that he has looked to the Saviour, trusted Him in the heart, and has been saved.

So we see that the Bible promises never picture salvation as a long, drawn-out process of those who plead long enough, who mourn long enough, who persist until they touch the heart of a careless and indifferent God. No, no, by all the promises of the Bible, the sinner that turns in his heart to trust Christ is instantly saved. So "praying through" for a lost sinner is never necessary to his salvation.

Do not misunderstand me: I did not say that those who wait long before God and pray much never get saved. I am sure that they often do. But they never get saved until they trust. And if they had put the trusting at the first end of their pleading instead of at the last end, they would have been saved at once and have saved themselves all that delay and that sinful rejection of Christ while they pleaded.

The one sure and blessed way to be saved is to take God's Word for it that when you in your heart turn from sin to trust in Christ Jesus, you already have everlasting life.

In November 1939, at Marquette Manor Baptist Church in Chicago, a young man came to the services and came forward wanting to be saved. He came from Tennessee where they were accustomed to the mourner's bench and to long waiting on God and begging God for salvation. His mother had shouted when she was saved, and he too felt he must shout or he would not know he was saved. I told him that he must trust in Christ, and then I asked dear Brother Frank Sheriff, secretary of the Christian Business Men's Committee, to take the Bible and show the young man how to be saved.

They went to the inquiry room and spent a good long while there together. After the services were dismissed, this young man came back with Mr. Sheriff. The Bible had done its blessed work. He shook my hand and said, "Brother Rice, I don't feel like I wanted to feel, but the Bible says I am saved!"

And so he was, you may be sure, if the Bible said he was saved. When he trusted in Christ he got everlasting life. And later, if he went on to serve the Lord and win souls and grow in grace, I am sure he had all the joy and blessed emotion that he needed. But the emotional crisis is not the sure proof of salvation. Simple trusting in Christ's Word, in His blood, in His love, in His atonement, is the one, instant, sure way to be saved.

III. Bible Examples of People Saved Instantly
Without "Praying Through"

The second way to prove from the Bible that a sinner does not need to "pray through" in order to be saved is by Bible examples. And Bible examples, just as surely as Bible precepts and promises, show that a sinner, when he is saved at all, is saved instantly, without any long period of mourning or pleading, trying to touch the heart of an indifferent God or trying to work up his own soul to the proper state so God can save him. Just so, the examples in the Bible prove that people who were saved, were saved instantly without "praying through."

How delightfully simple are the cases of salvation described in the Bible! Note in John 1:40–42 how Simon Peter was saved:

"One of the two which heard John speak, and followed him, was Andrew, Simon Peter's brother. He first findeth his own brother Simon, and saith unto him, We have found the Messias, which is, being interpreted, the Christ. And he brought him to Jesus."

When Peter got to Jesus he was saved, for he got to Jesus in the heart, as well as in the body.

Philip was saved, evidently, when Jesus "findeth Philip, and saith unto him, Follow me" (John 1:43).

Then we learn of the salvation of Nathanael. Philip, the new convert, went and got Nathanael and brought him to Jesus. One question to Jesus, and all his doubts were removed, and Nathanael was saved (John 1:45–49). In those cases there was certainly not any time of mourning and wailing and weeping and begging in order to get saved.

In the fourth chapter of John, the woman at the well of Sychar in Samaria was saved as Jesus talked to her. When Jesus led the woman to be convicted of her sins and said unto her, when she mentioned the Messiah, that "I that speak unto thee am he" (John 4:26), the woman at once left her waterpot and ran away to win others to Christ and to bring the men out of the city to see Him!

There was certainly not any mourner's bench and wailing and pleading and begging there before she was saved!

And we are told about the Samaritans of the city that many of them were saved even before they could get out of the city to see Jesus. And others, just as soon as they got out to the well and heard Him, were saved and told the woman so!

In Luke 18:13, 14, Jesus tells about the conversion of the publican in the temple in the following brief words:

"And the publican, standing afar off, would not lift up so much as his

eyes unto heaven, but smote upon his breast, saying, God be merciful to me a sinner. I tell you, this man went down to his house justified."

A prayer of seven words, and the poor sinner went home already saved! Certainly there was no so-called "praying through" there.

In Luke 23:42,43, we have the simple story of the conversion of the dying thief on the cross in these words:

"And he said unto Jesus, Lord, remember me when thou comest into thy kingdom. And Jesus said unto him, Verily I say unto thee, To day shalt thou be with me in paradise."

There, in a prayer of nine words, the dying thief was saved, and the entire account takes only two verses. And if there was ever a poor wicked sinner that ought to have to beg for salvation, it seems to me it would have been this man, a condemned criminal deserving to die by his own admission. Yet he simply called on Jesus and got salvation instantly.

In the book of Acts we find many examples of how people were saved. Poor Cornelius, in heathen darkness and ignorance, fasted and prayed and begged God, but it did no good. God told him to send for Peter, who would tell him words "whereby thou and all thy house shall be saved." Peter started a good sermon, but just as soon as he said that "whosoever believeth in him shall receive remission of sins," Cornelius and his whole family were converted. They trusted Christ and were instantly saved. All the weeping and mourning did not do any good for him, and it never did any good for anybody else, as far as getting him saved is concerned. I am glad Cornelius was earnest and sincere and sorry for his sins. I do not mind tears when a sinner turns to Christ. But I want us to remember that God is already, instantly ready to save anybody who will trust in Him.

In Acts 13:6–12 we have the story of the conversion of the deputy Sergius Paulus at Paphos in Crete. Paul and Barnabas preached to him, and we are told:

"Then the deputy, when he saw what was done, believed, being astonished at the doctrine of the Lord."

That was certainly an instantaneous conversion, wasn't it?

In Acts 16:14,15, we are told how Lydia was converted:

"And a certain woman named Lydia, a seller of purple, of the city of Thyatira, which worshipped God, heard us: whose heart the Lord opened, that she attended unto the things which were spoken of Paul. And when she was baptized, and her household, she besought us, saying, If ye have judged me to be faithful to the Lord, come into my house, and abide there. And she constrained us."

It was as simple as this: God opened her heart, and she believed and was saved. That seems to have been a very quiet conversion, but it was certainly genuine. And there was no long process of mourning and wailing or waiting and begging God in her case. God opened her heart, and she saw she was a sinner and trusted Christ, and Paul was convinced, and she was baptized.

Acts 16:32-34 tells of the conversion of the Philippian jailer and his whole household. Read it for yourself, and you will see that there was no time of mourning or weeping. In fact, the earthquake came at midnight (Acts 16:25,26), and after that the whole family was saved and baptized and Paul and Barnabas had their backs washed and supper prepared, and still it was not yet day. The whole family were taught the word of the Lord, were won to Christ, were taken out and baptized; the apostles had their backs washed and had eaten a good meal before morning!

No, the mourner's bench plan of salvation is not in the Bible. I mean that the Bible does not teach that anybody needs to take a long period of time to find God. God's way is for the sinner to turn his heart from his sins, penitently, to trust in Jesus Christ, and then he is instantly saved.

I mean no unkindness to good and earnest people who are anxious for sinners to be "genuinely saved." I am anxious too for them to be saved. But I remind you that the genuineness of their salvation does not depend on how long they pray. When God does the saving, He does it genuinely. A lady not long ago said about another, "I believe that she is *thoroughly saved.*" Well, "thoroughly saved" is the only kind of saved there is. God never does halfway save anybody, and God saves everyone who trusts Christ for salvation and does it thoroughly and eternally.

Someone says that when a child is born there must be a period of travail. Yes, but the child does not do the travailing. The mother does that. And the Bible does not teach that unsaved people should travail, but rather it says, "As soon as Zion travailed, she brought forth her children" (Isa. 66:8). Christians need to travail over lost sinners. But lost sinners simply need to repent and trust Christ. Lost sinners do not need to "pray through." They need simply to accept what Christ has already "paid through" for them. Salvation is instantly available for everyone who will accept it as a free gift of God, paid for by the blood of Christ.

IV. But Christians Ought Often to "Pray Through" With Long, Continued Supplications and Waiting on God Until God Answers Their Prayers

Again we remind you that what is seasonable and proper in one case is not seasonable and proper in other cases. The Scriptures certainly teach that the kind of prayer that is proper for a Christian is far different from the kind of prayer that is proper for a lost sinner on the question of salvation. On a matter which is already freely offered to everybody in the world, it is unbelief and rebellion not to believe God and accept what He offers. He has offered salvation to every person in the world who will receive it. But on other matters, we may never get the assurance of God's will and that He will give us certain things, unless we wait on God until He can work out His will in our lives. Persistent, believing, intercessory, agonizing prayer is proper for a Christian when he takes his burdens to God.

Note some Bible examples of such persistent prayer by people who were Christians:

Read how Jacob wrestled with God and prevailed. Genesis 32:24–29 tells the story as follows:

"And Jacob was left alone; and there wrestled a man with him until the breaking of the day. And when he saw that he prevailed not against him, he touched the hollow of his thigh; and the hollow of Jacob's thigh was out of joint, as he wrestled with him. And he said, Let me go, for the day breaketh. And he said, I will not let thee go, except thou bless me. And he said unto him, What is thy name? And he said, Jacob. And he said, Thy name shall be called no more Jacob, but Israel: for as a prince hast thou power with God and with men, and hast prevailed. And Jacob asked him, and said, Tell me, I pray thee, thy name. And he said, Wherefore is it that thou dost ask after my name? And he blessed him there."

There is good evidence to believe that Jacob had already trusted in the Lord. He had met God at Bethel as described in Genesis, chapter 28; but now, Jacob prevailed with God and got a new name and a new blessing and went out the next morning to meet Esau unafraid after an all-night time of prayer and wrestling with God.

Jacob certainly "prayed through" about the problem of meeting his bloodthirsty brother, who had sworn to kill him. Christians have a right to "pray through" about their problems and burdens.

Daniel set his face to seek the Lord by prayer and supplication with fasting and sackcloth and ashes (Dan. 9:3). Daniel "prayed through" until the Angel Gabriel came and made known to Daniel the thing he was so greatly concerned about—the future of the nation Israel which had so greatly sinned against God. Again in the tenth chapter, Daniel "prayed through," going for three full weeks without eating any pleasant bread, any meat or wine; and finally his prayer was answered, and divine revelation was given to him, and his heart's burden was eased.

Nehemiah "prayed through" about the sad condition of the desolate city of Jerusalem during the captivity. Nehemiah 1:4 says:

"And it came to pass, when I heard these words, that I sat down and wept, and mourned certain days, and fasted, and prayed before the God of heaven."

Some of Nehemiah's prayer is given to us; how contritely he pled with God! But his prayer was heard, the heart of the king was touched, and God sent Nehemiah back to build the walls of the city so dear to his heart, because he "prayed through."

When a group of Israelites were going back from Babylon to Jerusalem under Ezra the scribe, they proclaimed a fast at the River Ahava, and there they afflicted themselves and fasted and prayed and begged God for protection from the bandit bands that roamed the country, since they were ashamed to ask the king for soldiers, having told him that God would care for them. And they "prayed through," as Ezra 8:21–23 tells us, and God was entreated for them and protected them. They arrived safely and unharmed at Jerusalem.

The Jews fasted and prayed that God would spare their lives during the time of Queen Esther in Persia, and in three days and nights they "prayed through," and the Jews had salvation and then vengeance on their enemies.

The people of Nineveh fasted and prayed, and God repented of the evil that He thought to do to their great city and did it not. Their fasting was not in order to get saved, but that God would relent and not destroy the great wicked city as He had announced through Jonah that He would do.

In the New Testament it is the same way. Preceding Pentecost it is certainly fair to say that the disciples "prayed through." Acts 1:14 says:

"These all continued with one accord in prayer and supplication, with the women, and Mary the mother of Jesus, and with his brethren."

Supplication, that is, pleading, is certainly all right *for a child of God wanting to become a soul winner.* It is not in order *for a lost sinner wanting to be saved.* The sinner simply needs to trust and accept the salvation so freely offered. But the Christian needs God to work him over and prepare him for soul winning and endue him with power from on high, and he should "pray through."

Paul the apostle was converted on the road to Damascus. After his conversion he went three days and nights praying and fasting (Acts 9:9,11). Paul "prayed through" and got his eyesight back and was filled with the Holy Ghost to begin his marvelous ministry.

In Acts 13:1–4 we see again where a group of Christians "prayed through." They ministered unto the Lord and fasted until God told them they should send away Barnabas and Saul as missionaries. They "prayed through" for divine leading. And then again they fasted and prayed and "prayed through" for divine power on these preachers, and sent them forth.

In the twelfth chapter of Acts, verses 1 to 17, we see how a group of Christians gathered at the home of Mary, the mother of John Mark, and "prayed through" until the Apostle Peter was released from jail by an angel.

That was long-continued, heart-searching, heartbroken praying. And that is the example of New Testament Christians everywhere.

In this case I have given the examples first. But the precepts about Christians' "praying through" prove the same thing. God does want His own children, born-again Christians, to wait on Him and plead for the things they need, particularly for power and help in the things they cannot do themselves.

For example, in Luke 11:5–8, Jesus gave this story:

"And he said unto them, Which of you shall have a friend, and shall go unto him at midnight, and say unto him, Friend, lend me three loaves; For a friend of mine in his journey is come to me, and I have nothing to set before him? And he from within shall answer and say, Trouble me not: the door is now shut, and my children are with me in bed; I cannot rise and give thee. I say unto you, Though he will not rise and give him, because he is his friend, yet because of his importunity he will rise and give him as many as he needeth."

Notice the key word in verse 8: "Because of his *importunity* he will rise and give him as many as he needeth." Importunity is the way for a Christian to get things from God. And that passage evidently refers to a child of God wanting power to win others. A Christian has a right to go to God and beg for the bread of life to give others. Go, Christians, confess to God that "a friend of mine in his journey is come to me, and I have nothing to set before him." Concerning this matter of Holy Spirit power to win souls, do not take a denial. Bread for sinners is only given to those who learn the secret of "importunity." The sinner need never "pray through" to be saved; but a Christian who wants the supernatural, miracle-working power of the Holy Spirit has a right to wait on God, yea, is taught to do so by the plain word of our Saviour Himself.

Again Jesus taught importunate prayer in Luke 18:1–8 as follows:

"And he spake a parable unto them to this end, that men ought always to pray, and not to faint; Saying, There was in a city a judge, which feared not God, neither regarded man: And there was a widow in that city; and she came unto him, saying, Avenge me of mine adversary. And he would not for a while: but afterward he said within himself, Though I fear not God, nor regard man; Yet because this widow troubleth me, I will avenge her, lest by her continual coming she weary me. And the Lord said, Hear what the unjust judge saith. And shall not God avenge his own elect, which cry day and night unto him, though he bear long with them? I tell you that he will avenge them speedily. Nevertheless when the Son of man cometh, shall he find faith on the earth?"

Note that the sole end of the parable is "praying through." Jesus spoke this parable "to this end, that men ought always to pray, and not to faint."

Even a poor widow can plead with a judge that he may hear her cause and deliver her from her adversaries and give her justice. And shall not God's own children cry unto Him day and night? "And shall not God avenge his own elect, which cry day and night unto him, though he bear long with them? I tell you that he will avenge them speedily."

Verse 8 above hints that when the Saviour comes He will find little faith on the earth. People do not believe in prayer. People do not "pray through." People do not pay the price in heart-searching, in long hours, in fasting, in confession, in restitution. But when God's people really "pray through," then they can have revival, can have protection, can have provision, can have anointing of the Holy Spirit, can have anything God has for His people. "Pray through"!

The unconverted sinner needs simply to trust in Christ and instantly accept salvation. But one who is already a child of God has a right to camp on God's doorstep and persistently, insistently, plead the promises of God and refuse to take a denial, until that which is needed, that which is imperative to win souls and have revivals, is received from God.

Oh, may God's people be encouraged to pray, pray, pray—may they be encouraged to PRAY THROUGH!

Keep on praying
  Till you pray it through,
Keep on praying
  Till you pray it through.
God's great promises
  Are always true;
Keep on praying
  Till you pray it through.

CHAPTER XV

WHY FAST AND PRAY?

*Why Christians Should Sometimes Leave Off Sleep, Nice Clothes, Family
Life or Other Comforts to Pray and Do Nothing but Pray*

The greatest saints of God throughout the Bible often fasted. Fasting is
often connected with wholehearted prayer, with mourning, with repentance,
with seeking deliverance from enemies or wisdom from above. Moses
fasted forty days on Mount Sinai, and our Saviour fasted forty days in the
wilderness. The Bible tells how Joshua, David, Ezra, Nehemiah, Daniel, the
disciples of John the Baptist, Anna, the apostles, Paul and Barnabas, and
others fasted and prayed. Saints of God got their prayers answered when
they waited on God with fastings and prayer. Since Bible times, the greatest men of prayer have oftentimes fasted as well as prayed. A Christian is
in good company when he fasts and prays.

During the earthly ministry of Christ, the disciples of John the Baptist
fasted, the Pharisees fasted, and naturally inquiries were made concerning
the disciples of our Saviour. Jesus answered,

*"Can ye make the children of the bridechamber fast, while the bride-
groom is with them? But the days will come, when the bridegroom shall
be taken away from them, and then shall they fast in those days."*—
Luke 5:34,35.

So the Saviour not only fasted; He also taught His disciples to fast, and
they did fast after He was taken away.

The only restriction that our Saviour put upon fasting is that it was to be
sincere. Men should not disfigure their faces to appear unto men to fast. A
boastful, self-righteous flaunting of religious ceremonies such as that practiced by the Pharisees, hypocrites in the days of our Lord, is offensive to
God, to be sure. But hypocrisy in anything else is a sin as truly as in the case
of fasting. Christians should not fast as hypocrites, but they certainly should
fast as Jesus fasted, as Paul fasted, as Barnabas and many others fasted.

I. What Is Fasting and Prayer?

Fasting is such a lost art, so little practiced, so little taught, that we need
to consider here what is the meaning of fasting. How does fasting add to
prayer? Does it mean simply to abstain from food? Is there virtue in fasting
when we do not pray? What is the spiritual significance of fasting?

First, fasting means putting God first. There are times when one ought
to eat and praise God for the food as did David when he said, "Bless the
LORD, O my soul, and forget not all his benefits…Who satisfieth thy mouth

with good things; so that thy youth is renewed like the eagle's" (Ps. 103:2, 5). Sometimes eating is the will of God. There are times also when it pleases God for His child quietly and trustfully to lie down to sleep, laying aside all his burdens and sweetly resting in the arms of God's care. "He giveth his beloved sleep" (Ps. 127:2). David could say, "I laid me down and slept; I awaked; for the LORD sustained me" (Ps. 3:5). There are times when men should enjoy the pleasures of family life. "Marriage is honourable in all, and the bed undefiled" (Heb. 13:4). We are told that, "Whoso findeth a wife findeth a good thing, and obtaineth favour of the LORD" (Prov. 18:22). "Every good gift and every perfect gift is from above, and cometh down from the Father of lights, with whom is no variableness, neither shadow of turning" (Jas. 1:17). Let us enjoy the blessings of God, whether food or drink or rest or Christian fellowship or homelife or service. Let us give God the glory for them all. But certainly there are times when we should turn our backs upon everything else in the world but seeking the face of God. Such times should be times of fasting and prayer.

Fasting, then, should mean that one determines to seek the face of God and for a time, at least, to abstain from other things in order to give the whole heart to prayer and waiting on God. Fasting and prayer means to leave off the lesser blessings for the greater one, the lesser duty for the far more important duty. There are times when preachers should quit preaching, teachers should quit teaching, and all of us should leave off Bible study even, should even cease to win souls in order to pray. The apostles said, "We will give ourselves continually to prayer, and to the ministry of the word" (Acts 6:4). They put praying before preaching. That is what Jesus meant when He commanded the disciples not to depart from Jerusalem, but to tarry in Jerusalem as they prayed for the power of the Holy Spirit before Pentecost. Thus, fasting and prayer simply means to put prayer first, before the desire for food or before anything else that would take our energy or our attention too much from the matter of prayer.

Ordinarily, fasting means to abstain from food. But the same spirit will oftentimes lead to abstaining from other things as well. Sometimes those who fasted in Bible times fasted without any kind of drink, as well as without food. The men of Nineveh did "not feed, nor drink water" (Jonah 3:7). Queen Esther and her maidens and Mordecai and other Jews, before the days of Purim, when Jews were to be destroyed by the plot of wicked Haman, did not eat food nor drink water for three days (Esther 4:16). So when God planned to give the Law to Israel from Mount Sinai, the command was given to the people to wash their clothes and "come not at your wives" (Exod. 19:14, 15). And husbands and wives are commanded, "Defraud ye not one the other, except it be with consent for a time, that ye may give yourselves to fasting and prayer" (I Cor. 7:5). The spirit of fasting simply means that one, for the time being, is willing to abstain from otherwise normal and proper duties or pleasures that he may give himself wholly to the business of prayer. So fasting is really putting God first when one prays, wanting God more than one wants food, more than one wants sleep, more than one wants fellowship with others, more than one wants to attend to business. How could a Christian ever know that God was first in his life, if he did not sometimes turn aside from every other duty and pleasure to give himself wholly to seeking the face of God?

There are many other occasions in life when men do without food. At a football training table, men gladly deprive themselves of sweets and certain foods likely to hinder mental alertness and physical fitness and endurance. Should we do less for Jesus Christ? One can run a race better if he has not eaten just beforehand. Swimmers well know that it is dangerous to eat much before swimming lest they suffer from cramps. Public speakers and singers customarily do not eat in the evening until after the important period of concentration and perfect control necessary for their public appearance. If I can preach better without eating, then why cannot I pray better without eating? If a businessman can concentrate better on his figures, in some emergency, without having his stomach loaded with food, then why cannot a Christian pray better when all his energies are given to that one thing? When men are wholly absorbed in grief for a loved one, they are not hungry; they do not want to eat. Then when one is wholly absorbed in passionate and most earnest prayer, why should he not be glad to do without food?

In truth, when Christians fast, it is often true that they simply do not want to eat; they have no desire for food. Many, many times I have been so busy about the Lord's work and so absorbed in it that I had no taste for food. Fasting simply means putting God first in a very intense way for a period of time and for very definite purposes.

Second, fasting means *persistence* in prayer. We may pray *often*, but most of us do not pray *much*. Our prayers are transitory, indefinite and brief. On the other hand, to fast and pray simply means that one settles down to the business of praying with a persistence that will take no denial. The widow who haunted the unjust judge with her persistent pleading that he avenge her of her adversary (Luke 18:3) probably neglected her housework while she did it and possibly did not eat! I suppose even the unjust judge did not get to enjoy his food or his rest, so steadily did she pursue him with her urgent pleas! Real persistence in prayer, letting other things go by and giving God the right of way, often involves fasting. In fact, I think there is little point to fasting or depriving ourselves of other things simply as a matter of self-punishment, if we do not pray. If a man is to be just as absorbed in business as ever, with no more thought for God, then what good would it do him, spiritually, to do without food or drink or sleep? Fasting is the accompaniment of persistent, fervent prayer that will not be denied!

Third, fasting is the deliberate clearing of the way for prayer, laying aside weights and hindrances. In Hebrews 12:1,2 we are commanded: "Wherefore seeing we also are compassed about with so great a cloud of witnesses, let us lay aside every weight, and the sin which doth so easily beset us, and let us run with patience the race that is set before us, Looking unto Jesus the author and finisher of our faith." Since it is faith that the Holy Spirit is speaking about, and since all the holy examples and witnesses given were men of persistent, faithful prayer, we surely will make no mistake to interpret this verse as a command to lay aside hindrances to prayer. "Lay aside every weight." Eating may be good in its place, but certainly sometimes it is a weight that holds down our prayers. Sleep may sometimes be proper, but doubtless many, many times Christians sleep when they ought to be praying. Business in itself may be proper, and sometimes men ought to do with their might what their hands find to do; but business, "the care of this world, and the deceitfulness of riches, choke the word, and he becometh unfruitful" (Matt. 13:22). Fasting is simply laying aside every weight, every hindrance to prayer. A Christian ought to be willing, as often as necessary, to abstain from anything that hinders getting the answer to his prayers, to wait on God until everything that hides the face of God is removed, waiting before God until really he gets the full assurance that his prayer is heard and will be answered to the glory of Christ! When we fast and pray, we are simply trying to lay aside sincerely anything that hinders our prayers.

Fourth, to fast when we pray ought to be simply claiming the answer to our prayers. To fast when we pray should mean "I have set myself to seek God as long as necessary and as earnestly as necessary until He hears me and answers me." It requires faith to pray, for "he that cometh to God must believe that he is, and that he is a rewarder of them that diligently seek him" (Heb. 11:6). Then it requires *more faith* to fast when we pray. Fasting pictures greater desire, greater determination and greater faith. One who fasts thereby signifies his sincerity and his confidence that God can be reached and that God will answer and bless his sincerity and definiteness and willingness to know and do the will of God. Prayer is too often a shallow thing, a light and insincere thing. That is surely one reason why so many, many prayers are never answered. Fasting, then, should be simply an evidence of our earnestness, our fervor, our faith.

Fifth, fasting is very properly an expression of mourning. When people are overwhelmed with sorrow, they often do not eat. They have no desire for food: they could not enjoy it. Sometimes when people are overwhelmed with grief, the body will not digest food. Nature itself teaches that fasting is the proper accompaniment and expression of mourning.

In the Bible we have many examples of fasting as an expression of grief.

David fasted while he wept over the first child of Bathsheba when the babe was smitten by the Lord (II Sam. 12:16,21). The same spirit must have animated Samuel when he "cried unto the LORD all night" in grief over the rejection of Saul (I Sam. 15:11). That was the spirit of fasting, though the word is not used in that passage. The men of Nineveh fasted, with sackcloth and ashes, a symbol of the deepest mourning (Jonah 3:5–7). As people feast at weddings and other occasions of rejoicing, so they fast at occasions of mourning. Thus, the Saviour said that when the Bridegroom was taken away, His disciples would fast. Hence, those who are in sorrow do well sometimes to fast as they seek the comfort of God's face. Those who have sinned and grieve in penitence do well to fast as they turn their hearts from sin and confess their failures and faults and try to make restitution. Fasting fits exactly with repentance and with sorrow for sin.

II. Things We Can Get by Fasting and Prayer

Fasting is an aid and adjunct of prayer. Some things never come to a child of God "but by prayer and fasting." If prayer is good, then more prayer is better. If earnest prayer pleases God, then sometimes, surely, He is pleased when the prayer is so earnest that we do not want food nor drink nor sleep nor any other ordinary pleasure. If God is pleased for us to seek Him, then sometimes, surely, it pleases Him for us to lay aside every weight, abstain from everything that might absorb our energy and interest and thought, that we may give ourselves wholly to the matter of prayer. We name here some things that Christians have a right to seek by prayer and fasting; things which God has, in times past, given His people because of their prayer with fasting.

1. *Help in time of trouble often comes from fasting and prayer.* God says, "Call upon me in the day of trouble: I will deliver thee, and thou shalt glorify me" (Ps. 50:15). A time of trouble is a good time to pray. If it is a good time to pray and if the trouble is severe, then it is a good time to fast too. Joshua and the elders of Israel remained prostrate before the ark of God from morning until evening without eating after the Israelites were defeated by the men of Ai (Josh. 7:6). It was a time of distress, of defeat, of shame and of fear. The very destiny of the nation seemed at stake. When they fasted and prayed, God showed them the sin that hindered victory.

When in the days of the judges, the eleven tribes of Israel came up against Benjamin by God's command, and when forty thousand were slain in two days, "then all the children of Israel, and all the people, went up, and came unto the house of God, and wept, and sat there before the LORD, and fasted that day until even" (Judg. 20:26). In their defeat and sorrow they wept and called on God and fasted. God heard and delivered them and the next day gave them victory. The time of defeat is a fine time to pray with fasting!

When Queen Esther and Mordecai and the Jews in captivity were in danger of being blotted out of the race, they fasted and prayed. Their trouble led to the sincerity and fervor of their praying, such praying that they did not eat nor drink. When Ezra feared the brigands of the wilderness, he called a fast at the River Ahava (Ezra 8:21–23). The time of trouble is a proper time for fasting and prayer.

Let all those who are in trouble call upon God. If they find difficulty in getting an answer from Heaven, then let them fast and pray, sincerely laying everything else aside, as far as necessary, to seek God's face and find His will and blessing.

2. *To find what is wrong, what displeases God,* we should sometimes fast and pray. When Joshua and the elders of Israel did not know why God had allowed them to be defeated by Ai, they fasted and prayed until God showed them the sin of Achan and about the hidden wedge of gold, the silver and the Babylonish garment. Many a Christian who does not prosper could learn the reason if he would wait before God in such sincerity and abandon of self that he would not eat, would not sleep or would not carry on the regular affairs of life until God revealed what was wrong.

3. *Genuine repentance sometimes involves fasting and prayer.* One may confess his sins without repenting of them. Often, unless we deliberately take time for meditation and examination of our hearts and waiting on God, we have no real sense of sin, no genuine horror at our guilt. I know that in order to be saved, one may turn immediately to Christ, as soon as he knows himself a sinner and knows that Christ died for him, if he will. But alas, many times those of us who are already saved have trouble turning our hearts away from sin! I believe that in Bible times God's saints often took time to fast and wait before God in order that they might genuinely, with contrite hearts, forsake their sins and mourn over them. In Zechariah 12:10–14 we are told how at the second coming of Christ, the Jews will mourn over Christ "as one mourneth for his only son, and shall be in bitterness for him, as one that is in bitterness for his firstborn." And that mourning in Jerusalem over their sins will be as great as the mourning in the valley of Megiddo over the dead! "Every family will mourn [apart], and their wives apart." This evidently pictures the broken hearts of people who long to turn away from their sins and who take time to see the enormity of their sin in rejecting the Saviour. We are commanded, "Be afflicted, and mourn, and weep: let your laughter be turned to mourning, and your joy to heaviness. Humble yourselves in the sight of the Lord, and he shall lift you up" (Jas. 4:9, 10). I know God is merciful and ready to forgive instantly all who sincerely turn in the heart to Him. But I know too that oftentimes our pretended turning to God is insincere and shallow with no real sorrow for sin, no effort at restitution, and no genuine change in attitude of heart. The

ghastly wickedness of sin is hidden from us lighthearted moderns. Surely often it would please God if we would take time apart to search our hearts and find what displeases God and wholly forsake, as far as we can consciously do so, our sins. If we spend enough time in prayer we can learn the meaning of the old song,

Return, O holy Dove, return,
Sweet messenger of rest!
I hate the sins that made Thee mourn,
And drove Thee from my breast.

Fasting will help us to break up the fallow ground of our hearts.

4. *Fasting and prayer often lead to victory over sin.* The world has many Christians who have trusted Christ, who sincerely love Him, who are going to Heaven—yet Christians who have no daily victory over sin. Everywhere I go I find Christians who say they cannot quit cigarettes, they cannot control their tempers, they have trouble in surrendering even enough to give God regularly the tithe. Christians find it hard to forgive one another and are constantly falling under the temptation of Satan. Is there victory for such Christians? Yes, there is. But sometimes it is found only in the time of fasting and prayer, waiting on God and laying aside every weight, every duty, every pleasure that might interfere with our wholehearted prayers. Many times I have seen things happen in protracted seasons of prayer that would not happen in the ordinary course of events.

In an all-night prayer meeting, a number of men including a young preacher gave up tobacco. One Christian man confessed to his pastor his sin of enmity and gossip. A grown son, now on the foreign mission field, confessed to his violent temper and mistreatment of his mother and gained courage to right the wrong he had done. In days of fasting and prayer, when God is put first, when the heart has been searched, when sins have been confessed, when restitution has been made, when one's will is surrendered to God, then God has often done great things for the penitent beggar who waits before Him.

We need not think that our hunger gains any favor with God. No, God has abundant mercy for all our needs, and we cannot, need not, buy it. But on the other hand, God does want sincerity and fervor and single-heartedness in our praying.

Every Christian, I think, should occasionally fast and pray, waiting before God until he gets the victory that he needs. I remember with great joy one night when I waited before God alone in my room until 1:30, begging God for victory over some things in my own life and begging also for the power of the Spirit on the revival in which I was engaged. And God heard and answered in both matters, gloriously. If you do not have victory over sin, then wait before God; and pay whatever price is necessary to secure His favor and the assurance of His help.

5. *Heavenly wisdom received in prayer and fasting.* In Acts 13:1–3 we have a remarkable incident showing how men who fasted and prayed got direct leadership of the Holy Spirit. Here is that sweet passage:

"Now there were in the church that was at Antioch certain prophets and teachers; as Barnabas, and Simeon that was called Niger, and Lucius of Cyrene, and Manaen, which had been brought up with Herod the tetrarch, and Saul. As they ministered to the Lord, and fasted, the Holy Ghost said, Separate me Barnabas and Saul for the work whereunto I have called them. And when they had fasted and prayed, and laid their hands on them, they sent them away."—Acts 13:1–3.

Notice that "as they ministered to the Lord, and fasted" the Holy Ghost told them whom to send, that is, Barnabas and Saul. Notice again, "when they had fasted and prayed, and laid their hands on them, they sent them away." Twice in that short passage we are told that these prophets and teachers fasted. They fasted first as they prayed for wisdom. They fasted second as they prayed for power upon these men they were sending forth as the first foreign missionaries in New Testament times. And when these men laid their hands upon the heads of Paul and Barnabas and sent them away, they were "sent forth by the Holy Ghost." And marvelous wonders attended their ministry! We too could have plain leading, we could know the will of God, we could have a plain path for our feet, if we were willing to wait before the Lord, ministering unto Him, fasting and praying! You have a problem about raising your family, about making a living, about where you should serve for Christ, about what course you should take in some particular matter; does not God hear your prayer for wisdom? Do you have doubts and troubles and no assurance of mind? Then why not just set a time and wait before God until you get the answer? If it takes fasting as well as praying, if it takes giving up other matters, then do it and get the blessing that God has for you. You can find the will of God if you seek it sincerely, unstintedly and without limit in fasting and prayer.

6. *Intercession for others is answered when we fast and pray.* Most of our praying is for ourselves. Yet every Christian, surely, admits his responsibility to pray for others. Do you pray for your pastor; for the editor of *The Sword of the Lord;* for some foreign missionary? Do you pray regularly for some loved one who is unsaved? Do you pray for someone who has asked you to help bear the burden of his load day by day, whatever it is? Well, our own needs take up most of the time in our little, puny, short praying. If you would pray for others, pray happily, pray with assurance that you are heard, then take time to "pray through." And any long, extended time of fervent prayer may involve fasting as well as prayer. It takes more than a little short

prayer to get away from our own selfishness. We have, each one of us, so many needs that we will not do our duty in praying for others unless we take an extended time for it, unless we really wait before God long enough to get out of our selfishness and get victory over our own immediate needs. Would you be an intercessor? Do you want to learn to pray for others? Then set aside long periods of time in which to pray with sufficient time to search your heart and to know the mind of Christ. Take time without distraction for eating and drinking or sleeping perhaps, and God will surely give you part of the blessed burden that is on Jesus Christ, the burden that is for others.

7. *Holy Spirit power comes in answer to fasting and prayer.* There are many things for which we can pray and at once receive the answer. I believe that a sinner can trust in Christ and be saved at once, without delay. The thief on the cross had only to ask, and he was forgiven. The publican in the temple had only to say, "God be merciful to me a sinner," and went down to his house justified. I know of no Scripture that teaches that a lost sinner needs to beg and plead or afflict himself and so try to touch the heart of God in order to be saved. When the poor, sinful will is ready to surrender and put his trust in Christ, then God is immediately ready to forgive and save. However, though God is instantly willing to forgive the sinner, there are other matters about which we should expect to pray longer. Certainly one of the blessed teachings of the Saviour, emphasized many times, is that we should be persistent in prayer. The widow before the unjust judge prayed again and again (Luke 18:1–8). Jesus, teaching the disciples to pray, first gave them the model prayer, called the Lord's Prayer, and then told them about the neighbor who came and pounded on the door at midnight, saying, "Lend me three loaves; For a friend of mine in his journey is come to me, and I have nothing to set before him" (Luke 11:1–13). In that case, certainly the man asking for bread was asking for it for another who had none. And Jesus told exactly what He meant in that parable when He said in verse 13, "If ye then, being evil, know how to give good gifts unto your children: how much more shall your heavenly Father give the Holy Spirit to them that ask him?" Notice the Holy Spirit was given to them "that ASK him." To them that ask how? To them that ask like that neighbor who knocked on the door again and again and even then received only "because of his importunity." That illustrates a Christian's begging God for bread to take to sinners or, in other words, praying for the power of the Holy Spirit to make him a soul winner! And the word *ask,* I understand, is in the imperfect or continuing tense in the Greek, and it means to them that keep on asking, God will give the Holy Spirit.

Certainly before Pentecost, the disciples "continued with one accord in prayer and supplication" (Acts 1:14). And otherwise, I feel sure they would not have received the blessings that God gave them. They prayed, but they more than prayed; they begged God. That isn't all. They doubtless fasted as well. Jesus had said about His disciples, "But the days will come, when the bridegroom shall be taken away from them, and then shall they fast in those days" (Luke 5:35). Jesus had just been taken away, and now the disciples, children of the bridechamber, fasted as they prayed and begged God for the power to get about His business! They prayed, yes, but they fasted as they prayed. I do not know that it specially matters just that they did without food. What matters is that they turned their hearts wholly, unreservedly and without interruption to the business of getting all the power God had for them and to being possessed by and covered and filled with the Holy Spirit Himself!

When Peter came to preach the Gospel to Cornelius and his household, Cornelius said to him, "Four days ago I was fasting until this hour; and at the ninth hour I prayed in my house" (Acts 10:30). Perhaps that is part of the secret as to why Cornelius and his household were filled with the Holy Spirit at the same time they were saved. This is the only specific instance on record in the Bible, as far as I know, where people were filled with the Holy Spirit at the same time they were saved. Evidently, all the heart-searching, all the surrendering of the will, all the confession of sin, all the yielding of the heart that was necessary for Cornelius to be filled with the Holy Spirit was already done by the time he learned how to be saved!

When Paul was converted, he fasted and prayed three days and nights before he was filled with the Holy Spirit. Read carefully the ninth chapter of Acts, and you will see that Paul was converted as described in verses 4 and 5. Verse 9 tells that he went three days without sight, "and neither did eat nor drink." The angel told Ananias, "Behold, he prayeth," in verse 11. Those three days of fasting and prayer fitted Paul to be filled with the Holy Spirit, and in verse 17 we learn that Ananias went to him, sent by the Lord, "that thou mightest receive thy sight, *and be filled with the Holy Ghost.*" Certainly fasting and prayer are appropriate for Christians who want to be filled with the Holy Spirit.

Let us turn again to the sending forth of Barnabas and Paul in Acts 13:1–4. These prophets and teachers fasted until they knew the will of God. Then they fasted and prayed further until they could lay their hands upon Paul and Barnabas in power and they could go away "being sent forth by the Holy Ghost."

It was the experience of D. L. Moody, of R. A. Torrey, of Charles G. Finney, as it has been of many other Christians greatly used in soul winning, that they were filled with the Holy Spirit after a long season of waiting before God, finding the will of God, surrendering self, being molded on God's potter's wheel.

III. Revival Brought by Prayer and Fasting

Many an experience could I tell of victories and blessings that followed prayer and fasting. But the one dearest to my heart occurred in 1921. God spoke to my heart in the Pacific Garden Mission, and I gladly gave up college teaching to enter the ministry. God had called another young man named Ross from the cashier's window of a bank, and we two went to the Corinth Baptist Church, a rural church near Decatur, Texas, for evangelistic services. Ross preached and I led singing, and our hearts burned as we set out to win souls in that indifferent country community.

The church had been pastorless for months. I was told that it had been years since a soul had claimed Christ as Saviour in the entire community. There were two deacons, but only one of them came. We preached and sang in services Sunday morning and evening, and there was no move of any kind. There was no move on Monday night, nor on Tuesday night, nor on Wednesday night, nor on Thursday night, nor on Friday night! We preached, sang, made earnest intreaty with individuals, and all to no avail. There seemed to be no warming of Christians' hearts, no confession, no restitution, no burden for lost sinners. There seemed to be no conviction on the part of the lost, no seeking after God, and our pleading was answered by excuses and alibis or utter indifference!

We were two discouraged young preachers as we met out in a ravine Saturday morning to read the Bible together and to pray. Our hearts were heavy. We had left all to follow Jesus and to preach His Word, and now nothing seemed to happen! So we counseled what to do. I said, "I think we had just as well make up our minds either to close this effort and leave defeated, or to call a day of fasting and prayer and waiting on God for His blessing." Ross gladly agreed, and so we set Sunday as a day for fasting and prayer.

That Saturday evening as we announced to the people our conviction and set Sunday as a day for seeking God, some were moved, and God began to breathe on the people. We came early Sunday morning to pray before the Sunday school. But when the Sunday school and the morning preaching service were over, there remained only five of us for the season of fasting and prayer: Brother Ross, a visiting minister and his wife, a lone deacon who lived in the community, and I! All the others had gone home to their big Sunday dinners.

Nevertheless, we read the Bible, confessed our sins, and again and again the little circle of five bowed to pray. It had been announced that at 3:00 there would be another sermon, so perhaps twenty-five people came back for that. Then I stood before the people and asked, "What shall we expect of God tonight? We are spending this day in waiting on Him, confessing our sins, seeking His favor. Now let us ask something definite and expect His blessing tonight. What do you want?" I went around through the congregation and asked every person. They had no requests to make. Finally one woman said, "I would like to see one soul saved tonight, but I have no assurance that I shall."

I insisted we should expect God's blessing. Then the visiting minister said, "You preacher boys are young at this business. God isn't going to save souls here until these people get right with God. They never paid their former pastor what they promised. The two deacons have been angry with each other. I don't expect to see anybody saved."

Finally I turned to Brother Ross and said, "Ross, let's you and I go back to our ravine and pray together, and you and I will ask God for what we want and claim it and expect His blessing."

But Brother Ross was wise and said, "Let's do it here! What do you want to see tonight?"

"I want to see this many people saved," I said, lifting up ten fingers.

"Do you believe it?" Brother Ross asked me.

I was stumped. Wanting is not the same as believing. But like the father who cried to the Lord Jesus, "Lord, I believe; help thou mine unbelief" (Mark 9:24), I said to him, "I will believe it if you will!"

So we stood together before that congregation and shook hands, and Brother Ross announced that there would be at least ten people saved in the services that night and that all who wished to see it should be there. The visiting minister interrupted and said that we were younger at this business than he was, that we might encourage the people to believe there would be someone saved and then there would not be, and the people would believe that God does not answer prayer.

But I answered, "God *does* answer prayer. God will save ten people tonight! You see if He doesn't!"

The people were dumbfounded. They gathered in little groups to whisper. One man got his hat and left the house, and I heard him mumble to himself as he walked down the aisle, "If God saves ten souls here tonight, I'll never do another wrong thing as long as I live!"

I had not had breakfast nor dinner, and now I was too scared to want any supper! Brother Ross and I met in the little ravine to pray, and I remember telling God that I did not save myself, I did not call myself to preach. I reminded the Lord, "Lord, I told You in Chicago that if You wanted me to preach, You would have to save souls, that I could not keep going without souls being saved. Now it is Your reputation at stake, not mine. I never did tell the people I could save anybody. If I am going to serve You, 1 will have to know that You answer prayer." Then we agreed that not a single person should come on the grounds without an earnest effort being made to win him to Christ if he were unsaved. At sundown a rattling old buggy approached with a bony black horse, driven by a widow with a twelve-year-old son, and I went to talk to that boy about his soul.

A great crowd soon assembled that summer night, packing the little country church, with faces at all the windows on the outside looking in. I led a brief song service, and dear Brother Ross preached for a few minutes with power. He gave an invitation for people boldly and openly to come to accept Christ. After I had started the invitation hymn, "Jesus Is Tenderly Calling Thee Home," I turned to a man named Jernigan, a bootlegger, gambler, a drinking, profane man, who sat (of all places!) in the choir. In a moment with trembling lips he confessed his need for Christ and came with me down to tell the preacher of his sin and that here and now he was repenting and turning to trust Christ as his Saviour and to live for Him.

Back in the audience a woman screamed, "Oh, my boy! my boy!" and I saw her son coming out of the choir, climbing over the three front benches as if he had no time to slide out beside other people. Long that mother had been praying for her nineteen-year-old boy, and when the bootlegger came, he came too!

In a moment the aisles were full of people, some sinners coming weeping to find Christ, parents and loved ones coming with rejoicing over their own who were saved. That man who had said, "If God saves ten people tonight I'll never do another wrong thing as long as I live," elbowed his way down through the thronged aisle to the outside. Outside by a window he got his own seventeen-year-old son by the wrist as if he had been a little child and almost dragged him into the house. By the time the young man had gotten to the altar, he was weeping. I heard the father say, "Get down on your knees!" and the weeping sinner dropped to his knees. Then the father called for me. Soon the son had put his trust in Christ and was happily saved. Then the father, wiping his eyes with his shirt-sleeves, made his way outside again and got his other son, and the process was repeated. He too was saved!

How Heaven came down that night! The Spirit of God convicted some of the wild boys outside, and they came in the house weeping to find the Saviour. Some in the building, when approached about their souls, turned and ran, as if afraid for their lives, out into the dark!

The weeping, the pleading, the confession, the rejoicing went on and on until a little kerosene lamp with a tin reflector, hung on a wall bracket, burned out its kerosene and went out. Then another lamp flickered and went out. And nobody noticed until the last one went out! Then oil was borrowed from the farmer across the road; a lamp or two were filled; and at last, about 11:00, we decided to count our trophies that all could see that God had saved at least ten souls.

They came to stand boldly facing the congregation in a long line, twenty-three of them saved wonderfully that night.

I have seen more people saved in one service than that, but, oh, what a blessing that was to me as a young preacher just starting out! I know that real fasting and prayer and humiliation of mind as we wait on God will get the blessing God wants to give us!

Have you tried fasting and praying and waiting on God *until the victory came?*

Dear Christian, if you want help in trouble, then pray; and if the answer does not come easily and soon, fast and pray. Fasting and prayer, by which we mean wholehearted, surrendered, fervent, determined praying, will help you to find what is wrong, will help you to repent genuinely and to turn from sin, will help you to get victory over bad habits, grudges, daily temptation, will help you to find wisdom of God and the leadership of the Holy Spirit, will help you to intercede for others, and will open the way for you to receive the power of the Holy Spirit in abundance.

Dear child of God, do you feel led to try it? Then fast and pray until God meets you in blessing.

CHAPTER XVI

BIG PRAYERS TO AN ALMIGHTY GOD

"I am the LORD *thy God, which brought thee out of the land of Egypt: OPEN THY MOUTH WIDE, and I will fill it."*—Ps. 81:10.

"Call unto me, and I will answer thee, and shew thee GREAT AND MIGHTY THINGS, which thou knowest not."—Jer. 33:3.

The infinite, almighty God is able to give great answers to prayer. If there be a God, Creator of the heavens and earth, the Sustainer of all things, then it would be silly to quibble that He is unable to answer prayers, any kind of prayers, and answer them to any extent—provided only that to answer the prayers would be right. God cannot lie, cannot sin, cannot be tempted. Anything that is right, God can do in His infinite power and authority.

Not only has God the *power* to give mighty answers to prayer, but He has the disposition to do so. God *delights* to answer prayers for big things, because He is not only the infinite and almighty God, but He is the loving Father of His children. If the creation of the worlds proves God's power, then the giving of His own Son in redeeming love to save lost men proves His willingness to bless! "He that spared not his own Son, but delivered him up for us all, how shall he not with him also freely give us all things?" is the way the Holy Spirit Himself records this willingness of God to give mighty things, literally "all things," to His own (Rom. 8:32). God is able and He is willing to answer big prayers for mighty things.

This twofold position of God in regard to great answers to prayer is expressed in Isaiah 59:1, in these words, "Behold, the LORD's hand is not shortened, that it cannot save; neither His ear heavy, that it cannot hear." God is able; God is willing. His hand reaches out as far as ever in power, and His ear listens as willingly as ever in His kindness toward men.

How little our unbelieving hearts know about God's willingness to answer prayers wonderfully, mightily to His own glory! A dear friend who is now in Heaven was praying with me once about a series of problems and burdens. We had agreed about a number of things, and this friend apologetically said to the Lord in his prayer, "Lord, it may seem like we are asking an awful lot; but if You will hear us this one time, we will try not to ask You for so much anymore!" The Scriptures tell us that God laughs (Ps. 2:4). I wonder if He laughed then at the foolish idea of men that we might exhaust either God's infinite storehouse or His infinite love and patience. But I think more likely He was grieved and made sad at our childish unbelief. God has so much to give, and we need it so badly, and He would be so glorified before men at an opportunity to answer big prayers. Yet our unbelieving hearts ask so little! I think of every one of us it must be said that in our lives it is true as it was in Nazareth where "he did not many mighty works there because of their unbelief" (Matt. 13:58). And in Mark 6:5 we are told that Jesus could not do mighty works there, except heal a few sick people!

Oh, we ought to ask big things of God! Many sins are mentioned in connection with prayer. People are warned not to pray to be seen of men, not to ask for something to consume it upon their own lusts. We are warned of how unforgiveness, covetousness, disobedience, unbelief and wrong home-life hinder prayer. But of all the sins mentioned regarding prayer, not once does the Scripture hint that any man ever asked too much of God!

My six daughters sometimes gather around me, telling me how they need new shoes, money for music lessons and for many other things. Sometimes I have been compelled to say, "Go easy! I am not made of money. We will just have to get what we can afford and do without the rest." But I never read in God's Word where He ever told anybody, "Go easy! I don't have very much. I have already strained Myself giving to others. I cannot give as much as you ask." No, no!

One of our greatest sins about praying is that we do not ask for enough. We do not take what God is willing to give. We do not give God an opportunity to prove His love and power. God forgive us our little, stingy, unbelieving prayers!

I. God Invites and Commands Us to Ask Big Things

It is amazing how many places in the Bible God has given us promises that He is willing to answer prayers for mighty things. God seems to plead with us, to argue with us and urge us to give Him a chance to answer prayers for big things. And sometimes the Scripture gives a plain command about this, and to disobey is to sin. Here I give some Scriptures which I urge you to take much to heart. Let them transform your praying and your faith. These Scriptures show how eager God is to have you ask Him for big things.

1. *"I am the* LORD *thy God, which brought thee out of the land of Egypt: open thy mouth wide, and I will fill it"* (Ps. 81:10).

Here God first introduces Himself and gives His credentials as if He were a contractor bidding for a big construction job, and offers proof of His ability and resources to complete the contract. God seems to say, "Do you need a really big God to do something for you? Then call on Me, for I am the Lord thy God which brought thee out of the land of Egypt. I opened the Red Sea in answer to Moses' prayer. I brought all the plagues upon Egypt, from turning water to blood to killing the firstborn, and then I brought my people Israel out between the piled-up waters of the Red Sea! I fed them for forty years with manna from Heaven. I gave them rivers of water from a rock when Moses smote it at My command. I showed My mighty power by wondrous miracles as they journeyed, and then I caused the people to cross the flooded Jordan on dry ground while the waters piled up high on their right and ran away downstream on the left. I caused the walls of Jericho to fall down flat. That is the kind of God I am. Now if you want any big things done, you see I am able to do them."

It is as plain as day that the Lord here means that He is as willing now to do such mighty wonders as He was then! He is still the same kind of a God. He still can do mighty works if people will believe Him.

God seems to be so jealous about His own great name, and He constantly reminds us that He never changes. "I am the LORD, I change not," He says in Malachi 3:6. And in Hebrews 13:8 we are reminded of our Lord that He is "Jesus Christ the same yesterday, and to day, and for ever." So the Lord here says, "I am the LORD thy God, which brought thee out of the land of Egypt: open thy mouth wide, and I will fill it."

James 4:2 says, "Ye have not, because ye ask not." Then this Scripture must mean that "ye have little, because ye ask little." If we would open our mouths wider, we would get bigger bites from God!

It is impolite to be pigs at the table and take big bites, as all of us were taught when we were children. But this rule does not apply at God's table! God wants His people to open their mouths wide to receive the mighty blessings He is so able and so willing to bestow! Oh, beloved reader, open your mouth! Ask God for big things. He is able!

This verse of Scripture was one of the favorites of George Müller, the modern apostle of prayer who received and dispersed over seven million dollars for the Lord's work without ever asking a man for a penny, all of it received in answer to prayer. One by one he prayed into existence the orphan houses at Ashley Downs, Bristol, England, to care for more than two thousand orphan children. Day by day their food and clothes, their teaching and all their needs were met in answer to the prayers of this man of God. By prayer alone he supported hundreds of missionaries, printed multiplied millions of tracts, and circulated a multitude of copies of the Word of God. George Müller opened his mouth wide, and God proved Himself by filling it so often and answering particular prayers so definitely that George Müller came to say he could ask for one million dollars now with as much assurance of an answer as once he could ask for a pound (about $5).

Will you too open your mouth wide and let God fill it with mighty things?

2. *"Call unto me, and I will answer thee, and shew thee great and mighty things, which thou knowest not"* (Jer. 33:3).

Here God exhorts us to call on Him so He can give "great and mighty things, which thou knowest not."

Again God has in mind big prayers, asking great things from God. God had been dealing with Jeremiah on this matter of big prayers because the people of Israel were in such terrible need. In the preceding chapter, Jeremiah 32, we learn that the Chaldeans under Nebuchadnezzar had surrounded the city of Jerusalem, had thrown up mounts against the walls, ready to swarm over them and take the city. Famine and pestilence had already stricken the besieged people. Then Jeremiah cried out, "Ah Lord GOD! behold, thou hast made the heaven and the earth by thy great power and stretched out arm, and there is nothing too hard for thee" (Jer. 32:17). Then Jeremiah reminded God of how He had dealt with the children of Israel before in bringing them out of Egypt. And in verses 26 and 27 we find God's answer: "Then came the word of the Lord unto Jeremiah, saying, Behold, I am the LORD, the God of all flesh: is there any thing too hard for me?" (Jer. 32:26,27). God was going to allow Jerusalem to fall into the hands of Nebuchadnezzar, but it was only because of the unbelief and sin of the people, not because He was not able and not willing to deliver the people even in this dire extremity! God reminded Jeremiah, and through him He reminded the Jews and reminds all of us today, "Behold, I am the LORD, the God of all flesh." Then He asks us all, "Is there any thing too hard for me?" All of us must answer surely with Jeremiah, "Behold, thou hast made the heaven and the earth by thy great power and stretched out arm, and there is nothing too hard for thee." God is able to give us mighty things. So the Scriptures continue into the next chapter, and there we find this blessed promise of Jeremiah 33:3, "Call unto me, and I will answer thee, and shew thee great and mighty things, which thou knowest not."

Can you in these Scriptures see the hunger of God's heart for somebody who will believe Him, somebody who will give God a chance to do great and mighty things? Isn't there a pleading note in His inquiry of Jeremiah, "Is there any thing too hard for me?" How anxious God is to prove His mighty power. He only waits until we ask Him to give! Only as God's people really call upon Him for great and mighty things can God give these great and mighty things "which thou knowest not." God has greater things to give us than we can know how to pray for, and He will give them if we really call upon Him for mighty things and give Him a chance!

3. *"If ye have faith as a grain of mustard seed, ye shall say unto this mountain, Remove hence to yonder place; and it shall remove; and nothing shall be impossible unto you"* (Matt. 17:20).

The disciples had been unable to cast out the demon from the lunatic boy and asked Jesus why they could not cast him out. Jesus answered that it was because of their unbelief, and assured them that they were right to pray for big things, even so great as asking that a mountain be removed into the sea.

And then He gave that startling promise, *"...and nothing shall be impossible unto you"!*

Nothing is impossible to those who pray with faith! What an encouragement to ask for mighty things from God!

4. *"Jesus said unto him, If thou canst believe, all things are possible to him that believeth"* (Mark 9:23).

Here in Mark's account of the healing of the same lunatic boy, whom the disciples had tried and failed to heal while Jesus was on the Mount of Transfiguration, we are given an added promise. In Matthew we were told how Jesus promised the disciples that if they believed when they prayed, "nothing shall be impossible unto you." But here we are told how the Saviour addressed the father of the child himself and said to him, "If thou canst believe, all things are possible to him that believeth."

"ALL THINGS ARE POSSIBLE TO HIM THAT BELIEVETH." Again the dear Saviour seems to challenge us to ask for bigger things. The father of the child had said, "If thou canst do any thing, have compassion on us, and help us." But Jesus answered him in effect, "You have the *if* in the wrong place. There is no *if* about My power or about My compassion. The only *if* is whether you will believe. All things are possible to him that believeth"—to *anybody* that believeth!

5. *"Jesus answered and said unto them, Verily I say unto you, If ye have faith, and doubt not, ye shall not only do this which is done to the fig tree, but also if ye shall say unto this mountain, Be thou removed, and be thou cast into the sea; it shall be done. And all things, whatsoever ye shall ask in prayer, believing, ye shall receive"* (Matt. 21:21,22).

This is an entirely different occasion from that mentioned in Matthew 17:20,21, yet here the Saviour uses the same illustration and says again that not only can a fig tree be blighted but a mountain can be cast into the sea in answer to prayer. And then He adds the mighty promise, "And ALL THINGS, whatsoever ye shall ask in prayer, believing, ye shall receive." Plainly, this is an invitation to pray for anything, no matter how mighty, just so you believe in your heart that God will give it. The Lord Jesus pleads with us to ask for big things!

6. *"And Jesus answering saith unto them, Have faith in God, for verily I say unto you, that whosoever shall say unto this mountain, Be thou removed, and be thou cast into the sea; and shall not doubt in his heart, but shall believe that those things which he saith shall come to pass; he shall have whatsoever he saith. Therefore I say unto you, What things soever ye desire, when ye pray, believe that ye receive them, and ye shall have them"* (Mark 11:22–24).

This is Mark's account of the incident of the withered fig tree and the

Saviour's wonderful promise that mountains could be removed by faith. And here He adds this wonderful statement that "what things soever ye desire, when ye pray," we can have if we believe that we receive them!

7. *"And the apostles said unto the Lord, Increase our faith. And the Lord said, If ye had faith as a grain of mustard seed, ye might say unto this sycamine tree, Be thou plucked up by the root, and be thou planted in the sea; and it should obey you"* (Luke 17:5,6).

Here again the Saviour means to tell us that startling and wonderful miracles can be done in answer to the prayer of faith. We should ask for mighty things and believe God!

8. *"Now unto him that is able to do exceeding abundantly above all that we ask or think, according to the power that worketh in us, Unto him be glory in the church by Christ Jesus throughout all ages, world without end. Amen"* (Eph. 3:20,21).

God "is able to do exceeding abundantly above all that we ask or think." Able to do above all that we ask, able to do above all that we can even think! Not only able, but *abundantly able.* Not only abundantly able, but *exceeding abundantly able* to do above all that we ask or think! And then the Scripture tells us that that is according to the power that worked in Paul, and Paul prays that this same exceeding abundantly able God may be glorified in the church by Christ. That is, he prays that God's mighty power will be manifested in the church and notes that God will be able to answer prayer down through all ages and could answer prayers greater than anybody can ask or even think! This wonderful promise shows that God intended the marvelous answers to prayer to continue through all ages, having wonders done by the Holy Spirit who worked in Paul, and that these wonders should be done in the name of Jesus Christ, glorifying God. The next time you pray, remember that you have an exceeding abundantly able God who can give more than you can even ask or think. What a challenge to us to ask great things of God and glorify a great Saviour by letting Him manifest His power!

II. Bible Examples of Prayers Demanding Great Things From God

The Bible is a book of marvelous answers to prayer, of big faith and of a bigger God! And never is there a hint throughout the Bible that any man ever expected too much from God or that God was ever displeased because one asked for mighty things!

I mention here only a few illustrations that thrill the souls of men and help us to believe God!

1. First I mention the case of Joshua, who commanded the sun to stand still. In Joshua 10:12–14 we are told:

"Then spake Joshua to the LORD in the day when the LORD delivered up the Amorites before the children of Israel, and he said in the sight of Israel, Sun, stand thou still upon Gibeon; and thou, Moon, in the valley of Ajalon. And the sun stood still, and the moon stayed, until the people had avenged themselves upon their enemies. Is not this written in the book of Jasher? So the sun stood still in the midst of heaven, and hasted not to go down about a whole day. And there was no day like that before it or after it that the LORD hearkened unto the voice of a man: for the LORD fought for Israel."

Of course I believe this, and of course you do too if you are a child of God. If God made the sun and the earth, He was easily able to make the sun still in its relationship to the earth for "about a whole day." And this marvelous miracle was written of not only in the book of Joshua but written of by a contemporary writer in "the book of Jasher." That book has not been preserved for us and was not intended to be a part of the canon of Scripture, but was a trustworthy chronicle and added witness to this marvelous miracle. And every line of this divinely inspired account shows that God was pleased with Joshua's faith and answered him mightily!

2. But one of the most audacious prayers ever prayed was that of Elisha, the young prophet who had followed Elijah now for years acting as a servant for him. When his master, Elijah, was about to go to Heaven, Elisha, with a boldness that defied Elijah, abruptly dismissed every suggestion of unbelief and seemed almost to *demand* of God instead of pleading. May God bless our hearts as we read this sweet story again:

"And it came to pass, when the LORD would take up Elijah into heaven by a whirlwind, that Elijah went with Elisha from Gilgal. And Elijah said unto Elisha, Tarry here, I pray thee; for the LORD hath sent me to Beth-el. And Elisha said unto him, As the LORD liveth, and as thy soul liveth, I will not leave thee. So they went down to Beth-el. And the sons of the prophets that were at Beth-el came forth to Elisha, and said unto him, Knowest thou that the LORD will take away thy master from thy head to day? And he said, Yea, I know it; hold ye your peace. And Elijah said unto him, Elisha, tarry here, I pray thee; for the LORD hath sent me to Jericho. And he said, As the LORD liveth, and as thy soul liveth, I will not leave thee. So they came to Jericho. And the sons of the prophets that were at Jericho came to Elisha, and said unto him, Knowest thou that the LORD will take away thy master from thy head to day? And he answered, Yea, I know it; hold ye your peace. And Elijah said unto him, Tarry, I pray thee, here; for the LORD hath sent me to Jordan. And he said, As the LORD liveth, and as thy soul liveth, I will not leave thee. And they two went on. And fifty men of the sons of the prophets went, and stood to view afar off: and they two stood by Jordan. And Elijah took his mantle, and wrapped it together, and smote the waters, and they were divided hither and thither, so that they two went over on dry

ground. And it came to pass, when they were gone over, that Elijah said unto Elisha, Ask what I shall do for thee, before I be taken away from thee. And Elisha said, I pray thee, let a double portion of thy spirit be upon me. And he said, Thou hast asked a hard thing: nevertheless, if thou see me when I am taken from thee, it shall be so unto thee; but if not, it shall not be so. And it came to pass, as they still went on, and talked, that, behold, there appeared a chariot of fire, and horses of fire, and parted them both asunder; and Elijah went up by a whirlwind into heaven. And Elisha saw it, and he cried, My father, my father, the chariot of Israel, and the horsemen thereof! And he saw him no more: and he took hold of his own clothes, and rent them in two pieces. He took up also the mantle of Elijah that fell from him, and went back, and stood by the bank of Jordan; and he took the mantle of Elijah that fell from him, and smote the waters, and said, Where is the LORD God of Elijah? and when he also had smitten the waters, they parted hither and thither: and Elisha went over."—II Kings 2:1–14.

The story tells itself, but two or three comments may be helpful:

(a) Elisha would not be discouraged. He was accustomed to taking the words of Elijah as if they were direct from God, but here he point-blank refused to listen to Elijah's suggestion that he stay at Gilgal, or at Bethel, or at Jericho; no, "As the LORD liveth, and as thy soul liveth, I will not leave thee," he said.

(b) We surely must be convinced here that God does not always mean "no" when He seems to say "no." These discouragements were manifestly meant to prove Elisha just as Jesus temporarily discouraged the Canaanitish woman but was secretly pleased when she insisted and would not take "no" for an answer about the healing of her poor, devil-possessed daughter (Matt. 15:21–28). So if God does not at first answer your prayers, and if discouraging circumstances seem to indicate that He will not hear you, do not be discouraged. If you know that what you are asking will honor God, then demand it and expect it.

(c) Note the astounding request, "And Elisha said, I pray thee, let a double portion of thy spirit be upon me." Really, what he asked for was this: "Let me have twice as much of the power of the Holy Spirit as Elijah had!" Elijah had raised the dead; had prayed, and God had given a drought for three and a half years; had prayed again, and God had given rain. Elijah had had the most marvelous miracles since the time of Moses. And yet this bold young prophet demands that he shall have twice the measure of the Holy Spirit and His power which Elijah had! What a prayer!

(d) And even more astounding than the prayer is the fact that God answered it! The mantle of Elijah fell on Elisha! And while by careful comparison we find eight great miracles done by Elijah, we find sixteen great miracles done by Elisha after a double portion of the Spirit of God was on him in answer to this prayer! We will not count Elijah's answered prayers for drought and then for rain because they might be said to have happened through natural causes, not by a miracle, though in answer to prayer. Likewise, we will not count the miraculous revelation to Elisha of the plans of Benhadad, king of Syria, recorded in II Kings 6:8–12, since that, though a miracle and repeated several times, was not a *physical* miracle. Likewise, prophecy of seven years of famine is not counted (II Kings 8:1). But compare these lists of miracles and see that Elisha really got what he prayed for, a double portion of the Holy Spirit that empowered Elijah!

Miracles of Elijah

1. Fed by ravens (I Kings 17:1–6).
2. Widow's meal and oil replenished (I Kings 17:8–16).
3. Raises widow's son (I Kings 17:17–23).
4. Fire comes down from heaven and consumes his offering (I Kings 18:36–38).
5. Fed by angel (I Kings 19:5–7).
6. Calls fire down from heaven to consume captain and fifty men (II Kings 1:9–12).
7. Divides waters of Jordan (II Kings 2:8).
8. Elijah went up by whirlwind with chariot of fire into heaven (II Kings 2:11).

Miracles of Elisha

1. Parts the water and goes over Jordan on dry land (II Kings 2:14).
2. Heals water with salt (II Kings 2:21,22).
3. Bears tear forty-two children (II Kings 2:23–25).
4. Country is filled with water (II Kings 3:16–20).
5. Increase of widow's oil (II Kings 4:1–7).
6. Birth of son to barren Shunammite woman (II Kings 4:8–17).
7. Restores life to son of Shunammite (II Kings 4:18–37).
8. Heals noxious pottage (II Kings 4:38–41).
9. Feeds one hundred men with twenty loaves (II Kings 4:42–44).
10. Naaman's leprosy miraculously healed (II Kings 5:1–19).
11. Commands leprosy of Naaman to cleave to Gehazi (II Kings 5:20–27).
12. Makes lost axe float (II Kings 6:5–7).
13. Eyes of his servant opened; sees mountain full of horses and chariots of fire around Elisha (II Kings 6:13–17).

14. Brings blindness on Syrians (II Kings 6:18–20).

15. God miraculously scatters Syrians and fulfills Elisha's promise of food (II Kings 7:1–16).

16. Man brought to life by touching Elisha's bones (II Kings 13: 20,21).

Back of the scene, in my mind, I can see God looking on with delight! God was not insulted; He was *pleased* by the audacious boldness of Elisha's prayer! I am sure He was grieved at the unbelief of the other sons of the prophets, but He was pleased with Elisha. Praise God, Israel would not be left now without a believing prophet of God to show forth His power!

(e) And last, note that this bold young prophet, Elisha, walked right back to the Jordan River and demanded at once that God show Himself, that the God of Elijah should prove Himself the God of Elisha as well! Wrapping the mantle of Elijah together, he smote the waters of Jordan and cried out, "Where is the LORD God of Elijah?" and the waters stood back in a wall on either side, and he walked over.

Surely in a world where God's great soul winners have left the scene, God wants to raise up others with like power. The God of Spurgeon, of Wesley, of Charles G. Finney, of Dwight L. Moody; the God of R. A. Torrey and of Billy Sunday—where is He? Where is the Lord God of Moody? Evidently, He only waits until some man shall boldly, with a holy abandon that will not be denied, demand and claim the mighty power of God! The Lord's work languishes because we do not pray such big prayers! And we do not have mighty things because we do not ask for them!

Another illustration of how eager God is to give more than we can ask and how pleased He is with big prayers is given in II Kings 4:1–7. Here again Elisha, the man who demanded and received a double portion of the Spirit of God that rested on Elijah, is the hero of the story. As Elisha had called on Elijah, so this woman calls on Elisha.

Read the passage prayerfully:

"Now there cried a certain woman of the wives of the sons of the prophets unto Elisha, saying, Thy servant my husband is dead; and thou knowest that thy servant did fear the LORD: and the creditor is come to take unto him my two sons to be bondmen. And Elisha said unto her, What shall I do for thee? tell me, what hast thou in the house? And she said, Thine handmaid hath not any thing in the house, save a pot of oil. Then he said, Go, borrow thee vessels abroad of all thy neighbours, even empty vessels; borrow not a few. And when thou art come in, thou shalt shut the door upon thee and upon thy sons, and shalt pour out into all those vessels, and thou shalt set aside that which is full. So she went from him, and shut the door upon her and upon her sons, who brought the vessels to her; and she poured out. And it came to pass, when the vessels were full, that she said unto her

son, Bring me yet a vessel. And he said unto her, There is not a vessel more. And the oil stayed. Then she came and told the man of God. And he said, Go, sell the oil, and pay thy debt, and live thou and thy children of the rest."—II Kings 4:1–7.

How much oil did God give to the widow? Just as much oil as she had vessels for! God had more oil than she had vessels, and the oil did not stop flowing until there was nowhere else to put it.

When this poor mother said to her son, "Bring me yet a vessel"; and when he said to her, "There is not a vessel more"; and when the oil stopped flowing, oh, I am sure she wished she had borrowed more vessels! If she did not have enough to buy all her heart could desire, it was her own fault; for God surely showed that He could furnish the oil according to the vessels provided. And as it was, there was oil enough for her to pay the debt and then for the widow and her sons to live of the rest.

Dear Reader, does not God here teach us that if we would "borrow thee vessels abroad of all thy neighbours, even empty vessels; borrow not a few," we should have them filled? If we prepare the vessels, empty vessels, and not a few of them, the mighty God of Elijah will fill them in answer to prayer. The thought here is certainly kindred to Psalm 81:10, "Open thy mouth wide, and I will fill it." Bring the empty vessels, and God will fill them!

Time and space would fail us to call to your attention other such marvelous prayers and marvelous answers in the Bible. But for the strengthening of your faith in a mighty God who delights to answer big prayers, read the story of how Moses prayed and God opened the earth and swallowed up wicked men who challenged his leadership (Num. 16:25–35). Read how King Hezekiah prayed that heart-moving prayer of faith and how God heard, and "the angel of the LORD went forth, and smote in the camp of the Assyrians a hundred and fourscore and five thousand: and when they arose early in the morning, behold, they were all dead corpses" (Isa. 37:36). Read again how in Hezekiah's sickness when God Himself had told him to prepare to die, Hezekiah turned his face to the wall, ignored the warning of Isaiah, God's prophet, and so prayed that God sent Isaiah back to tell him, "I have heard thy prayer, I have seen thy tears: behold, I will add unto thy days fifteen years" (Isa. 33:1–5). Did ever a man pray so boldly! Then the sun turned ten degrees backward on the sundial (Isa. 38:8). Both these marvelous prayers and their mighty answers are recorded also in II Kings, chapters 19 and 20.

Any honest heart in reviewing these Scriptures must see that God intended us to be encouraged to pray great prayers. In I Kings, chapter 18, we read how God gave fire from Heaven on Mount Carmel and turned the hearts of all the nation back to God again in answer to Elijah's prayer. Then the three-and-a-half years' drought which had come in answer to Elijah's prayer was broken when he prayed again and the Lord gave rain. And how suggestive it is that Elijah is held up to New Testament Christians as our example in faith:

"The effectual fervent prayer of a righteous man availeth much. Elias was a man subject to like passions as we are, and he prayed earnestly that it might not rain: and it rained not on the earth by the space of three years and six months. And he prayed again, and the heaven gave rain, and the earth brought forth her fruit."—Jas. 5:16–18.

I suggest it would be a blessed exercise to spend some days in carefully rereading all the great answers to prayer which you can find in the Bible and in meditating upon the mighty promises of God.

III. The Blessings of Big Prayers

Small prayers are the sign of weak faith, and little faith grieves God and does great harm. Remember that Jesus said more than once, in reproof, "O ye of little faith"! (Matt. 6:30; 8:26; 14:31; 16:8; Luke 12:28). Big prayers show faith in God. And that not only pleases God but brings other blessed results.

1. Glorifies God, Shows His Great Power

First, big praying gives God a chance to show His mighty power and glorify His name. In Nazareth the Lord Jesus Himself could do no mighty works because of their unbelief (Mark 6:5). God is still able and is still willing to do mighty things, but there are so few people who ask God and believe God and expect big things. God is still the God who brought His people out of Egypt, but we do not open our mouths wide, and we do not get big bites from God. God still has plenty of oil, but we do not furnish the empty vessels.

When Elijah called down the fire from God on Mount Carmel by his prayers, then the people fell on their faces and cried out, "The LORD, he is the God; the LORD, he is the God"! (I Kings 18:39). And so today unbelief and modernism would be defeated and scattered, and multitudes would turn to God, if only there were an Elijah who believed God and could have God's mighty power!

Surely God must yearn over men and long to show His power and His love. The Scripture plainly says, "For the eyes of the LORD run to and fro throughout the whole earth, to shew himself strong in the behalf of them whose heart is perfect toward him" (II Chron. 16:9). God is anxious "to shew himself strong." Unbelief abounds because Christians do not give an example by asking great things of God and giving God an opportunity to manifest His mighty power.

We have just closed a campaign for trial subscriptions for *The Sword of the Lord* (December 1941), the weekly Christian paper I edit. I set a goal of five thousand trial four-month subscriptions. In the office my helpers put this goal in large letters on the wall and daily prayed for it, along with other needed blessings, in the prayer meeting each weekday morning at 10:00. Five thousand subscriptions is a good many, and my dear daughter Grace, a freshman in Wheaton College, said to me about two or three weeks ago, "Daddy, don't you think we set our goals too high sometimes and do not reach them?" That got on my mind and heart heavily. So in prayer I said to God, "Lord, hear my daughter's question. She is young; she hasn't tried You as often as I. Lord, prove the goal is not too high for You. Strengthen her faith; show her You answer her daddy's prayers!" I got victory about it and told her so. Now, this morning, bless God, a letter arrived in Toronto, where I write this, from my secretary at Wheaton, saying, "Praise the Lord! He sent us five thousand trial subscriptions! Through this morning's mail...the total reached five thousand *exactly.*" God gave exactly what we asked for, not one less nor more. (Later: As I told you in the chapter on "Definite Praying," when someone thought thirty of these subscriptions were given to "help God out," the workers prayed again and received thirty other subscriptions the next day!) My own faith is strengthened, and how happy I am for my dear children to see it. I know God will be more real to them and to my workers as He is to me today because of this remarkable answer to prayer. Big prayers, when answered, stop doubts and glorify God, strengthening Christians and convicting sinners.

2. Big Praying Prospers God's Work

Next, the work of God languishes because of our small asking. Missionaries are called home, fields are closed, church congregations dwindle, revival efforts fail, all because people do not ask for mighty things from God. The Spirit of God is not manifest because people do not ask for Him to show His power. There is no doubt that if there could come a wave of prevailing, mighty prayer, pleading with God, insisting on great things, we should have a mighty revival, and the work of God would prosper.

How the Lord's work prospers when we go to God with big requests! One case I shall never forget when God gave a wonderful answer to my prayer, unworthy and unbelieving as I am. In 1938, I believe, I was called to a city in a midwestern state for a revival campaign. After much urging, I felt led to go and expected great things from word I had received. But lo, when I arrived I found there had been no money to advertise the meetings, few knew about my coming, and besides, I was unknown. A crowd of not more than fifty, I judge, met me the first service. I had promised to stay about ten days, including one Sunday, away from my work in Dallas, my radio program and my paper. Crowds grew slowly; a few were saved. Then the pastor asked me to stay over the second Sunday. "I cannot get you a good offering unless you stay through Sunday," he said. I replied that I did not come for the offering, that I was needed at home for the Sunday night evangelistic services at our church, needed for my Sunday radio broadcast, and that I must plan to return after Friday night. Sadly the pastor told how a heavy debt had stripped the people, another payment was about due, and if I did not stay over Sunday he feared the people could not give much. I told him not to worry, that I should not; and after the service that Thursday night I went to my room.

There in my room I faced certain facts, and temptation assailed me. I had expected the offering that would be given me to go on a heavy printing bill. *The Sword of the Lord*, the weekly evangelistic paper which my heavenly Father helps me publish, has never quite paid expenses. The price of one dollar a year will not pay all the postage, printing and wages of workers for such a high-grade weekly paper unless the circulation runs above 10,000 copies weekly regularly. I had borrowed $450 at the urging of a good Christian lady, for six months. It was overdue, and I must renew the note or pay it. Besides, I owed the printer $270 for printing *The Sword of the Lord* after I had borrowed the $450. Then I owed $200 to another printer for tracts which I had been giving away by thousands. At least $920 needed to be paid soon, and now I was told that for my ten days' work it seemed there would be little pay. Satan taunted me with all the sacrifices I had made to carry on the burden of that soul-winning paper, putting into it thousands of dollars of money I could have used on my family. Satan reminded me that I had refused ever to set a price on my services, that I had no regular salary, and that now this was the way it would turn out!

With tears, that Thursday night I turned to prayer. I reminded God of a covenant I had made with Him in 1926 that He was to look after my business and I would trust Him and look after His, 'seeking first the kingdom of God and His righteousness,' and believing that what I needed He would supply. I remember that I said to God, "Lord, look on the heading of that paper; it has Your name on it, 'THE SWORD OF THE LORD.' Your name is in big type; mine, in small type. It is Your paper, not mine. I did not save myself; I did not call myself to preach. If You want a paper, You pay the bills. If You do not want that paper, then let it die. It is not my worry; it is Yours. I am not going to stay with this little meeting trying to get a bigger offering, and I am not going to fret or worry. Lord, it is up to You to pay those bills!" And so, at last, with peace I went to sleep.

The next night we had some people saved. They took an offering for me. For the ten days' time, the check was $25. They gave me what I asked for expenses, bare railroad fare, without Pullman berth. In sweet peace I took the train that night to Dallas. Though I sleep poorly, as a rule, unless I can stretch out and relax in a regular bed, that night I slept as sweetly as a child in the chair car. The next morning as my train, the Rock Island *Rocket,* left Wichita, Kansas, the porter came through the car holding a telegram, calling my name. I took the telegram, opened it and read from my secretary, "YOU HAVE JUST RECEIVED CHECK FOR ONE THOUSAND DOLLARS FOR YOUR WORK"!

I walked up and down the aisles clutching that telegram, laughing, praising God in my soul! I could hardly refrain from telling the porter, the hostess, the passengers, how God hears prayer! I told old Satan what a liar he was. I told my heavenly Father I would turn that blessed paper over to Him and that I knew now He would take care of the bills. I promised I would love Him better than before, and oh, may He help me to do it, always!

That thousand dollars came from a man I had never seen. I had never appealed to him, of course, never had written to him nor received a letter from him, nor have I had a letter or gift from him since, though I have since met the noble, good man. And bless God, I have never since been in distress about the printing bills for *The Sword of the Lord.*

How often the Lord's work suffers and languishes because we do not pray for big things and expect big answers from God! How God longs to bless His work when we believe Him for great things!

3. Big Prayers Get Christians What They Need

And last, God's people live in poverty, in sickness, in disappointment and defeat, because they do not pray for big things.

I have already told you how, when I preached on prayer in Wheaton, Illinois, the wife of a college professor came to me and said, "I have gone on living without the things I needed because I was afraid to ask God. I was ashamed of my rug with a hole in it but never thought that God would be pleased for me to ask for a new one. I am going home now and ask God for what I need!"

All over the world there are Christians who have no jobs because they have never asked for jobs. There are young people who cannot go to school because they have never taken the matter to God with large faith and insisted on God's showing His power. There are wives whose husbands are unsaved, there are fathers whose sons are drunkards; and yet they do not pray to God expecting mighty things, and so God does not show His power and do the things which He would so gladly do if people only prayed expectantly, prayed largely, opened their mouths wide so God could fill them!

In 1932 in Dallas, Texas, I had an old Dodge car that was worn out. The upholstering was frayed, the motor used far too much oil; and that winter we had to push the car downhill again and again to get it started. One Monday I nearly missed my radio broadcast; besides I was constantly embarrassed to have my wife and daughters and secretary pushing the car along the wintry streets, trying to get it started. So I said to Mrs. Rice, "I believe it would please God for me to ask Him for a new car." She agreed, and we laid the matter out before the Lord. I reminded God that He knew I was not laying by a penny and that I was working almost night and day trying to win souls. I reminded Him that the work was His work, not my own, and that in 1926 I had made a covenant with Him that I would look after His business and He should look after mine. And so I asked Him that in His own way He would provide me with a new automobile.

On Wednesday night I went to the service in a big furniture building where we were meeting, pending the erection of a building of our own. When the song service was done I went to the pulpit to teach the Scriptures, and a Mr. Reeves handed me an envelope containing some keys and a folded paper or two. I looked at him in bewilderment and then at the people who were looking on in great joy. They burst into laughter, and one and then another began to point to the curb out in front of the building. There stood a new Chevrolet four-door sedan, and in my hand I held the keys and warranty and title. As a surprise to me, the men in the church had bought the car. I think they could not have known about my prayer; certainly I had not told them. And I knew nothing of their plans.

When we went home that night I said to my wife, "If I had known that God was as willing as that to give me an automobile, I would not have been pushing that old wreck up and down these hills day after day trying to get it started!"

And how many of us, dear readers, do not have even what God wants to give us, because we do not expect much from God, do not pray big prayers. We do not open our mouths wide so He can fill them.

It is said that in a Southern state at the close of the Civil War a slave, the body servant to a Southern gentleman, was set free by Lincoln's proclamation. But his master said to him, "Sam, if you will stay with me and take care of me, I will see that you are cared for when I am gone." The old man loved his master and agreed to stay on with him, which he did until his master died.

Afterward the old man mowed lawns, chopped kindling, and ran errands until his legs were stiff and his body bent with rheumatism and with age. Then he could hardly get enough work to do to buy the poorest food. He lived in a little shack and hobbled about in rags. But an old friend of his master's family said to him one day, "Sam, you don't have to live this way: your master told me that he had deposited five thousand dollars in the bank for you. Go down to the bank and get some money to buy what you need!"

With much persuasion the timid old man decided to go to the bank. Turning his hat nervously in his hand, he inquired of the teller, "Did Marse

Tom sho nuff leave me some money in this here bank?" His name was inquired, and the bank clerk told him yes, that there was money at hand for him and that he might have it whenever he wished.

"How does I git it?" the old man asked. He was told how to write a check. He could not write, so the teller offered to write out the check and sign his name, and beside it the old man could make his mark.

"Could I have as much as fifty cents to get me a sack of meal?" he inquired, and the teller replied that he could have as much as he wanted within any reasonable limits, since there was five thousand dollars deposited to his account in the bank.

So the former slave instructed the teller to make out a check for fifty cents, and with trembling hands he made his mark beside his name. Then he took the bright fifty-cent piece and shuffled away to buy some meal and to live in his poor little shack in his rags and poverty, leaving $4,999.50 in the bank!

And how like us that is! Our heavenly Father says that the gold and the silver are His and the cattle on a thousand hills. He has lovingly invited us to tell Him all our needs—"what things soever ye desire when ye pray"— and promised us "great and mighty things, which thou knowest not" (Jer. 33:3), if we will only call upon Him. He asks us to open our mouths wide and let Him fill them. And yet we live at a poor dying rate in our poverty— physical, mental and spiritual poverty. We do not have because we do not ask. Our mouths are never full because we never open them wide!

On a Dallas, Texas, radio station one Sunday morning I used the above illustration in speaking on Psalm 81:10. In Fort Worth, thirty-two miles away, a poor, distressed Christian woman was up early to pray. Her prayer was about like this: "Oh, God, please give me two or three dollars to pay on the gas bill. My husband doesn't have a job, we are behind on the rent, the children do not have enough clothes for school, and I think it will break my heart if they cut off the gas and we have no heat in this winter weather. Please, Lord, I don't ask much; give me two or three dollars to pay on the gas bill so they won't cut off the gas!"

She arose from her knees, turned on the radio and listened to me in the morning broadcast when I urged Christians to open their mouths wide and told how this old man got fifty cents when he could have had any amount up to five thousand dollars.

She snapped off the radio and fell on her knees and began to pray. And this is the way she prayed this time: "Oh, God, forgive me for just asking for two or three dollars. You are not poor! You are able to give all we need. Then give my husband a job like other men have! Let us pay the rent and pay all of the gas bill. Give my children school clothes. Lord, many an unsaved mother sends her children to school well clothed. And You have plenty; give my husband a job and let us have what we need. And forgive me for asking so little and expecting so little!"

On the following Tuesday morning we had testimonies in a Bible conference service at Dallas. From Fort Worth came Mrs. Frank Williams. She stood, and with tears running down her cheeks, she told of the woman and her despairing cry for two or three dollars, then the change in her prayer. And then Mrs. Williams said, "This morning that man went back to work at a full-time job! Already arrangements have been made about the gas bill and the rent, and that mother's prayer has been answered!"

We have a great God. There is nothing too hard for God. He loves us. He wants us to have all we need. Will you today take to heart His blessed promises and begin to pray the kind of prayers that will allow God to do the wonderful things He wants to do for you? Remember what He has promised.

"I am the LORD thy God, which brought thee out of the land of Egypt: open thy mouth wide, and I will fill it" (Ps. 81:10).

"Call unto me, and I will answer thee, and shew thee great and mighty things, which thou knowest not" (Jer. 33:3).

CHAPTER XVII

DOES GOD WORK MIRACLES TODAY?

"If ye have faith as a grain of mustard seed, ye shall say unto this mountain, Remove hence to yonder place; and it shall remove; and nothing shall be impossible unto you."—Matt. 17:20.

"If thou canst believe, all things are possible to him that believeth."—Mark 9:23.

"And these signs shall follow them that believe; In my name shall they cast out devils; they shall speak with new tongues;

"They shall take up serpents; and if they drink any deadly thing, it shall not hurt them; they shall lay hands on the sick, and they shall recover."—Mark 16:17,18.

"Why should it be thought a thing incredible with you, that God should raise the dead?"—Acts 26:8.

Does God work miracles today? Yes, He does if He answers prayer! In the very nature of the case the question of answered prayer is one of miracles. An answer to prayer means there must be a personal God, who hears an individual cry and so orders events that the man who prayed gets what he would not get through natural means if he did not pray. An answer to prayer means that God supernaturally intervenes and gives what would not be given without this miraculous intervention.

The question as to whether God ever works miracles today is just a part of the age-old question as to whether God ever did work miracles. It is a part of the unbelief that denies God, denies the inspiration of the Bible, denies the virgin birth, the bodily resurrection and the atonement of our Saviour, and denies the need for and the possibility of an actual regeneration, the new birth. I say, To question whether God works miracles today is unbelief.

Yet the question deserves an honest investigation in the light of God's Word and in the light of facts wherever found. And no Christian need ever fear the truth, whether found in the Bible or in nature or in history.

I. The Bible Certainly Promises Miracles in Answer to Prayer and Faith

Anyone who takes the Bible at face value must see that Jesus promised miracles to those who should have faith for them when they prayed. Consider the following promises:

1. In Matthew 17:20 Jesus says,

"If ye have faith as a grain of mustard seed, ye shall say unto this mountain, Remove hence to yonder place; and it shall remove; and nothing shall be impossible unto you."

Beyond any doubt the subject of discussion here is miracles. Jesus had just performed a miracle in casting out a demon from a lunatic boy. Then He says that the disciples are to expect miracles, and if they have faith as a grain of mustard seed, they may easily have a mountain remove out of its place at their word! Certainly that would be a marvelous miracle. And then the Saviour generalizes His teaching in these strong words, "And nothing shall be impossible unto you." For those who have faith, nothing is impossible! For they have at their command the miracle-working power of God.

2. Jesus cursed the barren fig tree, and it withered away presently. How astonished the disciples were when they saw this miracle! Discussing it, Jesus said in Matthew 21:21,22:

"Verily I say unto you, If ye have faith, and doubt not, ye shall not only do this which is done to the fig tree, but also if ye shall say unto this mountain, Be thou removed, and be thou cast into the sea; it shall be done. And all things, whatsoever ye shall ask in prayer, believing, ye shall receive."

Again, the subject of discussion is miracles. Jesus had just worked a mighty miracle in drying up the fig tree from the roots by a word of command. And now He promises the disciples that they can do the same kind of physical miracles if they have faith and do not doubt. They can curse a fig tree or remove a mountain and cast it into the sea if they have faith. And again Jesus moves from the particular to the general and promises, "And all things, whatsoever ye shall ask in prayer, believing, ye shall receive." Certainly He here meant ALL THINGS, which involve miracles of every kind.

3. In Mark 9:14–29 we have the story of Jesus' casting out the dumb spirit of the lunatic boy as told by Mark. It was clearly a miracle. Regarding it Jesus said to the father of the boy,

"If thou canst believe, all things are possible to him that believeth."—Mark 9:23.

Note in this case the promise was not to the twelve disciples, but to the father, a stranger, evidently not even a preacher. And again Jesus promised a miracle to him if he had faith. But more than that, Jesus gave a general law, saying, "All things are possible to him that believeth." Here is a promise not only for the apostles but for this father. It was not only for the Jews but for Gentiles, and not only for that generation but for all generations, whoever had faith. "All things are possible to him that believeth." If the *whosoever* in John 3:16 is meant to involve anybody, in any generation, then the *him* in this verse is meant to involve any creature who trusts Christ in any generation. John 3:16 promises salvation to anyone who trusts in Christ for salvation, anytime, anywhere; and Mark 9:23 promises that literally ALL THINGS are possible to anyone, anywhere, who has faith for the all things. The Scripture does not mean that all who trust in Christ for *salvation* get miracles, but it certainly does mean that in any particular matter one who believes will find the thing possible that he has faith for.

4. In Mark 11:22–24 we have in slightly different words the promise of the Saviour when He discussed with the disciples the withered fig tree which He had cursed. There the Scripture says:

"And Jesus answering saith unto them, Have faith in God. For verily I say unto you, That whosoever shall say unto this mountain, Be thou removed, and be thou cast into the sea; and shall not doubt in his heart, but shall believe that those things which he saith shall come to pass; he shall have whatsoever he saith. Therefore I say unto you, What things soever ye desire, when ye pray, believe that ye receive them, and ye shall have them."

How wonderful that the Holy Spirit here gave us added light on what Jesus promised. Compare this passage with Matthew 21:21,22, and you will see that in Matthew 21:21 there might be some reason to suppose that Jesus was talking to the disciples, the twelve apostles, alone. But here in Mark 11:23 the Saviour plainly says, "Whosoever shall say unto this mountain, Be thou removed, and be thou cast into the sea; and shall not doubt in his heart, but shall believe that those things which he saith shall come to pass; he shall have whatsoever he saith." The promise is not only for the apostles; it is for *whosoever*. If *whosoever* in John 3:16 means anybody who trusts Christ for salvation, then *whosoever* in Mark 11:23 means anybody who will trust Christ for a miracle. If Jesus Christ is to be believed and if the Bible can be trusted, then anybody who has faith for a miracle will get one!

Of course, we must remember that faith is a gift of God and that the Holy Spirit will not help us to have faith about wicked things, things out of the will of God. Yet the point is quite plain here that a miracle was possible in the apostles' day, in answer to the prayer of faith, and that anybody else in the world in any day can have a miracle on exactly the same condition. The apostles did not move that mountain into the sea, and others have not done so yet. But the promise of Jesus Christ still stands, and miracles, He said, are possible for "whosover...shall not doubt in his heart, but shall believe that those things which he saith shall come to pass."

And then Jesus gave the general law of miracles in answer to prayer when He concluded, in Mark 11:24, "Therefore I say unto you, What things soever ye desire, when ye pray, believe that ye receive them, and ye shall have them." How blessed it is to remember that Jesus had specifically mentioned miracles here and that miracles were the topic of conversation and the thing He had in mind when He gave this blessed promise!

5. The night before Jesus was crucified, in the Upper Room He was talking to the saddened disciples; and He gave them there the marvelous promise of John 14:12–14, which says,

"Verily, verily, I say unto you, He that believeth on me, the works that I do shall he do also; and greater works than these shall he do; because I go unto my Father. And whatsoever ye shall ask in my name, that will I do, that the Father may be glorifed in the Son. If ye shall ask any thing in my name, I will do it."

This promise certainly involves miracles. The work that Jesus had been doing, these disciples should do too. But Jesus did not give the promise to the disciples only. Rather, the promise is to "[him] that believeth on me." Anybody who has enough faith in Christ can do His work, the same kind of work that Jesus had been doing. And then Jesus continued His blessed promise addressed to the disciples but evidently intended for everyone, "And whatsoever ye shall ask in my name, that will I do." That *whatsoever* must involve things reaching into the supernatural, things that could be done only by the miracle-working power of God. And verse 14 says, "If ye shall ask any thing in my name, I will do it." *Anything* means "anything." You can put any thing in the place of that word *anything,* and the promise is still literally true—and exactly what Jesus meant. You could read that promise, "If ye shall ask a miracle in My name, I will do it," and still you would not have changed the meaning a particle. *Anything* means "any thing," and a miracle is a *thing,* coming within this blessed promise. Certainly, then, the Saviour promised miracles to those who ask things purely in *His* name. That is, when one can ask a thing wholly in Jesus' name, or with His authority and for His sake, with His approval, then one can get it even if it be a miracle.

6. Jesus gave the Great Commission in Mark 16:15–18, and that Great Commission expressly mentions miracles:

"Go ye into all the world, and preach the gospel to every creature. He that believeth and is baptized shall be saved; but he that believeth not shall be damned. And these signs shall follow them that believe; In my name shall they cast out devils; they shall speak with new tongues; They shall take up serpents; and if they drink any deadly thing, it shall not hurt them; they shall lay hands on the sick, and they shall recover."

Note that this Great Commission is for "all the world," and it is for "every creature."

Notice that the promise is not only to the apostles, but verse 17 says, "These signs shall follow them that believe." This does not mean that "these signs shall follow them that believe for salvation." This is not a promise that these signs, miracles, shall follow every saved person. It is only a promise to people who have faith *for these signs.* One who trusts Christ for salvation, gets salvation. One who would have faith to cast out devils, would cast out devils; and one who had faith to speak in a foreign language that was new to him, would get power to do it exactly as the disciples did at Pentecost. "These signs shall follow them that believe" simply means what all these other promises of Jesus on the same line mean: "All things are possible to him that believeth." One who has faith for a thing can get it.

Even in apostolic times it was never true that every saved person worked miracles or had these signs following him. No, no. Only those had miracles who received faith for the miracles. One who has faith for salvation, gets salvation. One who has faith for a mountain to be cast into the sea, has a mountain cast into the sea. One who has faith for a revival, gets a revival.

I think it is important to remind you that the Lord Jesus never meant these miraculous signs to be the plaything of the curious or the charlatan. These signs were never to exalt men. No one in Bible times ever picked up a snake and let it bite him to show his faith. No one in Bible times drank poison to show that it would not harm him. Yet Paul, on the island of Melita, was bitten by a viper, a very poisonous snake, and by faith he shook off the beast into the fire and felt no harm (Acts 28:1–6). And in the same chapter, in Acts 28:8, we learn that Paul laid his hands upon the father of Publius and prayed for him and healed him. The apostles at Pentecost (and I think others) did speak with tongues that were new to them—that is, in foreign languages they had never learned—to preach the Gospel to people in their own languages in which they were born. And Paul cast a devil out of a fortune-telling girl as recorded in Acts 16:18. No doubt all these signs came as separate instances of separate faith for the particular occasion. And Mark 16:20 indicates that the same kind of thing happened in many, many cases. "And they went forth, and preached every where, the Lord working with them, and confirming the word with signs following." The book of Acts is principally the story of the lives of Peter and Paul, and we may be sure that God signally honored with supernatural manifestations the work of other of His servants everywhere they went—that is, as often as it could honor His name and as often as they had faith for it. Miracles were never done just to show off, never came just at anybody's whim, but were always the answer to somebody's faith for that particular instance.

Summing up these Scriptures, every honest reader of the Bible must agree that God did promise miracles to those who had faith for them.

II. Christianity, a Miracle Religion

You may have heathen religions without miracles. You may have the evolutionary theory without miracles. You may have modernism without miracles. You may have atheism without miracles. BUT YOU CANNOT HAVE CHRISTIANITY WITHOUT MIRACLES! Christianity is a miracle religion.

Every opponent of Christianity opposes it on the point of miracles. Evolutionists do not believe in a direct, immediate, supernatural, miraculous creation. They do not believe that God made something out of nothing, that He did it instantly and not by a process. They do not believe that God made man directly out of dust. Infidels do not believe that the Bible was directly, miraculously inspired of God. They may think good men wrote it; they do not think that God miraculously gave the Book, making it entirely different in kind from other books, and infallibly correct. Critics particularly deny the recorded miracles of the Bible, such as the Flood, the miracles of Jonah and the whale, and of the sun standing still for about a day in its relation to the earth in Joshua's time, for example. Those who do not believe that Christ is the Son of God, of course, mean that they do not believe in the miracles recorded about Him. They believe that there was a man named Jesus who lived, that He was a good man, a great teacher, a fine example. But they do not believe He was God incarnate in human form, that He was born of a virgin, without a human father, that He actually miraculously rose from the dead and ascended bodily into Heaven.

Christianity stands or falls on its miracles. Christianity is a miracle religion.

Other religions teach man to try to be good. Christianity teaches that a man must be supernaturally, miraculously born again, by direct act of God the Holy Spirit's making him a new creature. The Bible teaches clearly that God directly, supernaturally answers prayer, that the Holy Spirit of God literally dwells in the bodies of saved people, to direct them, to comfort them, to give them wisdom and power in a wholly supernatural manner.

Christianity is a religion of present-day miracles. For example, the creation of the universe, the ordering of the planets, the creation of animal life and plant life, the creation of man in the image of God were certainly miraculous. But people who doubt miracles forget that the miracle of creation continues every second. In Colossians 1:16, 17 the Scripture tells us:

"For by him were all things created, that are in heaven, and that are in earth, visible and invisible, whether they be thrones, or dominions, or principalities, or powers: all things were created by him, and for him: And he is before all things, and by him all things consist."

Christ Himself created all things. But that is not all: "by him all things consist." Christ is as miraculously sustaining and holding all things together this moment as He miraculously created them in the beginning! People think that unnumbered millions of stars, suns, planets and comets of the universe simply spin and revolve in their intricate patterns without supervision. That is silly. Christ not only created, but He sustains. His power keeps the earth in its annual journey about the sun. He Himself guides through the infinite trails of space comets which follow a known schedule but which are controlled by forces science cannot fathom nor find. If science has proved anything in the world, it has proved that perpetual motion from one initial start is utterly impossible. There must be a continuing source of energy. The Lord Jesus Christ Himself sustains, personally, the whole universe which He created. And so one who believes that Christ created the worlds must believe that He also sustains them.

Does the heart beat automatically with no supervision? Certainly human beings do not supervise nor control their heartbeats. Then does God keep life in the body? And when and where does a baby get its soul? Does that individuality, that personality that comprises a separate human being—does that come to the baby by chemical processes? Does it come by some mechanical act of nature? Isn't it more likely that the Christ who created the world and sustains it is still the only One who can give and who can sustain life? Then life every day is surrounded with invisible miracles. Christ is in His own creation, sustaining it, and "by him all things consist."

The Holy Spirit is a person. He is not simply nature. He is not simply a divine influence, but a person. The work of the Holy Spirit is as supernatural as the work of God the Father or as the work of Christ. And the Holy Spirit works constantly today His miracles in the lives of men. Note these miracles of the Holy Spirit:

1. He regenerates. The salvation of a soul is a miracle. It is not ordinary, but extraordinary. It is not human, but divine. It is not natural, but supernatural. A new creature in Christ is not the result of the working of any natural law. It is a direct intervention of God Himself through the Holy Spirit, making a spiritually dead person alive, making a child of Hell into a child of God.

2. The Holy Spirit after conversion lives in the body of the believer. After one is "born of the Spirit" (John 3:6), then his body is the literal home of the Holy Spirit (Rom. 8:9; I Cor. 6:19,20). The Holy Spirit is given to comfort the believer, to guide him into all truth, to empower him for service, to grow in him the Christian graces, or fruits, of the Spirit. And remember that all of this is not natural, but supernatural. It is not the result of the working of natural law, but it is the direct intervention of God the Holy Spirit who lives in every Christian. Every man who was ever called to preach had a miracle. Every Christian who ever had a direct leading of the Holy Spirit, instruction as to what he should do, was present at a miracle. Walking down an aisle in a strange audience, knowing almost no one present, I felt impressed to lay my hand upon a man's shoulder and ask him if he were saved. Immediately he began to tremble and then to weep and told me that he was not. In a moment or two he trusted in Christ and was

happily saved. There were few unsaved people present. What led me to select the one man who was already concerned of the few unsaved people in that great audience? Was it natural or supernatural? Was it human or divine? And yet many thousands of Christians have had leading as direct as that.

But we must remember that it is the Holy Spirit Himself who works miracles. It was the Holy Spirit who raised Christ from the dead, and in Ephesians 1:19,20 Paul prayed that New Testament Christians should know "what is the exceeding greatness of his power to us-ward who believe, according to the working of his mighty power, which he wrought in Christ, when he raised him from the dead." And Romans 8:11 says, "But if the Spirit of him that raised up Jesus from the dead dwell in you, he that raised up Christ from the dead shall also quicken your mortal bodies by his Spirit that dwelleth in you." The Holy Spirit raised up Christ from the dead. It is the same Holy Spirit that will raise our bodies.

But this Holy Spirit is the miracle-working One today. Acts 10:38 tells us,

"God anointed Jesus of Nazareth with the Holy Ghost and with power: who went about doing good, and healing all that were oppressed of the devil; for God was with him."

The healings and miracles that Jesus did were done by the power of the Holy Spirit. And we are commanded to be filled with the Holy Spirit, as Jesus was filled with the Spirit; and in His power we are to do His work.

First Corinthians 12:4–11 tells how the Holy Spirit distributes His gifts, severally as He will; and those gifts include prophecy, the gift of healing, the discerning of spirits, the power to speak foreign languages, the gift of physical miracles, etc. But all these gifts are miraculous, supernatural manifestations of the Holy Spirit. And then this startling statement is made in I Corinthians 12:7,

"But the manifestation of the Spirit is given to every man to profit withal."

Anytime the Holy Spirit manifests Himself, it is a supernatural, miraculous work. Not all Christians may have the same manifestation, but every Christian may have some manifestation of the Holy Spirit, we are told! So I say that Christianity is a matter of present-day miracles.

Do you believe there are angels? The Bible has a very clear teaching about angels. They are heavenly beings. According to the Bible they go and come without any regard to natural laws such as gravity and the limitations of time and space. Angels are messengers from God and report back to God. They are "all ministering spirits, sent forth to minister for them [us] who shall be heirs of salvation" (Heb. 1:14). Human beings do not often see these heavenly beings, but they are always about us. Jacob saw them more than once. Elisha saw them; and Joshua, Gideon, Samson's father and mother, Balaam, Daniel, Hagar, Zechariah, Joseph, Mary, Paul, and many others saw angels, according to recorded instances. Angels went to Sodom. Angels appeared at the open tomb of the Saviour. Angels appeared after He went away and reminded the disciples that Jesus would come again. The Scripture says that little children have guardian angels—"their angels do always behold the face of my Father which is in heaven" (Matt. 18:10). Psalm 34:7 tells us,

"The angel of the LORD encampeth round about them that fear him, and delivereth them."

So the plain teaching of the Scripture is that angels are all about us, invisible to us, but guarding us, ministering to us, protecting us. But if that is true, it is all miraculous. It is not natural, but supernatural. It is not human, but divine. It is not ordinary, but extraordinary.

The supernatural, the miraculous, is all about us though unseen by our blinded eyes and ignored by the unbelieving. Christianity is a miracle religion, and miracles are present-day facts.

The Bible itself shows that miracles were scattered throughout all human history until the last record of the Bible closed. There were miracles before the Flood, like the translation of Enoch, in the midst of wickedness. The divine revelation to Noah, the coming of animals into the ark, and the great Flood were all miraculous. After the Flood the confusion of tongues, the many miracles in connection with Abraham, the birth of Isaac, and the destruction of Sodom and Gomorrah followed. Jacob and Joseph had miracles, dreams, revelations from God. After the silent period in Egypt when revelation takes up the story again, there are miracles with Moses: the burning bush, the plagues in Egypt, the crossing of the Red Sea, the marvels of the wilderness period. Miracles continued with Joshua, then in the period of the judges. Miracles were given to Samson, Gideon and others. Throughout the kingdom period there were mighty miracles at the hands of the prophets: Elijah, Elisha and others, with King Hezekiah, with Jehoshaphat, and with an unnamed prophet that warned Jeroboam, and with others. There were miracles in the captivity as recorded in the book of Daniel. After the captivity, angels talked with Zechariah. There were visions and interpretations wholly miraculous. The New Testament starts with miracles and ends the same way. Miracles followed Peter, Paul, Stephen and Philip. The five narrative books of the New Testament—that is, the four Gospels and the book of Acts—are full of miracles. Miracles are in the first of the book of Acts, and then in the very last chapter the miracles promised in Mark 16:17, 18 followed Paul. Bitten by a serpent he suffered no harm, and he laid hands on the sick, and they recovered. But that isn't all. Many years later John, the beloved apostle, was on the isle of Patmos, and Jesus Christ appeared to him miraculously; and God revealed unto him the whole course of human history to the end. The Bible is simply a history of miracles.

There may have been brief periods when, because of unbelief and sin, there were no outward manifestations of the miracle-working power of God. There were relatively brief periods with no miracles recorded. But usually that is because there is no record of the entire period, such as the period between Malachi and the New Testament, the four hundred years in Egypt, etc. It would be presumptuous to say there were no miracles in those periods. We simply do not know of any.

Some say that miracles stopped with the closing of the canon of Scripture. But how foolish that is. Men are still born again when they trust in Christ, are they not? Then that is a miracle. Men still have the Holy Spirit dwelling in their bodies, do they not? Then miracles continue! The angel of the Lord still encamps around about them that fear Him and delivers them, does He not? Then there are present-day, living miracles.

Do you say the *physical* miracles ended? No! Bible prophecies foretell miracles for all the future. The return of Christ for His saints, the translation of living saints, the resurrection of Christian dead, the ascent in the air to meet Jesus, the marvelous events of the Tribulation Period as recorded in Revelation, the return of Christ to reign, the millennium of happiness on earth, the resurrection of the unsaved dead and their judgment, the destruction of the world by fire, its re-creation into a new earth surrounded by a new heaven—all these are miracles, physical miracles. The future is packed full of miracles according to the divine prophecy.

In fact, the Bible never hints that there was any period in which people could not have had miracles if they had trusted the Lord; and the Bible does not foretell any period in the future in which people will not have miracles if they believe God!

Christianity is a miracle religion. The Bible is a history of past miracles and a prophecy of miracles to come! Every saved soul has already had a spiritual miracle, and one day every saved person will have a physical, literal, miraculous resurrection, or translation, of his body, as wonderful as the resurrection of Jesus Christ and of the same order.

I believe if we are conscious that the Holy Spirit of God lives within us, that angels are all about us, that a miracle-working God still sustains all things, it will be easier for us to believe that God can and will answer our prayers, that He has a limitless ability and a limitless willingness to do what we need for us whom He loves so well!

III. Miracles of the Bible Are Given as Examples for Us

In the very nature of the case, the fact that the Bible is full of miracles must be intended to teach us that God is a miracle-working God. Why should God tantalize us with accounts of how He has blessed others, how He has heard their prayers, how He has healed their sicknesses, how He has provided for their needs, if He be not willing to do the same for us whenever it is right and good?

But the Scripture repeatedly tells us that these miracles are given for examples to us. For instance in Psalm 81:10 God tells us,

"I am the LORD thy God, which brought thee out of the land of Egypt: open thy mouth wide, and I will fill it."

What could the Lord here mean but this: that He who did miracles before is able to do them again! He who blessed Israel with mighty blessings will do the same for us if we trust Him. Evidently He means that all the wonders accompanying the deliverance of the people of Israel and their support and protection in the wilderness journeys are written to encourage us, and that therefore we should open our mouths wide in faith and receive like blessings when needed.

In I Corinthians 10:1–5 God reminds us again how the Jewish fathers were brought out of Egypt under a cloud, passed through the Red Sea and ate of manna and drank of the water out of the rock. Then verse 6 sums up the lesson, saying,

"Now these things were our examples, to the intent we should not lust after evil things, as they also lusted."

The miracles accompanying the birth of the Jewish nation "were our examples." And the way God punished them with plagues for their sins and miraculous manifestations are to warn us too, lest we should desire evil things as they did and be punished as they were.

Doesn't that plainly mean that the miracles of those days are meant for examples to us?

Again in the same chapter, verse 11 says,

"Now all these things happened unto them for ensamples: and they are written for our admonition, upon whom the ends of the world are come."

All these miracles and wonders, these blessings and cursings, "happened unto them for ensamples." Not only that, but "they are written for our admonition, upon whom the ends of the world are come." To the end of the world the miracles recorded in the Bible are for our admonition.

If the age of physical miracles is past, here would have been a good place for the Holy Spirit to have said so; but He did not. Instead, He said those miracles were sample miracles and that the accounts of them are for our admonition in these last days!

The translations of Enoch before the Flood and of Elijah later were evidently sample miracles, pointing toward the translation of every living saint at the return of Christ. And our translation will be exactly the same kind of literal, physical miracles as they had.

The plagues of Egypt are certainly types and samples of miracles that will occur during the Great Tribulation Period. The turning of water to blood, the great darkness, the hail and many others of the plagues of Egypt are to be repeated, as foretold in the book of Revelation.

The resurrection of Christ, that mighty miracle, is specially mentioned as a type and prophecy of future resurrections of all the saints. First Corinthians 15:20,23 says, "Now is Christ risen from the dead, and become the firstfruits of them that slept....But every man in his own order: Christ the firstfruits; afterward they that are Christ's at his coming." Christ is only the firstfruits. We will be the following harvest. Romans 8:11 again refers to this truth that our mortal bodies will be raised as the body of Christ was.

I am saying that the Bible miracles necessarily involve future miracles for the rest of us.

CHAPTER XVIII

MIRACLES TODAY, Continued

I. Some Objections Answered

Here we will notice a few of the principal arguments offered by those who say that the age of miracles is past, that God does not work miracles, especially physical miracles, today.

1. It is claimed that miracles were never given except to introduce a new epoch or dispensation. But a careful review of the miracles of the Bible proves that is not true. What epoch did Enoch begin? What age or dispensation did Elijah and Elisha usher in? The miracles in the book of Daniel—what age or epoch did they begin?

2. It is claimed that miracles were needed until the Bible was written but not after that date. But the Bible itself foretells miracles in all the ages to come: at the return of Christ, during the Tribulation Period, during the millennial reign of Christ, at the last judgment, and beyond. So miracles did not end with the Bible. And the Bible itself never hints that after the Scriptures were completed there would be no more need for miracles.

3. It is said that the miracles of healing particularly that Jesus performed were done only to prove His Messiahship, to prove His deity. But that is not the motive the Scripture mentions for His work. Acts 10:38 tells us Jesus "went about doing good, and healing all that were oppressed of the devil." He did not go about "proving His deity," but He went about doing good. And Mark 2:5 tells us that Jesus healed a man sick of the palsy "when Jesus saw their faith"! Why, that is the same reason He has promised to answer prayers for anything (Mark 11:24; Matt. 21:22)! Then Jesus healed that man for the same reason that He always answers prayer, the reason of faith. And when Jesus healed the son of the widow of Nain, the reason is given, "And when the Lord saw her, he had compassion on her, and said unto her, Weep not. And he came and touched the bier: and they that bare him stood still. And he said, Young man, I say unto thee, Arise. And he that was dead sat up, and began to speak. And he delivered him to his mother" (Luke 7:13–15). We do not need to look further when the Bible tells us Jesus' motive. He had compassion on the mother and raised her son! But the Lord Jesus still has compassion on people in trouble! Luke 14:1–5 tells how Jesus healed a man with the dropsy on the Sabbath Day and explained that He did it from the same motives as they would take an ox or an ass fallen into a pit and pull him out even if it were on the Sabbath Day. The motive was compassion!

Indeed, the Saviour did not do His miracles to prove His deity. When

Jesus healed two blind men, He "straitly charged them, saying, See that no man know it" (Matt. 9:30). Again He charged his disciples "that they should tell no man that he was Jesus the Christ" (Matt. 16:20). To the Mount of Transfiguration He took only three disciples and warned them not to tell of the miracle there (Matt. 17:9). When He healed the daughter of Jairus, "he suffered no man to go in, save Peter, and James, and John, and the father and mother of the maiden," and then "he charged them that they should tell no man what was done" (Luke 8:51–56).

It is generally believed that miracles came only in rare and isolated cases, and in some sense that was true. But certain kinds of miracles continued throughout the Bible times almost without interruption, we believe.

For example, prophecy—that is, receiving divine revelations concerning the future or at least divine revelations of knowledge not otherwise to be known—was prevalent throughout Bible times.

Abel doubtless had divine revelations about the coming Saviour and knew the meaning of a bloody sacrifice. Enoch was a prophet concerning even the second coming of Christ (Jude, verses 14,15). Noah was plainly a prophet of God in foretelling the future of his descendants (Gen. 9:24–27). God told Abimelech that Abraham was a prophet (Gen. 20:7). Isaac in blessing Jacob and Esau proved that he had the gift of prophecy (Gen. 27:26–40). Doubtless even Laban and Bethuel and their family had this gift of prophecy too, as we see from Genesis 24:60. Jacob and Joseph likewise had this same gift (Gen. 48:15–22; 49:1–29; 50:24,25). Even during the sad period of the judges there were prophets and prophetesses. David was a prophet (Acts 2:29,30). And the gift of prophecy certainly extended throughout Old Testament times, as far as we know, without any long interruption.

But this gift of prophecy is spoken of as the normal possession of New Testament Christians. Christians are commanded to covet to prophesy, though we are not to covet speaking in foreign languages (I Cor. 14:1). We are told that if all Christians prophesy, the unsaved will be convicted and all his doubts about God will disappear (I Cor. 14:24,25). We are told that "ye may all prophesy" (vs. 31). And again we are commanded, "Covet to prophesy" (vs. 39). Even women, who are expressly forbidden to teach or preach, may have the gift of prophecy (I Cor. 11:5). Do not be confused about the term *prophesy*. It means exactly the same in the Old Testament and in the New, and it is not preaching. Prophetesses never did preach.

But if the gift of prophecy is the normal thing for New Testament churches, then that means that the miraculous, supernatural working of God is to continue down through the ages in His church. Thus, when miracles are past, it is because the faith of God's people has waned.

The inspiration of the Bible was certainly miraculous, supernatural.

Every man who wrote a part of the Bible was moved by the Holy Ghost and given a supernatural, infallible revelation, speaking with the very words of God (I Cor. 2:13; Isa. 51:16; Jer. 1:9; Exod. 24:4). Again that increases the spread of miracles. Wherever there was a prophet writing part of the Book of God, then there was a marvelous miracle taking place.

But I believe that God's miracles concerning the Bible did not end when John wrote the last words of the book of Revelation long after Paul had been beheaded. For the Bible is itself a living miracle. "The word of God is quick, and powerful" (Heb. 4:12). The word *quick* here means "alive." It is the same word used about the living people in the phrase, "the quick and the dead," in Acts 10:42, in II Timothy 4:1, in I Peter 4:5. The Bible is a living thing. That means that the power of God is in the Word, and it is a living miracle. The things that the Bible does are miraculous things. If the saving of a soul, regeneration, is a miracle and if that is done by the Word of God used by the Holy Spirit, then the Word of God is miraculous even today.

Reverent students have long believed, as I do, that the preservation of the Word of God down through these centuries is miraculous and supernatural. How Satan hates the Bible! The conspiracies of Romish priests, burning multiplied thousands of copies, the putting to death of those that harbored the Bible and insisted on reading it—these could not do away with the Word of God. The assaults of the infidels, the attacks of atheists and modernists—these could not do away with the Bible. It could not be lost through mistranslation, through the errors of copyists, through the awful darkness and ignorance of the Dark Ages. The Bible has been preserved of God. It lives and abides forever. And that preservation is surely a miracle of God, such as other books do not have.

This supernatural, miraculously living Bible may be typified by the pot of manna which was collected and put within the ark of the covenant and there preserved miraculously from spoiling, century after century (Exod. 16:32–34; Heb. 9:4). The preservation of that manna, the bread from Heaven, was a living, physical miracle down through the centuries. If God had failed to sustain it miraculously one day, then it would have decayed and "stank" as the manna did that had been kept more than a day by the people. That was an everyday miracle. But the same kind of miracle lives today in the Bible, the Word. It is a miracle Book. It has life in it. It "is a discerner of the thoughts and intents of the heart" (Heb. 4:12).

Aaron's rod that budded was likewise miraculously preserved in the ark of testimony. The almond buds and blossoms that grew out of that dry stick seemed to have been miraculously kept fresh and unwithered through the centuries as a reminder of the miraculous sustaining of God's ministry and the supernatural power that was at the beck and call of Israel when in the will of God (Num. 17:8–10; Heb. 9:4). The preservation of that budded and blooming walking stick from an almond tree was a miracle every day that it was kept.

Likewise, the fire of the Lord that never went out on the altar and the Shekinah glory over the mercy seat where God dwelt, were living, day and night miracles down through the centuries in the Tabernacle and in the temple until the temple was forsaken by the Lord.

In Numbers 5:12–31 we have a remarkable teaching that God's miracle-working presence was with Israel all the time, to bring sin to judgment miraculously, to whisper to a husband if the wife was impure; and when she drank the bitter water, then if she were guilty of adultery "this water that causeth the curse shall go into thy bowels, to make thy belly to swell, and thy thigh to rot." And if she was not guilty there would be no evil effect. Surely that means that the living, miracle-working God was present continually to bring sin to judgment; and that this miracle would take place at the hand of whatsoever husband and wife and priest were called upon to make the test, down through the years! It is impossible to rule out miracles in the Christian religion. Where there is any manifestation of God, there is a miracle.

II. Many Authenticated Miracles in Modern Times

The Bible teaches that Jesus Christ is "the same yesterday, and to day, and for ever" (Heb. 13:8). The Lord Himself said, "I am the LORD, I change not" (Mal. 3:6). All God's promises about limitless answers to prayer that would involve the cursing of trees, the moving of mountains, or literally "WHAT THINGS SOEVER ye desire" or "if [we] shall ask ANY THING in my name," show that miracles will last as long as God's promises are true, whenever people are given faith to trust Him for miracles.

But this is not just a matter of theory; it is a matter of actual historical fact. In countless instances since the Bible was written, God has worked miracles; and these miracles have been witnessed by the best men and women of the centuries, who give their witness that they know God still answers prayer, even miraculously.

Dr. H. A. Ironside, in *Moody Church News*, November 1941, well says: "There are those who say today that miracles passed away with the apostles. That is not true. Many wonderful miracles have been wrought in answer to prayer during the last 1,900 years, and here and there throughout the world today God still acts in wonderful grace. Again and again God puts forth His hand in healing power, and people who have been given up by doctors have been marvelously recovered as God's people have prayed. Other signs and wonders, too, have accompanied Christianity. It really behooves us to be careful and not go to either of two extremes—let us not insist that the working of the Spirit of God in manifesting His power by miracles and signs is past; and, on the other hand, let us not say that He will always so act if we ask Him to do so. The measure in which He delights to work is left with Him."

Dr. W. B. Riley, writing on divine healing, says: "Justin Martyr, Irenaeus, Tertullian, Origen, Clement, and others tell us of cases of devils cast out, of tongues given, of poison failing of its effects, and of the sick raised to health in answer to prayer. Such authors as Waterland, Dodwell, and Marshall insist that miracles of healing did not fail until the rise of the Catholic Church, and we know from history that since that time they have appeared among God's most devout people—the Waldenses, Moravians, Huguenots, Friends, Baptists, and Methodists, not to speak of the experience of the Scotch Covenanters, Knox, Wishart, Livingstone, Welsh, Baillie, Peden, Craig; as also with George Fox, the father of Quakerism, and our own Baptist fathers, Powell, Knollys, and Jessey; and these were men that followed the letter of our text."

Other sources prove beyond any doubt that even among Catholics, and in the midst of much superstition and tradition, God has occasionally worked mighty miracles in answer to prayer.

Dr. Alexis Carrel, M.D., had in the *Reader's Digest* for March 1941 an article on "Prayer Is Power," and this scientist, Dr. Carrel, takes the position that miracles are a fact, often attested by intelligent, reliable people. The footnote to his article says:

"Dr. Alexis Carrel has long been impressed by the fact that many of life's phenomena cannot be scientifically explained. He knows, for example, that miracles of healing are possible; he spent weeks at Lourdes studying them, and will never forget seeing a cancerous sore shrivel to a scar before his eyes. Dr. Carrel concluded 33 years of brilliant biological research at the Rockefeller Institute in 1939. Among his many honors are the Nordhoff-Jung medal for cancer research and the Nobel Prize for success in suturing blood vessels. His *Man, the Unknown* was a best-seller in 1935."

This Nobel Prize winner, this Rockefeller Institute scientist, has seen miracles with his own eyes. "He knows, for example, that miracles of healing are possible"; saw actual miracles of healing at the Catholic shrine Lourdes, spent weeks studying them, "and will never forget seeing a cancerous sore shrivel to a scar before his eyes." So God still works miracles in answer to prayer.

Do you not believe that God works miracles of casting out devils in modern times? Then you are certainly behind the times and are not acquainted with the best in high-grade foreign missionary literature. For example, you need to read the story, *Pastor Hsi, One of China's Christians,* written by Mrs. Howard Taylor of the China Inland Mission. This Chinese Christian, Pastor Hsi, signed his name "Master of Demons" and again and again, repeatedly, by prayer, cast out devils, exactly in the fashion that Christ and His apostles did it in Bible times. Furthermore, these miracles have been attested by the leaders and the best missionaries of the China Inland Mission and by others. Similar cases have been reported from a number of mission fields. God still casts out devils in answer to prayer.

Can God raise the dead in answer to prayer? I answer that God can do exactly the same today in answer to prayer that He could do any other day in all of history. God has not changed. His power, His willingness, His compassion have not changed. His promises about wonders in answer to the prayer of faith still stand.

Dr. Charles A. Blanchard, late president of Wheaton College, Wheaton, Illinois, is the author of a blessed book, *Getting Things from God*, a book on prayer. The book is published by the Moody Press of Chicago. Dr. Blanchard gives in his book the remarkable story of a railroad engineer raised from the dead in answer to his wife's prayer. Dr. Blanchard says:

"A Railroad Engineer Testifies

"I was a few weeks ago in the Eighth Avenue Mission in New York. On the platform by me sat a gentleman, to whom I was introduced, but whom I had never before seen. When the meeting had progressed for an hour or so, Miss Wray, the superintendent, called upon him for a testimony. He said: 'Friends, about two and a half or three years ago I was in the hospital in Philadelphia. I was an engineer on the Pennsylvania Lines, and although I had a praying wife, I had all my life been a sinful man. At this time I was very ill. I became greatly wasted. I weighed less than one hundred pounds. Finally the doctor who was attending me said to my wife that I was dead, but she said: "No, he is not dead. He cannot be dead. I have prayed for him for twenty-seven years, and God has promised me that he should be saved. Do you think God would let him die now after I have prayed twenty-seven years, and God has promised, and he is not saved?" "Well," the doctor replied, "I do not know anything about that, but I know that he is dead." And the screen was drawn around the cot, which in the hospital separates between the living and the dead.

" 'To satisfy my wife, other physicians were brought, one after another, until seven were about the cot, and each one of them as he came up and made the examination confirmed the testimony of all who had preceded. The seven doctors said that I was dead. Meanwhile my wife was kneeling by the side of my cot, insisting that I was not dead—that if I were dead God would bring me back, for He had promised her that I should be saved, and I was not yet saved. By and by her knees began to pain her, kneeling on the hard hospital floor. She asked the nurse for a pillow, and the nurse brought her a pillow upon which she kneeled. One hour, two hours, three hours passed. The screen still stood by the cot. I was lying there still, apparently dead. Four hours, five hours, six hours, seven hours, thirteen hours passed, and all this while my wife was kneeling by the cot-side, and when people remonstrated and wished her to go away she said: "No, he has to be saved. God will bring him back if he is dead. He is not dead. He cannot die until he is saved."

"'At the end of thirteen hours I opened my eyes, and she said: "What do you wish, my dear?" And I said: "I wish to go home," and she said: "You shall go home." But when she proposed it, the doctors raised their hands in horror. They said, "Why, it will kill him. It will be suicide." She said: "You have had your turn. You said he was dead already. I am going to take him home."

"'I weigh now 246 pounds. I still run a fast train on the Pennsylvania Lines. I have been out to Minneapolis on a little vacation, telling men what Jesus can do, and I am glad to tell you what Jesus can do.'"

Dr. Blanchard was a great educator, a man of national prominence, a scholar, as well as a devout Christian. It was not hard for him to believe that God had answered the prayer of a wife for her unsaved husband and that he was brought back in order that he might be saved. And if it is hard for you to believe, then I ask you in the words of Paul the apostle, "Why should it be thought a thing incredible with you, that God should raise the dead?" (Acts 26:8).

If such an occurrence is rare, then it is equally rare that a woman should pray like that and believe God. God still answers prayer for those who trust Him.

In the little booklet called *The Finnish Gold Story*, Dr. S. D. Gordon, author of the famous "Quiet Talks" series, tells of a remarkable case of an outstanding miracle in Finland where in answer to a woman's prayer God actually multiplied the money which was put away to build a chapel, until there was enough to pay all the bills. It was in a time of real distress, it followed long and faithful prayer, and God was greatly glorified in this wonderful miracle.

Dr. Gordon himself had occasion to go to Finland, to meet the woman whose prayers had been answered; and from her he heard the details of the amazing story and then had the miracle confirmed by others who knew the facts. The woman was a postmistress, handled hundreds of thousands of dollars, was a responsible and intelligent public servant; and the most rigorous investigation convinced Dr. Gordon beyond any doubt that an actual physical miracle had been performed; that just exactly as the Lord Jesus multiplied the loaves and fishes to feed the five thousand, so He multiplied the money, in answer to prayer, to build His chapel. The story is too long to tell here, but it will enrich every heart who can get the book and read it.

Miracles of healing have been so many in modern times I will not take the time to mention many. Before me is a newspaper clipping dated June 14, 1939, furnished by the Associated Press. The headline says, "HER SIGHT RESTORED—AFTER 2 DAYS OF PRAYER." And then the clipping follows:

"Hemphill, Texas, June 14—(AP)—Mrs. Mattie Boyett, 69 years old, believes prayer restored her sight after fifteen years of blindness.

"Ill of an incurable malady, Mrs. Boyett prayed for 2 days and nights that she might see her grandchildren. She feared death was near.

"Monday she could see dimly. Tuesday her sight was stronger. A prominent Sabine County physician examined Mrs. Boyett. He said she apparently suffered from glaucoma but he could not account for her restored sight. He never had heard of a similar case.

"Mrs. Boyett lost the sight of an eye 32 years ago. A film grew over the other, and she was blind fifteen years. The film has disappeared. No physician has treated her eye for several years, she said."

Dr. W. B. Riley in his little book *Saved or Lost?* tells of the wonderful healing of Miss Hollister. He says:

"Miss Hollister, of Minneapolis, for seven years lay on a couch on the fifth floor in Syndicate Arcade, her right lower limb shriveled and drawn; and yet one day, as she and others prayed, Jesus of Nazareth, the Physician of all physicians, passed that way, and she heard Him say: *'I will; be thou whole.'* Instantly that weariness, that waiting, that affliction was at an end!

"From that moment she walked these streets on two good feet, entered this house of prayer scores and scores of times, bore her testimony in our prayer meetings again and again, as to how, by one touch, one speech from the Master's lips, her weariness and waiting were at an end!"

The book *The Ministry of Healing* by Dr. A. J. Gordon, late pastor of the Clarendon Avenue Baptist Church, Boston, the head of Boston Bible College, gives many marvelous and well-authenticated cases of healing and gives something of a history of divine healing down through the centuries. Miracles? Yes, God does work miracles in answer to prayer whenever it will please Him to do so and whenever someone prays the prayer of faith!

In the book *Early Recollections of Dwight L. Moody* by Honorable John V. Farwell, published by the Moody Press of Chicago, is the account of a miraculous healing to which Moody was a witness. Mr. Farwell was a leading philanthropist, a fervent Christian worker associated with D. L. Moody, a large backer of the Y.M.C.A. in those early days, the man for whom Farwell Hall in Chicago was named. Mr. Farwell says:

"Soon after this a devout Christian man from a neighboring state had business in our city, which detained him several months. He at once became very much interested in the Association (particularly the noon prayer meeting) and Mr. Moody's Mission School, and was abundant in labors with him in these two fields. He had had hip disease from his early youth and was then thirty-eight years old. The disease had caused the dislocation of the hip joint, making one leg some three inches shorter than the other. His walking about from house to house with Brother Moody in connection with the Mission Sunday School had made the disease much more painful than usual, until he had determined to have a surgical operation performed if it should promise any relief. On Saturday, he had made an engagement with a surgeon to that end, and was to have been examined on the Monday following. On Sunday evening after the usual labors of the day, he invited Brother Moody and myself to his room, as he had something very important to tell us.

"We all went from the Sunday School prayer meeting to his room, where with choked utterance he gave the following account of the Saturday night's experiences in that room (after giving us quite an extended account of his Christian experience, and his lameness which we had both noticed for months). He said he went from his bath to his room with the thought, 'Why cannot my hip be made whole as well as that impotent man's who lay at the beautiful gate of the temple?' Then he fell asleep convinced that there was no reason why he could not claim the promises for such a purpose. In his sleep he dreamed that the surgeon had opened his thigh with a knife and set the bone, in an incredibly short space of time, and waking out of his sleep he was astonished to find his pain all gone and still more to find that both limbs were of the same length when he got up to walk. We had not noticed that he had no cane on Sunday though we had noticed that his walk was changed and when we came to his room he astonished us by running upstairs two steps at a time, using one leg as well as the other. It will be fourteen years in June since this occurred, and you are the first person to whom I have mentioned it in writing, for this reason. For these fourteen years I have not seen any reason in the history of this brother, why God should so deal with him (as he purposely abstains from mentioning it) that might not be found in hundreds of other Christians, except his own statement of faith in God's promises for such a purpose."

In this case the healing was instantaneous, it was witnessed by thoroughly reliable Christian men, and on their authority we ought to believe it.

In the book *Miraculous Healing* by Dr. Henry W. Frost, bearing the special endorsement of Dr. Charles G. Trumbull, late editor of *The Sunday School Times*, Dr. Frost gives the story of six healings which he plainly marks as miraculous, since they were instantaneous and the healings were performed without the usual natural means. One instance was where he himself was instantly healed in answer to prayer when he had about given up to die. Another was the healing of Hudson Taylor, the founder of the China Inland Mission, which happened when only he and Mr. and Mrs. Taylor were present on a houseboat in China and Mr. Taylor was at the point of death. Another was of the marvelous healing of an insane woman. Another, yet, was the healing of a well-known Bible teacher who has recently gone to Glory. Another was the instant healing of Dr. Frost's own son after long prayer and after doctors had utterly failed.

In the little book *I Cried, He Answered,* published by the Bible Institute Colportage Association and compiled by Henry W. Adams, Norman H. Camp, William Norton and F. A. Steven, and with an introduction by Dr. Charles Gallaudet Trumbull, former editor of *The Sunday School Times,* are accounts of many marvelous answers to prayer. Some of these answers to prayer were direct miracles. Among them is this testimony:

"Optic Nerves Restored

"It was while at the Bible Institute (Chicago) in 1898 that I had serious trouble with the optic nerve, so that I was unable to study or read more than perhaps five minutes continuously. The retina of the eye became so exceedingly sensitive that even the light was painful.

"I was excused from all class work, and for the first time in my life began to think of calling upon God for divine healing. I had heard Dr. Torrey speak on this subject in the classroom; so I went to him and asked if he thought God would be pleased to intervene in my case. Dr. Torrey said he was sure that if I would take my stand on the promise in James 5:14–16, God would heal me.

"Accordingly, we arranged that at Dr. Torrey's home he would anoint me that day at noon. At the appointed hour together with Mrs. Curtis, we went to the home of our friend. After the anointing and prayer, I went directly to my study and took up all my class work.

"N. R. C."

God works miracles in answer to prayer!

Charles G. Finney, the great evangelist, in his autobiography tells of many miracles: men struck dead for opposing revivals; sinners falling in many, many cases, unable to lift themselves up; of the Holy Spirit's revealing to Finney and others what God would do. But here is Finney's account of how a woman, in answer to prayer, was instantly given the ability to read the Bible, when before she did not know even the alphabet:

"I addressed another, a tall, dignified-looking woman, and asked her what was the state of her mind. She replied immediately that she had given her heart to God and went on to say that the Lord had taught her to read, since she had learned how to pray. I asked her what she meant. She said she never could read and never had known her letters. But when she gave her heart to God, she was greatly distressed that she could not read God's Word. 'But I thought,' she said, 'that Jesus could teach me to read; and I asked Him if He would not be pleased to teach me to read His Word.' She said, 'I thought when I had prayed that I could read. The children have a Testament, and I went and got it; and I thought I could read what I had heard them read. But,' said she, 'I went over to the school ma'am and asked her if I read right; and she said I did; and since then,' said she, 'I can read the Word of God for myself.'

"I said no more but thought there must be some mistake about this as the woman appeared to be quite in earnest and quite intelligent in what she said. I took pains afterwards to inquire of her neighbors about her. They gave her an excellent character, and they all affirmed that it had been notorious that she could not read a syllable until after she was converted. I leave this to speak for itself: there is no use in theorizing about it. Such, I think, were the undoubted facts."

I have given these true accounts given by eyewitnesses of wonders that God has done, to encourage you to pray. Let no one tell you that God has changed His plan about answering prayer, that such answers are for another dispensation. "According to your faith be it unto you" (Matt. 9:29). "If thou canst believe, all things are possible to him that believeth" (Mark 9:23).

"And Jesus answering saith unto them, Have faith in God. For verily I say unto you, That whosoever shall say unto this mountain, Be thou removed, and be thou cast into the sea, and shall not doubt in his heart, but shall believe that those things which he saith shall come to pass; he shall have whatsoever he saith. Therefore I say unto you, What things soever ye desire, when ye pray, believe that ye receive them, and ye shall have them" (Mark 11:22–24).

CHAPTER XIX

HINDRANCES TO PRAYER

"...that your prayers be not hindered."—I Pet. 3:7.

"Behold, the LORD's *hand is not shortened, that it cannot save; neither his ear heavy, that it cannot hear: But your iniquities have separated between you and your God, and your sins have hid his face from you, that he will not hear."*—Isa. 59:1,2.

"For the eyes of the Lord are over the righteous, and his ears are open unto their prayers: but the face of the Lord is against them that do evil."—I Pet. 3:12.

"If I regard iniquity in my heart, the Lord will not hear me."—Ps. 66:18.

Daily, Regular Answers to Prayer Should Be Normal for All Christians

The normal Christian life is a life of regular, daily answers to prayer. In the model prayer Jesus taught His disciples to pray daily for bread and expect to get it and to ask daily for forgiveness, for deliverance from the evil one and for other needs and daily to get the answers they sought.

That is the way Jesus Himself lived, in daily unhindered communion with the Father, so that He could say to His Father and our Father, "I knew that thou hearest me always" (John 11:42). And all the teaching of the Lord Jesus about prayer shows that we too have a normal, day-by-day unhindered intercourse with God, asking and receiving, seeking and finding, knocking and having God open to us. He plainly said, "Hitherto have ye asked nothing in my name: ask, and ye shall receive, that your joy may be full" (John 16:24). When we are told in James 4:2 that "ye have not, because ye ask not," it is proper to infer that God intended *asking* to be followed by *having* and that the Christian in the will of God can live day by day in the fullness of joy of having his prayers answered.

It is perfectly normal for an obedient child to ask for food every meal time and get it, get all he wants, and eat until he is perfectly satisfied. And using that figure the Saviour said, "If ye then, being evil, know how to give good gifts unto your children, how much more shall your Father which is in heaven give good things to them that ask him?" (Matt. 7:11).

A depositor whose account is in good condition normally has every check he draws honored by the bank. Then why cannot a child of God day by day draw on the bank of Heaven, have his prayers answered as a matter of course, as a daily business? He can! When a Christian fails to have his prayer-check cashed, he should regard it as proof that something is wrong that needs attention at once.

When I turn faucets in bathroom or kitchen, I expect water to pour forth every time. If I turned the tap and water did not come, I would be surprised. Also I would know that something radical was wrong, and I would immediately set out to find out why the water did not run. If I press a light switch and the light does not shine, or if I plug in an electric motor and there is no power, I know that something is wrong, dead wrong, that the connection with the powerhouse is broken; and I set out to find what is wrong and to remedy it. Just so, every Christian ought to be in daily communion with God and ought to live the joyful life of answered prayer. And when anything hinders his prayers, the Christian ought immediately to be able to find out what is wrong and get it remedied.

Now the Scriptures above, at the head of this chapter, indicate that there are sins which hinder the prayers of Christians, sins that turn God's face away so that He will not hear, yea, sins which make it so that God cannot, in righteousness, heed the cry of His own child whom He loves! We are not left in the dark about these sins. God, in His wonderful love, has shown us in the Bible the things that grieve Him, the things that make it so He cannot fully answer our prayers.

Often we pray for daily bread or for other daily necessities, such as money for rent, or for a job, or furniture or clothes, things for which God tells us to pray; and yet no answer comes. Christians often pray for the conversion of loved ones, pray for revivals, pray for help in temptation—all matters about which every Christian certainly *has a right* to pray, matters about which God has *declared in His Word* that He is concerned and which He is anxious to give us; and yet Christians often do not get the answer to their prayers. Why? The answer is that many a *good* prayer cannot be answered by a holy God because of sins in the life and heart of the one who prays.

It may be that you have some of your prayers answered, or think you do. The dear Lord who "sendeth rain on the just and on the unjust" (Matt. 5:45) and is "kind unto the unthankful" (Luke 6:35) may give you many things that do not come because He respects your prayers and answers them, but because of His infinite mercy which is poured out even upon the vilest sinners. The God who still gives breath to the murderer, still gives food to the man who never prays, the God who gives all the bounties of nature to a sinning, Christ-rejecting race—that God still loves and cares for His children even when they live in sin and grieve His heart. So perhaps what God has been doing for you when you prayed was not at all the answer to your prayers but just such mercies as His infinite love and goodness provide for the most wicked of His creatures.

But whether God hears some of your prayers or none of them, your prayers are hindered if you do not day by day live in the fullness of answered prayer so that you can sing,

> **Nothing between my soul and the Saviour,**
> **So that His blessed face may be seen;**
> **Nothing preventing the least of His favor;**
> **Keep the way clear—let nothing between.**

Often we are painfully conscious that our prayers are not heard. Last night a man said to me as we parted at the close of the service in a great rescue mission, "Preacher, before you sleep I wish you would pray for me. My prayers never get higher than my head. God won't hear me." Is that your case? Do you feel, even as you call on God, that He is not pleased, that He will not hear, that there is no likelihood of your receiving the thing for which you ask? Then, oh, how important it is to clear the line between you and God so He will hear you. How important it is to confess and forsake everything that grieves the dear Holy Spirit and shuts up Heaven to your prayers and stops God's ears!

Let us now prayerfully examine the Word of God and search our hearts to see why our prayers are hindered and why God does not answer to give us what we ask.

I. Wrong Relationships of Wives to Husbands and of Husbands to Wives Hinder Prayer

In the matter of hindered prayer, we ought to begin where God begins. In I Peter 3:7, the Lord says, "...that your prayers be not hindered." Speaking first of the sins of a rebellious wife that hurt her prayers, He discusses that in detail. And then the Scripture speaks of the sins of a husband who does not take his proper, God-appointed place in relation to the wife, and warns both wife and husband that they are to obey God in this matter, "that your prayers be not hindered."

Will you read prayerfully these seven remarkable verses, which may show why God does not hear your prayer?

"Likewise, ye wives, be in subjection to your own husbands; that, if any obey not the word, they also may without the word be won by the conversation of the wives; while they behold your chaste conversation coupled with fear. Whose adorning let it not be that outward adorning of plaiting the hair, and of wearing of gold, or of putting on of apparel; But let it be the hidden man of the heart, in that which is not corruptible, even the ornament of a meek and quiet spirit, which is in the sight of God of great price. For after this manner in the old time the holy women also, who trusted in God, adorned themselves, being in subjection unto their own husbands: even as

Sara obeyed Abraham, calling him lord: whose daughters ye are, as long as ye do well, and are not afraid with any amazement. Likewise, ye husbands, dwell with them according to knowledge, giving honour unto the wife, as unto the weaker vessel, and as being heirs together of the grace of life; that your prayers be not hindered."—I Pet. 3:1–7.

Here God speaks to the wife about her duty to the husband. And in the matter of getting your prayers answered, it does not matter, says the Lord, what kind of husband you have: you must obey him; you must be subject to him. A woman must be subject to her husband, or her prayers are hindered. He may even be an unsaved man, one who will not obey the Word of God, who will not listen to the Bible, will not attend church; and yet a Christian woman is to be subject to such a husband, says the above Scripture, that her prayers be not hindered.

It is even inferred that the wife's prayer for the salvation of her husband may be blocked by her own disobedience. A woman may seek to use her influence with her husband by adorning her body, by the plaiting of her hair, by the wearing of gold, or by her neat and attractive dress; but the Lord here says that these things are not to be the beauty, the adornment, the attraction of a Christian woman. And they will not win her husband; they will not get her prayers answered. Rather, every Christian woman is to have that "ornament of a meek and quiet spirit, which is in the sight of God of great price" (vs. 4). It is not wrong to plait the hair or wear clothes; but the only ornament to win a husband for God is the ornament that will cause God to answer prayers, the ornament of a meek, obedient spirit.

In this matter, Sarah, the wife of Abraham, is held up as an example. She called Abraham lord, and she obeyed him. And God gave Sarah a baby when she was ninety years old, wonderfully answering her prayers. And so, argues the Word of God, Christian women, if their prayers are not to be hindered, must be subject to their husbands.

Many a Christian woman has wept as she told me how earnestly she prayed, how diligently she attended the house of God, how eagerly she did church work, and God seemed not to hear her prayers about an unsaved husband or son or daughter! It is a remarkable fact that in nearly every congregation of Christians are godly women, women who pray, who read their Bibles, who live lives more or less separated from worldliness in general, and yet who cannot get their prayers answered for the conversion of their loved ones. "Why? Why?" the cry comes. The answer is not found in the public church services. The answer is not found if you watch such good women singing in the choir, teaching in the Sunday school, attending Bible conferences, giving money to the poor. No, no! Our sins that hinder prayer are primarily home sins. The sins of Christians which hinder their prayers and stop Heaven and shut the ears of God and grieve Him till He turns His dear face away from His own born-again children, are not most often the sins of the tavern, nor of the dance floor, nor of the theatre. They are not the public sins so much as the private sins. They are not the sins in the church so much as in the homes!

You remember Achan and the wedge of gold and the two hundred shekels of silver and the Babylonish garment which he stole—treasures dedicated to God. When the curse of God was pronounced upon all Israel, Achan finally admitted, "They are hid in the earth, in the midst of my tent, and the silver under it" (Josh. 7:21). Achan's sin was not a public sin. Others never dreamed of it. It was a home sin.

And, dear wife who reads this, if you are guilty of this horrible sin of rebellion against the one whom you took with solemn vows as your husband, to honor, love and obey, then that sin today hinders your prayers! That rebellion is the secret of why God has turned away His face and many of your prayers go unanswered.

Rebellion is the sin of fallen angels. Rebellion is the sin which damns every Christ-rejecting sinner. Rebellion against authority is the heart of all crime, and every criminal in a penitentiary has been guilty first not of murder, nor of theft, but has been guilty first of rebellion against authority. This was the sin of the prodigal boy. Rebellion is the very heart of all sin. Dear Christian wife, God says to you that if you will not be subject to your husband, your prayers are hindered.

I dared not use this Scripture without an honest interpretation of it. The meaning surely is clear: rebellious wives have their prayers hindered.

And again, He says, "Likewise, ye husbands, dwell with them according to knowledge, giving honour unto the wife, as unto the weaker vessel, and as being heirs together of the grace of life; that your prayers be not hindered." Husbands too have their prayers hindered if they do not deal scripturally with their wives.

Husbands are (1) to dwell with their wives "according to knowledge"— that is, based on an understanding of the Scriptures relating to husband and wife; (2) "giving honour unto the wife, as unto the weaker vessel" and (3) "as being heirs together of the grace of life." Husbands, then, should take the place accorded them in the Scriptures as heads of the homes, high priests unto God, responsible for the home and for the children, like Joshua, who said, "As for me and my house, we will serve the LORD"; for "the husband is the head of the wife, even as Christ is the head of the church" (Eph. 5:23). Husbands are to "rule over" their wives (Gen. 3:16). A husband who does not dwell with his wife according to knowledge of the plain command of Scripture is likely to have his prayers go unanswered, hindered.

A husband is to remember that he is stronger than his wife. His life should be an example to his wife. The husband should be able to explain the Scriptures to his wife (I Cor. 14:35). The heavy responsibilities of earning a living, of disciplining children, winning the family to Christ, of religious instruction in the home and the family—these heaviest burdens ought to fall heaviest on the husband's shoulders. The man who shirks and avoids such responsibilities, leaving them for the weaker partner, sins before God and will have his prayers hindered.

And the husband should feel himself as one with his wife, one flesh. "No man ever yet hated his own flesh; but nourisheth and cherisheth it" (Eph. 5:29). The husband is to love the wife as Christ loved the church and gave Himself for it.

And this general surrender to God's pattern for the place of the husband in the home is essential to the full, happy life of daily answered prayer. The slacker husband will find that his prayers are hindered.

Discord in the home grieves God. And if there be children that rebel against parents, let them know that such rebellion turns away the face of God and stops His ears and hinders their prayers.

If an old-time revival of Bible Christianity can be had in the homes, how blessed, how far reaching will be the results! Heartfelt surrender to the will of God and obedience to His plan in the home is more important than any kind of public worship or any duties of citizenship. The hindrances to prayer are often in the relations of wives and husbands and of children and parents in the home.

II. Prayers Blocked by Wrongs Unrighted, Debts Unpaid, Offended Brothers Unreconciled

If a wife's prayers are hindered by the sin of rebellion against her husband, and the husband's prayers are hindered by not taking his scriptural position in the home and in relation to his wife; it is also true that every wrong against others which is not made right stands between the Christian and God to hinder his prayers.

This must be the meaning of our Saviour in Matthew 5:23,24 when He said,

"If thou bring thy gift to the altar, and there rememberest that thy brother hath ought against thee; Leave there thy gift before the altar, and go thy way; first be reconciled to thy brother, and then come and offer thy gift."

The Old Testament saint who came to present himself before God at the temple and offer a lamb for a sacrifice, represents a Christian in his prayers and service and praise. If the Hebrew saint were spiritually minded, he knew that that lamb represented Christ, the Lamb of God which should take away the sins of the world. He knew, if he were taught by the Holy Spirit, that the blood of that lamb pictured the blood of Calvary that would be shed for sinners. All his heart's devotion to God would be expressed by the offering of this lamb, all his hope of pardon, all his trust in the atoning blood, all his loving adoration. But the Lord Jesus plainly said that if one should bring a lamb for a sacrifice or any kind of an offering to God and there at the altar should remember a brother whom he had wronged or offended, then he must at once stop the sacrifice. 'Leave the lamb with its feet tied together on the ground before the altar! I will not receive it! I will not hear your prayers; I will not be pleased with your offerings. Nothing you can do for Me can be viewed with favor until you go and make right the wrong done your brother!' said the Saviour, in effect.

Some of you pray long, and God never hears you. Some of you give much money, and the sight of it is an abomination to God. Some of you work and toil doing "church work," and God hates it. Anything you can offer to God is hateful in His sight if you will not go and be reconciled to others you have wronged. There is a fundamental hypocrisy in any attempt at worship or service by those who do not honestly forsake sin and make an effort to undo the wrong that has been done, to pay debts that have been made, to ask forgiveness for sins committed against others.

Many of us cannot get our prayers heard because already the cry of others whom we have wronged has been heard by God. Cain tried to talk to God; but the blood of his slain brother, Abel, had cried out of the ground to God against Cain. Pharaoh in Egypt made fair promises, but already he was marked for destruction, and God brought along one crisis after another that forced Pharaoh to choose, knowing that Pharaoh would harden his heart and die under the wrath of God. The reason was that God had heard the groanings and the cries of the oppressed multitudes of the Israelites; of mothers whose babies were murdered; of toiling laborers who had to make brick without straw. May God pity Hitler if ever he tries to pray; for ringing in the ears of God already are the groans and pleadings of the martyred dead, the slaughtered Poles, the murdered Jews, the betrayed French, the starved Greeks, and the downtrodden millions of poor and oppressed in all of Europe!

God told the Jews in the days of Malachi that divorced wives had covered the altar of the Lord with tears until He would no longer regard the offering or receive it with goodwill at the hands of the Jews because He was a witness between the sin of the men who tried to pray and their treacherously divorced wives (Mal. 2:13, 14). And the Lord warns in Exodus 22:22, 23 that any afflicted widow or fatherless child could cry to God and that his faintest cry would be heard and God's wrath would wax hot against those who oppressed him. And verse 27 of the same chapter tells us that if the poor man should cry at all to God against those who take away his garment and covering, God would hear.

Do you then, dear Christian, believe that God will hear you pray when there are wrongs against others that you have not made right and debts that you have not paid?

God commands all men to repent, we are told. And repentance means a sincere heart-turning away from sin, a change of mind and disposition toward sin and toward God. How, then, could God be pleased to bless His own children who have not themselves honestly turned away from some sin in their own lives?

More than once when I have urged some businessman to come out to the services at the house of God, he has replied, "Well, if the members of that church would pay me what they owe me, I would feel a good deal more like going to their church." Anyone who is well acquainted with retail credit business knows that multitudes of church people will not pay honest debts unless the bill collector follows them up to get them. Sometimes Christians move out of apartments or houses owing back rent which they never pay. Some Christians owe long-standing bills to doctors, good physicians who cared for them in the time of deepest distress. Students leave Christian colleges with bills that they never pay. A brother borrows money from a Christian brother, promises to repay it within a certain time; and then the debt becomes so old that he is ashamed to pay it, and never does! I am not speaking about unusual circumstances. As a pastor, as an evangelist, as an editor, as a radio preacher, and as one who feels the heartbeat of multitudes through the thousands of letters that come to me each year, I know something of the shockingly lax standards of Christians about debt paying. I know of churches, more than one, who borrowed money in good faith on buildings and then in Depression years turned the buildings back to the creditor, buildings which were not useful for other purposes and had no sale, and then bought back the same buildings at reduced prices. The creditors in such cases took a net loss. They would rather have part of the money than none of it. But the result is that church loans are not counted good business loans in America!

From a small town in Texas a storekeeper who heard my radio broadcasts in Dallas wrote to me about as follows:

"Dear Brother Rice:

"The other day a man came into my store and handed me $25 to pay a debt that was ten years old. I had given up all hope of ever collecting the debt. I had tried again and again, and the debtor would make no effort to pay. When he came in to pay the debt, I told him frankly, 'That's $25 I never expected to see.' And he answered back, 'Yes, it's $25 I never intended to pay. But I've been hearing Brother John R. Rice on the radio. He showed me from the Bible that if I ever expected God to hear my prayers for the salvation of my children, to hear my call for daily help, I must make things right and be reconciled to those I had wronged. So I resolved to pay this debt. I must make it so God will hear my prayers and save my children!'"

The storekeeper then wrote me that he felt the money ought to go to God's cause since long ago he had marked it off his books as a loss. He said, "I have given $5 to a Methodist pastor here who I know preaches honestly that Christians must get right with others if they expect God to hear their prayers. I am sending you $10, and I will give the other $10 to the next preacher I hear who preaches that you must pay your honest debts if you expect God to hear your prayers."

I beg you that read this, if there are debts unpaid, that you go now and make them right at any cost so God will hear your prayers.

In a Sunday morning revival service in St. Paul, Minnesota, a number were led to trust happily in Christ. After the benediction, a woman with a troubled face came to me and said, "What did you do with my daughter? Where is she?" She was in the inquiry room being instructed by the pastor's wife with a group of other women and girls, I explained. And then I said, "Are you a Christian? Hadn't you better get this matter settled for yourself?"

"I don't know whether I am saved or not. I guess I'm not. I must talk to somebody." And she began to weep. We sat down together, and I asked her what her trouble was and why it was she could not know whether she was a Christian or not.

"Well, every time I start to pray," she said, "God says to me, 'What about that $800?' I never can get anywhere with my praying. God won't talk to me about anything else," she exclaimed.

"Well, what about the $800?" I asked.

Then she told me the sad story that she had never told another living soul. Her husband had died fourteen years before. She had two children. She knew of no way to make money. So when the children had gone to school, she set fire to the little home and burned it to the ground. The insurance company paid without question the full $800 of insurance. With that money she had moved to St. Paul, gotten the children in school, and gotten started in a livelihood. The lovely grown daughter who had that morning accepted Christ never dreamed it, nor did the son. Not a breath of suspicion had ever been attached to her. Yet God still remembered that she was a thief, that she was crooked; and every time she started to pray, God said to her, "What are you going to do about that $800?"

I told her that she must at once go to the officials of the insurance company and make confession.

"But I have no money; I could not pay it," she said. But I reminded her that she had beautiful clothes, that both she and her daughter now had good jobs and that if she had to pay it just a few dollars a week, she could begin to pay it and at least show good faith.

"But I would land in jail," she said. "I have broken the law, and they would brand me before the whole world as a thief. I can't do that," she said.

"But you are a thief, whether anybody knows it or not," I said. "And if you do not pay this honest debt, you will never have any peace with God. If you go to jail, then go to jail; and God will there give you peace in your mind and heart and hear you pray. As it is, God will never hear you pray as long as this wicked sin is between you and Him."

Again she objected, saying, "But I don't even remember the name of the insurance company. I do not know where its offices are. I could not pay them if I had the money."

"Just turn the thing around," I said. "If an insurance company owed you $800 and you did not know which insurance company it was, don't you believe that you could find out who it was?" She agreed that she would try mighty hard and she thought she could find out under those circumstances. So I showed her that she ought to try just as earnestly to find out so that she might confess a known sin and pay an honest debt and clear the way before God so He would hear her prayers which He had refused to hear for fourteen years!

Beloved reader, you may be God's own child, dear as the apple of His eye. You may be as dear to Him as David, a man after His own heart; or as Samson, a judge of Israel; or as Peter, the first apostle. But I warn you solemnly that God hates sin even in the dearest of His children. God demands that you forsake it, that you hate it, that you honestly try to make right the things you have done wrong.

Some things, of course, can never be undone. If you killed a man, you cannot bring him back to life. But as long as there is a sin which you could make right and have not honestly tried to do it, you are still as guilty as Satan; and every prayer you offer to God stinks with hypocrisy!

Oh, I long to see the kind of Christian lives that prove honest repentance! Zacchaeus, converted as he slid down a sycamore tree to face Jesus, made sudden high resolves that showed that he meant business. He said, "Lord, the half of my goods I give to the poor; and if I have taken any thing from any man by false accusation, I restore him fourfold" (Luke 19:8). He meant that beginning that very moment he would try to make right the wicked sins of his career as a crooked tax collector. No wonder that Jesus said, "This day is salvation come to this house."

The wicked jailer at Philippi, when he came trembling to lead Paul and Silas out of the wrecked jail following the midnight earthquake, was wonderfully saved by simply believing on the Lord Jesus Christ. And the same night, with scarcely an hour gone by, we suppose, he saw every member of his own family wonderfully converted. Do you know why? It was not simply because he was saved. Some of you who read this have been saved ten years, twenty years, thirty years. Yet you wives cannot win your own husbands. You parents cannot win your own children. But that poor, wicked jailer won every person in his household before morning, that same night. And I will tell you how he did it:

First, he took Paul and Silas the same hour of the night and was baptized. It was a wholesale turning of his life over to God in public profession and declaration.

Then he washed the stripes of Paul and Silas, long welts and cuts made by the Roman cat-o'-nine-tails, or scourge. I can imagine that with tears running down his old face, marked perhaps by years of sin, he said to Paul, "Oh, I'm so sorry I stood there and laughed while they beat you. I helped to tear your clothes off of you! I put you in the jail and in the innermost prison and fastened your feet in the stocks, and you had never wronged me. I treated you like a common criminal. God forgive me! I want to make it right the best I can!"

And then a midnight meal was prepared for these two preachers let out of jail in such strange circumstances. They had been put in the dungeon the night before without supper, and the jailer could not rest until he had made that right with a meal that showed his love.

It is not hard for me to believe that if there were a profligate, drunken son who had followed the father into all kinds of sin, when he saw what happened that strange night he may well have said to himself, "Well, the old man sure means business this time! Something surely has changed him. And if God can do that for Dad, He can do it for me, and I'm going too!" At any rate, the whole family was saved and baptized. What a happy scene they must have made, sitting around that table in the wee morning hours, the whole family saved, the whole family rejoicing after being baptized as a public profession of their faith!

Some of you pray and pray, but your prayers are not heard. You had as well never offer them anymore until you make a genuine effort to pay the bills you owe, to right the wrongs you have done, to apologize for sins committed, and to be reconciled with others.

Oh, what zeal we ought to have about making wrongs right! Jesus said, "Ye have heard that it hath been said, An eye for an eye, and a tooth for a tooth: But I say unto you, That ye resist not evil: but whosoever shall smite thee on thy right cheek, turn to him the other also. And if any man will sue thee at the law, and take away thy coat, let him have thy cloke also. And whosoever shall compel thee to go a mile, go with him twain. Give to him that asketh thee, and from him that would borrow of thee turn not thou away" (Matt. 5:38–42). You will never understand that passage until you remember that it is a matter of restitution God is talking about.

Under the Mosaic Law if a man put out his neighbor's eye, he was to be held and his eye put out. If one man's ox killed his neighbor's ox, he was to give the live ox for the dead. If one farmer's cattle ate his neighbor's crop, he was to make it good out of his own crop. And so the Saviour says if a man says that you owe it to him to let him hit you on the right cheek, then you are not only to allow that but to turn the other cheek also and so see that you satisfy your neighbor's claim against you. If he claims that you have his coat, then you make sure that you satisfy his claim perfectly so that your brother can have nothing against you. Give him your cloak also. If he says he has carried your burden a mile and you should go a mile with him, then offer to go with him two. In other words, a Christian should earnestly set out, at any cost, to be reconciled to people he has wronged.

Your hot words may have cut some dear one to the heart, and you have never confessed and asked forgiveness for that sin. You may have slandered some man of God, some innocent girl, or some thoughtless neighbor. I beg you, go be reconciled! Confess your wrong and earnestly try to make it right.

Someone hears me who has a mother or father far away. They long to hear from you. You have your own home, your own business, your own interests. They have now only memories of the past. How can God bless you who neglect heartbroken mothers and cause grief to those who gave everything for you?

Dear Christian, many times I have had to write letters asking forgiveness or write a check to pay an honest debt before I could have assurance that God would hear my prayers. Are your prayers hindered because there are those you have wronged with sins that you have never tried to undo? Then the Saviour said, "If thou bring thy gift to the altar, and there rememberest that thy brother hath ought against thee; Leave there thy gift before the altar, and go thy way; first be reconciled to thy brother, and then come and offer thy gift."

III. Unforgiveness Grieves God and Hinders Prayers

Unforgiveness in the heart of a Christian hinders the answer to his prayers. A grudge, a root of bitterness, or even hate, it may be, may be blocking the answer to your prayers.

In Matthew 6:9–13 we are given the model prayer, or the Lord's Prayer. And in that model prayer the Saviour taught us to pray daily, "And forgive us our debts, as we forgive our debtors." And when the prayer was finished Jesus added this plain, sharp word of warning,

"For if ye forgive men their trespasses, your heavenly Father will also

forgive you: But if ye forgive not men their trespasses, neither will your Father forgive your trespasses."—Matt. 6:14, 15.

Here it is clearly taught in the solemn words of our Saviour that Christians who will not forgive others will not be heard when they ask for forgiveness. And when we come to pray that our heavenly Father will take sins out of the way, will cleanse them and forgive them, not let them hinder our communion with Him or our service for Him, all our praying is useless unless we forgive others who may have wronged us.

You understand, I trust, that forgiveness of sins has two meanings in the Bible. In the first place, when a poor lost sinner comes to Christ and trusts Him for salvation, then all of his sins are forgiven and blotted out and will be remembered against him no more forever, as far as the damnation of his soul is concerned. "Blessed is the man to whom the Lord will not impute sin" (Rom. 4:8). In getting saved we do not get sins forgiven one at a time; but all at once the glorious transaction is finished, and all of our sins are laid on Jesus and forgiven, blotted out, never to be held against us anymore and never to endanger our poor souls again! What wonderful salvation! What marvelous mercy in the forgiveness of vile sinners!

But after one is already a child of God, after one is born again, after one has been made a partaker of the divine nature, he is still, while in this world, a sinner. "If we say that we have no sin, we deceive ourselves, and the truth is not in us" (I John 1:8). Paul, the mighty apostle, yet in the midst of his great ministry, claimed still to be the very chief of sinners (I Tim. 1:15). And David in that inspired Fifty-first Psalm, was led to write, "My sin is ever before me." And the Saviour in the Lord's Prayer is expressly teaching us that we ought daily to confess our sins and ask forgiveness. So besides the forgiveness of our sins we get in salvation, one can have and needs a day-by-day clearing of sin out of the way.

Although the Lord has forgiven all of our sins, yet He still hates sin. God hates sin in David or in Peter or in Paul; God hates it in you, beloved Christian. And if your sin is not confessed and cleansed day by day, it piles up between you and God to hinder your communion, to block your prayers, to taint your testimony, and to grieve the blessed Holy Spirit. So the Lord teaches us here to come daily and confess our sins, asking forgiveness.

The Scofield Reference Bible has wonderful helps; I use it constantly and recommend it. But no one man can know all about the Bible, and here the Scofield Reference Bible has a very foolish note, saying this is legal ground. No, this is not legal ground. This does not contradict Ephesians 4:32.

We should forgive others, Ephesians 4:32 tells us, because Christ has already forgiven us all of our sins in salvation so that they are not held against our souls' welfare. But here in Matthew 6:14, 15 the Saviour warns us that we should forgive others that we as Christians may have the daily cleansing, the daily renewal of fellowship, the daily fullness of the Holy Spirit which God desires for all His dear children, but which He cannot give without a daily confession and forsaking of sin.

When Jesus washed the disciples' feet, He said, "He that is washed needeth not save to wash his feet, but is clean every whit: and ye are clean, but not all" (John 13:10). He meant that the disciples (except Judas Iscariot) were already saved and all their sins were under the blood. But Christians walking in a dirty world need day-by-day confession of their defilement that they may have daily forgiveness and cleansing as the dear children of God in order to have His fullness and power and fellowship. The washing of the whole body, which these disciples already had, represents salvation, the forgiveness of all sin. That cleansing is once for all at regeneration. But the washing of the disciples' feet represented that day-by-day cleansing which is offered Christians who confess and forsake their sins (I John 1:9).

But unforgiveness blocks this daily cleansing and forgiveness and so hinders our prayers. Unforgiveness, holding grudges or enmity against others, may seem to be a very respectable sin. People who would never get drunk, who would not gamble, who would not steal, who scorn a lie, are yet guilty of this wicked sin. The temptation to this sin attacks preachers and soul winners who would never be tempted to grosser things. I know Christians who would never attend the theater nor belong to a lodge nor play a game of bridge, but who have been guilty of this horrible sin. In God's sight, it is truly hideous.

In Matthew 18:21–35 is the following remarkable teaching of our Saviour about the need for Christians to forgive others and of how God hates the wicked sin of unforgiveness:

"Then came Peter to him, and said, Lord, how oft shall my brother sin against me, and I forgive him? till seven times? Jesus saith unto him, I say not unto thee, Until seven times: but, Until seventy times seven. Therefore is the kingdom of heaven likened unto a certain king, which would take account of his servants. And when he had begun to reckon, one was brought unto him, which owed him ten thousand talents. But forasmuch as he had not to pay, his lord commanded him to be sold, and his wife, and children, and all that he had, and payment to be made. The servant therefore fell down, and worshipped him, saying, Lord, have patience with me, and I will pay thee all. Then the lord of that servant was moved with compassion, and loosed him, and forgave him the debt. But the same servant went out, and found one of his fellowservants, which owed him an hundred pence: and he laid hands on him, and took him by the throat, saying, Pay me that thou owest. And his fellowservant fell down at his feet, and besought him, saying, Have patience with me, and I will pay thee all. And he would not: but went and cast him into prison, till he should pay the debt. So when his

*fellowservants saw what was done, they were very sorry, and came and told
unto their lord all that was done. Then his lord, after that he had called him,
said unto him, O thou wicked servant, I forgave thee all that debt, because
thou desiredst me: shouldest not thou also have had compassion on thy fellowservant, even as I had pity on thee? And his lord was wroth, and delivered him to the tormentors, till he should pay all that was due unto him. So
likewise shall my heavenly Father do also unto you, if ye from your hearts
forgive not every one his brother their trespasses."*

How many times shall we forgive one who sins against us? Peter
thought seven times would be the perfect number; but Jesus answered back,
"I say not unto thee, Until seven times: but, Until seventy times seven." And
when you have forgiven the same person 490 times, no doubt you would
have lost count and would have conquered that wicked disposition to temper and bitterness in your own heart!

In the above parable, the Saviour illustrates our awful debt to God by the
man who owed his king ten thousand talents. Ten thousand talents would be
nearly twenty million dollars if they were silver talents, nearly three hundred million dollars if the talents were gold. In either case it would be an
unpayable amount, no doubt beyond the capacity of any man living in the
world at that time. So great is our sin toward God which needs forgiveness!

And then the sins of one against others are represented by the Saviour in
this parable by the debt of one hundred pence. And the servant who had
been forgiven ten thousand talents took his fellowservant by the throat, saying, "Pay me that thou owest," and would not give him time, but cast him
into prison until he should pay that trifling debt of a hundred pence, when
he himself had been forgiven ten thousand talents that he owed!

How trifling, how insignificant are all the sins that anybody ever did
against us compared to our horrible sins against God all the days of our
lives! This parable tells us how God sees the sin of unforgiveness.

And note the punishment of the wicked servant. Jesus said, "And his
lord was wroth, and delivered him to the tormentors, till he should pay all
that was due unto him."

Here the king delivered the evil servant "to the tormentors." And then
Jesus warns Simon Peter and the other disciples, in a lesson which is meant
for us Christians, "So likewise shall my heavenly Father do also unto you,
if ye from your hearts forgive not every one his brother their trespasses."
God will deliver His own children over to tormentors, will allow their
hearts to be miserable, their lives to be unhappy, their prayers to be blocked,
their homes to be accursed, if they do not forgive others! The Lord does not
mean that saved people will lose their salvation and go to Hell because
of unforgiveness, but He certainly does mean that here in this life they
will miss many, many blessings and suffer torment of soul because of the

horrible sin of unforgiveness. And how ashamed they will be when they face Jesus!

I have known brother who would not speak to brother; I have seen churches split into factions; I have seen homes broken; I have seen Christians so embittered by this horrible sin that they made shipwreck of all their lives. Terrible punishment will be the lot of every Christian who carries a grudge and unforgiveness in his heart.

And note that the Saviour said this forgiveness must be "from your hearts." To live nominally at peace is not enough. Sometimes a Christian will say, "Well, I will forgive her, but I will never forget." Or a brother may say, "I will forgive him, yes, because it is commanded me; but I will never have anything more to do with him." Such forgiveness is no forgiveness at all in God's sight. When God forgives, He forgets. How would you like for God to say about you, "Well, I will forgive your sins; but I never want to have anything more to do with you"? You know that is not forgiveness in a real, genuine sense. By God's grace, a Christian can so forgive that every memory brings a sweet sense of peace without any rancor or bitterness whatever.

If we want to be like Jesus, we must forgive. Dying on the cross, He prayed about the people who crucified Him, who mocked Him while He died, who gave Him vinegar mingled with gall when He was thirsty, who had spit in His face—for these He prayed, "Father, forgive them; for they know not what they do." One of the names of the Lord Jesus is "Prince of Peace." And if we forgive, we become Christlike. That is the reason why the Beatitudes say, "Blessed are the peacemakers: for they shall be called the children of God" (Matt. 5:9). Everyone who makes peace is that much like Jesus Christ. The Beatitudes promise that those who are pure in heart shall see God, that the meek shall inherit the earth; but they give the blessed promise to the peacemakers that they shall not only see God but shall be called His children, and shall not only inherit the earth, but even inherit Heaven as the heirs of God! How blessed to be a peacemaker, with forgiveness toward brethren, "even as God for Christ's sake hath forgiven you."

And that attitude of mind and heart which Jesus had is to be ours also. Stephen had it when, dying, he prayed about his tormentors, "Lord, lay not this sin to their charge" (Acts 7:60). And, oh, dear Christian, if you are to have your prayers answered, you too must learn to forgive!

When boiled down to its essence, unforgiveness is hatred. And I John 3:15 says, "Whosoever hateth his brother is a murderer." If you think a little grudge is very respectable, then you should remember that God looks into your wicked heart and calls it murder!

In Mark 11:22–24 is that marvelous promise about prayer that "whosoever" (anybody) can have "whatsoever" (anything) he asks, if he has faith.

But Jesus qualifies even that great promise by these words in the following verses: "And when ye stand praying, forgive, if ye have ought against any: that your Father also which is in heaven may forgive you your trespasses. But if ye do not forgive, neither will your Father which is in heaven forgive your trespasses" (Mark 11:25,26). It is obvious that every Christian who tries to pray with unforgiveness in his heart finds a great wall of his sins piled up between him and God which he cannot get removed and cannot get taken out of the way until he forgives all that others have done against him.

The Lord's Prayer is to be a daily prayer for daily bread and daily needs and confessing daily sins. And that indicates that every Christian every day ought to go about this important matter of seeing that all grudges are forgiven. Thus, Ephesians 4:26 commands us, "Let not the sun go down upon your wrath." A grudge, if left in your heart overnight, may so take root as to embitter your whole life and ruin your testimony. So daily, before sundown every day, search out your heart, judge every little grudge, every bit of enmity, every slightest passion of unforgiveness. Confess it to God as a sin and turn your heart away from it, and God will take it out and cleanse it. But if you do not forgive, neither will you be forgiven.

Have you honestly searched your heart as you have read this? Is there any root of bitterness, any of the sin of unforgiveness in your heart blocking your prayers?

CHAPTER XX

HINDRANCES TO PRAYER, Continued

I. Covetousness Puts One Under a Curse, Hinders Prayer

Covetousness too is a most respectable sin and is found in the "best families." But it is a sin that God hates terribly. It is literally idolatry (Col. 3:5), and the covetous man is an idolater (Eph. 5:5). And God's Word says that "the love of money is the root of all evil" (I Tim. 6:10)—that is, literally, that the love of money can lead to every kind of sin in the world.

Now the Scripture expressly says that covetousness is a sin that shuts the heavens against the Christian. In Malachi we read:

"Even from the days of your fathers ye are gone away from mine ordinances, and have not kept them. Return unto me, and I will return unto you, saith the LORD of hosts. But ye said, Wherein shall we return? Will a man rob God? Yet ye have robbed me. But ye say, Wherein have we robbed thee? In tithes and offerings. Ye are cursed with a curse: for ye have robbed me, even this whole nation."—Mal. 3:7–9.

Here is a startling statement that men actually rob God. They do it in tithes and in offerings. The tithe is the Lord's: not to give it is to rob God. The offerings also are the Lord's: not to give them also robs God. And the Lord says, "Ye are cursed with a curse: for ye have robbed me, even this whole nation."

Because of this sin of covetousness, the land of Israel was under a curse, the whole land. God had withheld the rain. He had not heard their prayers. They were under a curse and could not get the things they desired from God. And God gave them a challenge in the following verses:

"Bring ye all the tithes into the storehouse, that there may be meat in mine house, and prove me now herewith, saith the LORD of hosts, if I will not open you the windows of heaven, and pour you out a blessing, that there shall not be room enough to receive it. And I will rebuke the devourer for your sakes, and he shall not destroy the fruits of your ground; neither shall your vine cast her fruit before the time in the field, saith the LORD of hosts."

The simple matter of forsaking covetousness and bringing the tithes and offerings which He had expressly commanded as a token of His ownership of everything would enable God to hear their prayers, to bless their crops, and to pour out such blessings as they would not even be able to receive! The insect pests would be rebuked, the rain would come when needed, and it would be a happy land, God promised, if the people would prove God on this matter of tithes and offerings.

I well know that this was first addressed to the Jews. I have heard long arguments that the tithe was commanded only for Jews. But the truth of the matter is that proportionate giving is as clearly commanded in the New Testament as in the Old (I Cor. 16:2). Abraham, the tither, the man of faith, is held up as an example to New Testament Christians in this matter (Heb. 7:1–10). And the New Testament examples who are greatly praised went far beyond the tithe, as we see in the case of the woman who put in two mites (Mark 12:41–44) and in the cases of the saints at Jerusalem after Pentecost (Acts 4:34–37) and the churches of Macedonia (II Cor. 8:1–6). And besides, the promises given in the Old Testament about liberality have been abundantly proved true by literally thousands of New Testament Christians. I know that it pays in dollars and cents to bring God the tithes and offerings. And I have proved God, and He has opened the windows of Heaven as He promised.

And why should God demand more of an Old Testament Jew than of a New Testament Christian under grace? Should a Jew under law love God better? Should he trust Him further? Stealing, God-robbing, covetousness, is the same wicked sin in New Testament times as it was in Old Testament times. And those who sing "Oh, How I Love Jesus" but do not love Him a dime's worth out of a dollar will not get far in their praying. If you cannot trust God to supply your need and to repay you for all the tithes and offerings you bring in for Him, you have not much faith.

In Dallas, Texas, a good Christian woman, who had long proved how joyful and how prosperous it is to put God first with tithes and offerings, came to church one day with her heart all set on plans for some lovely clothes. Her husband's bimonthly paycheck had come Saturday night, and she had it in her purse at church, since he could not come. She thought to herself, *This one time I'll not put in the tithe; I will give a dollar, and the rest of the money we can use so well for things we need to buy.*

But that dear Christian woman was on the committee to prepare the bread and grape juice for the communion table that Sunday morning. As she filled the little glasses her heart remembered the strict injunction, "Let a man examine himself, and so let him eat." She dared not partake of the emblems representing the poured-out blood of the Saviour and His broken body with any known sin or rebellion in her heart. And the Spirit of God spoke insistently to her about how she had planned to withhold the tithe and use it for her own ends. She could have no peace in her heart; and she cried out to God, "Oh, heavenly Father, I cannot take the Lord's Supper until I know You are pleased with me!" So she solemnly promised God, "Lord, if You'll give me the joy in my heart again and let me know that You've forgiven me, that there is nothing between my soul and the Saviour, I promise You that before I leave the house of God today I'll get that check cashed

and turn in the tithe and offerings that I vowed to You that I would give."
And then in sweet peace and in remembrance of the death of our dear
Saviour, she took of the bread which pictured His broken body and of the
cup which pictured His poured-out blood. She came then to tell me, her pastor, of her victory; and the tears of joy rolled down her cheeks as she told
it! Oh, dear friend, God does not care so much about your money, but He
wants *you*. He wants your trust, your full surrender, your willingness to give
Him anything, everything, even yourself! How grieved He must be if any
child of His does not believe Him enough, does not love Him enough to put
Him first in money matters!

Many, many Christians have their hearts so set on material possessions,
on money, on business that God cannot answer their prayers. Are your
prayers hindered by this sin? Would God have to say to you, 'Ye are cursed
with a curse because ye have robbed Me'?

II. Self-Will, Rebellion, Disobedience Hinder Prayer

Dear Christian, I am probing in your heart and life, trying to help you
find the reasons for unanswered prayer. What sin of yours hinders your
prayers and shuts out the blessing God would give you?

Self-will is another horrible sin which means that God cannot have His
way in your life and cannot give you His best. I recall the case of Saul, the
first king of Israel, who was commanded to go out and utterly destroy the
Amalekites. God said to him, "Now go and smite Amalek, and utterly
destroy all that they have, and spare them not; but slay both man and
woman, infant and suckling, ox and sheep, camel and ass"! (I Sam. 15:3).
If that seems to you a hard command, then I remind you that you do not hate
sin as God does. This wicked, idolatrous nation had long deserved extermi-
nation. God's long-poured-out mercies had been rejected. If any of the
nation were left alive, they would be a temptation and snare to Israel. Even
their property should be destroyed as an awful reminder to Israel of how
God hated sin and was certain to punish it.

But Saul came back leading King Agag, alive, behind his chariot and
with a great number of sheep and oxen as a spoil, which he said he
intended to offer as sacrifices to God. But, oh, how the wrath of God
mounted up against Saul for his disobedience! Hear what God said to him
through Samuel:

*"And Samuel said, Hath the LORD as great delight in burnt-offerings and
sacrifices, as in obeying the voice of the LORD? Behold, to obey is better
than sacrifice, and to hearken than the fat of rams. For rebellion is as the
sin of witchcraft, and stubbornness is as iniquity and idolatry. Because thou
hast rejected the word of the LORD, he hath also rejected thee from being
king."*—I Sam. 15:22,23.

Immediately thereafter Saul pled with Samuel to go worship with him. Saul admitted his sin. He even laid hold upon the skirt of Samuel's mantle, as Samuel turned indignantly away, and rent the mantle. Despite all Saul's professed repentance, God rejected him as king. David was anointed to take his place, and Saul went steadily downhill until his suicidal death in disgrace, with his sons, who but for Saul's self-will might have reigned after him.

How moving is the story of how Saul tried to pray, but because of his self-will, his disobedience, God would not hear! God said to him, "Behold, to obey is better than sacrifice, and to hearken than the fat of rams." God does not want our money nor our work nor our promise one half as much as He wants our hearts surrendered to the will of God and an obedient, surrendered spirit. The Lord said through Samuel, "Rebellion is as the sin of witchcraft, and stubbornness is as iniquity and idolatry." Rebellion, stubbornness, self-will, in dealing with God is certain to block the answer to our prayers and shut up Heaven against us!

If there is a single matter, then, about which God has a controversy with you, I beg you, dear Christian, surrender your will at once, repent of your wicked rebellion, your self-will, your insistent disobedience. It is more important to hearken to God, to obey from the heart, than to give money, to sing, to pray, to preach or toil. It is a sad, sad fact that many active church people, some, no doubt, really born again, live at a far, guilty distance from the conscious presence of God and do not know the constant joy of answered prayer.

God called one man to preach; and he said, "Lord, I have no money to go to school. I must take care of my family. Lord, I'm too ignorant. But I will be a Sunday school superintendent." But God would not use him as Sunday school superintendent. God did not want work for its own sake; he wanted *obedience*.

A young friend of mine felt clearly led of God to preach the Gospel. He had been only to the eighth grade in school, was now married, and felt his ignorance, his limitations, his poverty. It was a long fight of unbelief that God could use him, of rebellion against the long years of preparation, of holding onto the career and money-making he had planned. But at last when he had surrendered tearfully to the full will of God, this young preacher told me, "Brother Rice, if I do not preach, I can't even live like a Christian!" He meant that God would not give him victory over sin, would not give him leading, would not give him happiness, would not answer his prayers, if he did not surrender to the full will of God.

A daughter was bitter over the death of her beloved mother. She complained and mourned and querulously asked, "Why? Why?" She felt that God had not been fair to her mother, had brought unnecessary suffering to herself; and there was rebellion in her heart against God. But the Bible lost its sweetness; the day-by-day conscious presence and fellowship with the Holy Spirit left her. God did not seem to hear her prayers, and doubts of every kind beset her. She could not find any peace until she confessed her sin to God and said, "Thy will be done," about her mother's death.

Beloved Christian, there is no way you can please God, no way you can have the sweet communion with Him to get your prayers answered, if you are in rebellion against the known will of God.

Has God turned His face away from you as He did from Saul, refusing to hear your prayers or bless you because of a stubborn self-will that rebels against God's plan for you? Oh, then I beg you, surrender today your poor will to God's good will. Trust Him! His will for you is wiser and sweeter and richer far and happier than any way you could plan! And no matter what other trouble or grief or loss might come, in His will you may always have the consciousness of His approving presence with the Holy Spirit ungrieved, manifesting Himself to you, and with the daily knowledge that your prayers are heard!

III. A Disinclination or Indifference Toward the Bible Makes Prayer an Abomination to God!

Proverbs 28:9 is a most searching Scripture. There God says, *"He that turneth away his ear from hearing the law, even his prayer shall be abomination."*

If your prayer is an abomination to God, then any happy fellowship, any oneness of purpose, any communion between you and God, is hindered.

Note that the Scripture does not refer primarily to infidels. One does not need to say that the Bible is false, that Christ was not born of a virgin, that He did not rise from the dead, that there is no real Heaven or a literal Hell, in order to come within the scope of this great hindrance to prayer. No, if only your heart is turned away from the Bible, if you have a disinclination to read it, if it is not interesting to you, if you do not meditate on it prayerfully, joyfully, then your prayer is an abomination, says God's Word.

Throughout the Bible, God stresses the fact that there is a close connection between the Word of God and spiritual prosperity. For example, Psalm 1:2,3 tells us of the blessed man who shuns evil companions:

"His delight is in the law of the LORD; and in his law doth he meditate day and night. And he shall be like a tree planted by the rivers of water, that bringeth forth his fruit in his season; his leaf also shall not wither; and whatsoever he doeth shall prosper."

Day-by-day blessing from God, spiritual prosperity, Christian fruit-bearing all depend upon delighting in the law of the Lord and meditating on it day and night. *Knowing* the Bible is not enough; *reading* the Bible is not enough; blessing depends on delighting in it and meditating on it.

In Joshua 1:8 the Lord spoke to Joshua, saying,

"This book of the law shall not depart out of thy mouth; but thou shalt meditate therein day and night, that thou mayest observe to do according to all that is written therein: for then thou shalt make thy way prosperous, and then thou shalt have good success."

Good success, prosperity, depended on having the Word of God in his mouth and meditating therein day and night so Joshua might make sure to observe everything in it. And then Joshua would make his way prosperous and have good success. But if Joshua had turned his heart away from hearing the law, he would not have been prosperous, he would not have succeeded, and the blessing of God would have failed. And does not that bear out the statement of Proverbs 28:9 that even the prayer of one who turns his heart away from hearing the law, is abomination? How could one who is disinterested in the Bible, who shuns it, one who has his heart turned away from it, please God in prayer? What claim could such an unspiritual heart, such an alienated child, have on God in prayer?

Then notice that one whose heart is alienated from the Bible, disinterested in the Word of God, finding no joy in God's promises, indifferent to the duty of obeying God's commands—notice that such a Christian cannot meet any of the conditions of successful prayer. All the promises in the Bible concerning answers to prayer involve in some way a heart that is eager to find the will of God in the Word of God. In John 15:7 Jesus promised, "If ye abide in me, and my words abide in you, ye shall ask what ye will, and it shall be done unto you." One who does not love the Bible, is not eager to read it, does not gladly heed its warnings and admonitions and commands, cannot meet that promise, because Christ's Word does not abide in him, and he is not really abiding in Christ in the sense of surrender to the will of Christ. And how can such a Christian come to ask anything of the Father in the name of Christ? One who does not know the Bible does not know the will of Christ. One who is not interested in the Bible is surely not much interested in the will of Christ. How could I genuinely ask anything in Jesus' name, if I can quote no authority from Christ giving me the right to ask it in His name? Therefore, the blessed promise that the Father will give you anything you ask in Christ's name, the promise of John 14:13,14, will not avail for the man whose heart is turned away from hearing the Word of God.

"If we ask any thing according to his will, he heareth us," says I John 5:14. But one who does not know the Bible, does not love it and does not meditate on it, will not have any assurance that what he asks is in the will of God. "All things are possible to him that believeth," said Jesus in Mark

9:23, but "faith cometh by hearing, and hearing by the word of God" (Rom. 10:17). One whose heart is turned away from the Bible is turned also from faith. He cannot call upon God in faith, since he does not use the means to grow faith, and since God's Holy Spirit will not encourage faith in such a disobedient heart. "Delight thyself also in the LORD; and he shall give thee the desires of thine heart," says Psalm 37:4. But a real delight in the Lord involves a delight in God's Word. How eager I am for a letter from home! And that is because I love my wife and daughters and long to see them. How anxiously a young woman awaits the postman, looking for a letter from her sweetheart who has been called away to the army. So if one really delighted in God, he would delight in His letter to us. God is so revealed in the Word that those in close fellowship with God must delight in His Word. Oh, then, Christian, if your heart has been turned away from the Bible, you are out of touch with all the promises of God for answers to your prayers! "He that turneth away his ear from hearing the law, even his prayer shall be abomination."

Even lost people wanting salvation do well to turn and read the Word of God. As you with an earnest heart seek to find God in the Scriptures, the Holy Spirit will reveal Him. The God who answers prayer is the God of the Bible. He is not only the God who wrote the Bible, but the God who yet today reveals Himself in the Bible and gives His blessings to those who love the Bible.

A disinclination to read the Word of God, to meditate on it, to learn it, to follow it, to search it out, shows sin in the heart. When a Christian, a born-again child of God, shows indifference to the Word of God, then we may know that he is living after the carnal, fleshly mind. For I Corinthians 2:14 says, "But the natural man receiveth not the things of the Spirit of God: for they are foolishness unto him: neither can he know them, because they are spiritually discerned." The blessed Holy Spirit has an affinity for the Word of God, which He inspired. The conscious fullness of the Spirit and the keenest delight in the Word of God go together. People who are full of the Spirit are also full of the Word of God. The natural mind is a stranger from God and is not interested in the Bible. And the carnal or undeveloped and untaught and unspiritual Christian is likely to have no taste for the Word of God. A state of disinterestedness in the Bible is an unspiritual state, a state of backsliding and sin.

A mother wrote in the flyleaf of her son's Bible when he went away from home, "This Book will keep you from sin, or sin will keep you from this Book." The Christian who loses interest in the Bible, cannot find time to read it, or takes exceptions to some of its teachings, may well search his heart; for in that heart are things that grieve God, that block God's blessing and make even his prayers an abomination to God.

Every Christian, then, should long for and earnestly seek a delightful familiarity, an unceasing interest in the Word of God. Set apart a time early in the day, I beg you, when you read the Scriptures, several chapters if possible, and meditate over them prayerfully, longing to find the mind of God, willingly surrendering yourself to all that you find in God's Word. If you surrender yourself and do not rush but meditate on the Word of God, you will find prayer forming in your heart. It is a prayer inspired by the Holy Spirit, a prayer that God will be pleased to hear. George Müller, the great English man of prayer, founder of the Bristol orphan houses, tells of the new ease and joy in prayer he had when he began first to read the Bible before prayer every day and let his prayers begin out of what the Spirit whispered in his heart as he read the Word of God. A daily quiet time of reading the Word of God, memorizing it, subjecting oneself to the searching, probing, judging, purifying action of God's Word, will mean rich prosperity in your prayer life. But "he that turneth away his ear from hearing the law, even his prayer shall be abomination."

IV. Any Unconfessed, Unlamented, Unrepented Sin Grieves God and Hinders the Prayers of His Children

I have given you some sample cases where particular sins are mentioned in God's Word as hindering our prayers. But I cannot mention every detail. God's Spirit must do that for you. But let us find a general rule which you can apply to your own heart and life and find what grieves God.

In Psalm 66:18 are these solemn words, "If I regard iniquity in my heart, the Lord will not hear me."

I want you to notice what God did NOT say. God did not say that if I *have sinned*, He will not hear me. No, no! Thank God, He did not say that; for if He had, then God could never hear a human being pray, for all of us have sinned. He did not even say that if at this moment there is any sin in the life, He would not hear us. For I John 1:8 teaches us plainly that all of us have (present tense) sin in our lives all the time: "If we say that we have no sin, we deceive ourselves, and the truth is not in us." The constant presence of human frailty, of bodily illness, the encroachments of age and infirmity, the limitations to our prayer and soul winning, all testify that we have sin, even now, and that we will have, until we are translated when Jesus comes or until we die. If Paul needed to say, "When I would do good, evil is present with me" (Rom. 7:21), so do the rest of us need to say it. I cannot come to God and ask anything of Him on the basis that I am sinless and perfect and that there is not in my heart, unknown to me, unseen to my neighbors, a single thing that is less than His best, a single thing that is not as pure as an angel or as Christ Himself. No, no! I *am* a sinner. But I can still get my prayers answered.

And then what does God say? If I *regard iniquity in my heart,* God will not hear me. I am a sinner, but, oh, I must not love sin. And if I hold any particular sin in my heart and love it and make an alibi for it and excuse it and cover it up—then that becomes a cause of controversy between me and God. God hates sin, but God has a remedy for sin. If we Christians confess our sins, He is faithful and just to forgive us our sins and to cleanse us from all unrighteousness, says I John 1:9. So it is not primarily the *fact of sin,* but it is *a love for sin, a willingness to sin, an excusing of sin* that make it so God cannot answer our prayers.

If you want to get along with God and keep sweet fellowship and have your prayers answered, then you must judge your sins. You must honestly confess your sins and take sides with God against them. There must be a wholehearted repentance—that is, the turning of the will away from all the things that grieve God. Otherwise, your will is dead set against the will of God. You cannot ask anything in the name of Christ, you cannot pray in the Spirit, you cannot pray according to the Word of God, your own conscience will not allow you to believe that God will bless you while you have set your own will up as an idol or when some secret sin has your heart's devotion which ought to be given to God alone.

Oh, dear child of God, if you would have God's blessing on your prayer life, then let your heart cry out in the words of the old song—

> **Return, O holy Dove, return,**
> **Sweet messenger of rest!**
> **I hate the sins that made thee mourn,**
> **And drove Thee from my breast.**

> **The dearest idol I have known,**
> **Whate'er that idol be,**
> **Help me to tear it from Thy throne,**
> **And worship only Thee.**

Maybe you loudly insist, "I don't see any harm in the theater." Perhaps you repeatedly say, "There is nothing wrong with a nice dance if you have it with nice people." Perhaps you say, "Well, if I never do anything worse than smoke a cigarette, I think I am pretty good." But the plain truth is, if you in your heart excuse your sin and "regard" it and love it, then it is an issue between you and God. And that controversy will block the answer to your prayers and will steal away your peace and leave you helpless and powerless like Samson with his hair cut off. Oh, dear friend, the smallest sin in the world, if it breaks your contact with God, will leave you powerless and your prayers without results.

It may be the love of money. It may be a shameful secret love has entered into your life. It may be a sin that nobody but God knows about.

But if you love a sin and hide it and take up for it, then your prayers will be hindered.

V. How to Get the Hindrances Removed

Are your prayers hindered? Well, thank God, there is a remedy. The hindrances can be torn down. Even this very day you may feel again the smile of God's face and hear the whisper of His Spirit and know that there is nothing between you and God.

In I John 1:9 we are given this blessed promise,

"If we confess our sins, he is faithful and just to forgive us our sins, and to cleanse us from all unrighteousness."

Confession—that is the remedy for your sin.

A Christian does not have to atone for his sins. In fact, no man can possibly atone for his sins. The atonement was completed by Jesus Christ; and thank God, on the cross He cried out, "It is finished"! Let no one, then, think that he must go through a long period of time, trying to earn God's favor and to lay up credit so that his prayers can be answered.

And the Christian is not to "do penance" for his sins. Paying money, doing without food, sleeping on boards, or fasting a certain number of days—these, as a matter of penance or suffering, trying to pay for sins, as a criminal spends a certain number of years in prison to "pay his debt to society," are not what God demands.

No, the dear Lord simply and plainly promises, "If we confess our sins, he is faithful and just to forgive us our sins, and to cleanse us from all unrighteousness."

I think that an honest confession of sin would involve the following matters:

First, an honest realization in the heart of one's failure and sin. Confession cannot be simply a matter of the lips. For the mouth to say, "I have sinned," when the heart still says, "but it was not very bad, and it was not altogether my fault," is not true confession of sin. Another way to say this is that the Christian must honestly judge his sin in the light of God's Word and the revelation of the Holy Spirit of how God feels toward the sin.

Second, honest confession would involve a penitent heart and sincere repentance. I think there could be no honest confession of sin, if there were not grief over it. The sin grieved the Holy Spirit, it wronged God, and by it the Christian who sinned was untrue to the Saviour he professed to love and serve. The Christian's testimony was injured before the world, his fellowship with God was broken, his usefulness was curtailed, and his prayers were hindered. All these things ought to cause the Christian sincere grief of heart over his own sin. I do not mean a morbid despair. I simply mean the godly sorrow that "worketh repentance" (II Cor. 7:10). And this grief of heart over sin will involve a revulsion, a turning away, a change of mind and attitude toward sin, which we call repentance. If the Christian is not sorry for his sins, in his heart, and does not honestly long to do better, then there is no genuine confession of sin.

Third, a confession, in the sense that is meant in I John 1:9, would involve a simple faith that God is willing to forgive and cleanse us as He has promised. We are God's own dear children. We are dear to His heart. For us He gave His own Son. He has already given us everlasting life and promised to take us home to Heaven. We have never deserved His mercy, and we do not deserve it now; but He loves us still. And so a Christian can confess his sin, safe in the assurance that God has promised to forgive and cleanse and God cannot lie. We are under a covenant relationship with Him. Our forgiveness is based on His faithfulness, not on our faithfulness.

So anytime a Christian is conscious of his sin, judges the sin and takes sides against it with a penitent heart, then he has a perfect right to trust the Lord for instant, complete forgiveness and for perfect cleansing.

Beloved Reader, you can know the sweet intimacy with God that you long for; you may know it this very day. You may then live a life of unhindered prayer and daily, glorious answers. So in the light of God's Word and submitting yourself to the searching of the Holy Spirit, I urge you today to confess honestly and to turn your heart away from every known sin and then claim the forgiveness and the cleansing which God has so freely promised to all of His own who confess their sins!

Is there nothing between your soul and the Saviour? Have you humbly searched your heart anew in the light of God's Word and found nothing to hinder your prayers? Oh, then, dear Christian, enter into your inheritance and begin the abundant life of prayer, asking and receiving that your joy may be full!

CHAPTER XXI

THE SIN OF PRAYERLESSNESS

"God forbid that I should sin against the LORD in ceasing to pray for you."—I Sam. 12:23.

Prayerlessness is a horrible sin. For the lost sinner it is a part of his wicked rejection of Christ. For the child of God it is identical with backsliding. Prayerlessness is another name for unbelief. Prayerlessness is the father and partner of every vile sin, as much as the saloon is the father of drunkenness and lust is the father of adultery. There is not a vile sin in the world but that prayerlessness is a part of it and that real prayerfulness would have prevented it or cured it. Of itself prayerlessness is, I have no doubt, worse than murder, worse than adultery, worse than blasphemy. It is more fundamental. It more clearly reveals the heart. In fact, while murder, adultery and blasphemy may catch a person unaware, trapped by the carnal mind, prayerlessness is the very heart of the carnal mind itself, a state of alienation from God.

My greatest sin, and yours, is prayerlessness. My failures are all prayer failures. The lack of souls saved in my ministry is primarily because of lack of prayer, not because of lack of preaching. The withering away of joy in my heart, sometimes, is the fruit of prayerlessness. My indecision, my lack of wisdom, my lack of guidance come directly out of my prayerlessness. All the times I have fallen into sin, have failed in my duties, have been bereft of power or disconsolate for lack of comfort, I can charge to the sin of prayerlessness. Oh! horrible sin, the lack of prayer!

What is wrong with the churches is lack of true prayer. What is wrong with the preachers is this same sin, prayerlessness. What is wrong with the pew is still that blighting sin, prayerlessness. For every sin, every failure, every lack, God had a remedy and cure if we had sufficiently and effectually prayed.

It is a sin when we pray and ask amiss that we might consume it on our own lust. It is a sin when we pray without faith. And it is sad beyond expression when wrong homelife, when wrongs unrighted, when unforgiveness or rebellion or distaste for the Bible or any secret love of sin hinders our prayers. But the greatest prayer sin of all is simply *not to pray!* Our greatest trouble is not that we pray wrongly. Our greatest trouble, our greatest sin, perhaps, is that we pray little or *do not pray at all!* We have, perhaps, our formal phrases in which we simulate prayer. But often they are really little different from the *Ave Marias* and *Pater Nosters* of our Catholic friends or the formal words on a Buddhist's prayer wheel. Prayer, in the sense of asking God for things as directly as a woman goes to the grocery store with her basket for groceries, or as a motorist drives into the gas station for gas and oil, or as a child says, "Pass the bread, please"—I say real prayer, definitely, directly, determinedly going to God to get things, is an unknown and unexperienced process to most Christians. And this prayerlessness is back of all the fruitlessness and powerlessness and joylessness in the average Christian life.

The disciples begged Jesus, "Lord, teach us to pray." They did not say, "Lord, teach us *how to pray*." They simply asked, "Lord, teach us *to pray*." Oh, that the people of God would forsake their sin of prayerlessness and get down to prayer.

I. Proof That Prayerlessness Is a Sin

Do we need to prove it? *Then first, prayerlessness is a sin since the Bible expressly calls it that.* Samuel said to the children of Israel,

"God forbid that I should sin against the LORD in ceasing to pray for you."—I Sam. 12:23.

The Holy Spirit of God put it in Samuel's heart to say it, and the same Holy Spirit of God had it recorded in the Bible for us, that to cease praying is a sin.

Second, many, many, many Scriptures command that Christians should pray. These Scripture passages even demand that we pray all the time, pray without ceasing.

First Thessalonians 5:17 says,

"Pray without ceasing."

And that verse has no immediate context. There are no modifications. There is the stark, bald command that Christians ought to pray literally without ceasing.

Again Jesus

"Spake a parable unto them to this end, that men ought always to pray, and not to faint."—Luke 18:1.

Men ought always to pray and *never give up!* That is the command of Jesus Christ; not to obey it is sin.

The Christian is commanded to put on the whole armor of God: the girdle of truth, the breastplate of righteousness, the shoes of the Gospel of peace, the shield of faith, the helmet of salvation and the sword of the Spirit,

"Praying always with all prayer and supplication in the Spirit, and watching thereunto with all perseverance and supplication for all saints."—Eph. 6:18.

There are many commands in the Bible that Christians should pray.

Jesus warns His disciples more than once to watch and pray lest they should enter into temptation.

We see that repeatedly God tells the Christian to pray without ceasing, that men ought *always* to pray and not give up, praying always with all prayer. And any violation of God's plain commands is a sin. When we do not pray, then, we are rebels, we are disobedient children, we are in sin.

And note, please, the measure of our sin of prayerlessness. We ought to pray all the time, never ceasing. Anything less than constant prayer is thus disobedience and sin. If for a short season of time we do not pray as we ought, then we have sinned. And if that sinful disregard of prayer continues, with small intermissions, through hours and days and weeks and months, even years, as is true in the lives of many Christians, then prayerlessness is a long, extended sin, is habitual sin, is veritably a life of sin. Long, continued prayerlessness is the same kind of extended sin that drunkenness or the dope habit is, in that it is repeated, extended and habitual.

But how could one pray without ceasing? Is not that an impossible standard? I answer no, that the Bible can be taken at face value. God's standards are proper standards, and God's words say what they mean and mean what they say. Prayer ought to arise from the heart like the fragrance from burning incense on an altar day and night, all the time. The soul of a Christian can be so possessed of God, so hungry for His presence, that both the conscious and the subconscious mind carry on the pleading, the searching for God's face and His will and way and work.

Here is an example. The baby sleeps in his crib, and when all the household is abed, Mother settles down to rest. In the night there is a tiny whimper, and instantly the mother is awake. She was *listening!* She was watching over the little one, even while she slept. Her soul was so set on the care of the little one that while her conscious mind slept, the subconscious being took over the listening post at her ear and watched through the darkness.

In the west Texas cattle country where I grew up, much of my boyhood work was done on a horse. Many a day I rode long hours, sometimes ten or twelve hours a day. Once after a long, heavy day it was far into the night when I, wearied to exhaustion, turned my sorrel horse homeward. As he followed the long road across a ranch pasture, I sat upright in the saddle, sound asleep. When he came to the gate and stopped, I awoke. When I had opened the gate, gone through and closed it, again I slept in the saddle until the tired horse stopped at the corral gate. My muscles did their accustomed work of years when my eyelids shut and I slept. But part of me was conscious of my horse, my feet in the stirrups, and the accustomed motion; and I awoke instantly when the horse stopped.

And dear friend, if a mother can be conscious of her babe when she sleeps, and a horseman can be conscious of his horse and maintain his equilibrium when he sleeps, cannot a Christian who with all his soul loves the Lord and longs for certain blessings which he seeks—cannot such a Christian still be conscious of God when he sleeps? One hypnotized carries out certain orders through the control of the subconscious mind. So it is foolish to say that we cannot do what God commands about prayer simply because our consciousness is directed to other business or because we sleep.

A few times—all too few, God forgive me!—I have waked from sleep to find myself in the very presence of God. Sometimes I have waked in the midst of conscious prayer. How great is our sin when we do not pray, since God has commanded us to pray without ceasing, to pray always, to pray with all prayer, always, for all the saints.

Every moment of prayerlessness, then, is a sin. Long, continued prayerlessness is continual sin, habitual sin, a very living in sin, because it is disobedience to the plain and oft-repeated command of our heavenly Father and of the Lord Jesus Christ.

Third, prayerlessness is a sin because it leaves the door open for all other sins.

That is made clear by the command of Jesus in Mark 14:38,

"Watch ye and pray, lest ye enter into temptation. The spirit truly is ready, but the flesh is weak."

We are to pray and to watch or continue attentively in prayer as the only sure preventative of entering temptation. Similarly the command is given in Luke 22:40, "Pray that ye enter not into temptation." If the disciples needed that warning in the Garden of Gethsemane with Jesus, how do we need it too!

In fact, in the Lord's Prayer, the model prayer for all who can truly call God "Our Father which art in heaven," we are expressly taught to pray,

"And lead us not into temptation, but deliver us from evil."

Prayer is the remedy for temptation. Prayer is the way to defeat the evil one.

In this connection it is well to remember that "the whole armour of God," which we are commanded to put on "that [we] may be able to stand against the wiles of the devil," and again, "that [we] may be able to withstand in the evil day," includes "praying always with all prayer and supplication in the Spirit, and watching thereunto with all perseverance and supplication for all saints" (Eph. 6:11–18). Prayer defeats Satan. By prayer one may be able to stand against the wiles of the Devil and to withstand in the evil day.

A Christian man who was enslaved by the tobacco habit said to me, "I can go about a half a day at a time, and then I just have to have a cigarette, it seems." He told me how he prayed every day about the matter and for hours would seem to have the victory, but before the day was gone he would again fall into temptation and sin. I showed him that he had been given the victory by prayer for a little time and that what he needed to do for continued victory was to pray more. He promised to pray every half-hour if need be, to take time out from his work and go alone until he had victory and to continue that until permanent victory came. And thus he conquered the thing that had enslaved him.

Would not your speech have been different, dear friend, if you had prayed like David, "Set a watch, O LORD, before my mouth," or, "Let the words of my mouth, and the meditation of my heart, be acceptable in thy sight, O Lord, my strength, and my redeemer" (Ps. 141:3; 19:14)? And if Peter had spent the time praying instead of sleeping in the Garden of Gethsemane, would not the outcome have been far better? Surely he fell into the snare because he did not pray. And so we too deny Jesus and curse and swear, it may be, before His enemies, because we are not strengthened in the secret place by prayer.

An old proverb says, "Satan trembles when he sees the weakest saint upon his knees." And well he may, if that saint really, directly, and persistently calls for God to help him against sin and to keep him out of temptation and to defeat the evil one.

The great John Bunyan, author of *Pilgrim's Progress,* wrote, "Prayer will make a man cease from sin, as sin will entice a man to cease from prayer" (*Works,* Volume I, page 65).

No doubt, then, all of our sins stem from our prayerlessness. No doubt in sincere and wholehearted prayer, in totalitarian prayer, is the remedy for and victory over our sins.

Fourth, for a final proof that prayerlessness is a sin, we need but examine the records concerning Bible Christians. How they prayed! If those who pleased God best prayed continually, prayed persistently, "prayed through" gloriously, then surely we sin when we do not pattern after them.

The best example is Jesus Himself. We are told that "he went up into a mountain apart to pray" (Matt. 14:23). People brought Him little children that "he should put his hands on them, and pray" (Matt. 19:13). In the Garden of Gethsemane He said, "Sit ye here, while I go and pray yonder" (Matt. 26:36). "He went out, and departed into a solitary place, and there prayed" (Mark 1:35). Again, "He departed into a mountain to pray" (Mark 6:46). Great multitudes came together to hear Him and to be healed, "and he withdrew himself into the wilderness, and prayed" (Luke 5:16). In the next chapter we are told, "And it came to pass in those days, that he went out into a mountain to pray, and continued all night in prayer to God" (Luke 6:12). And most of us forget that when Jesus was on the Mount of

Transfiguration and was glorified before the disciples, He had gone there to pray, and "as he prayed, the fashion of his countenance was altered" (Luke 9:28,29). Most of us have forgotten that Jesus was praying when the disciples asked Him to teach them to pray and He gave the Lord's Prayer. It was Jesus' praying that led to the great confession by Peter that Jesus was "the Christ of God," as you see in Luke 9:18–21. When Jesus said to His Father, "I knew that thou hearest me always" (John 11:42), He must have meant too that He prayed always. God forgive us that we do not pray as Jesus prayed. Our prayerlessness shows how we ignore God's commands to pattern after Jesus.

In Bible times the temple was literally "a house of prayer" and was intended to be that for all people. Bible Christians fasted, they prayed in sackcloth, they wept while they prayed, they often watched all night in prayer. Paul and Silas prayed at midnight in the jail at Philippi. A little group at the home of Mary prayed long hours until Peter was released from jail (Acts 12:3–17). Before Pentecost the apostles and Mary and the brothers of Jesus and some others "continued with one accord in prayer and supplication" (Acts 1:14), until the power of the Holy Spirit came upon them as promised. Later when the apostles called for some deacons to take over the business of waiting on poor widows they promised, "But we will give ourselves continually to prayer, and to the ministry of the word" (Acts 6:4)—prayer first, preaching second! When saintly men got together at Antioch, Barnabas, Simeon, Lucius, Manaen and Saul, they ministered to the Lord and fasted until the Holy Ghost said, "Separate me Barnabas and Saul for the work whereunto I have called them." And then we are told they prayed more and fasted more, "And when they had fasted and prayed, and laid their hands on them, they sent them away" (Acts 13:1–3). That is the secret of all great missionary movements—"prayer," "ministering to the Lord," "fasting," and again "prayer and fasting"! All of our alibis for the lack of the power of the Spirit of God which was manifest in New Testament times can properly be ignored. The real difference between New Testament churches and the churches of today, between New Testament preachers and the preachers of today, between New Testament Christians and the Christians of today is in the matter of prayer and the power that comes through prayer! If New Testament Christians had the right idea of serving the Lord, then we have the wrong idea. If they were right so to pray, then we are wrong not to pray as much as they did. If we do not follow the examples of the heroes of the Bible in prayer, then our prayerlessness is sin.

And if we compare ourselves with missionaries, Carey, Judson and Hudson Taylor, how glaring is the sin of our prayerlessness!

When our prayerlessness is compared with the prayers of Brainerd, who spent days in fasting and prayer, often kneeling in the snow in the primitive forests begging God for the salvation of Indians, how insincere seem our excuses for not winning souls. When we read of the long vigils of Charles G. Finney in woods or hayloft, or in days of fasting and prayer, ending in a new and fresh baptism of power again and again and in marvelous revivals and in hundreds of souls saved, how can we excuse our sin of prayerlessness! When we learn how George Müller prayed and fed thousands of orphan children, how he prayed and sent forth missionaries to the end of the world, how he prayed and gave Bibles and books and tracts by the multiplied thousands, receiving over seven million dollars from God without ever asking man for a penny, when he pleaded with God and argued with God and knew what it was daily to wait on God—compared with Müller, what sinners we are in our prayerlessness!

II. The Sad Results of Prayerlessness

Aside from the fact that our prayerlessness opens the door to all sin, I call your attention to some tragic results of our prayerlessness:

First, God's people do not get what they ought to have. Many do not have daily necessities because they do not pray as we are commanded to pray, "Give us this day our daily bread" (Matt. 6:11). No doubt many of the afflicted are still afflicted because they have not obeyed God's command, "Is any among you afflicted? let him pray." And many of the sick remain sick because they do not "call for the elders of the church, and let them pray over [them], anointing [them] with oil in the name of the Lord," as the Lord said, and so have not received the blessing promised that "the prayer of faith shall save the sick...and if [they] have committed sins, they shall be forgiven [them]" (Jas. 5:13–15). Many are undecided, in doubt about duty. They lack wisdom because they have not obeyed God when He commanded, "If any of you lack wisdom, let him ask of God, that giveth to all men liberally, and upbraideth not" (Jas. 1:5). Such Christians "have not, because they ask not" (Jas. 4:2). They do not ask, and therefore they do not receive. They do not seek, and therefore they do not find. They do not knock, and to them the door is not opened (Matt. 7:7, 8).

Sometimes there are other hindrances, but many, many times we simply have not because we ask not. Many of God's children go through this world as orphans, as if God did not love them, as if God were not able or were not willing to care for His own. How sad! Israel wandered forty years in the wilderness before entering the land of promise, which they could have had, which God wanted them to have, before. I waited to marry until I had finished college and paid up school debts, and then my bride told me she would have married me before if I had asked her! So much of the poverty and frustration and lack of victory and joy comes to Christians simply because they do not pray. Oh, the results of prayerlessness!

Many Christians die prematurely because they do not pray. There are a number of Bible examples of this. For example, II Chronicles 16:12, 13 tells us, "And Asa in the thirty and ninth year of his reign was diseased in his feet, until his disease was exceeding great: yet in his disease he sought not to the LORD, but to the physicians. And Asa slept with his fathers, and died in the one and fortieth year of his reign." Asa was sick. In his disease "he sought not to the LORD, but to the physicians," and he died. The clear implication is that if he had prayed, he would have lived.

In I Chronicles 10:13, 14 we are told about King Saul's death: "So Saul died for his transgression which he committed against the LORD, even against the word of the LORD, which he kept not, and also for asking counsel of one that had a familiar spirit, to enquire of it; And enquired not of the LORD: therefore he slew him, and turned the kingdom unto David the son of Jesse." Here it is clearly inferred that Saul died for his transgressions and particularly for asking counsel of a spiritualistic medium instead of praying to the Lord.

On the other hand, King Hezekiah was "sick unto death." God sent Isaiah to say to him, "Thus saith the LORD, Set thine house in order: for thou shalt die, and not live" (Isa. 38:1). But Hezekiah turned his face to the wall and prayed, and God raised him up and gave him fifteen years. Clearly Hezekiah would have died according to God's first plan. When he prayed, God changed His plan!

The Bible does not teach that one who prays may live forever without dying, but it certainly does teach that many die prematurely when they might live longer with great blessing if they had prayed.

Likewise, other people die because *we do not pray*. For example, God had planned to destroy the whole nation Israel and make of Moses and his family a new nation; but Moses prayed, and God did not do "the evil which he thought to do unto his people" (Exod. 32:9–14).

It seems likely that Abraham's prayer saved Lot alive out of Sodom. And we know God heard the prayers of Esther and her maidens and of Mordecai and his friends to save the lives of the Jews who were to be destroyed by Haman's conspiracy, as told in the book of Esther. God would stop the war and give us victory sooner if we prayed as we ought, and so millions of lives would be saved.

So, because of our prayerlessness we miss many, many blessings. People are sick when they might be well. Some die when they might live. Businesses fail when they might prosper. And people go hungry and without proper clothing who might be covered and fed to the glory of God if they would but pray.

Second, another sad result of our wicked prayerlessness is that God's work suffers and languishes. In II Chronicles 7:14 God plainly promises to hear His people when they come in humility and prayer and supplication and repentance. We know many, many revivals in Bible times came because of seasons of prayer and waiting on God. It is always true that we do not have revivals because we do not sincerely, with a holy abandon, pray, as well as obey God. Of course the right kind of praying would lead us to obedience and power.

The orphan houses in Bristol, England, founded by George Müller, prospered because of prayer. It was so manifest that no one could doubt that the only essential reason that God blessed and sent the means needed was that people expectantly, faithfully prayed. Müller asked nobody for money and often would not even let his needs be known except to God. What an example to prove that when the Lord's work languishes it is for lack of prayer! And of course I mean the work that is truly the Lord's work. I do not mean that we can by prayer contrary to the will of God get our own work to prosper by saying "in Jesus' name." But the work of the Lord's own planning languishes only when the people of God do not obediently pray.

Hudson Taylor and the China Inland Mission are a modern evidence that the work of God languishes only because of prayerlessness and prospers under prayer. When many denominational missions which depended upon denominational organization and promotion for their funds were being overwhelmed with debts and making retrenchments continually, the China Inland Mission, going only by faith, depending on God alone without any organization to raise money, prospered and increased, spreading the Gospel to millions and sending out continually new groups of workers who were cared for in answer to prayer.

In many, many cases when I have been used of God in a blessed revival campaign in some locality, one or two saintly Christians have told me, "I have been praying for two years that God would bring you here for these meetings," or, "This campaign is the answer to my daily prayer for years." Oh, if people would but pray, pray earnestly, pray effectively, pray with a holy abandon, God's work would not languish. The decay in the churches, the cooling of revival fires, the lukewarmness in the churches are the fruit of our prayerlessness.

Third, countless souls go to Hell because we do not pray. Nothing could more sharply show the wickedness of prayerlessness than this fact, that if Christians do not pray as they ought, many whom they might win, if they prayed, will go to Hell.

It is easy for us to see that people cannot be saved without the Gospel. The Bible so clearly says, "How then shall they call on him in whom they have not believed? and how shall they believe in him of whom they have not heard? and how shall they hear without a preacher?" (Rom. 10:14). If no one goes to preach the Gospel and if sinners do not hear the Gospel, then those who might be saved will not be saved. But it is equally true that if people go without prayer, their ministry will be ineffective, and in proportion as they pray themselves and as they are lifted up to God in earnest prayer by others, their ministry will be powerfully moved by the Spirit of God to the saving of souls. It is utterly impossible to disconnect revival fire and prayer. It is utterly foolish to suppose anyone will have a fruitful ministry that is not held up to God by earnest prayer, either by the minister alone or by his own prayers joined to the prayers of others. Oh, how many poor lost souls are in Hell today because someone did not pray!

III. What the Sin of Prayerlessness
Shows About Our Wicked Hearts

If a man kills somebody, that may show premeditated hate, deliberate murder, or it may show a sudden flare of temper in a fight, or it may show simply carelessness in driving. Or the killing may have been altogether accidental without any blame at all.

When a man gets drunk, it may show that he is diseased, enslaved by habit, which is really a sickness. Such a man may deserve more pity than blame, and he may be otherwise generous, honest, loved and greatly respected by those who know him. When a person commits adultery, it may show a long and deliberate course of sin and depravity, or it may simply be the result of a sudden gust of passion under unusual temptation, such as the person did not expect and under circumstances where most others might yield too. All these shocking outward sins show some sin in the heart. But they do not reveal as much wickedness as the sin of prayerlessness, for the sin of prayerlessness reveals some shocking things about the state of heart of all of us who do not pray constantly, who do not live in an attitude of unceasing prayer.

First, prayerlessness shows a lack of real enjoyment of God. We should honestly face the fact that most of us do not really enjoy prayer or we would pray more. We eat because we are hungry; the body demands food. We sleep because we are sleepy, or the body demands rest. We visit people because we enjoy fellowship. If we work harder and the body needs more food, we hunger for it and then eat more. If we are specially in love with someone, we long more for his companionship and spend more hours in his presence when possible. When we are unusually worn and tired, the body demands more rest, and we sleep longer if possible. And that simply illustrates the fact that if your heart were hungrier for God, you would pray more. If you really enjoyed His presence, you would seek it. If you enjoyed praying more than other things you do, then you would do more praying and less reading or playing or eating or sleeping. Prayerlessness proves that we do not really enjoy God.

Let us be honest, each one, in searching his own heart here. Do you not often pray simply as a matter of duty? Two days ago a young man came to me with great joy, saying, "Brother Rice, before I heard your message on prayer, prayer had become a burden to me. I prayed because I felt I ought, but it was hard, and I did not enjoy it. But now, thank God, it has become a joy to pray!" I am led to believe by the testimony of thousands of individuals that prayer to the average Christian is hard and burdensome. We pray little because we do not enjoy it. We pray as much as we do pray largely out of duty or absolute necessity. And our lackadaisical praying when we do pray, along with the fact that we really pray little at all, proves that our poor, wicked hearts do not feel at home with God, do not enjoy God, do not delight in His presence and conscious fellowship! And how wicked is that sin!

The complaint of Isaiah, quoted by the Saviour, was that "this people draweth nigh unto me with their mouth, and honoureth me with their lips; but their heart is far from me" (Matt. 15:8). And Jesus frankly addressed such people, "Ye hypocrites"! How many of us, I wonder, pray in a way that honors Christ with our lips and draw near to Him with our mouths, but our hearts are far away! Oh, if our hearts are not in our prayers, if we do not love to draw near to God, if we do not enjoy praying, if prayer is not sweet to us, how sinful are our wicked hearts!

No doubt much of the failure of what little praying we do is indicated by that sweet promise in Jeremiah 29:12, 13, "Then shall ye call upon me, and ye shall go and pray unto me, and I will hearken unto you. And ye shall seek me, and find me, when ye shall search for me with all your heart." Oh, God is not far off! God has toward us, as the preceding verse, Jeremiah 29:11, tells us, "thoughts of peace, and not of evil." God is more eager to hear than we are to pray, if only we shall search for Him with all our hearts!

Have you searched in your own heart about this matter whether you really enjoy the presence of God? If you enjoyed praying more than the other things you do, wouldn't you pray more?

Many a son or daughter, I suppose, loves Mother and Dad but has little in common with them and seeks rather the company of his or her own age group at the dance floor or movie. Perhaps there are honest, good men who love their wives after a fashion but find them drab and uninteresting and hasten away from home to company they enjoy better or hide themselves with a newspaper or book. How sad that any of us should be like that toward God! If we are saved, born-again children of God, then we love Him of course. In our hearts we have received the Spirit of adoption whereby we cry, "Abba, Father." But sad to say, many of us do not really enjoy our heavenly Father, and we spend little time in His company, little time or heart in asking for His blessings and receiving those He has offered. Our prayerlessness proves that we do not really enjoy God.

Second, prayerlessness proves our unbelief. Hebrews 11 says that "without faith it is impossible to please him: for he that cometh to God must believe that he is, and that he is a rewarder of them that diligently seek him." And Romans 10:14 says, "How then shall they call on him in whom they have not believed?" I suppose that primarily means that lost people do not really call on God for salvation unless in their hearts they believe that He is able and willing to save. Prayer is the proof of faith for a lost sinner. But is it not equally true that prayer is the proof of faith in a Christian? How can we pray if we do not believe it pays? How can we really pray much if we do not believe we get anywhere or get anything from God? When we are sick we go to the doctor first instead of praying first because really we have more confidence in the doctor than in God. We think of medicine before we think of prayer. And I do not mean that medicine and doctors and hospitals are to be avoided by Christians. God often uses means to do His blessed work. He uses Christians and personal soul winners to save sinners. He uses foods, medicines, treatments oftentimes to heal the sick. But is it not obvious that a child of God who really believes that the healing depends on God and that the healing, whether through doctors and medicine or without either, must come from God—isn't it obvious that one who believes that will pray before he does other things? I think there is no doubt that our prayerlessness proves that we really have little confidence in getting answers to our prayers. Prayerlessness is a proof of unbelief. And unbelief is a sin, a besetting sin which we are to lay aside, looking unto Jesus the Author and Finisher of our faith (Heb. 12:1,2).

I have known people who say, "Yes, I believe in prayer as much as anyone," or, "Sure, I have lots of faith in God," who when they were sick really depended on doctors, and when they were out of jobs really depended on employment agencies and who, when they were in need, called on relatives for help before they called on God! To them faith was just a certain feeling, a general doctrinal position.

But real faith, living faith, absolutely must express itself in calling on God for what we need and desire. From the sum total of our prayer let us subtract all the praying we do as a matter of duty and subtract all the praying we do to be seen of men, and the little that remains will be the actual measure of our faith in a God who hears and answers prayer! O God, forgive us of this sin of unbelief!

Third, our prayerlessness proves our laziness. Prayer is hard work. It demands thought, demands concentration, demands persistence. One who becomes great in prayer must overcome every kind of handicap and discouragement and temptation. Satan would keep us from prayer by making us too busy at other matters. Satan would stop our prayer with discouragement and unbelief. He would distract our minds. So real praying is work, hard work.

It is said of Jesus in the Garden of Gethsemane, that "being in an agony he prayed more earnestly: and his sweat was as it were great drops of blood falling down to the ground" (Luke 22:44). And many a saint of God has found himself likewise covered with perspiration from the earnest work, the concentration, the pleading of prayer. Brainerd, kneeling in the snow praying for the Indians on his heart, worked at his praying until he did not feel the cold. Charles G. Finney, kneeling on a buffalo robe in the hayloft after a meeting at night, prayed long into the wee hours and did not suffer from the upper New York state winter. I finished a game of college football with a broken nose, and in the labor and concentration of the game I felt no pain at all, though the blood ran down my jersey. In a time of great grief and trouble I went for days with practically no desire for food. Just so, many have learned to agonize in prayer, to labor, as Jacob wrestled with the angel at Penuel (Gen. 32:24–31).

Jacob *wrestled* with an angel of God in prayer (Gen. 32:24, 25). Rachel, the barren wife, prayed without ceasing that she might not be outdone by her mocking sister; and of her prayers she said, "With great wrestlings have I wrestled with my sister, and I have prevailed." And Paul tells of Epaphras, the great man of prayer who sent word to the Colossians, "always labouring fervently for you in prayers." And the word *labouring* means "to agonize, to contend, to wrestle." In fact, it is the Greek word from which we get our English word *agonize*. Oh, what labor real prayer is! And the fact that we do not pray proves that we are lazy, indifferent Christians with little heart for the work of God. We are fat, well fed, indolent, indifferent Christians, or we would pray. Prayerlessness proves laziness.

Fourth, our prayerlessness proves that God is not first in our love and interest and that other things come first. Prayerlessness is almost proof of idolatry. We read the newspapers instead of praying because we are more interested in the things the newspapers talk about than we are in the things we would talk to God about. We spend more time chatting with other people than we do in talking to God because we really think more of other people than we do of God. We Christian workers may even spend more time with our sermons, with our libraries, with our Christian visiting, with our church organizations because we care more about these incidental and secondary matters than we do about the main matters. Remember that the apostles said, "We will give ourselves continually to prayer, and to the ministry of the word" (Acts 6:4). Prayer first, preaching second! I think we preachers are often more concerned with our sermons than we are with getting people saved, more concerned with what we say to man than what we say to God, more concerned to please the ear than we are to save souls by the power of God which only comes through prayer.

Some Christians spend hours a day at hobbies, hobbies that in themselves are innocent and harmless and often useful. But count the time you spend on your hobby and compare it with the time you spend in prayer. Is your hobby of more interest to you than God and His Word and His blessings and His power? Reading is proper, and good reading is commended in the Bible, but compare your reading with your praying; which takes the precedence in your life? Does not our prayerlessness prove that we put prayer of less importance than nearly everything else? Does it not mean that our love, our interest, our desire is on other things first? Prayerlessness, I say, is almost a proof of our idolatry. And the little that we pray proves how little we are really interested in God's will for us and in bringing souls to Christ and advancing the work that is truly His.

Some will be tempted to say that they have so much work to do, good work, honorable, necessary work, that they cannot pray as much as my teaching here infers that they should. Well, we ought to be able to pray all the time. "Pray without ceasing," and, "Men ought always to pray, and not to faint," the Bible commands. That means praying while busy at all other things. But we ought also to have long seasons every day in which we would lay aside other matters and give ourselves altogether to prayer. And you need not say that is impossible, for the greatest men of God, the busiest, found time for that kind of praying.

If you will go through Paul's epistles and find how many people he addressed, reminding them that he prayed for them in every prayer or prayed for them every day, you will see that Paul was given to much prayer, hours of prayer, daily. And Jesus spent long seasons in prayer. He went up into a mountain to pray. He prayed all night in the wilderness. He prayed, perhaps, for hours in the Garden of Gethsemane.

Martin Luther said that he had so much work to do for God that he could never get it done unless he prayed three hours a day! How Martin Luther labored in prayer! Prayer to him was fighting, wrestling, agonizing. And once as he prayed, Satan became so real to him, taunting, tempting, interfering, that Martin Luther threw the ink bottle at him! And the splash on the wall has long been shown to visitors to remind us of how real was prayer to Martin Luther.

Preachers, especially evangelists, must get late to bed, and so often they are late risers. Speaking in the evenings and finding it hard to relax and sleep immediately after the greatest labor and excitement of the day, preachers get the best rest after midnight. But D. L. Moody arose regularly, we are told, at four o'clock in the morning that he might have at least a full hour with God in prayer and with the Bible before anybody else on the place should be awake. And Hudson Taylor had a custom of waking in the midst of the night to spend an hour or two undisturbed with God. C. T. Studd in Africa rose at 3:00 a.m. to pray. It is a remarkable fact that the men who have been the most abundant in labors for God have been the ones who really spent the greatest amount of time in prayer. Our excuses are really alibis. We do not pray more because we do not think prayer is as important as the other things which we do. We think sleep is more important than prayer. We think food is more important than prayer. We think visiting is more important than prayer. We think preaching is more important than prayer. Our prayerlessness really proves that other things come first in our estimation and in our love.

IV. How to Overcome the Sin of Prayerlessness

I feel I know all too little about prayer, and yet humbly I would make the following suggestions about how to overcome the sin of prayerlessness:

First, I would set apart a season of time early in every day to pray, along with meditation on the Bible. The earlier, the better. It ought to be before breakfast. One great missionary had a motto, "No Bible, no breakfast." If he couldn't find time to read the Bible and pray, then he would not take time to eat. Brother, that motto will make an impression on the callous carnality of us who put our stomachs before God if we will but adopt it! Put prayer really first by having a real season of prayer before anything else of importance in the day. You probably will have to rise earlier than you now rise to do it. You may have to leave off other matters of lesser importance. But "those that seek me early shall find me," says the Lord in Proverbs 8:17.

Second, make a habit of *"praying through"* about every burden and problem that comes to you. Sometimes we cannot in one day get the full answer to a great prayer, but we can every day, I believe, get a sweet peace to know that God has heard us and that we left the thing in the hands of our heavenly Father and He has smiled into our hearts and given us peace. You may not, as you pray in one given season, see the salvation of the man for whom you pray; but you can pray until you have sweet assurance that God has undertaken and will do the thing you desire. Or you can pray until God's Holy Spirit helps you see how you should modify your prayer to fit with the plan of God.

This kind of praying will mean that you do not continue bowed down under anxieties and worries. Leave every worry, every anxiety with Jesus every day.

Third, take time to pray about things as they come up. Years ago as a preacher I found it impossible to remember all the requests for prayer that would come to me in a day's time so as to pray for them before I slept or the next morning. So I formed a habit of stopping to pray for every case about which I was impressed that I ought to pray, at the time it was mentioned. And then I never promise to pray for any matter in the future except as God shall lay it on my heart and bring it to my mind. I have found a great peace in going to God with every burden the moment I feel the need for prayer about it. And one of the sweet and blessed results is a constant companionship and fellowship with God.

Fourth, leave off the formalities and let prayer be simply talking with God. Every Christian many times a day should stop and say, "Lord, I did wrong in that. Forgive me!" or, "Lord, help me to know what to say to this man." Connect prayer with every detail of your life. Hallesby, in his great book on prayer, says that we ought to pray about everyone we meet. Leave off the forms of set prayers and get accustomed to talking to God as simply as a little child to his mother or as a wife to her husband. Some people pray with all the stiffness and unreal formality of being introduced to the king and queen at court. When you pray you will do well to leave off the powdered wigs, the knee breeches, the formal introductions, the curtsies, and the bowing low and the walking out backward!

Fifth, I would set out to follow the Bible examples and teachings about prayer.

Jacob prayed all night; so did Jesus. Then I would enter into the fullness of prayer life by praying all night. I will never forget the fullness of blessing that came in some nights of prayer in the Galilean Baptist Church in Dallas, and when I prayed until two o'clock in the morning in a Y.M.C.A. at St. Paul, Minnesota, and when I prayed with a great group in the Peoples Church in Toronto, Canada, led by Dr. Oswald J. Smith, in a half-night of prayer. I think it is shameful that the great experiences of prayer in the Bible are not duplicated in the lives of modern Christians. By God's grace let us enter into these experiences.

Esther and her maidens fasted and prayed three days and nights. The people of Nineveh prayed without either eating or drinking for days until God heard and spared the city and saved them. The apostles fasted and prayed for ten days before Pentecost, as you see by comparing Matthew 9:14, 15 with Acts 1:13, 14. The Bible has many accounts of the saints who fasted while they prayed: Ezra and his companions, David, Paul and Barnabas fasted. Have you ever gone without meals or spent a day without food while you sought the bread from Heaven and while your mind was absorbed in God and seeking His power alone? If Pharisees entered into fasting as a form, a work of merit, cannot Christians fast and pray for a burden for souls and to be filled with the power of God?

Daniel went, he tells us, for three full weeks in which he ate no pleasant bread and ate no meat (Dan. 10:2, 3). And should not we sometimes have times of mourning, of confessing our sins, of waiting on God in which we might for weeks go eating only moderately, doing only such work as we must, until certain great problems are settled, certain victories won, certain blessings obtained? I recall in some of the most blessed of revival campaigns, some where great numbers were saved, that for days I felt little interest in food or sleep, I lost weight, I felt a constant burden of prayer until the victory was won and we began to see a breaking out of revival fires and the salvation of many. Would it not be blessed sometime to follow the permission given in I Corinthians 7:5 and by mutual, loving agreement husband and wife stay apart for a few days "that ye may give yourselves to fasting and prayer"?

I have known homes in which for a certain season the beds were quickly spread, the meals prepared were of the simplest, and there was little of the normal entertainment while the housewife felt led to give herself to an earnest burden of prayer.

Sometimes Bible characters kneeled in prayer. Peter, called to pray by the side of the dead Dorcas, put them all forth and kneeled down and prayed (Acts 9:40). But the same Peter simply stood and pronounced the curse of God upon Ananias and Sapphira, though it had in it the elements of prayer. Joshua stopped fighting only long enough to command the sun to stand still, which seemed a very bold prayer of great faith. Solomon stood in the temple with his hands stretched out and prayed at the dedication of the temple (II Chron. 6:12). Jesus sometimes stood to pray, but in the Garden of Gethsemane He fell on His face and prayed (Matt. 26:39). And from all this let us learn the lesson that prayer is not in the form. And let us get out of our ruts, pray when we stand or pray when we sit. In times of great emergency and distress, we ought surely to be on our very faces on the floor before God, pleading and waiting on Him. But at other times we ought like David to awake in the night, communing with our own hearts upon our beds (Ps. 4:4) and again pray at evening, morning and at noon (Ps. 55:17).

Let us seek to enter into all the wealth of prayer in the Bible. Let us pray as much as Bible characters. Let us weep as much as they wept. Let us fast as much as they fasted. Let us make prayer the biggest work of our lives and the greatest enjoyment, the unceasing activity.

Are you ready now to confess to God your sin of prayerlessness?

For a complete list of books available from the Sword of the Lord, write to Sword of the Lord Publishers, P. O. Box 1099, Murfreesboro, Tennessee 37133.

(800) 251-4100
(615) 893-6700
FAX (615) 848-6943
E-mail: 102657.3622@compuserve.com